The Death Drive

The Death Drive:

Philosophy, Literature, Theory

Edited by
Jeffrey R. Di Leo and Paul Allen Miller

BLOOMSBURY ACADEMIC
LONDON • NEW YORK • OXFORD • NEW DELHI • SYDNEY

BLOOMSBURY ACADEMIC
Bloomsbury Publishing Plc, 50 Bedford Square, London, WC1B 3DP, UK
Bloomsbury Publishing Inc, 1359 Broadway, New York, NY 10018, USA
Bloomsbury Publishing Ireland, 29 Earlsfort Terrace, Dublin 2, D02 AY28, Ireland

First published in Great Britain 2026

Cover image: Visage via Getty Images

A catalogue record for this book is available from the British Library.

A catalog record for this book is available from the Library of Congress.

ISBN: HB: 978-1-3504-6567-1
ePDF: 978-1-3504-6568-8
eBook: 978-1-3504-6569-5

Typeset by Deanta Global Publishing Services, Chennai, India

To our colleagues at the Society for Critical Exchange in gratitude for their commitment to the free exchange of ideas.

Contents

Acknowledgments viii

Introduction: The Death Drive *Jeffrey R. Di Leo and Paul Allen Miller* 1

Part I Freud on the Death Drive—Philosophical Readings

1 Take It to the Limit: Ontology beyond the Pleasure Principle *Paul Allen Miller* 23
2 Baudrillard on the Death Drive *Jeffrey R. Di Leo* 39
3 Trauma and the Breakdown of All Grammars: Listening to the Wound as Voice *María del Rosario Acosta López* 59
4 Death's Drive in Hegel and Freud *Shannon M. Mussett* 75
5 Aristotle's Erotic Sublime? *Emanuela Bianchi* 89

Part II Poetics of the Death Drive—Literary Connections

6 Moral Masochism, Sexuality, and the Death Drive: Freud and Late James *David Greven* 109
7 Elegy, Queerness, and the Lacanian Death Drive *Sara H. Lindheim* 125
8 Reading beyond the Death Drive: Living Phantasms *Daniel T. O'Hara* 139
9 Death—Automation—Language *Adriana Michele Campos Johnson* 151
10 Antigone's Gaza *Mario Telò* 165

Part III Critique of the Death Drive—Theoretical Confrontations

11 The Queer Life of Auto-repugnancy in Freud *Penelope Deutscher* 185
12 Labor and Desire *Peter Hitchcock* 203
13 Derrida's Cruelty Drive *Brian O'Keeffe* 217
14 Black *Ressentiment* and the Politics of the Death Drive: A Fanonian Meditation *Zahi Zalloua* 233
15 Paraontology and the Death Drive *Nicole Simek* 247

Notes on Contributors 261
Index 265

Acknowledgments

We would like to thank the contributors to this volume for sharing their essays and insights with us. Thanks also go to Orlando Di Leo for his help in preparing this manuscript for publication and to Ben Doyle of Bloomsbury for his editorial support. We are also happy to acknowledge the support of the McCausland College of the Arts and Sciences and the Department of Languages, Literatures and Cultures at the University of South Carolina.

Introduction

The Death Drive

Jeffrey R. Di Leo and Paul Allen Miller

The attack had been so sudden that there remained for an instant the marks of an astonished stupor, very childlike, yet death must have proposed, all of sudden, games so astonishing that his cheeks seemed emaciated, lips pulled back over the teeth in an infinite laugh.

—Jean Giono[1]

Acceleration, hoarding, vertiginous suspension, breathless looping, affective bulimia or binge eating, serial cutting, trying to enter or fold in upon oneself, autoimmune inflammation, the orgasm as unfinished, non-teleological pleasure.

—Mario Telò[2]

In Jean Giono's 1950 novel, *The Horseman on the Roof*, a young Italian nobleman with revolutionary republican intentions finds himself in the south of France in the middle of the 1832 cholera epidemic. His adventures are at times exciting. Likewise, the images of people committing desperate acts in a time of horror, even as others maintain a sense of honor and republican commitment, form an obvious allegory for Vichy France during the Second World War. Nonetheless, what remains most striking in the novel are the long, loving, lyrical descriptions of people dying in the most horrible ways, descriptions that in themselves are irreducible to whatever additional political or existential signification they may bear. The screaming, the facial contortions, the convulsions, and the milky white vomit and diarrhea of the stricken are etched again and again. There are haunting images of birds feeding on the dead and of children who have crawled away into cabinets to die. The corpse of a young aristocratic woman is vividly described lying face down in the doorway of her bedroom, her still beautiful hair matted to the floor with vomit. The hero, Angelo, like the reader, is both fascinated and repulsed by these images. Allegorically, the novel might be compared to Albert Camus's *La peste* (*The Plague*, 1947), which is roughly contemporary, but Camus's descriptions do not linger over the details of bodily decomposition: that is not where the novel's aesthetic force lies. In the end, for Giono, what drives the narrative forward is not the horror of dying from cholera (though horrible it is), but its attraction, the enjoyment that is inseparable from the grimace of death itself, and the ecstasy of unbelievable suffering he asks us to imagine again and again.

In 1920, in the aftermath of the First World War and another plague, the Spanish flu, Sigmund Freud published *Beyond the Pleasure Principle*. At this same time, he was composing "The Uncanny" and "A Child is Being Beaten." These essays ask: How do we explain uncanny and horrific cultural productions, if human beings are governed by the pursuit of pleasure? "Why would the subject repeat nightmares that show him harassed, with no recourse, the object of cruelty and abuse?"[3] The force that compels this uncanny repetition, Freud names the death drive (*Todestrieb*).

A drive is not a desire in the normal sense. It cannot be satisfied. It is not like wanting a bowl of ice cream, having one, and feeling better (at least momentarily). A drive does not remain merely empirically unsatisfied; it is an unending obsession, a compulsion.[4] It is a movement toward a form of dissolution and reconstitution: a threatening violation of the self's boundaries, a form of paroxystic suffering and enjoyment.[5] The Argentine-Mexican psychoanalyst Nestor Braunstein writes:

> If life is defined beginning with an inscription in the structures of subjectivity, which are transactions with the Other, that is, starting from the flesh becoming body due to the interference of the signifier in the vital processes, the movement of the drives can be seen as the force that propels the recovery of a state before the word, or the recovery of the Thing as the absolute object of desire; a *jouissance* of being, from which the subject comes to ek-sist.[6]

This ek-sistence is a form of ecstatic standing outside the self. It is the drive for a return to a lost state of plenitude in which the alienations that found our "selves" as autonomous egos are denied and overcome. At its simplest level, the death drive is the story of Freud's grandson, Ernst, compulsively reenacting his own abandonment through the *fort-da* game and taking comfort in a repetition that in itself signifies his destitution.[7] Such drives are incredibly powerful forces; they motivate behavior—war, rage, the savagery of self-harm—without ever being reducible to a game-theoretical model of comparative advantage. They exist, not as either the opposite or the object of reason, but as its obscene obverse, as the smear of enjoyment that motivates, shapes, and channels the *logoi* of embodied, empirically existent human beings.

The death drive's essence, as we see in countless sociocultural phenomena, is insistence and repetition directed toward an aim that is never fully reached.[8] That aim is denominated by Jacques Lacan *jouissance*, which we translate as "enjoyment" to distinguish it from pleasure. Pleasure operates within the law. It respects decency and moderation. It can be reasoned with. *Jouissance* is a form of ecstatic transgression that by definition knows no satisfaction and cannot be reduced to a rational expression. It is literally unspeakable, a kind of shudder, a convulsion.[9]

The pleasure principle is far from scandalous. It is the bedrock of most psychological theories. Whether behaviorist, Freudian, or cognitive, the assumption is that people do things that give them pleasure and avoid those that produce pain, discomfort, and anxiety. These same assumptions underlie utilitarianism, classical economics, and most normative conceptions of rationality. Our pursuit of pleasure (*Lust*) is tempered by our desire to avoid displeasure (*Unlust*). Freud calls the latter the "reality principle." We make trade-offs and substitutions. We accept a lesser or deferred pleasure to avoid future pain. The pleasure and reality principles are not opposites but complements. They function in tandem. Reality is not an unmovable or incomprehensible real, beyond our ability to conceive it, but a rational limit placed on pleasure that ensures we can continue to pursue it. According to the reality principle, in an ideal environment, where each of us possessed the same opportunities, the same information, and the same calculative ability in our pursuits of pleasure, we would all make the same "rational" choices.

And yet we know this is not the case. People engage in all sorts of behaviors that neither procure them pleasure (at least not in the normative sense) nor maximize utility.[10] They do so often with full knowledge of the consequences. Entire swathes of cultural production are predicated on our fascination with sexualized violence and death, from tragedy to opera to horror. At the same time, people develop compulsions they know are self-destructive: traumatically abused spouses move from one abuser to the next; people knowingly engage in high-risk sexual behaviors; children of abuse compulsively inflict that abuse on others. We have an insatiable need for spectacles of violence: from gladiators to mixed martial arts to splatter films. It's the horrific auto accident you can't look away from. It's the people who, while claiming to be horrified by pedophilia, spend countless hours obsessing over internet fantasies of pedophiles and child cannibals secretly ruling the world (Q-Anon). It's the thrill of the rampaging, murderous mob. This set of phenomena, their traumatic origins, the search for control through repetition, and the ultimate inability of these compulsions to be accounted for by a rational, utilitarian calculus of pleasure were the focus of *Beyond the Pleasure Principle*.[11]

The dominant form of psychoanalysis in the United States and Britain in the years after the Second World War largely ignored the death drive. It focused on Freud's theory of libido up to the First World War and neglected the metapsychological works of his later period.[12] The unconscious, on this classical reading, consists of those desires for pleasure which, while part of our biological endowment, have either been repressed or turned in other directions (per-verted, sublimated), whether because of physical and social limitations or as the effects of past trauma. By coming to recognize them and gaining conscious control over them, we can, according to normative analysis, dissolve symptoms, remove resistances, work to strengthen the ego, and produce responsible citizens.[13] "Where id was, ego shall be!"[14] I may want to cross the street because I desire to acquire a piece of candy (or money, or a sexual partner, etc.), but if I am a well-adjusted individual and I see there is a large truck coming at a high rate of speed, I will decide to delay my gratification. Freud, in *Beyond the Pleasure Principle*, calls this classic libidinal compromise "the economic standpoint," because it involves a series of trade-offs as we try to maximize the return on our libidinal investment.[15] This, of course, is precisely the form of normalizing psychoanalysis criticized by Michel Foucault.[16]

What worries Freud in *Beyond the Pleasure Principle*, however, is less the economy of the mind that focuses on acquiring pleasure and avoiding pain, even when that mechanism goes awry, than how we understand the person who sees the truck and goes anyway. What about the person who pushes them? The person who watches again and again the video of them being run over? The person who sees the video and imitates the same? We can of course say that each of these people must receive pleasure from their acts or they would not have done them, and on a certain level, this is true. But is it the same pleasure as the person who carefully crosses the street to get the piece of candy? Does it conform to the pleasure principle as Freud articulates it?[17]

We run the risk of tautology here. If we maintain everyone does everything because they think it will maximize their pleasure, what are we actually saying? We find ourselves claiming that everything is pleasure, which means pleasure is nothing in particular. We wind up contending that the abused spouse returns to her abuser out of pleasure, that mass murder is a form of pleasure, that suicide is pleasure.[18] And perhaps, on one level, this is so, but what does pleasure mean if it can no longer be meaningfully discriminated from its contrary? Can we then speak of either a pleasure or a reality principle in any significant sense? What Freud comes to realize is that rather than speaking of all behavior as motivated by pleasure, which as an explanatory principle is negligible, we should rather assume the existence of a world prior to our libidinal investment, and therefore prior to its division into the fungible, exchangeable units of pleasure and pain, which can enter this rational calculus. We must assume the existence of a world that is beyond the pleasure principle.

In Freud's own words, "Es bleibt genug übrig": once all the economic calculations have been made, "there remains enough left over," there remains a sufficient margin of what "seems more original, more instinctual, and more impulsive than the pleasure principle,"[19] an indigestible remainder. That remainder would necessarily be "beyond," "on the other side of" (*jenseits*) the pleasure principle (*des Lustprinzips*). It is not completely separate because it constitutes the background that makes the pleasure principle's articulation possible.[20] The prospect of such a beyond, moreover, exercises a force of attraction. It beckons as the return to a primal unity, a before and beyond the compromises that led to "civilization" and our "discontents":[21] an enjoyment beyond pleasure and pain. Yet this return to the unbounded would mean the disintegration of the rational ego and the end of the self-protective boundary between same and other: a moment of self-shattering ecstasy or inconceivable immortality.[22]

This force of attraction, this impulse to return, is precisely the death drive (*Todestrieb*): a drive beyond the instantiation of all current goods. It is beyond good and evil and thus makes possible their conceptualization and reconceptualization.[23] It introduces the possibility of a radical decision, of a fundamentally free act not already determined by reality's dictates.[24] Like Julia Kristeva's semiotic, before the imposition of the limit, the death drive recalls the Demiurge's creation of the phenomenal world in Plato's *Timaeus* through the repeated impressing of form on a substance without qualities.[25] This is the moment of determination qua determination, the imposition of the Law as Law, the original Oedipal moment, which has its own before and beyond.[26] Beyond the pleasure principle and its economic calculations lies the unnameable, a region of passion and enjoyment: the choric site on which love, friendship, and politics are erected, the ground on which an economy of exchange takes root.[27] It is the drive for reunion with this ground that fuels our *jouissance*. As Freud recognized in the penultimate chapter of *Beyond the Pleasure Principle* when he recalls Aristophanes' myth of the Androgyne, pleasure is but the intelligible surface of a fundamental drive to heal the wound of separation, to see ourselves in the face of the other, to find our exemplar.

In Freud's foundation myth in *Totem and Taboo* (1913), it is the murder of the father of the primal horde, the obscene and violent father of enjoyment, by his sons that founds civilization. In the fear and horror ensuing from their act, the brothers establish a pact, a form of law that inaugurates the Symbolic field of regulated exchange founded upon the incest taboo and the worship of the first father as a tribal totem. Parricide thus figures in many cultural mythologies as both the ultimate crime and a universal (repressed) desire. It is smeared with the stain of obscene enjoyment, with the fantasy of a world without law, in which each of us, for a moment, becomes the tyrant.[28]

In the end, the English translation "beyond" for *Jenseits des Lustprinzips* is problematic. One is never "beyond" but "on the other side of" the pleasure principle. Freud does not posit access to a world in which calculations of pleasure versus pain cannot take place, but a world irreducible to those calculations. The masochist certainly receives pleasure from pain, but the practicing masochist has a "safe word," a signal the game has gone too far and pulls it back within posited limits. What Freud asks us to imagine is a moment on the other side of the game, not one completely beyond pleasure. Pleasure and its beyond form a kind of Moebius strip in which each side folds back upon the other.[29] As Slavoj Žižek reminds us, even "the very renunciation to pleasures brings about a paradoxical surplus enjoyment, an 'enjoyment in pain,' in displeasure, baptized by Lacan *jouissance*, the 'impossible'/traumatic/painful enjoyment beyond the pleasure principle."[30]

For Lacan, this enjoyment finds its archetypal expression in the figure of Antigone,[31] to whom he devoted a portion of his seventh seminar on the ethics of psychoanalysis.[32] Antigone incarnates, for him, the possibility of a moment before and beyond the Oedipal world of law. She represents an ethics beyond the economic standpoint. She is beautiful and terrifying.[33] Sophocles' *Antigone* is for Lacan the ultimate psychoanalytic text because it poses a question only the late Freud can answer: Why does Antigone refuse to heed Creon's decree forbidding the burial of Polynices? Why does she knowingly and willingly embrace death?[34]

When the play opens, Antigone confronts her sister Ismene with the news that Creon has decreed their brother's body is to be left unburied. She and Ismene are conceived in this speech in line 1 as a unit: not separate individuals, but one substance from a common womb (*autadelphon*), the same womb that is the origin of Oedipus's evils. The experiential reality of that unity is characterized by the presence of *atē* in line 3, which is defined paratactically in lines 4–5 as "pain," "shame," and "dishonor." *Atē* appears fourteen times in the play. It denotes both a limit and a space beyond, "the horrifying, lethal, and at the same time fascinating borderline that we approach when the reversal into bliss is imminent."[35] According to the chorus, it represents an inhuman desire that causes one to misrecognize good and evil, to misrecognize pleasure. It represents a border upon whose crossing grandeur is predicated, but beyond which one cannot live:

> Far-ranging hope is a source of pleasure for many, for others the trickery of nimble desire creeps up on the man knowing nothing, before he should burn his foot on the hot fire.

> From this, in wisdom, a small saying appears: "the bad then seems good to one whose entrails the god turns toward *atē*." He acts only a very short time beyond *atē*.[36]

Antigone is directed "towards *atē*." Her desire is outside, *ektos*, the limits of the human:[37] a return to the oneness of the flesh, "a desire which is beyond desire itself and into the drive."[38] In this world, there is no substitution, no bargaining. This self-enclosed world is beyond the law Creon seeks to instantiate by forbidding the burial of Polynices.[39] In her choice of death, Antigone rejoins an incestuous beyond that submerges individuality, a region whose economy cannot be measured by the calculus of the pleasure principle.[40]

This implacable insistence, this drive, Lacan argues, is the source of her beauty and the beauty of tragedy generally.[41] Lacan refers to this beauty as Antigone's "éclat" or "splendor." "It's she who fascinates us, in her unbearable splendor, in the ways she holds us and forbids us, in the sense that this intimidates us, in the way she is disconcerting—this so terribly voluntary victim."[42] Her beauty is both endlessly fascinating and horrifying, like the death drive itself.[43] It is a form of unspeakable enjoyment that speaks to our alienation and separation, our desire for the illegal, the excessive, and traumatic. It is a tear or hole in the symbolic fabric of the world that would render our separate, subjective existence impossible. It is something we desire and despise. It threatens our existence and, as recognized individuals in a law-bound community, it endlessly beckons as the possibility of absolute transcendence and the end of desire.[44]

While strictly speaking enjoyment beyond the pleasure principle is unspeakable, one of the ways it manifests itself within symbolic structures is in the abject or grotesque. There is a paradoxical sense in which the death drive is also a creative force. In this, it is closely related to the concept of the abject developed by Kristeva. The abject repulses us. It reminds us of our material contingency, the unsealed and threatened natures of our bodies: blood, semen, excrement.[45] It is a source of fascination and aggression.[46] It is not an object per se but the evocation through *jouissance* of a pre-objectal world, a world before our existence as autonomous beings operating within the bounds of laws and norms. The abject manifests itself within the normative world as something beyond and hence threatening it—as something fascinating and repugnant.[47] It threatens to destroy the possibility of a regulated exchange between the pleasure-motivated ego and the world that enfolds it.[48] Abjection is the process of separation that creates defined subjects and objects. It is a return of the repressed, a moment when the expelled returns. "Abjection is a resurrection that passes through death (of the ego). It is an alchemy that transforms the death drive into a surge of life, of new meaning."[49]

The ironic pendant or complement of the abject is the sublime. In Immanuel Kant and Edmund Burke, the sublime is an experience that exceeds the bounds of subjective existence, producing a fracture or moment of ontological rupture that does violence to our imagination.[50] As Henry Sussman observes, the sublime in its "unmediated Being-there anticipates the Lacanian Real":[51] it is beyond the law and hence beyond the pleasure principle. It is both erotic and criminal. It "terrifies and thrills . . . with an awareness of the close proximity of life to death."[52] The tragic, the sublime, and the abject eroticize the boundaries of subjective existence and their transgression, producing "a disconcerting mixture of pain and pleasure."[53]

A psychoanalysis that embraces Antigone and the death drive does not seek the reduction of the id to the control of the disciplinary ego but a moment of radical externality to the fantasy construction of the self. As Lacan notes, the achievement of this externality is predicated on Freud's recognition that it is not sufficient for the analyst to circulate within the constituted field of discourse and to assume the position of an other to whom the analysand speaks. To take up such a posture is to continue to operate within the very system of given goods, of economic trade-offs between the pleasure and the reality principles, that had led the patient to misrecognize their desire, to accept the compromised goods on offer, and so to suffer from their symptoms. Under such conditions, as Freud notes, even though the analyst may offer the "correct" interpretation and the patient may accept it, the symptom often persists (even if in changed form) and the analytic scene repeats. In this repetition is revealed a moment of compulsion, of force and drive that exceeds the economic standpoint and thus cannot be totalized under the profits and losses of our existing discursive and disciplinary apparatus.[54] It is in this moment of radical externality that we find the possibility of a traumatic and ecstatic "enjoyment" or *jouissance*.[55]

In the end, what is beyond the pleasure principle is beyond signification. It is beyond the possibility of conceptualizing in terms of the rational or rule-based schema of disciplinary and professional norms. It must be understood as a form of nonexistence or death, as the crossing of a mute barrier whose transgression is impossible to conceive and yet reveals the contingency of our linguistic and material structures.[56] The death drive is not a dark mysterious force that lurks within us. Rather, as Freud conceptualizes the possibility of a metapsychology beyond the pleasure principle, it figures the repetitive insistence of the signifier, the blank materiality of language revealed in its traumatic repetition, in its compulsive emptying of the content and limits of the Symbolic as we traverse the fantasy constructions that knit it and ourselves together.[57]

Analytic practice, consequently, seeks less to dissolve the symptom through its assimilation to an external truth than to enjoy it: to see in the symptom a moment inassimilable to the reigning structure of reality, a repetitive moment of the alien, of what cannot be totalized in the logic of signification.[58] The suffering symptom lies beyond the pleasure principle. It is not something re-pressed that will provide liberation if ex-pressed. It is rather the sign of experience's limit, the scar of what must be excluded to make it cohere.[59]

This, then, is a volume explicitly staged on the ground where the death drive, after its Freudian theorization, has been reinterpreted by various psychoanalysts, most notably Lacan, Joan Copjec, Melanie Klein, Jacqueline Rose, and Žižek, and philosophers, most notably, Jacques Derrida, Gilles Deleuze and Félix Guattari, and Herbert Marcuse. Today it is enjoying a renaissance among political theorists (Judith Butler, Jacques Rancière), queer theorists (Laurent Berlant, Lee Edelman), Afropessimists (Calvin Warren), and posthumanist thinkers (Rosi Braidotti, Tracy McNulty). In this period of global crisis, ecological and political, we see individuals and states indulging in destructive behaviors that can be interpreted through the lens of the death drive. Yet

Freud's *Todestrieb* also possesses a disruptive aesthetico-political force that unsettles well-established modes of social being. In its rush toward an imagined origin, the death drive is the disavowed psychological principle that shapes—and threatens—modern relationships with antiquity as well as the very desire for historical reconstruction.

It should be noted, however, that the death drive has always been an unwelcome guest in the more "respectable" clinical circles of psychoanalysis. It was not well received in the International Psychoanalytical Association or embraced by Anna Freud. It was difficult to domesticate and did not offer demonstrable clinical results that stood up to the scrutiny of the Anglo-American psychological and psychiatric establishment. Indeed, as Freud himself admits—and as we have already outlined above—the death drive is before and beyond representation itself. It challenges the basic economic and rationalistic assumptions that underlie the most conventional aspects of a medicalized model of clinical practice.

Nevertheless, contributions to the present volume, which is organized in three parts, take up the death drive as a psychological, aesthetic, and political principle in a range of cultural phenomena. Death-driven feelings manifest themselves through the representation of the experiences of human and nonhuman agents but also, nonrepresentationally, in verbal form. These chapters by some of today's leading thinkers and theorists pose a series of crucial questions. How does recognizing those death-driven feelings change our perspective on these phenomena? How do they relate to the mechanisms of "immunity" and "auto-immunity," which theorists see operating in the bio- and necropolitical actions of modern states? Has death gone viral? In what ways do these feelings point to reimaginings of the social (the couple, family, and reproduction)? How does a new emphasis on the death drive—in its various theorizations—help us reimagine our relationship with the fundamental structures of our culture from the origins of metaphysics to contemporary popular culture?

Part I of the present volume, entitled "Freud on the Death Drive—Philosophical Readings," opens with Paul Allen Miller's "Take It to the Limit: Ontology beyond the Pleasure Principle." In this chapter, Miller rereads the central "speculative" portion on what Freud terms the primal "vesicle" in *Beyond the Pleasure Principle*, from three perspectives. First, he looks closely at several passages in *Beyond the Pleasure Principle* that surround the story of the vesicle and point to a moment before the economic, before the process of exchange and compromise that is eternally at work in the dynamic between the *Lustprinzip* and the *Realitätprinzip*. He then turns to Derrida's reading of this same text, "Spéculer sur Freud," in which he argues specifically that within *Beyond the Pleasure Principle* Freud never, in fact, does go "beyond," not because there is nothing beyond the eternal calculus of costs and benefits, negative and positive reinforcements, pleasure and pain, but because beyond the moment, beyond the *topos*, in which we can make the calculation of exchanging quantities, is a world *beyond* representation, a world prior to and beyond the constitution of reality as a discrete object of experience, a choric world without defined boundaries and qualities. To the extent we can and do talk about this world, write about it, and assign differential signifiers to it, then it is already saturated with pleasure and pain. It is a post-traumatic world that bows before the hegemony of its own prior constitution, the thetic moment whose compulsive repetition imposes order on chaos and is always already beyond it.

In the penultimate movement, Miller takes up a brief hint in Derrida's essay, where he argues that it is Plato who stands "Derrière Freud," and particularly the Plato of the *Philebus*, a dialogue which strives to answer the ethical question of what is the best life, by posing the ontological question of what lies between the limit and the unlimited, between the one and the many, or of how the ontic world can be understood in its inherent existential and epistemic precarity. Miller closes with some reflections on the ethical and political sense of the understanding of pleasure, enjoyment, death, and the sublime to be derived from this triple reading of what Freud terms his great moment of "speculation, often far-fetched speculation."

The next chapter in this section, Jeffrey R. Di Leo's "Baudrillard on the Death Drive," discusses how Jean Baudrillard turns the death drive loose on capitalism. Not only does the death drive, as a deconstructive process, offer an alternative account of value to capitalist notions, it also serves as a radical way of understanding culture and its processes. Nevertheless, the price of producing an alternative to capitalism for Baudrillard is a steep one: it asks us to turn psychoanalysis against itself. The radicality that is required to undermine the negation of death that grounds capitalism requires that the death drive be viewed, according to Baudrillard, "as acting against the scientific positivity of the psychoanalytic apparatus as developed by Freud." According to him, by interpreting the death drive against Freud and psychoanalysis, it becomes a notion that "goes far beyond all previous points of view and renders all previous apparatuses, whether economic, energetic, topological or even the psychical apparatus itself, useless." This chapter examines the value and limits of Baudrillard's alternative to capitalism through his radicalization of Freud's death drive.

In this section's third chapter, "Trauma and the Breakdown of All Grammars: Listening to the Wound as Voice," María del Rosario Acosta López explores the breakdown that trauma entails in Freud's text, both at an epistemological and at an aesthetic level. Trauma, as described by Freud, confronts us with a type of damage whose experience reveals itself as inarticulable by virtue of being profoundly paradoxical. It is paradoxical not only because it resists being conceptualized as an experience (thus exposing the limits of our capacity for processing and, accordingly, for listening and remembrance), but also because sense itself as a possibility—the possibility of "making sense" of what has happened—is broken by its occurrence (which is in fact both the absence of its occurrence and, simultaneously and paradoxically, its compulsive repetition). Her reading of Freud, then, aims to develop a wider understanding of the damage associated with trauma, which in turn sheds light on the kind of challenges that trauma poses to the question of listening in contexts of traumatic violence. These, she argues, are challenges that may go unnoticed when trauma is approached from other perspectives and that a philosophical gaze can help us not only to identify but also to understand in depth. More importantly, López demonstrates how an (aesth) ethical response to these challenges produces, in the very experience of listening, grammars that render it audible (in and as a breakdown of sense). A philosophical approach to listening to trauma is connected therefore to the conditions of possibility of its audibility, to what is perceived (or not) as legible, and as "making sense."

The fourth chapter in this section focuses on how the inorganic serves not only as life's engine but also as a dead core driving organisms toward demise. In "Death's Drive in Hegel and Freud," Shannon M. Mussett compares G. W. F. Hegel's *The Philosophy of Nature* (1830) and Freud's *Beyond the Pleasure Principle*. Despite their vastly different frameworks questioning the origin and purpose of life, Mussett argues that Hegel and Freud take seriously the notion that life may actually be in the service of something beyond or before itself. To explore this overlap, Mussett addresses the emergence of the organic from the inorganic, with particular emphasis on the inorganic conceived as what is dead. Once life appears, the role of drives becomes a central concern. Hegel and Freud conceive of drives as conservative, but Hegel locates the motive force in the preservation of the genus, where Freud finds it in individual germ cells. This shift in focus, maintains Mussett, has far-reaching implications for the optimistic conclusions of the former and the pessimism of the latter.

The final chapter in this section inquires into the fate of Eros in Aristotle. In "Aristotle's Erotic Sublime?," Emanuela Bianchi brings us back to the question of the sublime, which we described earlier as the ironic pendant or complement of the abject. However, unlike Miller, who takes up pleasure, enjoyment, death, and the sublime in relation to Plato, Bianchi takes this same journey through the much less traveled path of Aristotle. While Eros has a central philosophical function in Plato, it all but disappears in the thought of Aristotle, replaced by the more rational and reciprocal relation of *philia*. Foregrounding Eros's ancient epithet *lusimelēs*, unbinder of limbs, and noting Aristotle's elision of this epithet, Bianchi shows how Aristotle divests Eros of its destructive and disaggregating qualities, what Freud would later name the death drive, at the same time as it undergoes a certain sublimation in his philosophy. Picking up the thread of the key Aristotelian concept of *lusis*—unbinding, loosening, solving—central in both the *Poetics* and the *Metaphysics*—Bianchi shows that this sublimation is inevitably accompanied in his thought by the abjected threat of the disaggregating organism and the maternal body, in a return of the repressed.

If the philosophical assemblage of Plato, Aristotle, Hegel, and Baudrillard provides the contours of Part I, then the next section, where figures ranging from Sophocles and Tibullus to Henry James and Saul Bellow converge, might be deemed more poetic in its configuration. Part II, entitled "Poetics of the Death Drive—Literary Connections," begins with David Greven's "Moral Masochism, Sexuality, and the Death Drive: Freud and Late James." According to Greven, James's notoriously difficult late work, especially the novels *The Golden Bowl* (1904) and *The Wings of the Dove* (1902), links sexual experience and an inexorable movement toward death, prefiguring Freud's theories of the death drive and Lacan's reworking of them. Specifically, the idea of sex as unspeakable in *The Golden Bowl* and a means to financial security in *The Wings of the Dove* denatures sex and sexuality in a manner that evokes the death drive's movement toward the cessation of pleasure and an embrace of inorganic nothingness. James and Freud, argues Greven, jointly theorize moral masochism as a cultural death drive that categorizes sexuality as an unpleasure to be staved off, an appointment endlessly deferred along with meaning.

In the next chapter, Sarah Lindheim turns to some of the poetry of Tibullus to provide insight into the death drive. In "Elegy, Queerness, and the Lacanian Death Drive," Lindheim reads Tibullus Book 2 through the lens of Edelman's queer Lacanian death drive, tracing out the narrativization of the death drive in the poems. Lindheim's interpretation significantly alters how we think about both Latin love elegy and the scholarly reception of Tibullus Book 2. First, it suggests that these six oft-maligned Tibullan elegies are more disruptive to their contemporary Augustan sociopolitical order than any other text we possess from the period, including Ovid. Second, it argues that the text's nihilistic disruption to the self and the social order explains why and how readers turn away from it. Finally, Lindheim considers what alternatives embracing (rather than denying) the death drive offer a reader of Tibullus, but also by extension any subject operating within the Symbolic structures by which a society conceptualizes totalizing meaning.

Inspired by French psychoanalyst André Green's work on the death drive, Daniel T. O'Hara, "Reading beyond the Death Drive: Living Phantasms," the third chapter in this section, critically follows the transformations of the death drive in several arts including film (director Martin McDonagh's *The Banshees of Inisherin* [2022]), modern poetry (Ezra Pound's "Histrion"), and the contemporary novel (Saul Bellow's *Ravelstein* [2000]). One of Green's observations about the death drive utilized in these readings is that it, in the words of O'Hara, "creates the phantasm of heroic, albeit tragic, defeat," or what he terms *death narcissism*. For Green, says O'Hara, "the defenses of turning-around-upon the self and the reversal into the opposite, primary defenses of the ego, which result from death narcissism, the ego's perverse masochistic love of itself as suffering, exhibit what we can know via clinical experience (and its artistic elaborations) of the death drive." "Phantasms," writes O'Hara of Green's account, "are perceived as external objects as they play host to otherwise unconscious memories of experience and earlier wish-fulfillment dream images." Moreover, just as repressed fantasies come to haunt the mind, so too do these phantasms as blank-faced perceptions, something that is on display in a variety of artworks. In sum, the aim of O'Hara's critical pilgrimage is to delineate how, while Orpheus may be torn apart, Death *lives on*, via its repeated transfigurations.

Like Di Leo's contribution, the next chapter takes up the relationship between the death drive and late capitalism. However, the latter is not viewed through the aim of ending capitalism, but is rather a commentary on the poetics that is established through the interaction of capitalism with the death drive. In "Death—Automation—Language," Adriana Michele Campos Johnson begins with Catherine Malabou's contention that Freud had trouble reckoning with the form-giving capacity of destruction and that he was unable to represent the death drive in a fashion that wasn't bound to sexuality/life/love. His death drive in fact, she says, represents elasticity rather than confronting the possibility of a direct negative plasticity. The chapter will take up two stagings of the death drive in late capitalism to ask precisely how the *Todestrieb* gives and is given form in each. On the one hand, Jonathan Beller's *The Message is Murder: Substrates of Computational Capital* (2017) offers us a poetics of the automaticity and abstraction of capitalism, which deadens life and language as it drives toward machinic life; on the other, China Mieville's *Embassytown* turns on a poetics of breakdown, the cut, and an unexpected plasticity and becoming-life of infrastructure. Language—messages, communication, but also fabulation—is at the heart of both.

The final chapter in this section takes us back to Sophocles's *Antigone* and forward to how it informs contemporary political conflicts. In "Antigone's Gaza," Mario

Telò asks how our view of Antigone, Lacan's death-driven heroine, changes in light of Gaza's apocalyptic destruction. Telò offers a provisional answer by juxtaposing moments of Sophocles' play with the overdetermined collapse in Gaza, a target of the "instinct of aggression and self-destruction" that, for Freud, makes and unmakes the human. He is interested in elemental and environmental marginality and opacity, the cave and the tunnel and the dust stirred up by the auto-immunitarian, fundamentally death-driven violence of the nation-state, whether perpetrated by Creon or Israel. Animated by the fantasy of reappropriating ancestral land, of reconstituting a lost wholeness, the foundational project of Israel is arguably grounded in a different death-driven impetus, which could be said to mobilize Antigone's connection with the inorganic cave, a wish to reconnect with her father/brother, with the familial origin that turns nonexistence into existence, or brings nonlife (in)to life. The psychic motion of the Lacanian Antigone, her familial and political orientation toward the Real of death, argues Telò, tropes, through displacement, the disavowed "self-destructive instinct" of the state as it protects its integrity by suppressing dissent—the irruptions of disagreement that aggravate its illusory pursuit of immunity and self-possession.

The final section, Part III, is entitled "Critique of the Death Drive—Theoretical Confrontations." The first chapter of this section is Penelope Deutscher's "The Queer Life of Auto-repugnancy in Freud." According to Deutscher, the many resources of Freud's *Beyond the Pleasure Principle* include its capacity to understand life in terms of a self-resistant auto-repugnancy, as suggested by the Derridean term, "lifedeath." Against the backdrop of Lee Edelman and Derrida's readings of this dimension of Freud, Deutscher asks how the concept of auto-repugnancy (life that is always already resistant to life) challenges the stigmatized category of "anti-life," and thereby contributes to the critique of reproductive futurism and the latter's dialogue with afro-pessimism.

In "Labor and Desire," Peter Hitchcock examines the roots of the death drive in Karl Marx's *Capital* (1867). For Hitchcock, the fundamental problem from a psychoanalytic perspective of commodity fetishism, as outlined in chapter one of Capital, is that proletarian investment in the commodity begins as a displacement of desire. This displacement of desire in the commodity, however, does not interrogate the logic of desire in proletarian being itself: a logic that pivots precisely on the death of that very subject. This logic of proletarian desire, argues Hitchcock, is itself a death drive—an objective fiction of class that is elaborated within an altogether different dimensionality than the revelation of a hidden content in the fetishized form of the commodity. The desire of labor is not to make proletarians, for the latter exist only as the sign of subjugation and immiseration. The point of proletarian subjectivity is its own destruction, its historical negation, its death. For Hitchcock, it is blind to any other purpose. For the bourgeoisie as a class, Thanatos is singular and absolute. It is the death of the other. The only drive greater than its own is proletarian, and capital as capital, not as individual psychology, will not cease to perpetuate it. The focus of Hitchcock's analysis is not the violent joy that arises in overcoming proletarian subjectivity, but rather what happens to this proletarian desire, this desire of labor, if that overcoming does not take place? He provides a few examples from film culture where a displaced object of desire for class sublation comes into view, and violently so. The incidence of misrecognition is, as he argues, deeply symptomatic.

In the next chapter in this section, we return to Derrida, albeit not to understand the death drive, but to displace it. In "Derrida's Cruelty Drive," Brian O'Keeffe provides a close reading of a lecture Derrida gave to the States General of Psychoanalysis, where he engages with Freud's death drive and then displaces Freud in the name of what he names the "cruelty drive." The lecture, "Psychoanalysis Searches the State of its Soul: The Impossible Beyond of a Sovereign Cruelty," has received very little attention, even among Derrida scholars. What O'Keeffe seeks to clarify is how Derrida's raising of the issue of cruelty makes for a decisive intervention into Freud's meta-psychoanalytic texts, constituting in fact what could well be called a "deconstruction" of Freud's *Beyond the Pleasure Principle*.

The penultimate chapter in this section and this volume takes up the Black subject of the death drive. In "Black *Ressentiment* and the Politics of the Death Drive: A Fanonian Meditation," Zahi Zalloua begins by situating the death drive as social death in Frantz Fanon's elaboration of the "zone of nonbeing," a concept that continues to elicit interpretations from new and seasoned readers of *Black Skin, White Masks* (1952). Zalloua then turns his attention to the affective register, to civil society's libidinal economy, attending to the circulation of Black *ressentiment* as a response not only to negrophobia but also to liberal democracy's brand of negrophilia, encapsulated in its promotion of identity politics and the neoliberal grammar of victimhood. Finally, he returns to the politics of the death drive and considers its valences, focusing on the ways supplementing the death drive with a Fanon-inflected, dialectized vision of Black *ressentiment* ruthlessly troubles narcissistic investments in the solidity of identity, none more appealing than that of the victim.

Finally, this section as well as the volume closes with Nicole Simek's examination of suicidal political revolt through the lens of the death drive. In "Paraontology and the Death Drive," Simek opens with the example of eighteenth-century Guadeloupean revolutionary Louis Delgrès. She then examines the death drive's bearing on our understandings of slavery and of the modes of death-bound subjectivity that emerge in its afterlife. How, she asks, might we situate the death drive in relation to the Critical Black Studies notion of the paraontological—that disruptive negativity associated in Fred Moten's work with Blackness, disorder, and dehiscence? What does it mean to claim, as Moten does, that "the freedom drive is a death drive"? Lastly, what does it mean, asks Simek, to repeat Delgrès in a contemporary landscape burgeoning with memorializations of his suicide? Is it to repeat a deathly drive for self-possession? To reenact an instance of subjective destitution? Or to foster an ethico-politico-libidinal transformation and reinvestment in an ethical cause?

In sum, given the many different philosophical, literary, and theoretical dimensions of the death drive introduced in the present volume, it is clearly a concept of wide and deep valences that are by no means limited to Freudian psychoanalytic theory—even if its roots can be traced back to the analysis of a child playing a game. Not only does the death drive play a generative and significant role in many areas of contemporary literary and cultural theory such as biopolitics (Di Leo and Telò), decolonial studies (Simek and Zalloua), deconstruction (Deutscher, Miller, O'Keeffe, and Telò), Marxism

(Di Leo and Hitchcock), queer theory (Deutscher, Greven, Lindheim, and Telò), and trauma studies (Miller, Lopez, O'Hara, Johnson, and Zalloua), but it also provides a heuristic for understanding a wide range of literature and the other arts. This volume explores some of the uses of this heuristic to examine a variety of the death drive's manifold theoretical valences.

Notes

1 Jean Giono, *Le hussard sur le toit* (Paris: Gallimard, 1950), 276.
2 Mario Telò, *Archive Feelings: A Theory of Greek Tragedy* (Columbus: Ohio State University Press, 2020), 4.
3 Braunstein, *Jouissance*, 39; cf. Rossella Valdrè, *Psychoanalytic Reflections on the Freudian Death Drive: In Theory, the Clinic, and Art* (London: Routledge, 2019), 17–18.
4 Slavoj Žižek, *Enjoy Your Symptom: Jacques Lacan in Hollywood and Out* (New York: Routledge, 1992), 48; Slavoj Žižek, *The Parallax View* (Cambridge: MIT Press, 2006), 62.
5 Nestor Braunstein, "Desire and Jouissance in the Teaching of Lacan," in *The Cambridge Companion to Lacan*, ed. Jean-Michel Rabaté (Cambridge: Cambridge University Press, 2003), 103; Juan David Nasio, *Psychoanalysis and Repetition: Why Do We Keep Making the Same Mistakes?*, trans. David Pettigrew (Albany: SUNY Press, 2019), 36–8.
6 Braunstein, *Jouissance*, 56–7.
7 Sigmund Freud, *Beyond the Pleasure Principle* (1920), trans. James Strachey (New York: Norton, 1961), 8–11; Ellie Ragland-Sullivan, *Jacques Lacan and the Philosophy of Psychoanalysis* (Urbana: University of Illinois Press, 1986), 81.
8 Joan Copjec, *Imagine There's No Woman: Ethics and Sublimation* (Cambridge: MIT Press, 2002), 38–9; Žižek, *The Parallax View*, 62; Braunstein, *Jouissance*, 239.
9 Braunstein, *Jouissance*, 20–3, 53, 127; John M. Mellard, *Beyond Lacan* (Albany: SUNY Press, 2006), 163.
10 Valdrè, *Psychoanalytic Reflections on the Freudian Death Drive*, 19.
11 See Freud, *Beyond the Pleasure Principle*; Valdrè, *Psychoanalytic Reflections on the Freudian Death Drive*, 31.
12 The Kleinians were a major exception. In the French tradition and among those who trace their genealogy to Lacan, the death drive is central. Rob Weatherill, "Preface," in *The Death Drive: New Life for a Dead Subject?*, ed. Rob Weatherill (London: Rebus Press, 1999), 2–10; and Duncan Barford, "In Defence of Death," in Weatherill, *The Death Drive*, 12. Lacan of course was eventually expelled from the IPA.
13 Much of Anna Freud's work, which became the basis for American Ego Psychology, grew out of her experience working with children during the Blitz in Britain. Her focus on producing normal citizens who can function in a democracy is inseparable from the traumas of war, exile, and the scars of Austrian fascism. See Elana Shapira, "Introduction: Austrian Emigrés and Exiles and the Legacy of Psychoanalysis in Britain," in *Freud and the Emigré: Austrian Emigrés and Exiles and the Legacy of Psychoanalysis in Britain, 1930s–1970s*, ed. Elana Shapira and Daniela Finzi (Cham: Palgrave Macmillan, 2020), 19–20; Michal Shapira, "Anna Freud Shaping Childhood

Education and Promoting 'Democratic Citizenship' in Britain," in Shapira and Finzi, *Freud and the Emigré*, 150, 153–4; and Mitchell G. Ash, "Whose/Which 'Freud'? Social Context and Discourse Analysis of the 'Controversial Discussions,'" in Shapira and Finzi, *Freud and the Emigré*, 171.

14 Sigmund Freud, "XXI. The Dissection of the Psychical Personality," in *New Introductory Lectures on Psychoanalysis* (1932), *The Standard Edition of the Complete Psychological Works of Sigmund Freud*, ed. and trans. James Strachey, volume XXII (London: Hogarth Press, 1964), 80.

15 Freud, *Beyond the Pleasure Principle*, 1.

16 Michel Foucault, *History of Sexuality. Volume I: An Introduction*, trans. Robert Hurley (New York: Random House, 1978), 7, 158–9; Frédéric Gros, "Introduction," in *Foucault et la philosophie antique*, ed. Carlos Lévy and Frédéric Gros (Paris: Kimé, 2003), 12; Jacques Derrida, *Résistances de la psychanalyse* (Paris: Galilée), 139–40.

17 Barford, "In Defence of Death," 13.

18 Barford, "In Defence of Death," 16.

19 Freud, *Beyond the Pleasure Principle*, 17; translation altered.

20 Barford, "In Defence of Death," 34.

21 Sigmund Freud, *Civilization and Its Discontents* (1929), trans. James Strachey (New York: Norton, 1961).

22 Weatherill, "Preface," 1, "The theory of the death drive concerns extremes: on the one hand, an impossible excess of pleasure, and on the other, an ineluctable, morbid repetition of the same." See also Rik Loose, "Toxicomania and the Death Drive in Lacan," in Weatherill, *The Death Drive*, 61. Inasmuch as Freud contends that the unconscious cannot figure its own death, a vision of immortality often stands in its stead (Christian Kläui, *Tod—Hass—Sprache. Psychoanalytisch* [Vienna: Verlag Turia+Kant, 2017], 23–32).

23 Jacques Lacan, *Le séminaire livre VII: L'éthique de la Psychanalyse*, ed. Jacques-Alain Miller (Paris: Seuil, 1986), 269–70, 370–1.

24 Lacan, *Le séminaire livre VII*, 30; Copjec, *Imagine There's No Woman*, 44; Žižek, *The Parallax View*, 92.

25 Julia Kristeva, *La révolution du langage poétique: L'avant-garde à la fin du XIXe siècle: Lautréamont et Mallarmé* (1974; Paris: Seuil, 1985), 23–6, 48; Judith Butler, "Bodies that Matter," in *Bodies that Matter: On the Discursive Limits of Sex* (London: Routledge, 1993).

26 Braunstein, *Jouissance*, 28–9, 263.

27 Jacques Lacan, *Le séminaire livre II: Le moi dans la théorie de Freud et dans la technique de la Psychanalyse*, ed. Jacques-Alain Miller (Paris: Seuil, 1978), 257, 288; Fredric Jameson, "Imaginary and Symbolic in Lacan," in *The Ideologies of Theory*, volume 1 (Minneapolis: University of Minnesota Press, 1988), 94; Braunstein, *Jouissance*, 23.

28 Slavoj Žižek, *The Sublime Object of Ideology* (London: Verso, 1989), 124–5, and *Looking Awry: An Introduction to Jacques Lacan through Popular Culture* (Cambridge: MIT Press, 1991), 134–5.

29 Jeanne Wolff Bernstein, "Unexpected Antecedents to the Concept of the Death Drive: A Return to the Beginnings," *Recherches en psychanalyse* 28 (2019): 98–103.

30 Žižek, *The Sublime Object of Ideology*, 182.

31 Miriam Leonard, "Precarious Life: Tragedy and the Posthuman," in *Antiquities Beyond Humanism*, ed. Emanuela Bianchi, Sara Brill, and Brooke Holmes (Oxford: Oxford University Press, 2019), 87–8.

32 See Paul Allen Miller, *Postmodern Spiritual Practices: The Construction of the Subject and the Reception of Plato in Lacan, Derrida, and Foucault* (Columbus: Ohio State University Press, 2007), chapter 3; Paul Allen Miller, "Enjoyment Beyond the Pleasure Principle: Antigone, Julian of Norwich, and the Use of Pleasures," *The Comparatist* 39 (2015): 47–63; and Paul Allen Miller, "Confession and Repetition: Foucault, Lacan, and the *History of Sexuality*," in *Bloomsbury Handbook on Psychoanalysis, Classics, and Classical Reception*, ed. Richard Armstrong, Paul Allen Miller, Daniel Orrels, and Vanda Zajko (London: Bloomsbury, forthcoming).

33 Lacan, *Le séminaire livre VII*, 352; Žižek, *The Sublime Object of Ideology*, 113 and Slavoj Žižek, "From Antigone to Joan of Arc," *Helios* 31 (2004): 54.

34 Patrick Guyomard, *La jouissance du tragique: Antigone, Lacan et le désir de l'analyste* (Paris: Aubier, 1992); Judith Butler, *Antigone's Claim: Kinship Between Life and Death* (New York: Columbia University Press, 2000); Miriam Leonard, "Lacan, Irigaray, and Beyond: Antigones and the Politics of Psychoanalysis," in *Laughing with Medusa: Classical Myth and Feminist Thought*, ed. Vanda Zajko and Miriam Leonard (Oxford: Oxford University Press, 2006), 121–40; and Žižek, *The Sublime Object of Ideology*; Žižek, *Enjoy Your Symptom*; Žižek, "From Antigone to Joan of Arc," 51–62; and Žižek, *The Parallax View* have all offered theoretical readings of *Antigone* that respond to Lacan.

35 Žižek, *Looking Awry*, 25.

36 Sophocles, *Antigone*, lines 615–25.

37 Lacan, *Le séminaire livre VII*, 270.

38 Charles Freeland, *Antigone, in Her Unbearable Splendor: New Essays on Jacques Lacan's Ethics of Psychoanalysis* (Albany: SUNY Press, 2013), 156.

39 Lacan, *Le séminaire livre VII*, 277–80.

40 Lacan, *Le séminaire livre VII*, 277–80.

41 Jacques Lacan, *Le séminaire livre VIII: Le transfert*, ed. Jacques-Alain Miller (Paris: Seuil, 1991), 154.

42 Lacan, *Le séminaire livre VII*, 290.

43 Lacan, *Le séminaire livre VII*, 327.

44 Braunstein, *Jouissance*, 23, 58; Žižek, *Enjoy Your Symptom*, 134.

45 Julia Kristeva, *Pouvoirs de l'horreur: Essais sur l'abjection* (Paris: Seuil, 1980), 65.

46 Kristeva, *Pouvoirs de l'horreur*, 9–10. Compare Telò on the "sticky imagery of liquid emissions" in the death of Antigone and Haemon (*Archive Feelings*, 246–9).

47 Kristeva, *Pouvoirs de l'horreur*, 17, 20, 79–80.

48 Kristeva, *Pouvoirs de l'horreur*, 66.

49 Kristeva, *Pouvoirs de l'horreur*, 22.

50 Joel Black, *The Aesthetics of Murder* (Baltimore: Johns Hopkins University Press, 1991), 69–70; Meili Steele, *Theorizing Textual Subjects: Agency and Oppression* (Cambridge: Cambridge University Press, 1997), 15.

51 Henry Sussman, *Psyche and Text: The Sublime and the Grandiose in Literature, Psychopathology, and Culture* (Albany: SUNY Press, 1993), 29.

52 Black, *The Aesthetics of Murder*, 109.

53 Genvieve Lloyd, *Reclaiming Wonder: After the Sublime* (Edinburgh: Edinburgh University Press, 2018), 57.

54 Jacques Lacan, *Le séminaire livre I: Les écrits techniques de Freud*, ed. Jacques-Alain Miller (Paris: Seuil, 1975), 350; Lacan, *Le séminaire livre II*, 89; Freud, *Beyond the Pleasure Principle*, 14–17.

55 Braunstein, *Jouissance*, 20–4, 127, 148–9, 158, 217.

56 Lacan, *Le séminaire livre II*, 23, 257, 288, 448.
57 Guyomard, *La jouissance du tragique*, 48; Žižek, *Enjoy Your Symptom*, 48; Braunstein, *Jouissance*, 42–3.
58 Nasio, *Psychoanalysis and Repetition*, 36.
59 Sherry Benstock, *Textualizing the Feminine: On the Limits of Genre* (Norman: University of Oklahoma Press, 1991), 167–8; Žižek, *Looking Awry*, 44.

Works Cited

Ash, Mitchell G. "Whose/Which 'Freud'? Social Context and Discourse Analysis of the 'Controversial Discussions.'" In *Freud and the Emigré: Austrian Emigrés and Exiles and the Legacy of Psychoanalysis in Britain, 1930s-1970s*, edited by Elana Shapira and Daniela Finzi, 161–78. Cham: Palgrave Macmillan, 2020.

Barford, Duncan. "In Defence of Death." In *The Death Drive: New Life for a Dead Subject?*, edited by Rob Weatherill, 12–39. London: Rebus Press, 1999.

Benstock, Sherry. *Textualizing the Feminine: On the Limits of Genre*. Norman: University of Oklahoma Press, 1991.

Bernstein, Jeanne Wolff. "Unexpected Antecedents to the Concept of the Death Drive: A Return to the Beginnings." *Recherches en psychanalyse* 28 (2019): 98–103.

Black, Joel. *The Aesthetics of Murder*. Baltimore: Johns Hopkins University Press, 1991.

Braunstein, Nestor. "Desire and Jouissance in the Teaching of Lacan." In *The Cambridge Companion to Lacan*, edited by Jean-Michel Rabaté, 102–15. Cambridge: Cambridge University Press, 2003.

Butler, Judith. "Bodies that Matter." In *Bodies that Matter: On the Discursive Limits of Sex*, 3–27. London: Routledge, 1993.

Butler, Judith. *Antigone's Claim: Kinship Between Life and Death*. New York: Columbia University Press, 2000.

Camus, Albert. *La peste*. Paris: Gallimard, 1947.

Copjec, Joan. *Imagine There's No Woman: Ethics and Sublimation*. Cambridge: MIT Press, 2002.

Derrida, Jacques. *Résistances de la psychanalyse*. Paris: Galilée, 1996.

Foucault, Michel. *History of Sexuality. Volume I: An Introduction*, translated by Robert Hurley. New York: Random House, 1978.

Freeland, Charles. *Antigone, in Her Unbearable Splendor: New Essays on Jacques Lacan's Ethics of Psychoanalysis*. Albany: SUNY Press, 2013.

Freud, Sigmund. *The Standard Edition of the Complete Psychological Works of Sigmund Freud: Totem and Taboo: Some Points of Agreement between the Mental Lives of Savages and Neurotics* (1913), translated by James Strachey, volume 13, 1–192. London: Hogarth Press, 1953.

Freud, Sigmund. "'A Child is Being Beaten': A Contribution to the Study of the Origin of Sexual Perversions" (1919). In *The Standard Edition of the Complete Psychological Works of Sigmund Freud*, edited and translated by James Strachey, volume 17, 175–204. London: Hogarth Press, 1955.

Freud, Sigmund. "The Uncanny" (1919). In *The Standard Edition of the Complete Psychological Works of Sigmund Freud*, edited and translated by James Strachey, volume 17, 217–56. London: Hogarth Press, 1955.

Freud, Sigmund. "On Narcissism: An Introduction" (1914). In *The Standard Edition of the Complete Psychological Works of Sigmund Freud*, edited and translated by James Strachey, volume 14, 67–102. London: Hogarth Press, 1957.

Freud, Sigmund. *Beyond the Pleasure Principle* (1920), translated by James Strachey. New York: Norton, 1961.
Freud, Sigmund. *Civilization and Its Discontents* (1929), translated by James Strachey. New York: Norton, 1961.
Freud, Sigmund. "XXI. The Dissection of the Psychical Personality." In *The Standard Edition of the Complete Psychological Works of Sigmund Freud: New Introductory Lectures on Psychoanalysis* (1932), edited and translated by James Strachey, volume 12, 57–80. London: Hogarth Press, 1964.
Freud, Sigmund. *The Interpretation of Dreams* (1900), translated by James Strachey. New York: Avon Books, 1965.
Giono, Jean. *Le hussard sur le toit*. Paris: Gallimard, 1950.
Gros, Frédéric. "Introduction." In *Foucault et la philosophie antique*, edited by Carlos Lévy and Frédéric Gros, 7–13. Paris: Kimé, 2003.
Guyomard, Patrick. *La jouissance du tragique: Antigone, Lacan et le désir de l'analyste*. Paris: Aubier, 1992.
Jameson, Fredric. "Imaginary and Symbolic in Lacan." In *The Ideologies of Theory*, volume 1, 75–115. Minneapolis: University of Minnesota Press, 1988.
Kläui, Christian. *Tod—Hass—Sprache. Psychoanalytisch*. Vienna: Verlag Turia+Kant, 2017.
Kristeva, Julia. *Pouvoirs de l'horreur: Essais sur l'abjection*. Paris: Seuil, 1980.
Kristeva, Julia. *La révolution du langage poétique: L'avant-garde à la fin du XIXe siècle: Lautréamont et Mallarmé* (1974). Paris: Seuil, 1985.
Lacan, Jacques. *Le séminaire livre I: Les écrits techniques de Freud I* (1953–54), edited by Jacques-Alain Miller. Paris: Seuil, 1975.
Lacan, Jacques. *Le séminaire livre II: Le moi dans la théorie de Freud et dans la technique de la psychanalyse* (1954–55), edited by Jacques-Alain Miller. Paris: Seuil, 1978.
Lacan, Jacques. *Le séminaire livre VII: L'éthique de la psychanalyse* (1959–60), edited by Jacques-Alain Miller. Paris: Seuil, 1986.
Lacan, Jacques. *Le séminaire livre VIII: Le transfert* (1960–61), edited by Jacques-Alain Miller. Paris: Seuil, 1991.
Leonard, Miriam. "Lacan, Irigaray, and Beyond: Antigones and the Politics of Psychoanalysis." In *Laughing with Medusa: Classical Myth and Feminist Thought*, edited by Vanda Zajko and Miriam Leonard, 121–40. Oxford: Oxford University Press, 2006.
Leonard, Miriam. "Precarious Life: Tragedy and the Posthuman." In *Antiquities Beyond Humanism*, edited by Emanuela Bianchi, Sara Brill, and Brooke Holmes, 77–93. Oxford: Oxford University Press, 2019.
Lloyd, Genvieve. *Reclaiming Wonder: After the Sublime*. Edinburgh: Edinburgh University Press, 2018.
Loose, Rik. "Toxicomania and the Death Drive in Lacan." In *The Death Drive: New Life for a Dead Subject?*, edited by Rob Weatherill, 60–96. London: Rebus Press, 1999.
Mellard, John M. *Beyond Lacan*. Albany: SUNY Press, 2006.
Miller, Paul Allen. *Postmodern Spiritual Practices: The Construction of the Subject and the Reception of Plato in Lacan, Derrida, and Foucault*. Columbus: Ohio State University Press, 2007.
Miller, Paul Allen. "Enjoyment Beyond the Pleasure Principle: Antigone, Julian of Norwich, and the Use of Pleasures." *The Comparatist* 39 (2015): 47–63.
Miller, Paul Allen. "Confession and Repetition: Foucault, Lacan, and the *History of Sexuality*." In *Bloomsbury Handbook on Psychoanalysis, Classics, and Classical Reception*, edited by Richard Armstrong, Paul Allen Miller, Daniel Orrels, and Vanda Zajko. London: Bloomsbury, forthcoming.

Nasio, Juan David. *Psychoanalysis and Repetition: Why Do We Keep Making the Same Mistakes?*, translated by David Pettigrew. Albany: SUNY Press, 2019.
Ragland-Sullivan, Ellie. *Jacques Lacan and the Philosophy of Psychoanalysis*. Urbana: University of Illinois Press, 1986.
Shapira, Elana. "Introduction: Austrian Emigrés and Exiles and the Legacy of Psychoanalysis in Britain." In *Freud and the Emigré: Austrian Emigrés and Exiles and the Legacy of Psychoanalysis in Britain, 1930s-1970s*, edited by Elana Shapira and Daniela Finzi, 1–34. Cham: Palgrave Macmillan, 2020.
Shapira, Michal. "Anna Freud Shaping Childhood Education and Promoting 'Democratic Citizenship' in Britain." In *Freud and the Emigré: Austrian Emigrés and Exiles and the Legacy of Psychoanalysis in Britain, 1930s-1970s*, edited by Elana Shapira and Daniela Finzi, 141–60. Cham: Palgrave Macmillan, 2020.
Steele, Meili. *Theorizing Textual Subjects: Agency and Oppression*. Cambridge: Cambridge University Press, 1997.
Sussman, Henry. *Psyche and Text: The Sublime and the Grandiose in Literature, Psychopathology, and Culture*. Albany: SUNY Press, 1993.
Telò, Mario. *Archive Feelings: A Theory of Greek Tragedy*. Columbus: Ohio State University Press, 2020.
Valdrè, Rossella. *Psychoanalytic Reflections on the Freudian Death Drive: In Theory, the Clinic, and Art*. London: Routledge, 2019.
Weatherill, Rob. "Preface." In *The Death Drive: New Life for a Dead Subject?*, edited by Rob Weatherill, 1–11. London: Rebus Press, 1999.
Wohl, Victoria. "Sexual Difference and the Aporia of Justice in Sophocles' *Antigone*." In *Bound by the City: Greek Tragedy, Sexual Difference, and the Formation of the Polis*, edited by Denise Eileen McCoskey and Emily Zakin, 119–48. Albany: SUNY, 2009.
Žižek, Slavoj. *The Sublime Object of Ideology*. London: Verso, 1989.
Žižek, Slavoj. *Looking Awry: An Introduction to Jacques Lacan through Popular Culture*. Cambridge: MIT Press, 1991.
Žižek, Slavoj. *Enjoy Your Symptom: Jacques Lacan in Hollywood and Out*. New York: Routledge, 1992.
Žižek, Slavoj. "From Antigone to Joan of Arc." *Helios* 31 (2004): 51–62.
Žižek, Slavoj. *The Parallax View*. Cambridge: MIT Press, 2006.

Part I

Freud on the Death Drive—Philosophical Readings

1

Take It to the Limit

Ontology beyond the Pleasure Principle

Paul Allen Miller

> Let us picture a living organism in its most simplified possible form as the irritable substance of an undifferentiated vesicle. Then the surface turned towards the external world will be from its very situation differentiated and will serve as an organ for receiving irritation/stimuli. . . . It would be easy to suppose, then, that as a result of the ceaseless collisions of external stimuli on the surface of the vesicle, its substance to a certain depth may have become permanently modified, so that excitatory processes run a different course in it from what they run in the deeper layers. A crust (*Rinde*) would thus be formed which would at last have been so thoroughly "burned through" by stimulation that it would present the most favorable possible conditions for the reception of stimuli and become incapable of further modification.[1]

Halfway through Freud's *Beyond the Pleasure Principle* (1920) we are presented with what could be understood as a brief science-fiction novella: the origin of differentiation, we might even say *différance*, on the cellular level. In the beginning was the vesicle (*Bläschen*), a small fluid-filled sac or pustule, separated from the surrounding oneness by the barest of membranes. It is, save for this membrane, undifferentiated (*undifferentiertes*) from its encompassing environment. Nonetheless, this world is clearly pictured as hostile. The vesicle is the recipient of constant collisions. Strachey's neutral translation of the German adjective *reizbar* as "susceptible to stimulation" hardly does justice to the image, for, while *Reiz* often means "stimulus," or "charm," or even "attraction," *reizbar* is normally translated as "irritable," "touchy," or "high strung." The image then is not of clinical stimulus and response (unless perhaps we remember that a *stimulus* was originally in Latin a "goad or prod" used on livestock and slaves), but of a virgin, unmarked surface that is receiving various impacts. Those collisions sear or burn that surface, creating a scarring, a scab, a crust (*Rinde*) on the outer surface that signifies a definitive differentiation between the interior of this ball or bubble, which floats almost weightlessly in an undefined fluid or space, and the hostile external world that pelts, goads, wounds it, but at the same time charms it, stimulates it, excites it. Is this pleasure or is this pain, and how could this one-celled ur-ancestor of us all—this blister, this bubble, this utricle (*Bläschen*)—tell the difference?

In the beginning, Freud tells us, was trauma, and that trauma is prior to consciousness, prior to sense perception, and hence prior to both the pleasure and the reality principles, indeed prior to reality as a definable state itself.[2] In this moment of trauma, of limitation and delimitation, of scarring—dare we call it castration?—the process of differentiation begins both internally and externally. Freud spins an entire narrative in which the sensitive surfaces of these floating vesicles draw within, leaving only sensory organs—like insect antennae[3]—on the surface to assay the external world, to identify and package these stimuli, to bind the energy that bombards our scarred and sensitive membranes and makes the dominance or *Herrschaft* of the pleasure principle possible. As this differentiation and complexification proceeds apace, these vesicles become internally specialized, constantly absorbing these blows, metabolizing them, internalizing them, and recommunicating them to the surface. A process of economic exchange is engendered, quantities created, boundaries marked, and a world of defined things, the ontic world of subjects and objects we all believe we know comes into being. It all begins in a wound, that is a charm (*Reiz*), a stimulus that is a goad and an attraction, a blow that both moves and is absorbed, as the sensitive surface, our external membrane, both tries to preserve and return to its antecedent moment of all but unmarked clarity—a bubble floating in an undifferentiated amniotic sea, the original oceanic feeling—to a moment before and beyond the pleasure principle, and hence before and beyond the constitution of the same and the other, of the one and the many, of the ontic and the ontological, of life and death.

In what follows I want to reread this novella from three perspectives. First, I want to look more closely at several other passages in *Beyond the Pleasure Principle* that surround the story of the vesicle and point to a moment before the economic, before the process of exchange and compromise that is eternally at work in the dynamic between the *Lustprinzip* and the *Realitätprinzip*. I then want to turn to Derrida's reading of this same text, "Spéculer sur Freud," in which he argues specifically that within *Beyond the Pleasure Principle* Freud never, in fact, does go "beyond," not because there is nothing beyond the eternal calculus of costs and benefits, negative and positive reinforcements, pleasure and pain, but because beyond the moment, beyond the *topos*, in which we can make the calculation of exchanging quantities, is a world beyond representation, a world prior to and beyond the constitution of reality as a discrete object of experience, a choric world without defined boundaries and qualities.[4] To the extent we can and do talk about this world, write about it, and assign differential signifiers to it, then it is already saturated with pleasure and pain. It is a post-traumatic world that bows before the hegemony of its own prior constitution, the thetic moment whose compulsive repetition imposes order on choric chaos and is always already beyond it. In the penultimate movement, I shall then take up a brief hint in Derrida's essay, where he argues that it is Plato who stands "Derrière Freud," and particularly the Plato of the *Philebus*, a dialogue that strives to answer the ethical question of what is the best life by posing the ontological question of what lies between the limit and the unlimited, between the one and the many, or of how the ontic world can be understood in its inherent existential and epistemic precarity. I will then close with some brief reflections on the ethical and political sense of the understanding of pleasure, enjoyment, death, and the sublime to be derived from this triple reading of what Freud terms his great moment of "speculation, often far-fetched speculation."[5]

One

To return then to Freud, as we always must, there are three passages to which I would like to draw your attention that will stand as synecdoche for the many more. *Beyond the Pleasure Principle* opens with the assertion that its eponymous principle is believed without hesitation by analysts to regulate all psychic operations, leading to a reduction of tension or excitement. This notion, in turn, introduces an economic or exchange aspect (*ökonomischen Gesichtpunkt*) into psychic life, one that is inherently metapsychological (*metapsychologischen*) because it derives from an a priori determination that psychology itself cannot explain. For this economic model depends on a quantitative and proportional relationship that exists between pleasure and pain as forms of bound and unbound excitation. It presumes, in short, the prior existence of bounding, of the limit.[6]

Freud insists these are empirical observations, not part of a philosophical system, yet they depend on the assumption of a world made up of discrete entities that can enter into quantitative relations with one another, which is not in itself self-evident. Thus, the condition of possibility for a legible psyche, we are told, is the hegemony of the pleasure principle. The existence of this principle assumes the existence of an economic model that makes "proportional" calculations of relative quantities of pleasure and pain, calculations based on what Freud will shortly name the reality principle.[7] Yet the possibility of those calculations depends on a prior moment of legibility in which pleasure and unpleasure have already been rigorously distinguished. And there's the rub. Freud tells us we do not know what pleasure and unpleasure really are. Nonetheless, he has concluded that pleasure and unpleasure exist in relation to "the available life (*Leben*) in the soul" that is not "otherwise bound," and that an increase in this quantity means a symmetrical increase in pain, and a decrease, an increase in pleasure.[8] At the same time, he concedes that this does not mean we are dealing with stable, unchanging quantities but a dynamic relationship in time, a process of literal *différance* as the founding distinctions that make possible psychic life are produced.[9]

There is thus a limit that it seems cannot be breached, and it is that limit that renders the basic principle of psychoanalysis (but really of all post-enlightenment psychology), pleasure or, in another vocabulary, positive reinforcement, definable in terms of ontology or precise quantities. The economy of exchange is something that takes place in time and only occurs against a limit. That limit is its law but also necessarily posits a beyond the limit cannot explain. And so, we are told analysis can go no further, but yet we are only at the beginning. What would it mean to go beyond, to *be* beyond the limit?

In section 2, Freud recounts the myth of the *fort/da* game: the strange story of how, through a play of absence and presence, here and there, Freud's young grandson masters his mother's temporary absence, one which will all too soon be permanent, by reenacting it. Although the child's sounds are barely articulated, Freud emphasizes his verbal development is delayed—nonetheless, from the barest phonemic difference (*ooo* and *da*), he repeats the trauma of absence by casting his bobbin away and shouting (*ooo*/*fort*), and then, with great satisfaction, reeling it back (*da*). In doing so, he seems to soothe himself, as do the victims of trauma who reenact wounding moments in their dreams and rituals and find a measure of ironic mastery by inscribing both difference (*fort*/*da*) and repetition into their very flesh, the tender rind of these vesicles. Thus, we see the victims of trauma—the abused child, the battered spouse—return to the scene of their victimization and often victimize others in a seemingly senseless repetition. The question section 2 poses with special poignancy is: How can these moments of repeated traumatization be reconciled with the mastery (*Herrschaft*) of the pleasure principle? Even as we know that many seemingly unpleasant experiences form the basis, as Freud acknowledges, of the highest art, scenes which we repeat over and over, from *Oedipus* to *Hamlet* to *Tosca*.

Freud steps right up to the limit and tries to peer beyond it. Yet, he pulls back, "even under the mastery of the pleasure principle itself, there are ways and means enough of making what is unpleasant in itself into the object of recollection and psychic processing."[10] The world beyond the pleasure principle is a world beyond the economy of exchange and substitution. It is therefore a world beyond signification, beyond the acceptance of the name for the thing, beyond the acceptance of discontinuity in our experience, and hence beyond our separation from the sensuous manifold, the caesura that makes thought possible. The world beyond the pleasure principle is, therefore, fundamentally unable to be thought, and so the mastery of the pleasure principle always returns, endlessly repeating itself in the moment of its own beyond. As Freud acknowledges in the final sentence of section 2, there is a fundamental difficulty in imagining the ground from which the pleasure principle sprang, a moment before the limit.[11] This world of the "unlimited" is what Žižek gestures toward in his use of the term "desert of the real." It is a form of nonexistence and death.[12] The world in which the membrane of our vesicle ceases to hold.

In section 3, Freud's focus turns to the problem of repetition in the analytic setting, specifically the ways in which analysis reanimates past wounds, the deliberate, clinical repetition of *Unlust*. He compares analytic technique to people who keep repeating the same bad decisions again and again. Freud, in this section, posits the existence of a repetition compulsion, which "places itself over" the pleasure principle.[13] Yet every time we encounter this *Wiederholungszwang*, it is always already entangled with moments that can be recuperated under the dialectic of pleasure and pain, moments that presume their capacity to enter into proportional exchange with one another and be converted from one to the other.

The repetition compulsion, Freud tells us, almost never exists in its pure state because, in and of itself, it is before and beyond the economic aspect of the psyche. It exists only as a repetition of pure negation and determination that creates the ontic world and so allows the process of exchange to be engaged. It recalls the Demiurge's repeated stamping of indeterminate choric space in Plato's *Timaeus* that creates the phenomenal world as if he were impressing a preexisting form on a substance without qualities. This is the moment of determination qua determination, the imposition of the Law as Law, the original Oedipal moment, which has its own before and beyond.

In Freud's own words, "Es bleibt genug übrig": once all the economic calculations have been made, "there remains enough left over," there remains a sufficient margin of what "seems more original, more instinctual, and more impulsive than the pleasure principle" (1961: 17, translation altered), an indigestible remainder.

Two

> Différance, the pre-opening of ontico-ontological difference . . . and of all the differences that follow in the wake of Freudian concepuality, as they, and this is only one example, organize themselves around the difference between "pleasure" and "reality" : the difference between the pleasure principle and the reality principle, for example, is not only nor even primarily a distinction, an exteriority, but the original possibility, in life, of the detour, of différance (*Aufschub*)[14] and of the economy of death.[15]

As early as "Freud and the Scene of Writing," Derrida was interested in the ontological implications of *Beyond the Pleasure Principle*, its place within a Western tradition of thinking the origins of difference and the ontic, of how the world became not one. More than ten years later, he would return to it in "Spéculer sur Freud," the second movement of *La carte postale*. Here Derrida not only asks what it would mean to be beyond the pleasure principle, but he also interrogates what precisely is "'the logic' of the *beyond* or rather of the *not beyond*."[16] Translation cannot fully capture Derrida's second formulation, *pas au-delà*. *Pas* is, of course, half of the standard French negation *ne pas*, which is often shortened in colloquial speech to *pas*. But *pas* also means "step" and is cognate with English *pace*. The metaphor at the heart of the negation then is the image of "not a single step." There is a line, and neither the action referenced nor the actor has exceeded it by even a pace. Thus, when Derrida gives the alternative of beyond or not-beyond, the not-beyond immediately transforms itself into the step beyond, which is, in fact, the logic of the beyond and the fundamental ontico-ontological problem posed by *Beyond the Pleasure Principle*, even as it claims to eschew philosophical pretensions:[17] for the moment one has taken the step beyond, one is returned within. There is no thinkable "beyond" that by the act of thought, by becoming the object of articulated thought—as opposed to an intuition, sensation, or dream—does not cease to be beyond, but now falls within the field of the delimited. Hence, the logic of the beyond *is* the logic of the not-beyond. And yet the step is there: the repeated action that seems to go nowhere, that is always recuperated. One might even say a *Wiederholungszwang*, that in its repetition is never completely included within the "not beyond," in the same way as the repetition itself, while saturated with pleasure and recuperated within the "not beyond," always has a remainder—"Es bleibt genug übrig"—which cannot be precisely located but only reveals itself in the temporality of differentiation, in the movement of the step.

The logic of the beyond/not beyond, Derrida continues, spreads beyond (*déborder*, the image is of a flood), the logic of position: "Without substituting itself for [the logic of position], above all without opposing it, opening another relation, a relation without relation or common measure, to what it (*franchit*) crosses over with its step (*pas*) or from which it frees itself (*s'affranchit*) in one stroke (*coup*)."[18] The logic of the beyond/not beyond overflows a logic of position—a thetic logic, in which things are posited and positions assumed, theses defended (from the Greek *tithēmi*, "to put or place"), and oppositions created. The *au-delà/pas au-delà* certainly does not replace thetic logic. It does not oppose the logic of position as a thesis does an antithesis. Yet, it is also not without relation to thetic positionality, although it possesses no common measure with it. It happens in another place, in a different temporal movement, at another scene.

The step (*pas*) that enters the space of position (a *topos* rather than a *chora*), the stroke (*coup*) that enters that space as a determination or negation (*pas*), insofar as it is the act of entering itself rather than the difference it produces, insofar as it is the movement of oversweeping, going beyond the bounds of position, then that act necessarily enters into a relationship with thetic positionality. Nonetheless, as an action that must be repeated, since its consummation is also its recuperation (it assumes the position), then precisely in its temporal movement of determination it happens at another scene, on another plane whose geometry cannot be determined. Its relation to thetic positionality is a relation without relation (*rapport sans rapport*) in the same manner as Freud's death drive cannot occupy a position within the thetic logic of the pleasure and the reality principle, within the economic rationality of *Lust* and *Unlust*, without ceasing to give positive evidence of its existence, except in the figure of repetition itself. It is for this reason that Derrida refers to Freud's style in *Beyond the Pleasure Principle* as athetic. Freud's text, Derrida argues, speculates but never defends a thesis, never occupies a singular position but rather constantly steps up and over the line, only to see the line itself reconstituted on the other side. "Even the method/gait/step (*démarche*) of the text is diabolical. It imitates a progression (*marche*), does not cease from moving forward (*marcher*) without advancing; it regularly sketches out one more step (*pas*) without gaining an inch of territory."[19]

Indeed, as Derrida notes, death is both inscribed within the pleasure principle and uninscribable:[20] for what is beyond the pleasure principle is fundamentally illegible because it does not and cannot occupy a position within the psychic or (for that matter) any other economy. To the extent the death drive forms the object of a thesis, it no longer exists as a separable phenomenon from the pleasure principle, even if it cannot be fully inscribed within it. The reality principle opposes the pleasure principle only on the same ground. It is its mirror image since there can only be opposition on a common terrain.[21] Death has no position on this terrain. Rather, its silence is the condition of possibility for the opposition to arise in the first place. The pleasure principle, in its mastery, always returns to itself, but yet this return always also includes the radically other in the very movement of re-turning. "Without doubt in the return to itself, it allows the haunting of something *radically different* (*tout autre*) . . . to be implicated."[22]

There is thus no contradicting the pleasure principle. Every action can ultimately be recuperated on some level as either the attempt to procure what the subject wants (pleasure) or to avoid the opposite (unpleasure), and so every articulable position within such a rationality must already assume its mastery (*Herrschaft*), must already assume the possibility of the reduction of the psychic to pleasure and pain, to a series of pluses and minuses or ones and zeroes, and this hegemonic rationality can be met only with either silence or the creation of another space, a different rationality, another scene.[23] The pleasure principle on its own terms becomes the author of all that seems to escape it; even the most excruciating choice functions as its ratification, a kind of tautology[24]—because people act to pursue pleasure, then every act must be for pleasure.[25] At the same time, this asserted mastery always depends on a prior moment of differentiation that is beyond it, unstateable within it.[26]

This prior moment is what Freud terms "binding" (*Bindung*), a form of determination in which the energy flows that constitute life (*Leben*) are partitioned, given firm bounds. Hence, a certain membrane demarcating inside from outside arises, and the vesicle is created: the distinction of even the most primitive organism from its environment, which is the necessary predicate of pleasure and its opposite. This act of partition, the movement of differentiation, is both within and beyond the pleasure principle. "Freud has situated the *Bindung* before pleasure and before sexual pleasure. In view of this pleasure, but before and without it. The within and the beyond of sexuality work silently."[27] The binding itself, the fundamental step or stroke of determination that makes pleasure and its beyond possible, establishes a measure of control through the imposition of a bounded space demarcating life from death, the inside of the vesicle from the outside, and hence the possibility of scarring, of internal differentiation, of stimulus and response. Nonetheless, this binding can only work if it also includes the possibility of the loss of control, of free energy, the return of life to silence and death at the end of a long detour, after a series of economic exchanges, negations, and determinations—a set of steps.[28] A binding that does not assume the possibility of a return to the unbound is not a binding at all. In this resides the possibility of freedom, of a fundamental reshaping of our existence and the ontic world, of a beyond to come.

Freud's logic is thus not psychological but ontological or metapsychological. As Derrida argues in the penultimate section of "Spéculer sur Freud," "Platon derrière Freud":

> whatever Freud's reservations or distances with regard to the question of philosophy, *Beyond* . . . belongs to the tradition of the *Philebus*. The inheritance is assured, Plato is behind Freud. Or if one prefers, Socrates, with all the inversions brought on by the structure of a legacy. It's also the *Philebus* that we are reading through the scene of *Beyond* . . . . We would be able to verify this step by step (*pas à pas*) [negation by negation?].[29]

Let us be clear. What Derrida and we are talking about in these discussions is, on some level, the closure of metaphysics, the constitution of our representational universe. There is a logic to the epistemic world in which we live, a rational world that, as I argued in "Plato as World Literature," and as was perhaps most forcefully depicted by Heidegger, first manifests itself decisively in Plato. This is not to say that the creation of this world was the intention of Plato or that reading his often complex, ironic, and poetic texts as the scene of the creation of such a logic is the only or even best way to understand them as texts. Nonetheless, the elaboration of this moment exists: it constitutes what Derrida himself calls Platonism as opposed to Platonic textuality; and the world of Platonism, its understanding of truth and being, of what it means to see and think in the world, is decisively different from that found in Homer and the Presocratics, let alone Confucius, the Vedas, or Aztec mythology.[30] Moreover, one of the most crucial articulations of this logic can be found within the *Philebus*, which, as Derrida shows, Freud both reproduces and tries to think beyond, to peer over the limit, as indeed does Plato himself:

> The athetic style of *Beyond* . . . sets adrift the *Philebus*, which proceeds only through "theses" and a series of "*logoi*" from the first word to the last when Socrates asks—it's his last word—that they "let him go." But this drift is itself programmed by the discourse on the *apeiron*, the indefiniteness of the limit and the mixture.[31]

While Plato in the *Philebus* asks us to think about both pleasure and knowledge, and which is the good, he more profoundly demands that we see each of these as composites, as the product of a middle space between the limit and the unlimited, and thus always situated in relation to a beyond that threatens the seemingly stable unities of our rational discourse with being annihilated.

Three

> With matters arranged thus, it is necessary that we place ourselves to seek always on each occasion one idea concerning each thing—to find the idea present—then if we should interchange two with one, if they are so in some manner, but if not, to examine three or some other number, going back to each one to do similarly, until you might see the one at the origin that is not only one, but both many and unlimited, and also one might see their quantity.[32]
>
> I must point out again that what we call reality is thought of in Plato as a mixture of *peras* (limit, end) and *apeiron* [unlimited, infinite].[33]

The *Philebus* begins in *medias res*. Socrates asks Protarchus if he will be taking up the argument where Philebus left off since the latter has reached his limit. Socrates then asks if Protarchus would like him to summarize the argument, literally to bring the whole of it under one head (*sungkephalaiōsōmetha*). Whereupon he sums up Philebus's position that all living things enjoy pleasure, "as many as are harmoniously (*sumphōna*) together in this kind (*genos*)." Socrates does not dispute this argument directly, but he contends that "thinking, knowing, and remembering and all the related things of this kind (*sungenē*)" are better, at least for those able to partake of them. Protarchus then takes up the baton.

What we see in this opening, with Plato's typical poetic aplomb, is a foreshadowing of all the major themes of the dialogue: what is the good life for humans, pleasure or contemplation; how are things brought together under a single heading or grouped into a kind or genus; and is it possible to come to an end of such discussions or are they themselves unlimited, even if they also contain discrete units that form relays within a progression? It is perhaps not insignificant that the word that is used for Philebus giving up the discussion (*apeirēken*) puns on the very notion of the unlimited (*apeiron*), even as it signifies both the limit of his participation and the moment of continuation as the baton is passed to Protarchus.

It would be possible to give many other similar instances of the *Philebus*'s ironic textual poetics. Like Freud's text, the *Philebus* seems to undo and multiply its theses, its thetic moments, even as it advances them, both positing and disposing.[34] But for the moment, I will schematize ruthlessly: Socrates moves quickly to press Protarchus on the question of whether all pleasures are one, insofar as they *are* pleasures, or are there different kinds of pleasure? Equally, he is willing to grant that there are different forms of thought, so that his own position may be internally divided as well.

The introduction of the question of divisible kinds leads, then, to a discussion of the classic problem of the one and the many: is it merely a sophistic ploy to demonstrate that the same thing is both many and one (e.g., pleasure), a kind of party trick that young people use to confute their elders as Aristophanes suggests in the *Clouds*, or is there an actual question of what it means to be one, how a "one" could itself be made up of many things, and how the existence of those many things assumes both the imposition of a limit, a division that makes counting and quantification possible, and of what is beyond or before the limit, the unlimited.[35] Thus, in the quoted passage, Socrates tells us that it is a gift from the gods to recognize that each thing, insofar as it is one, can be divided into its component parts, and each of those components can in turn be divided, and so we continue until we can count up all the many, and only then do we release them into the unlimited. Thus, on the one hand, there are actual unities, and these unities can then be delimited into smaller parts, which are further divisible into still smaller parts, each of these divisions being the imposition of a limit, until such time as we reach the unlimited, the level beyond which any sort of unity ceases to exist.[36] On the other, it is through the imposition of the limit on the unlimited that units are first created, units that can then be collected with others to make more complex mixtures that eventually create a unified composite of the many into the one at the other end of the process.[37]

Socrates invites us to consider speech or music. In each case, we have a continuous column of sound that is divided into tones and rhythmic units—phonemes and notes—each of which can be subdivided until we reach a place where we return to the original undifferentiated column of sound, once we have completely dissolved the ordered arrangements we call music and speech. From there, one can repeat the process in reverse, build phonemes, words, sentences, and entire discourses, or notes, chords, phrases, melodies, and vast symphonic compositions to produce the unities that we all believe and understand to exist: music and speech. The problem of sophistic confutation comes not from the question of the one and the many per se, but from the assumption that it is always one or the other, that there is a logical contradiction between these two positions, when in fact the entire phenomenal world, to the extent that we accept that the entities we perceive and discuss are real, consists of things that are in fact both.[38]

Rational thought can only play itself out between the boundaries of the one and the unlimited. Pleasure and pain, for example, are both real, and they both are able to be exchanged with and converted into the other as complex composites that allow the world to be divided into intelligible, quantifiable entities. Yet that division and then those exchanges are only possible in relation to another scene, that of the unlimited, in which our selves and the ontic world of discrete phenomena cease to exist.

With these divisions established, Socrates returns to the question of pleasure versus knowledge, and he notes that neither of them can be the good, since each presumes the existence of the other: for no one would call either knowledge, which has no component of pleasure, nor pleasure, which is completely ignorant, the good; but insofar as our knowledge is truly good it should give us pleasure of some kind, and insofar as we pursue pleasure, it presumes a certain knowledge or even expertise, but the absolutely good would be that to which nothing could be added and nothing taken away, and so must presume both.

There are, then, in fact, two unlimiteds, or perhaps two infinities, which is another possible translation of the *apeiron*. The first unlimited is both the unquantifiable and also a realm of constant flux. It is the virgin, choric realm, like Kristeva's semiotic, before the imposition of the limit.[39] The second is the final "one," what Plato terms the good, that which is lacking nothing and exists as a kind of impossible totalization of all the other entities, all the other ones, all the other moments where lines have been drawn and types stamped, that by definition exceeds them and ultimately subsumes them. Another word for this might be *cosmos*, the Greek word for an ordered whole, but that ordered realm only exists within a bounded space and so can never really be *the* one, and the process of collection and assembly always leads to another moment of division, another step beyond the economic model that makes all our ones and zeroes possible. As Protarchus says in the last line of the dialogue, "There is still a little missing, Socrates. Surely you will not give up before we do. But I will remind you of what is left."[40]

Near the end of the dialogue, there comes a very odd moment where Socrates is trying to define an order of the different kinds of cognition and enjoyment, and he tries to imagine what an unmixed pleasure might be—one that held no element of pain, no moment of depletion before the pleasures of repletion.[41] He asks us to picture a moment of pure whiteness, as a source of pleasure and beauty that is without admixture.[42] Whenever I read this passage, I am always reminded of Rauschenberg's 1951 *White Painting*. There is, here, a moment of death and *jouissance* that Lacan would later identify as the essence of the death drive, in both the painting and Socrates' formulation.

Four

In his seventh seminar, Lacan identifies psychoanalytic ethics with Antigone's "no."[43] Antigone, he says, does not teach us an ethics of "biens," that is to say both "goods" in the Aristotelian since of virtues and "goods" in the sense of commodities that can be traded, exchanged, quantified, and possessed. Her "no" is not a compromise with the reality principle. It is not an attempt to maximize utility. She embraces death, like she embraces her dead brother, for no other reason than she does not accept the world of laws and limits Creon embodies. She does not cede on her desire. Such a "no," for Lacan, is the beginning of any ethics worthy of the name because it alone does not accept the world of given goods but asks the much more fundamental question: What would the world look like if none of these goods existed, if we discarded this economic model and started again?

Such a figure, as Žižek has noted, does not just bring us an ethics, but it also assumes a politics. One of his preferred examples is the Baader-Meinhof Group in the German Federal Republic of the 1970s. This was a small group that launched a terror campaign aimed at former Nazis, who occupied positions of power in the West German establishment, and German support for the Vietnam War. These too were people who refused to accept the goods on offer. But in the end, even Žižek is not a real terrorist, except perhaps of the spirit, and the failure of the Red Army Faction speaks for itself. They did not produce the revolution they hoped for. Still, Žižek's basic point remains. If we are not willing to question the limit, to go beyond the pleasure principle, beyond Antigone's veil of *atē*, if we are not willing to see that the world of stable entities on which our realities are predicated is in fact produced, is the product of certain delimitations that could be drawn otherwise, then we will never be able to assume an ethical stance that is not also a rationalization of the economic.[44] We will never be able to change the basic calculations and relations of power that delimit the world as it currently exists and for whom it exists.

As Plato, Derrida, and Freud teach us, each in their own way, each in the process of gesturing toward the limits and determinations that constitute the given, it is only beyond the closure of metaphysics, beyond the pleasure and the reality principles, that knowledge which does not seek to ratify the given is possible. Such knowledge depends upon the possibility of redrawing the fundamental lines that define the phenomenal, of reconfiguring what counts as an entity, and of what counts as real. This is as true for abstract concepts like democracy and freedom as it was at one time for phlogiston and classical mechanics, and as it has been true for the unconscious and sexuality. Ours is no longer the world imagined by Linnaeus, Newton, or Adam Smith. As Foucault reminds us, one of the fundamental questions we should ask is why is there not only the real, but why is there also truth?[45] Truth can never be perfectly congruent with the real, or the truth would simply be what is, and error would be inexplicable. New knowledge could not exist. Rather, our truths depend very much on the "ones" and the "manys" we identify, and the relations between those unities that produce an ordered and quantifiable world, one in which we not only seek pleasure and avoid pain, but also one in which we attempt to imagine new orders, new entities, and hence new objects of knowledge, new delimitations, and new pleasures—a poetic world.

Freud's *Beyond the Pleasure Principle*, with its positing of a death drive saturated with enjoyment, is a moment in which the closures that constitute our experiential world become visible, our reality begins to tremble, and the scars on the rind of our vesicle can be seen. Derrida's reading, in its refusal to accept the givenness of Freud's discourse, makes visible the radicality of his athetic style, but Derrida and Freud both continue to operate within and gesture beyond a unity that Plato himself first imagined in the *Philebus*, even as he too posited an "unlimited" that is "beyond" or, perhaps, "*à-venir.*" Indeed, what is truly still "to come" is never already here, never within the limit. In the end, as Derrida reminds us in *Spectres de Marx*, what we are searching for, as we seek the good, as we seek justice without limit, is

> Not for calculable equality . . . nor for the symmetrical and synchronic compatibility or imputability of subjects and objects, not to render a justice that would limit itself to sanctioning, to restitution and rectification, but for justice as the incalculability of the gift and the singularity of the an-economic ex-position to others.[46]

Inshallah. So be it. Amen.

Notes

1 Sigmund Freud, *Beyond the Pleasure Principle*, trans. James Strachey (New York: Norton, 1961), 20; translation modified.
2 Freud, *Beyond the Pleasure Principle*, 23.
3 Freud, *Beyond the Pleasure Principle*, 22.
4 See Paul Allen Miller, "The Platonic Remainder: *Khora* and the *Corpus Platonicum*," in *Plato and Derrida*, ed. Miriam Leonard (Oxford: Oxford University Press, 2010), 321–41; Judith Butler, "Bodies that Matter," in *Bodies that Matter: On the Discursive Limits of Sex* (London: Routledge, 1993), 3–27.
5 Freud, *Beyond the Pleasure Principle*, 18.
6 Freud, *Beyond the Pleasure Principle*, 1.
7 I want to have a given sensual satisfaction (*Lust*). I know that this satisfaction will cost x quantity of discomfort (*Unlust*). A calculation is then made whether, to paraphrase the Beatles, the *Lust* you take is equal to the *Unlust* you make. This is Freud the behaviorist (1).
8 Freud, *Beyond the Pleasure Principle*, 2; translation modified.
9 See Jacques Derrida, *Positions* (Paris: Minuit, 1972), 30–9, 56–7; Jacques Derrida, *La carte postale: de Socrate à Freud et au-delà* (Paris: Aubier-Flammarion, 1980), 425; Jacques Derrida, *Résistances de la Psychanalyse* (Paris: Galilée, 1996), 41–8.
10 Freud, *Beyond the Pleasure Principle*, 11; translation altered.
11 "May an economically directed aesthetics deal with these endless cases and situations, which have yield of pleasure as their final outcome; they are of no use for our purpose since they presuppose the existence and dominance of the pleasure principle and they give no evidence of the operation of tendencies beyond the pleasure principle, that is, which were more original than it and independent of it" (Freud, *Beyond the Pleasure Principle*, 11; translation modified). Note: they give no evidence because they presume it. This passage seems to validate Lacan's claim that *Beyond the Pleasure Principle* and metapsychology show that psychoanalysis had reached a point of stagnation and needed reformulation. See Jacques Lacan, *Le séminaire, livre II. Le moi dans la théorie de Freud et dans la technique de la psychanalyse*, ed. Jacques-Alain Miller (Paris: Seuil, 1978), 20–3.
12 See Slavoj Žižek, *Welcome to the Desert of the Real* (London: Verso, 2002).

13 Freud, *Beyond the Pleasure Principle*, 16; translation modified.
14 Cf. Freud, *Beyond the Pleasure Principle*, 4.
15 Jacques Derrida, "Freud et la scène de l'écriture," in *Écriture et difference* (Paris: Seuil, 1967), 295.
16 Derrida, *La carte postale*, 278.
17 Freud, *Beyond the Pleasure Principle*, 1.
18 Derrida, *La carte postale*, 278.
19 Derrida, *La carte postale*, 287, cf. 294.
20 Derrida, *La carte postale*, 344.
21 Derrida, *La carte postale*, 304–5.
22 Derrida, *La carte postale*, 314.
23 Derrida, *La carte postale*, 314.
24 Derrida, *La carte postale*, 369–70.
25 This is of course the failure of all forms of determinism. They are impossible to contradict. And yet such formulas are common in social science and psychology, which presume rational actors, self-interest, and the maximization of utility or, in more extreme variants, the preservation of a genetic endowment through the reproduction of the species. Every seeming counterexample to these explanations can always be shown to rest either on a lack of appropriate information—the consumer, voter, or subject did not understand their true interests—or can be shown actually to serve the stated principle: they took pleasure in their pain, their seeming self-sacrifice accrued to the benefit of their offspring, the species, and so on. All such systems of explanation effectively deny the possibility of real ethical or political choice. They are all-encompassing mechanisms, and as such, they explain nothing but simply reiterate their founding assumption.
26 Derrida, *La carte postale*, 372.
27 Derrida, *La carte postale*, 429, cf. 420–1.
28 Derrida, *La carte postale*, 365, 377.
29 Derrida, *La carte postale*, 425.
30 See Marcel Detienne, *The Masters of Truth in Archaic Greece*, trans. Janet Lloyd (New York: Zone Books, 1996); Michel Foucault, *Leçons sur la volonté de savoir. Cours au Collège de France, 1970–71. Suivi de "Le Savoir d'Oedipe,"* ed. Daniel Defert (Paris: Hautes Études/Gallimard/Seuil, 2011).
31 Derrida, *La carte postale*, 425.
32 See Plato's *Philebus* section 16d.
33 Hans-Georg Gadamer, "Reply to Nicholas P. White," trans. Roger C. Norton and Dennis J. Schmidt, in *Platonic Writings, Platonic Readings*, ed. Charles L. Griswold Jr. (New York: Routledge, 1988), 265.
34 And I have plans to someday do a full philosophical commentary on the *Philebus*, which it should be pointed out in the late Academy was the culminating dialogue of the philosophical curriculum.
35 A. J. Festugière, *Contemplation et vie contemplative selon Platon*, second edition (Paris: Vrin, 1950), 196–7; Auguste Diès, "Notice" (1941), in *Platon, Oeuvres completes*, tome 9.2 (Paris: Société d'Edition, 1966), xxii, xxv; Hans-Georg Gadamer, *Plato's Dialectical Ethics: Phenomenological Interpretations Relating to the Philebus*, trans. Robert M. Wallace (New Haven: Yale University Press, 1991), 120–1, 129–30.
36 J. C. B. Gosling, *Plato:* Philebus, *Translated with Notes and Commentary* (Oxford: Clarendon Press, 1975), xiv.

37 Nicolas-Isidore Boussoulas, *L'être et la composition des mixtes dans le "Phlèbe"* (Paris: Presses Universitaires de France, 1952), 57–8, 65; Dorothea Frede, "Disintegration and Integration: Pleasure and Pain in Plato's *Philebus*," in *The Cambridge Companion to Plato*, ed. Richard Kraut (Cambridge: Cambridge University Press, 1992), 428; Cynthia Hampton, *Pleasure, Knowledge, and Being: An Analysis of Plato's Philebus* (Albany: SUNY Press, 1990), 87–8.

38 Hampton, *Pleasure, Knowledge, and Being*, 34; Cynthia Hampton, "Overcoming Dualism: The Importance of the Intermediate in Plato's *Philebus*," in *Feminist Interpretations of Plato*, ed. Nancy Tuana (University Park: Penn State University Press, 1994), 226.

39 Diès, "Notice," xxvii–xxx; Gadamer, "Reply to Nicholas P. White," 260; Hampton, *Pleasure, Knowledge, and Being*, 43; Gadamer, *Plato's Dialectical Ethics*, 131, 138.

40 See Plato's *Philebus* section 67b.

41 See Plato's *Philebus* section 53a-b.

42 Festugière, *Contemplation et vie contemplative selon Platon*, 301; Hampton, *Pleasure, Knowledge, and Being*, 70; Frede, "Disintegration and Integration," 439.

43 See Jacques Lacan, *Le séminaire livre VII: L'éthique de la psychanalyse*, ed. Jacques-Alain Miller (Paris: Seuil, 1986).

44 Slavoj Žižek, *Enjoy Your Symptom: Jacques Lacan in Hollywood and Out* (New York: Routledge, 1992), 77–78; Slavoj Žižek, *The Sublime Object of Ideology* (London: Verso, 1989), 117.

45 Michel Foucault, *Subjectivity and Truth: Lectures at the College de France 1980–1981*, ed. Frédéric Gros, trans. Graham Burchell (London: Palgrave Macmillan, 2017), 237.

46 Jacques Derrida, *Spectres de Marx* (Paris: Galilée, 1993), 48.

Works Cited

Boussoulas, Nicolas-Isidore. *L'être et la composition des mixtes dans le "Phlèbe."* Paris: Presses Universitaires de France, 1952.

Butler, Judith. "Bodies that Matter." In *Bodies that Matter: On the Discursive Limits of Sex*, 3–27. London: Routledge, 1993.

Derrida, Jacques. "Freud et la scène de l'écriture." In *Écriture et difference*, 293–340. Paris: Seuil, 1967.

Derrida, Jacques. *Positions*. Paris: Minuit, 1972.

Derrida, Jacques. *La carte postale: de Socrate à Freud et au-delà*. Paris: Aubier-Flammarion, 1980.

Derrida, Jacques. *Spectres de Marx*. Paris: Galilée, 1993.

Derrida, Jacques. *Résistances de la Psychanalyse*. Paris: Galilée, 1996.

Detienne, Marcel. *The Masters of Truth in Archaic Greece*. Translated by Janet Lloyd. New York: Zone Books, 1996.

Diès, Auguste. "Notice" (1941). In *Platon, Oeuvres completes*, tome 9.2, vii–cxii. Paris: Société d'Edition, 1966.

Festugière, A. J. *Contemplation et vie contemplative selon Platon*, second edition. Paris: Vrin, 1950.

Foucault, Michel. *Leçons sur la volonté de savoir. Cours au Collège de France, 1970–71. Suivi de "Le Savoir d'Oedipe."* Edited by Daniel Defert. Paris: Hautes Études/Gallimard/Seuil, 2011.

Foucault, Michel. *Subjectivity and Truth: Lectures at the College de France 1980–1981.* Edited by Frédéric Gros. Translated by Graham Burchell. London: Palgrave Macmillan, 2017.

Frede, Dorothea. "Disintegration and Integration: Pleasure and Pain in Plato's *Philebus*." In *The Cambridge Companion to Plato*, edited by Richard Kraut, 425–63. Cambridge: Cambridge University Press, 1992.

Freud, Sigmund. *Beyond the Pleasure Principle.* Translated by James Strachey. New York: Norton, 1961.

Gadamer, Hans-Georg. "Reply to Nicholas P. White," translated by Roger C. Norton and Dennis J. Schmidt. In *Platonic Writings, Platonic Readings*, edited by Charles L. Griswold Jr., 258–66. New York: Routledge, 1988.

Gadamer, Hans-Georg. *Plato's Dialectical Ethics: Phenomenological Interpretations Relating to the Philebus.* Translated by Robert M. Wallace. New Haven: Yale University Press, 1991.

Gosling, J. C. B. *Plato: Philebus, Translated with Notes and Commentary.* Oxford: Clarendon Press, 1975.

Hampton, Cynthia. *Pleasure, Knowledge, and Being: An Analysis of Plato's Philebus.* Albany: SUNY Press, 1990.

Hampton, Cynthia. "Overcoming Dualism: The Importance of the Intermediate in Plato's *Philebus.*" In *Feminist Interpretations of Plato*, edited by Nancy Tuana, 217–42. University Park: Penn State University Press, 1994.

Lacan, Jacques. *Le séminaire, livre II. Le moi dans la théorie de Freud et dans la technique de la psychanalyse.* Edited by Jacques-Alain Miller. Paris: Seuil, 1978.

Lacan, Jacques. *Le séminaire livre VII: L'éthique de la psychanalyse.* Edited by Jacques-Alain Miller. Paris: Seuil, 1986.

Miller, Paul Allen. "The Platonic Remainder: *Khora* and the *Corpus Platonicum*." In *Plato and Derrida*, edited by Miriam Leonard, 321–41. Oxford: Oxford University Press, 2010.

Žižek, Slavoj. *The Sublime Object of Ideology.* London: Verso, 1989.

Žižek, Slavoj. *Enjoy Your Symptom: Jacques Lacan in Hollywood and Out.* New York: Routledge, 1992.

Žižek, Slavoj. *Welcome to the Desert of the Real.* London: Verso, 2002.

2

Baudrillard on the Death Drive

Jeffrey R. Di Leo

In 1976, Jean Baudrillard published *Symbolic Exchange and Death* (*L'échange symbolique et la mort*), where he challenged the Marxist theoretical tradition by favoring symbolic exchange over economic exchange. For Baudrillard, the symbolic exchange of precapitalist societies is much less limited than the economic exchange of capitalist and socialist societies. Rather than emphasizing the values of utility, production, and instrumental rationality, Baudrillard instead argues that we should look to the values of giving, expenditure, and sacrifice. In part, these latter values are derived from the anthropology of Georges Bataille, which, Baudrillard argues, posits an alternative form of economy that replaces the capitalist imperatives of labor, savings, and utility with ones derived from the pleasure humans find in things such as waste, sacrifices, expenditure, and festivities. Through Bataille, Baudrillard comes to view humans as characterized by an excess of drives, needs, fantasies, energies, and desires, which is a way very different from the one envisioned by Sigmund Freud and psychoanalysis.

Nevertheless, if Bataille can be described as a direct route to Baudrillard's notion of symbolic exchange, then Freud along with Ferdinand de Saussure and Marcel Mauss are each indirect—albeit equally important—routes. I say this because whereas the symbolic exchange aspects of Bataille's thought are directly cited and utilized by Baudrillard, those of Freud, Saussure, and Mauss only bolster his theory of symbolic exchange when the respective theories from these thinkers are deconstructed and, thereby, "radicalized." In the case of Freud, it is his theory of the death drive; in the case of Saussure, it is his theory of the anagram; and in the case of Mauss, it is his theory of the gift. "Indeed," writes Baudrillard, "we must switch the targets of each of these three theories, and turn Mauss against Mauss, Saussure against Saussure and Freud against Freud."[1] Specifically, in the case of Mauss, his notion of the "gift" must be subjected to "the principle of reversibility." Then, the resultant "counter-gift," writes Baudrillard, "must be imposed against all of the economistic, psychologistic and structuralist interpretations for which Mauss paved the way."[2] For Saussure, his linguistics must be set against his work on anagrams, including his "restricted hypotheses concerning the anagram."[3] Finally, in the case of Freud, his "death drive must be pitched against every previous psychoanalytic edifice, and even against Freud's version of the death drive."[4]

Baudrillard contends that by subjecting key hypotheses in the work of Mauss, Saussure, and Freud to "paradox and theoretical violence," we find that these "hypotheses describe, in their own respective fields . . . a functional principle sovereignly outside and antagonistic to our economic 'reality principle.'"[5] Thus, not only are the economic foundations of traditional Marxism, including capitalism and socialism, *dismantled* through the "reversibility of the gift in the counter-gift, the reversibility of time in the cycle, the reversibility of production in destruction, the reversibility of life in death, and the reversibility of every term and value of the *langue* in the anagram,"[6] but so too are the respective theoretical foundations of the fields of anthropology, linguistics, and psychoanalysis. In the wake of the dismantlement, radicalization, and deconstruction of these domains, the form of the symbolic is "inevitably" revealed. It is a form that is "[n]either mystical nor structural," but rather "assumes the form of extermination and death."[7]

In *Symbolic Exchange and Death*, Baudrillard pushes things such as death to the limit. By doing so, he contends, they "quite naturally . . . collapse and are inverted."[8] In the case of death, its form is inevitably revealed in economics, psychoanalysis, linguistics, and anthropology. However, it soon becomes apparent in *Symbolic Exchange and Death* that Baudrillard's conception of death is very different from that of not only Freud in particular but also of Western thought in general. "Death," writes Baudrillard, "*ought* never to be understood as the real event that affects a subject or a body."[9] Rather, death ought to be understood "as a *form* in which the determinacy of the subject and of value is lost."[10] The reversibility that is inevitably revealed by playing death against death ends both death's determinacy *and* indeterminacy. It also ends, he contends, "bound energies in stable oppositions, and is therefore in substantial agreement with theories of flows and intensities, whether libidinal or schizo."[11]

For Baudrillard, the unbinding of "energies," which is the inevitable consequence of practicing reversibility, results in "the impossibility of distinguishing libidinal economy from the political economy of the system of value; and the impossibility of distinguishing capitalist schizzes from revolutionary schizzes."[12] In this regard, the former impossibility has parallels to the work of Jean-François Lyotard's *Libidinal Economy* (*Economie Libidinale*), published two years before *Symbolic Exchange and Death*, and the latter impossibility has parallels to Gilles Deleuze and Félix Guattari's *Anti-Oedipus: Capitalism and Schizophrenia* (*L'Anti-Oedipe*), published four years earlier. But here's the rub for Baudrillard: while "the system is master [and] like God it can bind or unbind energies," it is still not capable of reversibility—and "can no longer avoid" it.[13] "Reversibility alone therefore, rather than unbinding or drifting," concludes Baudrillard, "is fatal to it."[14] For him, the fatality of reversibility is "exactly what the term symbolic 'exchange' means."[15]

In the remainder of this chapter, I would like to focus on the reversibility of Freud, which for Baudrillard means that the "Freud of the death drive must be pitched against every previous psychoanalytic edifice, and even against Freud's version of the death drive."[16] While the reversibility of Freud is significant as one of several fatal reversibilities that work in tandem in *Symbolic Exchange and Death* to undermine the notion of economic exchange, this is not the only reason it is worth a closer look. It is also significant because it presents a hypothesis regarding death after the death drive. And while this hypothesis contains aspects of subsequent biopolitical and thanatopolitical speculation, it also points to a very different possible approach to work in these areas—one that I believe has been largely ignored because Baudrillard's theses on death after the death drive in *Symbolic Exchange and Death* have not been seriously and extensively engaged or discussed.

Part of the reason for this is simple: a biopolitical or thanatopolitical Baudrillard does not fit the image of him in the English-speaking world, where he is heralded and read as one of the major theorists of postmodernity.[17] Moreover, as Baudrillard himself says, the arguments made in *Symbolic Exchange and Death* have never really been taken seriously, including the ones regarding death.[18] As evidence for this in the English-speaking world, where his work is generally engaged with much more seriousness than in the French-speaking world, consider that *Symbolic Exchange and Death* would not be available in English in its entirety until 1993, which, for those who are counting, is nearly two decades after its original publication. By this time, Baudrillard's image as a postmodern provocateur was firmly in place and was being further solidified by the publication of controversial books at the time, such as *The Gulf War Did Not Take Place* (*La Guerre du Golfe n'a pas en lieu*), which was published in 1991.

Moreover, the little that was published in English prior to 1993 omitted his extensive arguments about death and focused instead on his statements regarding the end of production and the order of simulacra. The first selection from *Symbolic Exchange and Death* in English was published in 1983 in the Semiotext(e) volume, *Simulations*, and included the majority of Chapter 2, "The Order of Simulacra,"[19] along with the entirety of the first chapter of his 1981 book, *Simulacra and Simulation* (*Simulacres et simulation*), which is entitled "The Precession of Simulacra."[20] The second selection from *Symbolic Exchange and Death* was published in 1984 in the edited volume, *The Structural Allegory: Reconstructive Encounters with the New French Thought*, edited by John Fekete, under the title "The Structural Law of Value and the Order of Simulacra." It included the book's "Preface" and brief selections from Chapter 1, "The End of Production," and Chapter 2, "The Order of Simulacra."[21] This, in turn, was reprinted verbatim in 1988 in another volume, *Jean Baudrillard: Selected Writings*, edited by Mark Poster, albeit with a new title, "Symbolic Exchange and Death." Then, a few years later, in 1990, a new selection from and translation of Chapter 1, "The End of Production,"[22] was published in *Revenge of the Crystal: Selected Writings on the Modern Object and Its Destiny, 1968–1983*, edited by Paul Foss and Julian Pefanis.

In short, these were the only selections from *Symbolic Exchange and Death* available to English readers from 1976 to 1993. For the most part, they conform to the image of Baudrillard as a postmodern theorist who is especially adept at articulating two of the features attributed to postmodernism by Fredric Jameson: flatness and depthlessness. For Jameson, postmodernism effects a kind of superficiality or flatness that resists interpretation; that is, it is anti-hermeneutic. Moreover, it effects a kind of addiction to the image or reproduction without a model or referent in the real, which is, in short, the logic of Baudrillard's simulacra.[23] What is missing, though, from these selections from *Symbolic Exchange and Death* is Baudrillard's extensive commentary on death, the dead, and the death drive, which arguably is his most lasting philosophical contribution—albeit one that goes against the grain of most Western thought in this area.

Freud on Life and Death

In *Beyond the Pleasure Principle*, which was first published in 1920, Freud introduces the death instinct. "If we are to take it as a truth that knows no exception that everything living dies for *internal* reasons—becomes inorganic once again—then we shall be compelled to say that 'the goal of all life is death,'" writes Freud, "and, looking backwards, that 'what was inanimate existed before what is living.'"[24] He would later formally link the "life instinct" (Eros) to the "death instinct" (Thanatos). Together, they are the only basic instincts. "The aim of the first of these basic instincts," he writes twenty years later in *An Outline of Psychoanalysis* [1940], "is to establish even greater unities and to preserve them thus—in short, to bind together; the aim of the second, on the contrary, is to undo connections and so to destroy things."[25]

For Freud, "the final aim of the destructive instinct is to reduce living things to an inorganic state."[26] Along with these two primal forces is the "pleasure principle," which Freud describes as "a tendency operating in the service of a function whose business it is to free the mental apparatus from excitation or to keep the amount of excitation in it constant or to keep it as low as possible."[27] As to whether the pleasure principle "requires a reduction, or perhaps ultimately the extinction, of the tension of the instinctual needs (that is, a state of *Nirvana*) leads to problems that are still [as of 1940] unexamined in the relations between the pleasure principle and the two primal forces, Eros and the death instinct."[28]

In 1933, he published his *New Introductory Lectures on Psychoanalysis*, which were meant to supplement his *Introductory Lectures on Psycho-Analysis* that were delivered in successive Winter Terms in 1915–16 and 1916–17. These later dates are important as they indicate a time period prior to the establishment of his theory of the death instinct. Therefore, one of the functions of the *New Introductory Lectures on Psychoanalysis* is to "introduce entirely new material and theories," which, in the case of his new introductory lecture on his theory of instincts, requires him to, as James Strachey says, "plunge into theoretical and metapsychological discussions of a difficulty which had been studiously avoided fifteen years earlier."[29]

In the new introductory lecture entitled "Anxiety and Instinctual Life," Freud associates instincts such as the death drive with mythology:

> The theory of instincts is so to say our mythology. Instincts are mythical entities, magnificent in their indefiniteness. In our work we cannot for a moment disregard them, yet we are never sure that we are seeing them clearly.[30]

He also says that in both the realm of mental life and the realm of vegetative life, the instincts reveal a compulsion to repeat:

> The instincts rule not only mental but also vegetative life, and these organic instincts exhibit a characteristic which deserves our deepest interest. . . . For they reveal an effort to restore an earlier state of things. We may suppose that from the moment at which a state of things that has once been attained is upset, an instinct arises to create it afresh and brings about phenomena which we can describe as a "compulsion to repeat."[31]

Thus, for Freud, examples of the instinctual compulsion to repeat include "the whole of embryology," "[t]he spawning migrations of fishes, [and] the migratory flights of birds."[32] Moreover, for him, it is possible that "all that we describe as manifestations of instinct in animals, take place under the orders of the compulsion to repeat, which expresses the *conservative nature* of the instincts."[33]

The latter point, that is, the conservative nature of the instincts, coupled with the compulsion to repeat, is important to Freud because he believes that it helps us to understand the death drive. Specifically, it helps us to understand what it is that the death instinct wants to *restore*. In "Anxiety and Instinctual Life," he writes,

> If it is true that—at some immeasurably remote time and in a manner we cannot conceive—life once proceeded out of inorganic matter, then, according to our presumption, an instinct must have arisen which sought to do away with life once more and to reestablish the inorganic state. If we recognize in this instinct the self-destructiveness of our hypothesis, we may regard the self-destructiveness as an expression of a "death instinct" which cannot fail to be present in every vital process. And now the instincts that we believe in divide themselves into two groups—the erotic instincts, which seek to combine more and more living substance into ever greater unities, and the death instincts, which oppose this effort and lead what is living back into an inorganic state. From the concurrent and opposing action of these two proceed the phenomena of life which are brought to an end by death.[34]

While one might be led to believe that Freud is arguing like Arthur Schopenhauer that the only aim of life is death, he does not believe this to be the case. Rather, in his defense, he says, "there is life as well as death."[35] For Freud, both the *life instinct* (Eros) and the *death instinct* (Thanatos) have their own aim. Nevertheless, at this relatively late point in his work (1933), Freud concedes that he is not sure how the life instinct and the death instinct are "mingled in the process of living."[36] In other words, for Freud, it is still to be determined "how the death instinct is made to serve the purposes of Eros, especially by being turned outwards as aggressiveness."[37] At this point, Freud seems content with the conclusion that his work on the death drive has "confirmed by sober and detailed research"[38] not natural science, but rather the philosophy of Schopenhauer. He also appears content to leave it to others to sort out how the process of living mingles with our two basic instincts: the death drive and the life drive. It is here, over forty years later, that Baudrillard seeks to complete Freud's research agenda for the death drive by thinking through some of the implications and paradoxes of Freud's work on life and death.

Freud against Western Thought

For Baudrillard, Freud's death drive is a decisive break from Western thought from "Christianity to Marxism and existentialism," wherein death is either "openly denied and sublimated, or it is dialectized."[39] Briefly, then, a note or two on each of these areas of Western thought as viewed by Baudrillard:

Christianity—in the case of Christianity, it was from the start, according to Baudrillard, "established on the bipartition of survival, or the afterlife, from life, the earthly world and the Kingdom of Heaven," and the power of the Church was "based on the management of the imaginary sphere of death."[40]

Marxism—in the case of Marxism, death was either "integrated as historical negativity or conquered in the being of class."[41] More generally speaking, writes Baudrillard, "the whole Western practice of the domination of nature and the sublimation of aggression in production and accumulation is characterized as constructive Eros: Eros makes use of sublimated aggression for its own ends and, in the movement of becoming . . . death is distilled as negativity into homeopathic doses."[42]

Existentialism—in the case of existentialism, Martin Heidegger, for example, speaks of "Authentic being-towards-death—which is to say, the finitude of temporality—is the hidden basis of Dasein's historicality."[43] According to Baudrillard, the notion of death as authenticity brings with it "a relation to a system that is itself mortifying, a vertiginous escalation, a challenge which is in fact a profound obedience."[44] Nevertheless, for Baudrillard, the "terrorism of authenticity through death remains a secondary process in that, by means of dialectical acrobatics, consciousness recuperates its 'finitude' as destiny."[45] Thus, in the existentialist notions of the "anguish of death as a test of truth" and "human life as being-towards-death," Baudrillard locates a complicated dialectics of death, which he finds "extremely Christian" and "constantly mixed up with "existential Christianity."[46]

Additionally, even *revolutionary* Western thought is characterized by a dialectics of death and the abolition of death. Revolutionary Western thought, writes Baudrillard, "oscillates between the *dialecticisation* of death and the *rationalist* objective of the abolition of death: to put an end to it as a 'reactionary' obstacle in solidarity with capital, with the help of science and technics, *en route* to the immortality of generic man, beyond history, in communism."[47] "Death," he continues, "like so many other things, is only a superstructure, whose exit will be governed by the revolution of the infrastructure."[48]

In contrast, however, Freud's death drive for Baudrillard presents a notion of death radically different from its Christian, Marxist, existentialist, and revolutionary forms. Specifically, it is a notion of death *with neither a dialectic, sublimation, nor denial.* These three points are important to Baudrillard as they are used to differentiate Freud's notion of death as a principle that is indestructible and in opposition to Eros from the notions of death in previous Western thought. Moreover, Freud's indestructible death principle is one wherein the notions of class, subject, and history are not relevant. Nevertheless, for Baudrillard, Freud's death drive still has a well-known precursor in ancient thought that begs to be explained away in view of the thesis that the death drive marks a profound break from Christianity and Western metaphysics.

This ancient precursor is Manichaeism, a religion that originated in Babylonia in the third century of the common era. Manichaeism generally contends that the framework of world conflict and redemption hinges on the opposition of good and evil, which are identified as light and darkness. Manichaeism spread from the Middle East to both Britain and China and was once one of the most popular religions in the world. Nevertheless, all of the major religions at the time, including Buddhism, Christianity, Islam, and Zoroastrianism, regarded Manichaeism as a heresy.

For Baudrillard, the duality of the Eros and Thanatos drives in Freud "reawakens the ancient Manichaean version of the world, the endless antagonism of the twin principles of good and evil."[49] But as Baudrillard points out, Manichaeism "was unbearable to the Church, who will take centuries to exterminate it and impose the pre-eminent principle of the Good (God), reducing evil and death to a negative principle, dialectically subordinate to the other (the Devil)."[50] By reawakening this ancient dualism in the death drive, Freud is also reawakening "the nightmare of Lucifer's autonomy, the Archangel of Evil,"[51] which includes forms such as black magic, Jansenist theory, and the Cathars. In short, for Baudrillard, *associating* the death drive with the dualisms of Manichaeism is tantamount to *disassociating* it from the Church, Christianity, Western metaphysics, and the dialectic, which here includes dialectical materialism.

This reawaking of the Manichaean dualities is most evident for Baudrillard in *Beyond the Pleasure Principle*, where neither the drives of Thanatos nor Eros dominates each other. It is in this early work by Freud on the death drive where its Manichaeism is in most direct evidence. In later work, such as *Civilization and Its Discontents* from 1929, Baudrillard argues that the death drive comes to subordinate the life drive. In this work, the duality of Eros and Thanatos "completes itself in a cycle dominated solely by the death drive."[52] "Eros," argues Baudrillard, "is nothing but an immense detour taken by culture towards death, which subordinates everything to its own ends."[53] Still, this later version of the duality of life and death is not one that reverts to an inverted dialectic between life and death. Why? Because the aim of Eros, as stated earlier in the passage from *An Outline of Psychoanalysis*, "is to establish even greater unities and to preserve them thus—in short, to bind together," which is directly opposed to the aim of the death drive, which "is to undo connections and so to destroy things."[54] Thus, for Baudrillard, the death drive through a repetitive cycle dismantles "the constructive, linear or dialectical finalities of Eros," which is ultimately a victory for "the viscosity of the death drive and the elasticity of the inorganic" over the resistance against it asserted by the "structuration of life."[55]

On the one hand, for Baudrillard, *disassociating* the death drive from the Church, Christianity, Western metaphysics, and dialectics is just to assert one sense of its *radicality*. And, to be sure, *Symbolic Exchange and Death* articulates this sense of Freud's radicality very well. On the other hand, this particular sense of radicality is not the one that Baudrillard utilizes in his own notion of death. Rather, it is another one, namely, the sense of radicality that comes by way of the application of the principle of reversibility, which, as noted earlier, involves not turning Freud against Western thought, but rather pitting Freud against Freud. Thus, for Baudrillard, "the death drive must be interpreted against Freud and psychoanalysis if we wish to *retain* its radicality."[56] Let's now turn to some of the ways in which Baudrillard turns Freud against Freud in order to retain the radicality of the death drive—a radicality that Baudrillard seems to believe has been diminished or lost over the course of the half century between the publication of

Symbolic Exchange and Death in 1976 and Freud's introduction of the death drive in *Beyond the Pleasure Principle* in 1920.

Freud against Freud

For Baudrillard, both the *duality* of the drives associated with Eros and Thanatos and the *counter-finality* repetition of the death drive in dismantling the finalities of Eros are indicative of an aspect of Freud's thought that cannot be reduced to any of the "intellectual apparatuses" found in Western thought. In a way, if Baudrillard concluded his commentary on Freud's death drive here, it would be sufficient to demonstrate the radicality of his work with respect to his intellectual predecessors. But this is not enough for Baudrillard as he insists that based on its dissociation and irreducibility to any of the intellectual apparatuses of Western thought, it is "absurd to give [Freud's death drive] the constructive status of 'truth': the 'reality' of the death instinct is indefensible."[57] Given then that the status "truth" cannot be conferred on the death drive, and that the death drive does not allow for any type of dialectical recovery, Baudrillard wonders if in the final analysis, the death drive in Freud is only a rationalization of death.

Nevertheless, for Baudrillard, there still must be some way "to remain faithful to the intuition of the death drive."[58] He contends that the *only* way to do this is by allowing the death drive "to remain a deconstructive hypothesis, that is, it must be adopted solely within the limits of the deconstruction that it carries out on all prior thought."[59] Moreover, according to Baudrillard, the concept of the death drive holds no special status that makes it immune to deconstruction, that is, no special status "other than as the ultimate subterfuge of reason."[60] Therefore, the principle of deconstruction must also be applied to the very concept of the death drive. So, in short, the further radicality of Freud's work can only be ascertained by deconstructing the very concept of the death drive, which is exactly what Baudrillard does in *Symbolic Exchange and Death*.

Baudrillard proceeds with this "deconstruction" by pointing to the tension in Freud between speaking of the death drive as both a speculative hypothesis *and* a positivist fact. Freud's *positivism* is on view for Baudrillard in statements from *Beyond the Pleasure Principle*, such as one that was cited earlier, where he says, "If we are to take it as a truth that knows no exception that everything living dies for *internal* reasons—becomes inorganic once again—then we shall be compelled to say that 'the goal of all life is death,' and, looking backwards, that 'what was inanimate existed before what is living.'"[61] Elsewhere, however, in the same work, the notion of the death drive as a speculative hypothesis or rationalization regarding death is also offered by Freud:

> The dominating tendency of mental life, and perhaps of nervous life in general, is the effort to reduce, to keep constant or to remove internal tension due to stimuli (the "Nirvana principle," to borrow a term from Barbara Low [*Psycho-Analysis*, 1920])—a tendency which finds expression in the pleasure principle; and our recognition of the fact is one of our strongest reasons for believing in the existence of death instincts.[62]

These two passages from Freud are indicative for Baudrillard of the difficulty of eliminating positivism from the death drive "in order to turn it into a 'speculative hypothesis' or 'purely and simply a principle of psychical functioning.'"[63] Additionally, and perhaps more importantly, in both of these passages, that is, the more positivistic one and the more speculative one, "death alone is finality."[64]

It is here, at the point where the duality of Eros and Thanatos is overcome by the finality of death, that Baudrillard adds another layer to Freud against Freud: if the first layer involves pitting the positivist Freud against the speculative Freud, then the second layer pits the scientific Freud against the mythologizing Freud. Regarding this second layer, Baudrillard contends that if *only* death is finality, then this also brings with it "death as anterior, as psychical and organic destiny, almost like programming or genetic code, in short, as a *positivity* that, unless we believe in the scientific reality of this pulsion [or drive], we can only take it as a myth."[65] Regarding the latter, recall that it was noted earlier that in "Anxiety and Instinctual Life," Freud associates instincts such as the death drive with mythology. "The theory of instincts," he says, "is so to say our mythology."[66] "Instincts," he continues, "are mythical entities, magnificent in their indefiniteness."[67]

Now that the organic destiny of death and the scientific reality of the death drive in Freud have been put to the side for a moment, Baudrillard speculates on what it means to regard the death drive as a myth:

> If the death drive is a myth, then this is how we will interpret it. We will interpret the death drive, and the concept of the unconscious itself, as myths, and no longer take account of their effects or their efforts at "truth." A myth *recounts* something: not so much in the content as in the form of its discourse. Let's make a bet that, under the metaphoric species of sexuality and death, psychoanalysis tells us something concerning the fundamental organization of our culture, that when the myth is no longer told, when it establishes its fables as axioms, it loses the "magnificent indefiniteness" that Freud spoke of. "The concept is only the residue of a metaphor," as Nietzsche said. Let's bet then on the *metaphor* of the unconscious, on the *metaphor* of the death drive.[68]

In addition, if the death drive is a metaphor, then for Baudrillard it is a metaphor for *both* the political-economic system and this system's double, that is, the doubling of the political-economic system into a "radical counter-finality."[69] It is at this point that Baudrillard contends that the radicality of Freud's death drive has been restored simply by regarding it as a deconstructive process.

For Baudrillard, as a metaphor, the death drive must be regarded as "nourishing repressive violence and presiding over culture like a ferocious super-ego, the forces of life inscribed in the compulsion to repeat."[70] Moreover, all cultural sublimation must be viewed as "a long detour to death."[71] And for Baudrillard, all of this is true of our culture. "Death undertakes to abolish death," he says, "and, for this very purpose, erects death above death and is haunted by it as its own end."[72] As a metaphor, the term "drive" refers to

> the contemporary phase of the political-economic system . . . where the law of value, in its most terroristic structural form, reaches completion in the pure and simple compulsive reproduction of the code, where the law of value appears to be a finality as irreversible as a pulsion [or drive], so that it takes on the figure of a destiny for our culture.[73]

But if all of this (and more) is what the myth of the death drive reveals, what happens when it is viewed as based on biology, science, and objectivity? While the implications are different from the implications of the death drive as myth, they are nevertheless just as radical. For Baudrillard, to regard the death drive objectively is to regard it as a species of Western thought and reason. As such, viewed from the perspective of science, death becomes both just another of the conceptual objects it produces as well as one of the axioms (viz., the separation of the dead) upon which science can be legitimated. Here Baudrillard claims that in science, dead or inorganic objects are *good* scientific objects, whereas living or organic objects are *bad* ones. This claim, however, is an arbitrary one, produced "through its own phantasm of repression and death."[74] But even if it is an arbitrary one, it is still the one wherein the death drive can be associated with good scientific objects and the legitimation of science. Thus, concludes Baudrillard, "being nothing but the cyclical repetition of the non-living, the death drive contributes to biology's arbitrariness, doubling it through a psychoanalytic route."[75]

Thus, if following the path of the death drive as myth elevates its radicality for Baudrillard, then so too does following the path of the death drive as objectivity—albeit in a different way. Namely, by letting the air out of the tires of science and biology through the assertion of their relative arbitrariness. The force of Baudrillard's arguments here is bolstered more than anything else by the findings of anthropology, wherein it has been established that "not every culture produces a separate concept of the non-living; only our culture produces it, under the sign of biology."[76] This, in turn, provides a fitting segue to the final section of this chapter, where we take up Baudrillard's notion of symbolic exchange and death, which arguably is one that is beyond both the death drive *and* biopolitics. But, to close out and affirm the anthropological basis of Baudrillard's arguments regarding the arbitrariness of biology (and science), consider that he argues that if we stop discriminating against cultures that do *not* produce a separate concept of the nonliving, then this "would be enough to invalidate the concept of the death drive, which is ultimately only a theoretical agreement between the living and the dead, with the sole result that science loses its footing amongst all the attempts at articulation."[77] So what are these cultures that do *not* produce a separate concept of the nonliving, and why does Baudrillard believe that accounting for them produces a notion of death beyond the death drive?

Symbolic Exchange beyond Biopolitics

According to Baudrillard, at the "core of the 'rationality' of our culture" there is an "exclusion that precedes every other."[78] It is an "exclusion more radical," he says, "than the exclusion of madmen, children or inferior races, an exclusion preceding all of these and serving as their model: the exclusion of the dead and death."[79] With this comment from *Symbolic Exchange and Death*, Baudrillard is well aware that he is evoking Michel Foucault's genealogies of discrimination, and in fact describes them as "among the masterpieces of . . . cultural history."[80] But by arguing that death is an exclusion that precedes and serves as the model for all of the ones Foucault discusses, Baudrillard is indirectly challenging him.

Nevertheless, in the same year that he published *Symbolic Exchange and Death*, Baudrillard directly challenges the foundations of Foucault's work by attempting to publish a long review-essay of his recently published book, *The Will to Knowledge* (*La Volonté de savoir*, 1976), which appeared in English a few years later as *The History of Sexuality, Volume 1: An Introduction* (1978). Baudrillard sent his review-essay, entitled "Forget Foucault" ("Oublier Foucault"), which among other things questioned the place of the dead and death in Foucault's oeuvre, to the French journal *Critique*, which was founded by Georges Bataille—and at the time had Foucault on its editorial board. Not only was the essay never published in *Critique*, but Foucault was invited to reply to it but remained silent. Baudrillard's essay, however, would come out a few months later as a book under the same title.[81]

The point here is that while Baudrillard is mostly quiet in *Symbolic Exchange and Death* about his disagreements with Foucault, only briefly mentioning his work three times in the book, *Forget Foucault* reveals that his disagreements are significant and extensive. It begins with Baudrillard's counter-genealogy of discrimination, which claims

> There is an irreversible evolution from savage societies to our own: little by little, *the dead cease to exist*. They are thrown out of the group's symbolic circulation. They are no longer beings with a full role to play, worthy partners in exchange, and we make this obvious by exiling them further and further away from the group of the living.[82]

Baudrillard argues that we must juxtapose the evolving location of cemeteries from the heart of the village or town to locations further and further from the living against the fact that "[e]ven madmen, delinquents and misfits can find a welcome in . . . new towns."[83] This leads him to assert that in the rationality of modern society "*it is not normal to be dead*."[84]

These observations regarding the abnormality of death echo Baudrillard's non-biological and nonscientific conception of death. "Death," he argues, "is ultimately nothing more than the social line of demarcation separating the 'dead' from the 'living': therefore it affects both equally."[85] He supports his argument for death as a social relation by pointing out the following:

> Savages have no biological concept of death. Or rather, the biological fact, that is, death, birth or disease, everything that comes from nature and that we accord the privilege of necessity and objectivity, quite simply has no meaning for them. . . . They have never "naturalized" death, they know death (like the body, like

> the natural event) is a *social relation*, that its definition is social. In this they are much more "materialist" than we are, since for them the real materiality of death, like that of the commodity for Marx, lies in its *form*, which is always the form of a social relation.[86]

Moreover, as a form of social relation, there is no concept of the irreversibility of death. Rather, death is regarded as something "that is *given* and *received*, and that is therefore reversible in the social exchange."[87] Additionally, there is also no opposition between birth and death, and no opposition between life and death. Ultimately, what separates the savages[88] who do not oppose life against death from those like us who separate life from death is that symbolic "exchange does not come to an end when life comes to an end."[89] "Symbolic exchange," says Baudrillard, "is halted neither by the living nor by the dead (nor by stones or beasts)."[90]

Regarded as an absolute law, the notion that symbolic exchange cannot be halted by either the living or the dead is a direct attack by Baudrillard on structures or apparatuses, such as psychoanalysis, that locate "their archetype in the fundamental distinction between life and death."[91] It is also an attack on structures or apparatuses that are fascinated with the *real* and the *imaginary*. According to Baudrillard,

> the price we pay for the "reality" of this life, to live it as a positive value, is the ever-present phantasm of death. For us, defined as living beings, death is our imaginary.[92]

But for those who believe that symbolic exchange cannot be halted by either the living or the dead, the real and the imaginary are of no theoretical import.[93] For Baudrillard,

> the symbolic everywhere put an end to the fascination with the real and the imaginary, to the closure of the phantasm drawn up by psychoanalysis, but where, at the same time, psychoanalysis locks itself up by establishing, through a considerable quantity of disjunctions (primary and secondary processes, unconscious and conscious, etc.), a psychical reality principle of the unconscious inseparable from psychoanalysis's own reality principle (the unconscious as psychoanalysis's reality principle!) and thus in which the symbolic cannot but put an end to psychoanalysis too.[94]

In short, not only is Baudrillard asking us to abandon distinctions between life and death, conscious and unconscious, and real and imaginary, he is also asking that we abandon their associated political economy in favor of the type of economy found in Bataille mentioned earlier.

Whereas the psychoanalytic vision of death is one where drives are constrained by repetition and where the final equilibrium is set by the inorganic continuum, Bataille's vision of death is one of a "paroxysm of exchanges, superabundance and excess."[95] "Death as excess" is for Bataille "always already there," says Baudrillard. It "proves," continues Baudrillard, "that life is only defective when death has taken it hostage, that life only exists in bursts and in exchanges with death, if it is not condemned to the discontinuity of value and therefore to absolute deficit."[96] "To will that there be life only is to make sure that there is only death," says Bataille.[97] For Baudrillard, this means "death is not the breakdown of life, that it is willed by life itself, and that the delirial (economic) phantasm of eliminating [death] is equivalent to implanting [death] in the heart of life itself—this time as an endless mournful nothingness."[98]

In sum, for Baudrillard, Bataille's notion of death as excess amounts to a kind of anti-economy, wherein

> Only sumptuous and useless expenditure has meaning; the economy has no meaning, it is only a residue that has been made in the law of life, whereas wealth lies in the luxurious exchange of death: sacrifice, the "accursed share," escaping investment and equivalence, can only be annihilated. If life is only a need to survive *at any cost*, then annihilation is a *priceless* luxury. In a system where life is ruled by value and utility, death becomes a useless luxury, and the only alternative.[99]

Unlike Freud, who missed "the curvature of life in death," Bataille recognizes the excess, vertigo, and paroxysm of death. For Freud, the final economy of life is viewed under the sign of repetition, whereas for Bataille and Baudrillard, "[d]eath is neither resolution nor involution, but a reversal and symbolic challenge."[100] For them, "life and death are exchanged at the highest price with death."[101] And again, this is a "vision of death that removes it from psychoanalysis and its individual and psychical domain."[102]

It is also one that removes it from biopolitics, in particular the kind discussed by Foucault in *The History of Sexuality, Volume 1*, which involves "a power to *foster* life or *disallow* it to the point of death."[103] "Now it is over life, throughout its unfolding," comments Foucault, "that power establishes its dominion; death is power's limit, the moment that escapes it; death becomes the most secret aspect of existence, the most 'private.'"[104] To be sure, from Baudrillard's perspective, the notions of life and death utilized by Foucault in his biopolitics are predicated on the determinacy and autonomy of life and death—notions which he rejects in favor of "the radical indeterminacy of life and death, and the impossibility of their autonomy in the symbolic order."[105] Thus, even though symbolic exchange as developed by Baudrillard involves extensive considerations of life and death, it is very much unlike what we have come to recognize or acknowledge as biopolitics. If anything, if we describe Bataille's, and therefore Baudrillard's, form of economics as *anti-economics* because of their relationship to capitalist economics, then it might be fitting to describe their biopolitics too as *anti-biopolitics*, namely, one wherein life and death are marked by radical indeterminacy.

Conclusion

"The great trick of capitalism," writes Gilles Dostaler and Bernard Maris, "is to channel, to divert, the forces of annihilation, the death drive, towards growth."[106] In their book, *Capitalism and the Death Drive: Freud and Keynes* (*Capitalisme et pulsion de mort*, 2009), Dostaler and Maris argue that capitalism is grounded in the negation of death and is accumulated as a defense against death. But in the hands of Baudrillard, the death drive is turned loose on capitalism. Not only does the death drive, as a deconstructive process, offer an alternative account of value to capitalist notions, it also serves as a radical way of understanding culture and its processes.

Nevertheless, the price of producing an alternative to capitalism is a steep one: it asks us to turn psychoanalysis against itself. The radicality that is required to undermine the negation of death that grounds capitalism requires that the death drive be viewed "as acting against the scientific positivity of the psychoanalytic apparatus as developed by Freud."[107] According to Baudrillard, by interpreting the death drive against Freud and psychoanalysis, it becomes a notion that "goes far beyond all previous points of view and renders all previous apparatuses, whether economic, energetic, topological or even the psychical apparatus itself, useless."[108] In Baudrillard's hands, the imaginary and the real, whether in Lacanian terms or others, play no theoretical role and are useless in understanding the way in which life and death undermine capitalism. The symbolic for Baudrillard is the sphere where life and death are radically indeterminate and where their autonomy is not possible. Once the symbolic enters the system of capital—one that "adds up living and capitalizes life" and one wherein "the death drive is the only alternative"[109]—catastrophe becomes unavoidable. "Nothing," writes Baudrillard, "not even the system, can avoid the symbolic obligation, and it is in this trap that the only chance of a catastrophe for capital remains."[110] For Baudrillard, this catastrophe is one that involves systemic suicide:

> The system turns on itself, as a scorpion does when encircled by the challenge of death. For it is summoned to answer, if it is not to lose face, to what can only be death. The system must *itself commit suicide in response to the multiplied challenge of death and suicide.*[111]

It is perhaps here—in the image of the system of capital like a scorpion taking its own life rather than accepting the *revolt* of symbolic death—that Baudrillard the philosopher comes to also be like the scorpion.

If indeed the death drive marks the limit of psychoanalysis and is something that "must be wrested from psychoanalysis and turned against it,"[112] and if the death drive has become a "meta-economic, metapsychical, meta-energetic, [and] metapsychoanalytic" notion where the dead and death are beyond determinate life and death, consciousness and unconsciousness, the real and the imaginary, and biopolitics and thanatopolitics, then what remains of philosophy that is grounded on these concepts after Baudrillard? As perhaps the ultimate antiphilosophical meta-philosopher of the late twentieth century, Baudrillard picks the Western philosophical cabinet clean in his analysis of death. But his analyses in *Symbolic Exchange and Death* marked the apex of his philosophical speculation on death—after which, he largely abandons this line of speculation on death and the dead for other provocations.[113] Moreover, and arguably, he also abandons symbolic exchange as a revolutionary and radical alternative to capitalism. I'll leave it to others to decide if, based on the lack of interest in his work in this area by Foucault and others, he killed it off like the scorpion encircled by challengers—or whether his work on the dead and death succumbed to some other form of fatality. Nevertheless, it remains one of the most devastating, radical, and revolutionary readings of the death drive to date—one that incredibly asks us to go beyond biopolitics almost before there was anything like biopolitics. Finally, if Foucault is correct in his call for us to think historically about neoliberalism in his 1978–9 lectures on the birth of biopolitics,[114] then Baudrillard's critique of Western notions of economic exchange, utility, production, and instrumental rationality in *Symbolic Exchange and Death* offers an alternative historical account of both the birth of biopolitics *and* neoliberalism, namely one where the death drive can and should play a prominent role.

Notes

1 Jean Baudrillard, *Symbolic Exchange and Death*, trans. Iain Hamilton Grant (Los Angeles and London: Sage Publications, 1993), 22–3.
2 Baudrillard, *Symbolic Exchange and Death*, 23.
3 Baudrillard, *Symbolic Exchange and Death*, 23.
4 Baudrillard, *Symbolic Exchange and Death*, 23.
5 Baudrillard, *Symbolic Exchange and Death*, 23.
6 Baudrillard, *Symbolic Exchange and Death*, 23.
7 Baudrillard, *Symbolic Exchange and Death*, 23.
8 Baudrillard, *Symbolic Exchange and Death*, 26.
9 Baudrillard, *Symbolic Exchange and Death*, 26n2.
10 Baudrillard, *Symbolic Exchange and Death*, 26n2.
11 Baudrillard, *Symbolic Exchange and Death*, 26n2.
12 Baudrillard, *Symbolic Exchange and Death*, 26–27n2.
13 Baudrillard, *Symbolic Exchange and Death*, 27n2.
14 Baudrillard, *Symbolic Exchange and Death*, 7n2.
15 Baudrillard, *Symbolic Exchange and Death*, 27n2.
16 Baudrillard, *Symbolic Exchange and Death*, 23.
17 While the dominant view is that Baudrillard is a postmodern theorist, there are some who argue his work has nothing to do with postmodernism. For Baudrillard as a postmodern theorist, see, for example, Steven Best and Douglas Kellner's *The Postmodern Turn* (New York: Guilford Press, 1997) and *The Postmodern Adventure* (New York: Guilford Press, 2001) as well as Douglas Kellner's *Jean Baudrillard: From Marxism to Postmodernism and Beyond* (Palo Alto: Stanford University Press, 1989), and for Baudrillard as not a postmodern theorist, see, for example, Mike Gane's *Baudrillard, Critical and Fatal Theory* (London: Routledge, 1991) and his edited volume, *Baudrillard Live: Selected Interviews* (London: Routledge, 1993).
18 In an interview with Anne Laurent, Baudrillard says, "*L'échange symbolique et la mort* is the last book that inspired confidence. . . . Everything I write is deemed brilliant, intelligent, but not serious. There has never been any real discussion about it" (Jean Baudrillard, "This Beer Isn't a Beer: Interview with Anne Laurent [1991]," in *Baudrillard Live: Selected Interviews*, ed. Mike Gane [London and New York: Routledge, 1993], 189).
19 The chapter from *L'échange symbolique et la mort* that appears in the Semiotext(e) volume *Simulations* is also entitled "The Order of Simulacra." However, the final

section of this chapter, entitled "Kool Killer, or The Insurrection of Signs," is omitted in the Semiotext(e) volume *Simulations*.

20 The chapter from *Simulacra and Simulation* that appears in the Semiotext(e) volume *Simulations* is also entitled "The Precession of Simulacra." It appears in its entirety in the Semiotext(e) volume *Simulations*.
21 The text from this chapter is drawn from pages 7–19, 77–9, 85–7, 89–90, 92, 93–4, 96–7, 98, 107–8, 110–12, 114, and 116–17 of Jean Baudrillard, *L'échange symbolique et la mort* (Paris: Éditions Gallimard, 1976).
22 Notably missing from this version of Chapter 1 of *L'échange symbolique et la mort* is the first section, "The Structural Revolution of Value," and the final two sections, "Political Economy as a Model of Simulation" and "Labour and Death."
23 Fredric Jameson, *Postmodernism, or, The Cultural Logic of Late Capitalism* (Durham: Duke University Press, 1991), 6, 18.
24 Sigmund Freud, *Beyond the Pleasure Principle* (1920), trans. James Strachey (New York: Liveright Publishing Corporation, 1950), 50.
25 Sigmund Freud, *An Outline of Psychoanalysis* (1940), trans. James Strachey (New York: W. W. Norton & Company, 1949), 20.
26 Freud, *An Outline of Psychoanalysis*, 20.
27 Freud, *Beyond the Pleasure Principle*, 86.
28 Freud, *An Outline of Psychoanalysis*, 109.
29 James Strachey, "Editor's Note," in *New Introductory Lectures on Psychoanalysis*, ed. and trans. James Strachey (New York: W. W. Norton & Company, 1965), 3.
30 Sigmund Freud, "Anxiety and Instinctual Life" (1933), in *New Introductory Lectures on Psychoanalysis*, ed. and trans. James Strachey (New York: W. W. Norton & Company, 1965), 95.
31 Freud, "Anxiety and Instinctual Life," 106.
32 Freud, "Anxiety and Instinctual Life," 106.
33 Freud, "Anxiety and Instinctual Life," 106.
34 Freud, "Anxiety and Instinctual Life," 107.
35 Freud, "Anxiety and Instinctual Life," 107.
36 Freud, "Anxiety and Instinctual Life," 107.
37 Freud, "Anxiety and Instinctual Life," 107.
38 Freud, "Anxiety and Instinctual Life," 107.
39 Baudrillard, *Symbolic Exchange and Death*, 169.
40 Baudrillard, *Symbolic Exchange and Death*, 165.
41 Baudrillard, *Symbolic Exchange and Death*, 169.
42 Baudrillard, *Symbolic Exchange and Death*, 169.
43 Martin Heidegger, *Being and Time*, trans. John Macquarrie and Edward Robinson (New York: Harper & Row, 1962), 438 [sec. 74]. Cited by Baudrillard, *Symbolic Exchange and Death*, 210n22.
44 Baudrillard, *Symbolic Exchange and Death*, 210n22.
45 Baudrillard, *Symbolic Exchange and Death*, 210n22.
46 Baudrillard, *Symbolic Exchange and Death*, 210n22.
47 Baudrillard, *Symbolic Exchange and Death*, 210n22.
48 Baudrillard, *Symbolic Exchange and Death*, 210n22.
49 Baudrillard, *Symbolic Exchange and Death*, 169.
50 Baudrillard, *Symbolic Exchange and Death*, 169.
51 Baudrillard, *Symbolic Exchange and Death*, 169.
52 Baudrillard, *Symbolic Exchange and Death*, 170.

53 Baudrillard, *Symbolic Exchange and Death*, 170.
54 Freud, *An Outline of Psychoanalysis*, 20.
55 Baudrillard, *Symbolic Exchange and Death*, 170.
56 Baudrillard, *Symbolic Exchange and Death*, 174; my emphasis.
57 Baudrillard, *Symbolic Exchange and Death*, 170.
58 Baudrillard, *Symbolic Exchange and Death*, 170.
59 Baudrillard, *Symbolic Exchange and Death*, 170.
60 Baudrillard, *Symbolic Exchange and Death*, 170.
61 Freud, *Beyond the Pleasure Principle*, 50.
62 Freud, *Beyond the Pleasure Principle*, 76.
63 Baudrillard, *Symbolic Exchange and Death*, 172.
64 Baudrillard, *Symbolic Exchange and Death*, 172.
65 Baudrillard, *Symbolic Exchange and Death*, 172.
66 Freud, "Anxiety and Instinctual Life," 95.
67 Freud, "Anxiety and Instinctual Life," 95.
68 Baudrillard, *Symbolic Exchange and Death*, 172.
69 Baudrillard, *Symbolic Exchange and Death*, 172.
70 Baudrillard, *Symbolic Exchange and Death*, 172.
71 Baudrillard, *Symbolic Exchange and Death*, 172.
72 Baudrillard, *Symbolic Exchange and Death*, 172.
73 Baudrillard, *Symbolic Exchange and Death*, 172.
74 Baudrillard, *Symbolic Exchange and Death*, 173.
75 Baudrillard, *Symbolic Exchange and Death*, 173.
76 Baudrillard, *Symbolic Exchange and Death*, 173.
77 Baudrillard, *Symbolic Exchange and Death*, 173.
78 Baudrillard, *Symbolic Exchange and Death*, 147.
79 Baudrillard, *Symbolic Exchange and Death*, 147.
80 Baudrillard, *Symbolic Exchange and Death*, 147.
81 Jean Baudrillard, *Oublier Foucault* (Paris: Éditions Galilée, 1977). An English translation of it appeared a few years later as "Forgetting Foucault," trans. Nicole Dufresne, *Humanities in Society* 3, no. 1 (1980): 87–111. This translation was later reprinted in Jean Baudrillard, *Forget Foucault*, intro and interview by Sylvère Lotringer (Los Angeles: Semiotext(e), 2007).
82 Baudrillard, *Symbolic Exchange and Death*, 147.
83 Baudrillard, *Symbolic Exchange and Death*, 147.
84 Baudrillard, *Symbolic Exchange and Death*, 147; italics in original.
85 Baudrillard, *Symbolic Exchange and Death*, 150.
86 Baudrillard, *Symbolic Exchange and Death*, 151–2.
87 Baudrillard, *Symbolic Exchange and Death*, 152.
88 The use of the terms "savage" and "primitive" in *Social Exchange and Death* is unsettling and, arguably, inappropriate. However, it also appears to be deliberate. According to William Pawlett, Baudrillard uses these terms deliberately, aiming to achieve three objectives: (1) to draw attention "to the disreputable past of anthropology," (2) to offend liberal and humanist sensibilities wherein people feel guilty about their positions of power and wealth and use politically correct language to assuage their guilt, and (3) to foreground the radical difference between Western practices and non-Western practices (William Pawlett, *Jean Baudrillard* [London and New York: Routledge, 2007], 50).
89 Baudrillard, *Symbolic Exchange and Death*, 155.

90 Baudrillard, *Symbolic Exchange and Death*, 155.
91 Baudrillard, *Symbolic Exchange and Death*, 154.
92 Baudrillard, *Symbolic Exchange and Death*, 154.
93 This includes Jacques Lacan's *Imaginary Order*, that is, the preverbal order wherein the infant identifies itself as an entity unified with both its biological dependence on its mother and its surroundings; and the *Real Order*, that is, the order beyond the Imaginary and the structure and representation of the Symbolic, which is only accessible in *jouissance* (fleeting moments of joy and terror). Also, Baudrillard's notion of the symbolic is very different from the *Symbolic Order* of Lacan, that is, the order that emerges with the acquisition of language, wherein the subject only interacts with the world through various forms of representation and structures of meaning. Regarding the Lacanian *Real Order*, Baudrillard writes, it "is no longer given as substance, nor as a positive reference; it is the always lost object that cannot be located, and of which there is nothing ultimately to say. A delimited absence in the network of the 'symbolic order,' this real retains however the charm of a game of hide-and-seek with the signifier which traces after it" (Baudrillard, *Symbolic Exchange and Death*, 208n10). Still, comments Baudrillard, at least there is something more going on in Lacan in contrast to Claude Lévi-Strauss, whose idealism leads him to reduce the symbolic to the imaginary (Baudrillard, *Symbolic Exchange and Death*, 209n10).
94 Baudrillard, *Symbolic Exchange and Death*, 154.
95 Baudrillard, *Symbolic Exchange and Death*, 175.
96 Baudrillard, *Symbolic Exchange and Death*, 175.
97 Baudrillard, *Symbolic Exchange and Death*, 175; Baudrillard quoting Bataille.
98 Baudrillard, *Symbolic Exchange and Death*, 175.
99 Baudrillard, *Symbolic Exchange and Death*, 176.
100 Baudrillard, *Symbolic Exchange and Death*, 177.
101 Baudrillard, *Symbolic Exchange and Death*, 177.
102 Baudrillard, *Symbolic Exchange and Death*, 179.
103 Michel Foucault, *The History of Sexuality, Volume 1: An Introduction*, trans. Robert Hurley (New York: Pantheon Books, 1978), 138.
104 Foucault, *The History of Sexuality*, 138.
105 Baudrillard, *Symbolic Exchange and Death*, 179.
106 "La grande ruse du capitalism, nous le verrons, est de canaliser, de détourner les forces d'anéantissement, la pulsion de mort vers la croissance" (Gilles Dostaler and Bernard Maris, *Capitalisme et pulsion de mort: Freud et Keynes* [Paris: Albin Michel, 2009], 9; my translation).
107 Baudrillard, *Symbolic Exchange and Death*, 179.
108 Baudrillard, *Symbolic Exchange and Death*, 174.
109 Baudrillard, *Symbolic Exchange and Death*, 197.
110 Baudrillard, *Symbolic Exchange and Death*, 58.
111 Baudrillard, *Symbolic Exchange and Death*, 58.
112 Baudrillard, *Symbolic Exchange and Death*, 174.
113 This shift is already apparent in *Seduction* (*De la seduction*, 1979), the major work that follows *Symbolic Death and Exchange*. Here Baudrillard now argues that the death drive is but one of two major oppositions in Freud, the other being seduction, which is the "lost object" of psychoanalysis. Whereas the death drive was discussed earlier in *Symbolic Death and Exchange*, this new book, *Seduction*, aims to focus on the other side of the opposition: "The Freudian *oeuvre* unfolds between two

poles that radically put into question the intermediary construction, these poles being seduction and the death drive. We have already spoken in *Symbolic Exchange and Death* of the latter, considered as an inversion of the earlier psychoanalytic apparatus (topical, economic). Regarding the former, which after numerous turns links up with the death drive by some secret affinity, one has to say that it appears as psychoanalysis' lost object" (Jean Baudrillard, *Seduction*, trans. Brian Singer [New York: St. Martin's Press, 1990], 55).

114 In general terms, *biopolitics* in view of Foucault's work comes to refer to the management of populations and the resources necessary for their survival through various types of accounting and record-keeping by the state. Its development coincides, argues Foucault, with the emergence of a new type of economic man (*homo oeconomicus*). Whereas the classical conception of economic man was "the man of exchange, the partner, one of two partners in the process of exchange," the *neoliberal* conception of economic man "is not at all a partner of exchange," but is rather "an entrepreneur," that is, "an entrepreneur of himself, being for himself his own capital, being for himself his own producer, being for himself the source of [his] earnings" (Michel Foucault, *The Birth of Biopolitics: Lectures at the Collège de France 1978–1979*, ed. Michael Senellart, trans. Braham Burchell [New York: Palgrave Macmillan, 2008], 225–6). Thus, *neoliberal society*, the hyper-driven market society wherein economic man operates as an entrepreneur, comes to bear in significant ways on any and all considerations of *biopolitics*.

Works Cited

Baudrillard, Jean. *L'échange symbolique et la mort.* Paris: Éditions Gallimard, 1976.

Baudrillard, Jean. *Oublier Foucault.* Paris: Éditions Galilée, 1977.

Baudrillard, Jean. *De la seduction.* Paris: Éditions Galilée, 1979.

Baudrillard, Jean. "Forgetting Foucault," translated by Nicole Dufresne. In *Humanities in Society* 3, no. 1 (1980): 87–111.

Baudrillard, Jean. *Simulacres et simulation.* Paris: Éditions Galilée, 1981.

Baudrillard, Jean. *Simulations.* Translated by Paul Foss, Paul Patton and Philip Beitchman. Foreign Agents Series. New York: Semiotext(e), 1983.

Baudrillard, Jean. "The Structural Law of Value and the Order of Simulacra," translated by Charles Levin. In *The Structural Allegory: Reconstructive Encounters with the New French Thought*, edited by John Fekete, 54–73. Minneapolis: University of Minnesota Press, 1984.

Baudrillard, Jean. *Revenge of the Crystal: Selected Writings on the Modern Object and Its Destiny, 1968–1983.* Edited and translated by Paul Foss and Julian Pefanis, 99–128. London: Pluto Press, in association with the Power Institute of Fine Arts, University of Sydney, 1990.

Baudrillard, Jean. *Seduction.* Translated by Brian Singer. New York: St. Martin's Press, 1990.

Baudrillard, Jean. *La Guerre du Golfe n'a pas eu lieu.* Paris: Éditions Galilée, 1991.

Baudrillard, Jean. *Symbolic Exchange and Death.* Translated by Iain Hamilton Grant. Los Angeles and London: Sage Publications, 1993.

Baudrillard, Jean. "This Beer Isn't a Beer: Interview with Anne Laurent" (1991). In *Baudrillard Live: Selected Interviews*, edited by Mike Gane, 180–90. London and New York: Routledge, 1993.

Baudrillard, Jean. *Simulacra and Simulation.* Trans. Sheila Faria Glaser. Ann Arbor: University of Michigan Press, 1994.
Baudrillard, Jean. *The Gulf War Did Not Take Place.* Translated by Paul Patton. Bloomington: Indiana University Press, 1995.
Baudrillard, Jean. *Forget Foucault.* Intro and interview by Sylvère Lotringer. Los Angeles: Semiotext(e), 2007.
Best, Steven, and Douglas Kellner. *The Postmodern Turn.* New York: Guilford Press, 1997.
Best, Steven, and Douglas Kellner. *The Postmodern Adventure.* New York: Guilford Press, 2001.
Deleuze, Gilles, and Félix Guattari. *L'Anti-Oedipe.* Paris: Les Éditions de Minuit, 1972.
Deleuze, Gilles, and Félix Guattari. *Anti-Oedipus: Capitalism and Schizophrenia.* Translated by Robert Hurley, Mark Seem, and Helen R. Lane. Minneapolis: University of Minnesota Press, 1983.
Dostaler, Gilles, and Bernard Maris. *Capitalisme et pulsion de mort: Freud et Keynes.* Paris: Albin Michel, 2009.
Foucault, Michel. *La Volenté de savoir.* Paris: Éditions Gallimard, 1976.
Foucault, Michel. *The History of Sexuality, Volume 1: An Introduction.* Translated by Robert Hurley. New York: Pantheon Books, 1978.
Foucault, Michel. *The Birth of Biopolitics: Lectures at the Collège de France 1978–1979.* Edited by Michael Senellart. Translated by Braham Burchell. New York: Palgrave Macmillan, 2008.
Freud, Sigmund. *An Outline of Psychoanalysis* (1940). Translated by James Strachey. New York: W. W. Norton & Company, 1949.
Freud, Sigmund. *Beyond the Pleasure Principle* (1920). Translated by James Strachey. New York: Liveright Publishing Corporation, 1950.
Freud, Sigmund. *Civilization and Its Discontents* (1929). Translated by Joan Riviere. London: Hogarth Press, 1955.
Freud, Sigmund. "Anxiety and Instinctual Life" (1933). In *New Introductory Lectures on Psychoanalysis*, translated and edited by James Strachey, 81–111. New York: W. W. Norton & Company, 1965.
Gane, Mike. *Baudrillard, Critical and Fatal Theory.* London: Routledge, 1991.
Gane, Mike, ed. *Baudrillard Live: Selected Interviews.* London: Routledge, 1993.
Heidegger, Martin. *Being and Time.* Translated by John Macquarrie and Edward Robinson. New York: Harper & Row, 1962.
Jameson, Fredric/ *Postmodernism, or, The Cultural Logic of Late Capitalism.* Durham: Duke University Press, 1991.
Kellner, Douglas. *Jean Baudrillard: From Marxism to Postmodernism and Beyond.* Palo Alto: Stanford University Press, 1989.
Lyotard, Jean-François. *Economie Libidinale.* Paris: Les Éditions de Minuit, 1974.
Lyotard, Jean-François. *Libidinal Economy.* Translated by Iain Hamilton Grant. Bloomington: Indiana University Press, 1993.
Pawlett, William. *Jean Baudrillard.* London and New York: Routledge, 2007.
Strachey, James. "Editor's Note." In Sigmund Freud, *New Introductory Lectures on* Psychoanalysis, edited and translated by James Strachey, 3–4. New York: W. W. Norton & Company, 1965.

3

Trauma and the Breakdown of All Grammars

Listening to the Wound as Voice

María del Rosario Acosta López

My relation to *Beyond the Pleasure Principle* (1920) is inflected by a philosophical interest in the question of trauma. To be more precise, after working with survivors of State and para-State violence (police torture in Chicago and paramilitary violence in Colombia),[1] I have been searching for ways to understand the kind of damage that trauma inflicts on its survivors. More specifically, I have inquired about the relation between such damage and the (in)capacity for testimony, together with the conditions for listening required by that relation. There are certain types of violence, I have argued, that involve not just "*an assault on life but on the conditions of production of sense that make life legible*."[2] Hence, in order to hear those voices that come from contexts of "traumatic violence" (my suggested designation), our examination must look beyond the conditions of possibility for testimony and consider the (aesthetic, ethical, epistemological) conditions of possibility that render such a voice audible and legible *as* testimony.[3]

It is at this point that I have found Freud's genetic analysis and conceptualization of "traumatic neurosis" particularly helpful. Trauma, as described in *Beyond the Pleasure Principle*, confronts us with a type of damage whose experience reveals itself as inarticulable by virtue of being profoundly paradoxical. It is paradoxical not only because it resists being conceptualized *as* an experience (thus exposing the limits of our capacity for processing and, accordingly, for listening and remembrance), but also because sense itself as a possibility—the possibility of "making sense" of what has happened—is broken by its occurrence (which is in fact both the *absence* of its occurrence and, simultaneously and paradoxically, its compulsive repetition).

My work on Freud, then, aims to develop a wider understanding of the damage associated with trauma, which in turn sheds light on the kind of challenges that trauma poses to the question of listening in contexts of traumatic violence. These, I argue, are challenges that may go unnoticed when trauma is approached from other perspectives and that a philosophical gaze can help us not only to identify but also to understand in depth. My fundamental intention here is to outline and analyze these challenges by reading Freud in *Beyond the Pleasure Principle* as a "phenomenologist" of trauma.

Freud's account of traumatic experience is crucial precisely because it seems to test the limits of any phenomenology—and thus, as I will suggest, to expose the breakdown of all grammars presumed to be already available for its elucidation. My claim, then, is that in considering contexts of traumatic violence, a philosophical reading of Freud can steer us toward a deeper understanding of the radicality of traumatic damage; moreover, since his analyses bring forth the singularity of this experience—and its paradoxical experiential structure—they allow us to gauge the extent of the challenges it poses to our usual understanding of experience, memory, and history—and most importantly, therefore, to the kind of listening required in order to construct memory and history *at the site of trauma*.[4]

Before I begin, a methodological clarification: this chapter does not purport to engage in conversation with psychoanalytical accounts of trauma or to undertake an exegetical review of Freud's work in search of an exhaustive reconstruction of his theory of traumatic neurosis. My reading of Freud—and, more specifically, of *Beyond the Pleasure Principle*—follows a very particular direction in trauma studies, inspired among others by the work of Cathy Caruth and what she describes as the necessarily *literary* dimension of traumatic experience.[5] Authors such as Shoshana Felman, Françoise Davoine, and Elizabeth Rottenberg have shed further light on this dimension in conversation with Caruth and her work,[6] and more recently Rosaura Martínez-Ruiz has framed it within a political perspective that has also proven to be considerably important to my work.[7] In Caruth's account, this literary dimension also entails a reading of Freud whose attentiveness ventures beyond what the text says and considers its silences and what they reveal. Caruth listens to Freud's text and senses therein a register of trauma that Freud has been unable to name and whose latency resonates in his writing; this is why this manner of thinking about trauma exceeds the merely theoretical. Caruth's interpretative strategy, and her capacity to listen to the text beyond what it says, decisively marks my own way of working, my relation to Freud's text, and, above all, my particular approach to the task of listening to traumatic violence.[8]

A Double Breakdown: An An-Economic Compulsion and the (De)Structure of Experience

It all begins, as we know, with the recurrent dreams that assailed those suffering from what Freud calls the "war neurosis." These dreams are the symptoms of a kind of wound that, although *invisible*—since *visible* "wounds or injuries," Freud reminds us, actually "work as a rule against the development of neurosis"[9]—seems to pervade the life—better said, the *dream* life—of many soldiers returning from the battle lines during the First World War. While the dreams seem to be the only "experience" that connects these soldiers to their "memories" of the war (which they seem rather reluctant to revisit in waking life, according to Freud), they "repeatedly bring the patient back into the situation of his accident, a situation from which he wakes up in another fright."[10] Now, fright, Freud explains, is itself nothing but the sign—and the experience—

of a lack or an absence; unlike anxiety, which describes a particular "state of expecting the danger or preparing for it, even though it may be an unknown one," "fright . . . is the name we give to the state a person gets into when he has run into danger *without being prepared for it*."[11]

Thus, the soldiers' dreams are enigmatic at least on three different levels: first, because they seem to refer to something rather indeterminate—unlike fear, these dreams do not have an "object," nor do they envision one in anticipation, as "anxiety" does; second, because of the kind of experience they awaken—and which, as we will see shortly, is not strictly speaking an "experience"; and third, because it is in a *dream*, and not in waking life, that a "fixation to the moment at which the trauma occurred" is expressed.[12]

If in cases of hysteria the trigger for a pathological response in the patient is a special kind of memory of the event ("Hysterics suffer mainly from reminiscences [*Reminiszenzen*]" is the famous line from the introduction to *Studies in Hysteria* that Freud returns to in this context),[13] the returning soldiers do not seem to experience a form of *remembering.* "I am not aware," he writes, "that patients suffering from traumatic neurosis are much occupied in their waking lives with memories of their accident."[14] Quite otherwise, what seems to be repeatedly experienced *in waking life* is fright, a sense of *unpreparedness* for a looming event that somehow leads to an experience of *reliving* (repeating)—not the past accident itself but one's condition right before its occurrence. "This astonishes people far too little," writes Freud:

> Anyone who accepts it as something self-evident that their dreams should put them back at night into the situation that caused them to fall ill has misunderstood the nature of dreams. It would be more in harmony with their nature *if* they showed the patient pictures from his healthy past or of the cure for which he hopes.[15]

The enigma of the soldiers' dreams creates a quandary for psychoanalytic theory to the extent that it seems to undermine Freud's "belief in the wish-fulfilling tenor of dreams."[16] Traumatic neurosis, in other words, threatens the standing of what Freud has described from the onset of *Beyond the Pleasure Principle* as the first "economic" principle of psychoanalysis, based on his earlier study of the workings of the pleasure principle.[17] As Freud is about to acknowledge a few pages ahead—and it is also telling, as Caruth points out,[18] that he first needs to take a break (through a digression inspired by a child's game) and *defer* confronting this seemingly inevitable conclusion—"it is impossible to classify" these dreams "as wish-fulfilments."[19] "This would seem to be the place" he then continues, "at which to admit for the first time an exception to the proposition that dreams are fulfilments of wishes,"[20] and thus "that there really does exist in the mind a compulsion to repeat which overrides the pleasure principle."[21]

All of this leads Freud to conclude—at least speculatively, as he warns us at some point in the essay, since he seems to be operating with no ground, given that the ground itself has been shaken by the evidence presented by traumatic neurosis—that beyond the pleasure principle there must be an *an-economic compulsion* at work here, whose function does not necessarily contradict but is at least "independent of . . . and seems to be more primitive than, the purpose of gaining pleasure and avoiding unpleasure."[22]

Traumatic neurosis is the result of "a disturbance on a large scale in the way an organism *administers* [*Betrieb*] its energy,"[23] and its analysis must carefully consider the "violent" [*gewaltsame*] consequences of such a disturbance.[24] However, Freud is now in a position to see that traumatic neurosis is *not only* a radical disturbance in the life of the psyche and its "economies," but *also* a radical disturbance in the way that psychoanalysis had been conceptualizing and explaining the very *structure* of experience and mental processes.

In the case of trauma, therefore, we are dealing with disturbance at two different levels, for in addition to the kind of breakdown that trauma itself brings about in an individual psyche (to be examined in further detail below), we also have Freud's conceptual unpreparedness to deal with this experience, which calls for a radical shift in the categories available for "making sense" of it. Listening to trauma, then, requires us to understand that any response to such an experience must *heed* its claims on us at these two different levels, one experiential and the other conceptual—or, in a broader sense, *grammatical.*

Witnessing Trauma: Toward a Memory of the Unforgettable

Let us first take a closer look, then, at Freud's account of trauma, now that its standing as a puzzle for psychoanalytic theory has come into view. Since the function of dreams can no longer be described as simply determined by the pleasure principle, Freud now needs to examine their potential role in a task that "must be accomplished before the dominance of the pleasure principle can even begin." "We may assume," he writes, that "these dreams are endeavoring to master the stimulus retrospectively, by developing the anxiety whose *omission* was the cause of the traumatic neurosis."[25]

There are at least two paradoxical aspects of this "task." On the one hand, there is something profoundly paradoxical about a *compulsion* whose ultimate task would be to *retrospectively master* the kind of unpreparedness that allowed an accident to traumatically impact the mind in the first place. First, because the relation between compulsion and mastery is far from clear: How can mastery be attained through the workings of a repetition that seizes one as a "fatality"[26] or a "compulsion of destiny,"[27] as Freud puts it? Second, because *retrospectivity* here cannot rely on a linearly structured experience, and thus on a stable temporality that would support it. What is being "looked back at" here is not a forgotten—but formerly actualized—past that could be *traced back* to a source and *undug*; rather, what we are dealing with in the case of trauma is a sort of *structural deferral*—a belatedness or afterwardness [*Nachträglichkeit*] of the very ability to experience an event as such. There is no past to be recovered here yet because the accident was not an event for the mind and *is yet to be worked through* as an experience.

As Rottenberg has explained in detail, this *latency* is not a feature of the traumatic *event*, but rather a structural constituent of trauma—the delay, as she writes, is not "empirical"[28] but rather "structural."[29] What comes into view here, then, is a kind of "untimeliness" that, from this point onward, becomes integral to Freud's definition of trauma:

> [W]hat Freud calls "trauma" is an inherent belatedness in relation to the event. Trauma is *nachträglich* or delayed as such; it is not the event but precisely the missing of the event. *A traumatic "event" is a missed event.* Thus, in *Beyond the Pleasure Principle, Nachträglichkeit* is what *structures* the traumatic "event." For this reason *Nachträglichkeit* can no longer be linked to a specific event like the retardation of puberty. *Nachträglichkeit* becomes, rather, *the structure of delay as such*, i.e., the structure that determines a trauma.[30]

This brings us to the second paradoxical aspect of the task mentioned above—or, better said, to the other side of the same paradox, since what we are dealing with here will ultimately reveal itself as the *paradoxical structure of traumatic experience* altogether. Freud explains the repetition compulsion that drives the dream life of those who have endured trauma as an attempt to prepare for the experience of an event that, strictly speaking, has *not yet* happened and whose *omission*, as we have seen, is the actual cause of the neurosis. According to Caruth, this leads Freud to develop a paradoxical conception of *experience* that fluctuates at the interstice between the *too soon* and the *too late* of an encounter.[31] The accident is, strictly speaking, *yet* to be lived as an actual experience, and hence, Caruth writes, "what returns to haunt the victim is not only the reality of the violent event, but also the reality of the way that its violence has not yet been fully known."[32]

For this reason, Caruth adds, trauma must be understood as a "breach in the mind's experience of time, self, and the world"[33] that subsequently motivates a radical reexamination of our conceptions of the past and the present—and so also, necessarily, of memory and history. As Caruth phrases it elsewhere, the paradox can also be described as a simultaneous *absence and excess of memory*, the impossible encounter between *amnesia and hypermnesia*.[34] If compulsive repetition makes it impossible for the mind to relate to the event as a past actuality—and thus as something that we can *remember*—it also makes it impossible for it to leave that event behind and deal with it in the present. The result, then, would be an *indelible (although unconscious) form of memory*.

A brief look at a few passages from *Beyond the Pleasure Principle* will allow us to understand how Freud means to account for this possibility. First, there are those key passages at the beginning of section IV where Freud introduces clarifications that he will elaborate on later in his "Notes on the Mystic Writing Pad." "Consciousness," he writes here,

> is not the only distinctive character which we ascribe to the processes in that system [the perceptual-consciousness system]. On the basis of impressions derived from our psycho-analytic experience, we assume that all excitatory processes that occur in the other systems leave permanent traces behind in them which form the *foundation of memory*. Such memory-traces, then, have nothing to do with the fact of becoming conscious; indeed they are often most powerful and most enduring when the process which left them behind was one which never entered consciousness.[35]

Consciousness must be understood as operating independently from memory if it is to remain constantly open to new excitations coming from the "outside" rather than becoming quickly saturated by an ongoing influx of stimuli. This, Freud explains, is also the reason why complex organisms develop a shield that protects them against overwhelming exposure to external stimuli. In this way, then, the psyche creates an "inside" for itself by setting up the kind of resistances that are ultimately needed for the operation of memory as *remembrance.* "Memory as writing in the psychic apparatus is possible," Martínez-Ruiz reminds us, "if and only if there is resistance to inscription."[36] That is, resistance is what makes it possible for consciousness to experience memory traces by creating the pathways that may allow it to make its way back to the original trace, free from the risk of saturation that would ensue if the system required all memories to first go through consciousness. Freud writes: "It may be supposed that in passing from one element to another, an excitation has to overcome a resistance, and that the diminution of resistance thus effected is what *lays down a permanent trace* of the excitation, that is, a facilitation."[37]

The protective shield against stimuli, Freud then adds, which is the result of a portion of organic matter becoming "inorganic," succeeds in protecting living organisms from being "killed by the stimulation emanating from an external world charged with the most powerful energies." Thanks to it, "the energies of the external world are able to pass into the next underlying layers, which have remained living, with only a fragment of their original intensity." "By its death," he then elaborates in a somewhat dramatic tone, "the outer layer has saved all the deeper ones from a similar fate—*unless, that is to say, stimuli reach it which are so strong that they break through the protective shield.*"[38] The latter, as we know by now, is the case with trauma:

> We describe as "traumatic" any excitations from outside which are powerful enough to break through the protective shield. . . . Such an event as an external trauma is bound to provoke a disturbance on a large scale in the functioning of the organism's energy and to set in motion every possible defensive measure. At the same time, the pleasure principle is for the moment put out of action. There is no longer any possibility of preventing the mental apparatus from being flooded with large amounts of stimulus, and another problem arises instead—the problem of mastering the amounts of stimulus which have broken in and of binding them, in the psychical sense, so that they can then be disposed of.[39]

This, then, is how the psyche may come to find itself engaged in a singular effort of remembrance that overrides the pleasure principle.

One of the great difficulties in listening to trauma survivors is that, more often than not, what we hear from them are not "memories" in the strict sense, but rather the marks left behind by their "unforgettable" absence. The event that we assume to be the nucleus of a trauma is not available as such to the survivor—at least not in our usual ways of understanding the availability, and thus the *communicability*, of our experiences—since it is, in a way, unlocatable both spatially and temporally. Thus, it cannot be located as a memory *to be remembered*; its irruption was so violent that it cannot be retraced and so it "lives on," somehow, in the latency of its obsessive return as present. In Martínez-Ruiz's words, once again:

> [T]rauma in Freud's theory is not living through a horrifying event, but the ongoing eternal present of seeking out the actual experience of the traumatic. In other words, traumatic neurosis is the non-experiencing of the traumatic and the paradoxical compulsion to return and seek out that experience.[40]

As I have argued, this means that trauma calls for an analysis and critique of the kind of violence that lodges itself in the psyche all the more tenaciously precisely because it leaves no traces of its breach—a violence that, paradoxically, leaves an absence as its only (un)traceable trace.[41] This sort of "originary" or "structural" erasure (for lack of better words to describe it) only helps to ensure the pervasiveness of such violence and renders its indelible effects all the more unlocatable.

There is a relation, then, between trauma and a certain experience of the *unforgettable*, and we must regard this relation as significant—as both a difficulty and a potentiality—in our efforts to elucidate, listen to, and remember the traumatic. "An unforgettable life or event," Walter Benjamin writes, is one "whose character demands not to forget them" "even if all humanity had forgotten them." It is then something, Benjamin adds, that demands to be remembered even if no human psyche could be regarded as empirically capable of its remembrance: "this predicate [the unforgettable] would not represent a mistake, but rather a demand that men do not respond to and, additionally, perhaps the indication of a sphere capable of responding to this demand: the sphere of a divine memory."[42] As my analysis elsewhere suggests, this is precisely the crux of the *aesth-ethical* challenge that confronts us as we embrace the task of listening to trauma.[43]

The voice that summons us out of this paradoxical call should not then lead us to paralysis. We may instead understand it, with Benjamin, as an indication that there is such a "sphere"—not necessarily "divine," but certainly one that we are yet to imagine—a singular modality of memory—and of listening—that is capable of responding to the demand that comes from its interpellation.[44] Our challenge, then, can be phrased in the following questions: How are we to listen to the truth of a voice that addresses us from out of this *non-place/non-time*? How can we construct conceptions of memory and history that resonate with this paradoxical encounter between the amnesia of the not-yet and a compulsory hypermnesia? How can we preserve such specific and singular modes of temporality without reducing them to a pathology that needs to be overcome? And how can we insert into history the mark of a non-experience, of something that strictly speaking has not-yet happened and yet stubbornly returns as something unforgettable? In Caruth's words: "How can we think of a history thus constituted, multiply and heterogeneously, around the site of a wound? This is the enigma at the heart of Freud's notion of traumatic repetition, and of the nature of the deferred experience that is central to it."[45]

Trauma as Testimony: The Voicing of the (Tree's) Unheard(-of) Wound

This all takes us to a second dimension of the paradoxical structure opened up by trauma, one that may not have been spelled out by Freud himself, but that would have to follow if we take the consequences of his analysis seriously enough. Traumatic neurosis, as we have seen, introduces a radical breach not only in our experience of the world but also in the very structure of experience. Trauma therefore poses a philosophical and epistemological challenge since it puts into question all the conceptual tools and frameworks of meaning that we have at our disposal to make sense of experience to begin with. Thus, Caruth writes,

> what is at the heart of Freud's writing on trauma, both in what it says and in the stories it unwittingly tells, is that trauma seems to be much more than a pathology, or the simple illness of a wounded psyche: it is always the story of a wound that cries out, that addresses us in the attempt *to tell us of a reality or truth that is not otherwise available.*[46]

As Caruth very clearly emphasizes, in the paradox that comes into view "by the ways it simultaneously defies and demands our witness,"[47] trauma forces us to rethink the very same notions of reference and representation that we usually presuppose in making sense of experience. How to *re-present* that which, in the strict sense, is yet to have been *present*? This is where the *literary* as a necessary complement—or indeed as essential—to trauma becomes fundamental for Caruth: trauma compels us to engage in a form of theory "that does not eliminate reference but precisely registers, in language, the impact of an event."[48] To be sure, trauma and its testimony are not a challenge by virtue of their "unrepresentability," as some voices in trauma studies might tend to assume, but rather because they call on us to revisit the very "mode of representation" at play in our listening—the very grammars that organize our sense.[49]

Trauma brings about what Nelly Richard, in theorizing post-dictatorial trauma in Chile, has aptly called a "catastrophe of meaning."[50] There are certain types of violence, Richard argues, that cause "the collapse of traditional categorial orders," all the while introducing unprecedented, unheard-of forms of violence whose excess has not yet been—and perhaps is not entirely meant to be—made intelligible. Not only are these realities abominably original,[51] but their originality is also meant to remain unthought, hidden, for only as such can traumatic forms of violence and the structures they bring about preserve the full force of their operativity. They do so, above all, through the pernicious strategy of stripping these unprecedented realities of their *audibility* within a regime of the perceptible and the intelligible that violence seeks to control and determine in advance. In this way, traumatic forms of violence could be understood, as I was suggesting above, as doubly destructive, since they saturate every space wherein sense can be produced and strip those subjected to it of any possibility to participate in this production other than through subtractive operations.[52]

Not in vain, as Caruth explains, the truth of trauma is one that speaks *another kind of voice* and opens *another form of insight*, one that urges us to imagine and produce the adequate grammars by which to convey and bear witness to its own most unknowability:

> A discourse [that is] not simply spoken *after* the catastrophe, but spoken *on the site of the* catastrophe, the words of the encounter establish an opening, not only through their meaning, but in the performance of a command that breaks their meaning, and in the question that this disruption opens.[53]

This would be an experience of language that, paradoxically, must somehow *name* the catastrophic *breach and disruption* of language that trauma survivors live through and with.[54] The challenge therefore seems here to be twofold. First, it concerns our capacity to *listen* to the disruption and breakdown of language in trauma: How are we to make these fractures of meaning available in the absence of resources for comprehension and expression? Second, it concerns the possibility of moving from a language of trauma to one that testifies to it: How can we find a passage from a language of trauma to what Caruth calls "the language of the address"? The task in this case is not to re-signify something that has been ripped out of language, but rather to seek new forms of representation that can bear witness to such a catastrophic disruption of meaning. Our task, in that sense, would be to search for new languages or modes of signification, new frameworks of meaning that can testify *to* trauma without remaining trapped within its radical unknowability; that can listen to trauma *as* testimony rather than having to translate it into (what is usually already legible as) testimony.

One could also put this in terms of a distinction between the task of *giving meaning* to trauma and the always-failed attempt to *make sense* of what happened. Martínez-Ruiz, who calls attention to this distinction in her analysis of Freud's notion of traumatic neurosis, explains that the first of these alternatives opens to a future within the present of trauma and its singular space/time structures, while the second remains trapped in the impossibility of producing a past that thus returns only as absent in the form of a repetition compulsion. She writes:

> It is the time and space of listening that give meaning to trauma, and not only in a semantic sense, I would also suggest in a phenomenological one, since understanding trauma ushers in the time of what is to come, breaking with the repetition compulsion of a suspended present that is trying to make sense of the past.[55]

This is why the task of listening, as I want to understand it here, is not simply concerned with recovering what remains inaudible in trauma, but is rather an effort to engage with the *unheard-of* in trauma. My use of the expression "unheard-of" seeks to retain the double meaning of the Spanish term "*lo inaudito*," which can be understood as something that remains unheard—or has not yet been heard—but is also ethically outrageous in its abominable, "unheard-of" originality. Such an account of traumatic experience as unheard-of provides us with another conceptual background through which to understand the unpreparedness discussed by Freud in *Beyond the Pleasure Principle*. The lack of psychic preparation for an excessive event can then also be understood as a lack of semantic resources that could allow us to elaborate it as a memory. Trauma is then unheard-of by virtue of its radically unprecedented violence—a violence that does not yet allow itself to be named because its excess, as we have seen, leaves no recognizable trace that might enable us to register it as "representable." This "not yet" that spans and binds the realms of the barely sensible, the linguistically expressible, and the morally comprehensible is therefore one of the structural features that determine traumatic experience.

To listen to the unheard-of: this, then, is the task that calls us on. And there is a source to this call: a *voice* that demands to be heard in the absence of an established frame of audibility—at least within our customary languages. On the other hand, this voice also addresses *us* as those who are responsible before something that, were it to remain unheard, would also remain excluded, condemned to an "ethical loneliness."[56] The only alternative to such loneliness is the opening of a shared world that is inaugurated, each time, in an act of *radical listening*,[57] that is, a listening that is capable of producing, in its practice, the grammars that make it possible. Listening is here an opening to the possibility of sense in contexts that brutally uproot it. Thus, in the face of traumatic violence—which defines in unprecedented ways both our capacity to make sense and the ethical imperative to name the damage—we are called upon to deal with this question as fundamental: How are we to listen to the voice that speaks from trauma?

In *Beyond the Pleasure Principle*, Freud turns to a literary image to refer to this "voice" of trauma, to its particular kind of call and, above all, to the compulsion that marks its (re)appearance in the audible register:

> The most moving poetic picture of a fate such as this [such as that of compulsive repetition] is given by Tasso in his *Gerusalemme Liberata*. Its hero, Tancred, unwittingly kills his beloved Clorinda in a duel while she is disguised in the armour of an enemy knight. After her burial he makes his way into a strange magic forest which strikes the Crusaders' army with terror. He slashes with his sword at a tall tree; but blood streams from the cut and the voice of Clorinda, whose soul is imprisoned in the tree, is heard complaining that he has wounded his beloved once again.[58]

Freud does not dwell on this image and, to an inadvertent reader, the mention of Clorinda's voice can easily fall to the side as a mere illustration of the hold of compulsive repetition on psychic life. Clorinda's voice provides an image—it allows us to imagine and therefore do more than *talk*; indeed, in using it as an illustration, Freud could be said to reduce it to a mechanism for *visualizing* the phenomenon of compulsive repetition that he has only begun to explore in the text. It certainly turns out to be an effective—and simultaneously compelling—mechanism for understanding what Rottenberg describes as the *unlocatability* of trauma through the image of a voice that both is and is not Clorinda's, that speaks from a wound that is no longer the original accident, and that abides in the latency of repetition as the sole available way of making its claim known.

However, we should not read past the sounding, audible character of the voice that speaks out of the traumatic wound. A voice that replicates and echoes itself is more than a voice that repeats itself. Or else we might say that the kind of repetition that a voice performs in the realm of sound does not allow itself to be understood simply as a "compulsion."[59] Clorinda's voice *resonates* through the wound in the tree, and this tree is here an-other body that resonates with her, traversed by the voice of her wound, by the wound of her voice: the wound that *becomes a voice* by restaging its occurrence. Thus, repetition is not—or is at least not simply reducible to—compulsion, for the resonance of its call already displaces the mere reproduction of the violence that originated it and opens toward what Caruth—following Felman—describes as a "testimonial event."[60]

But there is more: to remain attentive to the singular "topology"[61] of sounds captured by the description of trauma as a voice that enunciates itself out of the latency of its call—a call that is *always already* displaced and therefore *remains* unheeded—is also a way to insist on the ethical imperative at stake in listening to its testimony. Even in the absence of interpellation there is a voice, and its mere resonance already involves us in an "ethical bond."[62] The opening of the scene of listening—the scene of a wound becoming audible—reinstates the appeal to others that traumatic violence seeks to annihilate. Hence the importance of approaching trauma through listening, both in practice and conceptually. To center listening as an act that opens sense allows us to attend to the voice that speaks out of the traumatic wound in its singularity, as a *voice* and not as a semantic act: as *resonant* audibility. As Martínez-Ruiz emphasizes, what Freud discovers after experiencing the failures of hypnosis is precisely the fact that, in the case of trauma, "semantic communication does not in itself hold any healing power; something else is needed: the power of iteration as repetition in difference."[63]

It is no coincidence, then, that alongside the enigma posed by the soldiers' dreams and the compulsively repeated terror that they reexperienced upon waking, Freud found himself considering another form of repetition in *Beyond the Pleasure Principle*. As he watched his grandson play by making an object disappear and then reappear, Freud encountered a form of repetition that opens—and does so precisely by the act of voicing a sound ("*fort!*")—a different path for the elaboration of loss (the mother's departure and later death).[64] This form of repetition is not merely reproductive: it is generative. As Caruth writes, such forms of playful repetition do not respond to the death drive but rather manifest a drive to live; they thereby signal toward—although Freud himself does not theorize it in these terms—a possible way of testifying to catastrophe without reproducing it:

> Like the soldiers' dreams, the game thus reenacts the memory of a painful reality. What is most surprising in the child's game, is that this re-enacting . . . links the repetition to a creative act of invention. In the introduction of the child's game, Freud's original question, *what does it mean for life to bear witness to death?*, is thus linked to another question: *What kind of witness is a creative act?*[65]

To listen to trauma *as* testimony also entails listening to the voice that stages itself in and *as* repetition, in a creative act that entails testifying (from) the wound. By staging a scene that is first and foremost a space of listening, such repetition engages us on a path from compulsion to working through.

Notes

1 I refer here to my work on several reports for the Colombian National Center for Historical Memory (Centro Nacional de Memoria Histórica), which included holding extensive memory workshops with communities of survivors of paramilitary violence between 2012 and 2013, and to a series of projects on liberatory memory in the city of Chicago, where I worked with survivors of police torture (see Chicago Torture Justice Center [http://chicagotorturejustice.org/] and Chicago Torture Justice Memorials [https://chicagotorture.org/]) during the years of 2015 and 2019. For a more detailed account of this work, my involvement, and the history of the connections between the two, see María del Rosario Acosta López, ed., "'Making Memory' Historical Memory in Colombia and Its Legacies," in *Memory Work in Colombia: Past and Present Experiences, Legacies for the Future* (The World Humanities Report: South America [CHCI], 2023), https://worldhumanitiesreport.org/wp-content/uploads/2023/06/WHR-Colombia-Memory_1.Acosta-English-2.pdf.

2 María del Rosario Acosta López, "*Gramáticas de lo Inaudito* as Decolonial Grammars: Notes for a Decolonization of Memory," *Research in Phenomenology* 52 (2022): 208.

3 See, in particular, María del Rosario Acosta López, "Grammars of Listening: or on the Difficulty of Rendering Trauma Audible," *Royal Institute of Philosophy Series Supplement* 93 (2023): 153–70. I describe these conditions as "grammars of listening" to capture the sense in which they organize—and predetermine—what becomes audible and, therefore, capable of being believed, remembered, historicized.

4 These are the questions that orient my forthcoming book, *Gramáticas de la escucha. Hacia una memoria de lo inaudito* (Barcelona: Herder, 2026), whose first chapter is entirely devoted to a reading of Freud's *Beyond the Pleasure Principle*, through which I attempt to "set the stage" for a philosophical exploration of the aforementioned questions. What follows is an abbreviated, English-language version of that first chapter. I am thankful to Tupac Cruz for his assistance in translating some passages from the chapter into English and helping me establish a final shape for this condensed version of my argument. An earlier incarnation of this chapter was presented as a lecture in the context of my seminar *Grammars of Listening*, taught in the spring of 2021 during my tenure as International Chair of Contemporary Philosophy at the University of Paris 8. I thank all the participants of that seminar for their insightful questions and comments; I am particularly grateful to Ben Brewer for his attentive copyediting of my lectures.

5 See Cathy Caruth, *Unclaimed Experience: Trauma, Narrative, and History* (Baltimore: John Hopkins University Press, 1996), 3.

6 See Shoshana Felman, *The Juridical Unconscious: Trials and Traumas in the Twentieth Century* (Cambridge, MA: Harvard University Press, 2002); Soshana Felman and Dori Laub, *Testimony: Crises of Witnessing in Literature, Psychoanalysis, and History* (New York: Routledge, 1991); Françoise Davoine and Jean-Max Gaudillière, *History Beyond Trauma: Whereof One Cannot Speak, Thereof One Cannot Stay Silent* (New York:

Other Press, 2004); Elizabeth Rottenberg, "Freud's Other Legacy," *Parrhesia* 21 (2014): 13–22, and *For the Love of Psychoanalysis: The Play of Chance in Freud and Derrida* (New York: Fordham University Press, 2019).

7 See Rosaura Martínez-Ruiz, "Collective Working-Through of Trauma or Psychoanalysis as a Political Strategy," *Psychoanalysis, Culture, and Society* 25 (2020): 594–611, and her recently published *Trauma o en busca de la agencia perdida. Una aproximación desde la escucha y lo psicopolítico* (Madrid: Akal, 2025).

8 On Caruth and how I understand her work, see María del Rosario Acosta López, "Grammars of Addressing: On Memory and History in Cathy Caruth's Work," *Diacritics* 49, no. 2 (2021): 147–57.

9 Sigmund Freud, "Beyond the Pleasure Principle" (1920), in *The Standard Edition of the Works of Sigmund Freud*, volume 18 (London: Hogarth, 1953), 12.

10 Freud, "Beyond the Pleasure Principle," 13.

11 Freud, "Beyond the Pleasure Principle," 12.

12 Freud, "Beyond the Pleasure Principle," 13.

13 See Sigmund Freud and Josef Breuer, "Preliminary Communication," in *The Standard Edition of the Complete Psychological Works of Sigmund Freud*, trans. James Strachey in collaboration with Anna Freud, volume 2 (London: The Hogarth Press, 1953–74), 7.

14 Freud, "Beyond the Pleasure Principle," 13.

15 Freud, "Beyond the Pleasure Principle," 13.

16 Freud, "Beyond the Pleasure Principle," 13.

17 Freud, "Beyond the Pleasure Principle," 7.

18 See Cathy Caruth, *Literature in the Ashes of History* (Baltimore: Johns Hopkins University Press, 2013), Chapter 1.

19 Freud, "Beyond the Pleasure Principle," 32.

20 Freud, "Beyond the Pleasure Principle," 32.

21 Freud, "Beyond the Pleasure Principle," 22. See also: "But we come now to a new and remarkable fact, namely that the compulsion to repeat also recalls from the past experiences which include no possibility of pleasure, and which can never, even long ago, have brought satisfaction even to instinctual impulses which have since been repressed" (20).

22 Freud, "Beyond the Pleasure Principle," 32.

23 Freud, "Beyond the Pleasure Principle," 29; translation modified.

24 Freud, "Beyond the Pleasure Principle," 30.

25 Freud, "Beyond the Pleasure Principle," 32.

26 Freud, "Beyond the Pleasure Principle," 22.

27 Freud, "Beyond the Pleasure Principle," 23.

28 Rottenberg, "Freud's Other Legacy," 19.

29 Rottenberg, "Freud's Other Legacy," 19.

30 Rottenberg, "Freud's Other Legacy," 20.

31 Caruth, *Unclaimed Experience*, 4.

32 Caruth, *Unclaimed Experience*, 6.

33 Caruth, *Unclaimed Experience*, 4.

34 Cathy Caruth interviewing Bessel van der Kolk in *Listening to Trauma: Conversations with Leaders in the Theory and Treatment of Catastrophic Experience* (Baltimore: John Hopkins University Press, 2014), 157.

35 Freud, "Beyond the Pleasure Principle," 24–5.

36 Martínez-Ruiz, "Collective Working-Through of Trauma," 602.

37 Freud, "Beyond the Pleasure Principle," 26.
38 Freud, "Beyond the Pleasure Principle," 27; my emphasis.
39 Freud, "Beyond the Pleasure Principle," 29–30.
40 Martínez-Ruiz, "Collective Working-Through of Trauma," 601.
41 See Acosta López, "Gramáticas de lo inuadito," 210ff.
42 Walter Benjamin, "The Task of the Translator," in *Selected Writings*, volume 3, ed. Howard Eiland and Michael W. Jennings (Cambridge, MA: Harvard University Press, 2003), 151.
43 See María del Rosario Acosta López, "Gramáticas de lo inaudito. Aproximaciones estéticas a la memoria después del trauma," *Calibán RLP* 21, no. 2 (2024): 110–17; and "On *Aesth-ethic* Activism as Epistemic Resistance: In Conversation with José Medina," *Social Epistemology* (forthcoming).
44 On Benjamin's response to these questions, see María del Rosario Acosta López, "Storytelling as Grammars of Listening: On Trauma, Violence, and History in Walter Benjamin's 'The Storyteller,'" *Journal of Continental Philosophy* 3, no. 1 (2023): 135–57; *Gramáticas de la escucha*, forthcoming, Chapter Two.
45 Caruth, *Unclaimed Experience*, 4.
46 Caruth, *Unclaimed Experience*, 4.
47 Caruth, *Unclaimed Experience*, 5.
48 Caruth, *Unclaimed Experience*, 74.
49 Caruth, *Unclaimed Experience*, 183. See Caruth, *Unclaimed Experience*, 177, where Caruth explains the insufficiency and inadequacy of a limited focus on the silence and unrepresentability of trauma, which fails to capture the complexity of Freud's analysis.
50 Nelly Richard, *Fracturas de la memoria. Arte y pensamiento crítico* (Buenos Aires: Siglo XXI editores, 2007), 113.
51 I am borrowing here Hannah Arendt's phrase from "Understanding and Politics," *Essays in Understanding* (New York: Schocken, 2004), 309.
52 As a side note, and although I cannot argue this adequately here (I have made a point of developing it elsewhere in my work), it is important to keep in mind that, while destroying and expropriating entire worlds of sense is a goal of what I have been calling here "traumatic forms of violence" (whose links to colonizing forms of violence I have examined elsewhere; see Acosta López, *Gramáticas de lo inaudito*, 210–12), they do not necessarily succeed in doing so. The force displayed by testimony as resistance to these forms of violence is never to be taken for granted, since it is born in conditions designed precisely to curtail it. Of course, these are also precisely the conditions under which the most admirable forms of subversion and creativity come into play. Those who give testimony in conditions such as those mentioned above, under violence from agents of the State or the para-State, enact resistance where everything—including the mechanisms designed to "give voice" to victims—is designed to silence, erase, or frame survivors' memory as "illegible" (inaudible). In spite of it all, they do speak—and the question is then: How are we to listen to them?
53 Caruth, *Unclaimed Experience*, 35.
54 See also Bessel van der Kolk's response to Caruth's interview: "[W]e now understand that the breakdown occurs at the core level integration. As a result, you continue [after the traumatic experience] to have emotions without context, to have visual images without context, you continue to have sound that is associated with terror, but no context in which this terror relates to the past, or to the present. So the big issue is that you *lose your symbolic capacity*." Caruth, *Listening to Trauma*, 155; my emphasis.
55 Martínez-Ruiz, "Collective Working-Through of Trauma," 601.

56 Jill Stauffer's notion of "ethical loneliness" has fundamentally informed my work on these issues. See *Ethical Loneliness: The Injustice of Not Being Heard* (New York: Columbia University Press, 2015).
57 See María del Rosario Acosta López, "Grammars of Listening," 162ff.
58 Freud, "Beyond the Pleasure Principle," 22.
59 See here Adriana Cavarero's work on the voice as echo, in *For More than One Voice: Toward a Philosophy of Vocal Expression* (Stanford: Stanford University Press, 2005), 165–72; and my reading of her work in connection to trauma, in María del Rosario Acosta López, "Being Robbed of One's Voice: On Listening and Political Violence in Adriana Cavarero," in *Political Bodies: Writings on Adriana Cavarero's Political Thought*, ed. Paula Landerreche Cardillo and Rachel Silverbloom (Albany: SUNY, 2024), 237–64.
60 A testimonial event is one that manages to both approach and keep open, through the manner of acting of the one who listens, the singular wound of this particular event. See Caruth, "The Body's Testimony," 261. According to Caruth, this is connected to the "literary effect" of certain modalities of testimony, modalities by virtue of which testimony achieves effects that reach beyond its stated content.
61 See Juan Diego Pérez, "Hacia una (re)vocalización del trauma. Una crítica a Caruth desde la ética de la escucha," *Perífrasis* 9, no. 18 (2018): 128.
62 Pérez, "Hacia una (re)vocalización del trauma," 128.
63 Martínez-Ruiz, "Collective Working-Through of Trauma," 603.
64 Freud, "Beyond the Pleasure Principle," 14–16.
65 Caruth, *Listening to the Ashes of History*, 4–5.

Works Cited

Acosta López, María del Rosario. "Grammars of Addressing: On Memory and History in Cathy Caruth's Work." *Diacritics* 49, no. 2 (2021): 147–57.

Acosta López, María del Rosario. "*Gramáticas de lo Inaudito* as Decolonial Grammars: Notes for a Decolonization of Memory," translated by J. Rios-Acuña. *Research in Phenomenology* 52 (2022): 203–22.

Acosta López, María del Rosario. "Grammars of Listening: or on the Difficulty of Rendering Trauma Audible." *Royal Institute of Philosophy Series Supplement* 93 (2023): 153–70.

Acosta López, María del Rosario. "*Haciendo memoria*. La 'memoria histórica' en Colombia y sus legados." In *Memory Work in Colombia: Past and Present Experiences, Legacies for the Future*, edited by María del Rosario Acosta López. The World Humanities Report: South America (CHCI), 2023.

Acosta López, María del Rosario, ed. "'Making Memory' Historical Memory in Colombia and Its Legacies." In *Memory Work in Colombia: Past and Present Experiences, Legacies for the Future*. The World Humanities Report: South America (CHCI), 2023. https://worldhumanitiesreport.org/wp-content/uploads/2023/06/WHR-Colombia-Memory_1.Acosta-English-2.pdf.

Acosta López, María del Rosario. "Storytelling as Grammars of Listening: On Trauma, Violence, and History in Walter Benjamin's 'The Storyteller.'" *Journal of Continental Philosophy* 3, no. 1 (2023): 135–57.

Acosta López, María del Rosario. "Being Robbed of One's Voice: On Listening and Political Violence in Adriana Cavarero." In *Political Bodies: Writings on Adriana*

Cavarero's Political Thought, edited by Paula Landerreche Cardillo and Rachel Silverbloom, 237–64. Albany: SUNY, 2024.

Acosta López, María del Rosario. "Gramáticas de lo inaudito. Aproximaciones est-éticas a la memoria después del trauma." *Calibán RLP* 21, no. 2 (2024): 110–17.

Acosta López, María del Rosario. *Gramáticas de la escucha. Hacia una memoria de lo inaudito*. Barcelona: Herder, 2026.

Acosta López, María del Rosario. "On *Aesth-ethic* Activism as Epistemic Resistance: In Conversation with José Medina." *Social Epistemology*39, no. 4 (2024): 358–71.

Arendt, Hannah. "Understanding and Politics." In *Essays in Understanding*, 307–27. New York: Schocken, 2004.

Benjamin, Walter. "The Task of the Translator." In *Selected Writings*, volume 3, edited by Howard Eiland and Michael W. Jennings. Cambridge, MA: Harvard University Press, 2003.

Caruth, Cathy. *Unclaimed Experience: Trauma, Narrative, and History*. Baltimore: John Hopkins University Press, 1996.

Caruth, Cathy. *Listening to Trauma: Conversations with Leaders in the Theory and Treatment of Catastrophic Experience*. Baltimore: John Hopkins University Press, 2014.

Caruth, Cathy. "The Body's Testimony: Dramatic Witness in the Eichmann Trial." *Paragraph* 40, no. 3 (2017): 259–78.

Cavarero, Adriana. *For More than One Voice: Toward a Philosophy of Vocal Expression*. Stanford: Stanford University Press, 2005.

Davoine, Françoise, and Jean-Max Gaudillière. *History Beyond Trauma: Whereof One Cannot Speak, Thereof One Cannot Stay Silent*. New York: Other Press, 2004.

Felman, Shoshana. *The Juridical Unconscious: Trials and Traumas in the Twentieth Century*. Cambridge, MA: Harvard University Press, 2002.

Felman, Shoshana, and Dori Laub. *Testimony: Crises of Witnessing in Literature, Psychoanalysis, and History*. New York: Routledge, 1991.

Freud, Sigmund. "Beyond the Pleasure Principle" (1920). In *The Standard Edition of the Works of Sigmund Freud*, volume 18, 7–33. London: Hogarth, 1953.

Freud, Sigmund, and Josef Breuer. "Preliminary Communication." In *The Standard Edition of the Complete Psychological Works of Sigmund Freud*, translated by James Strachey in collaboration with Anna Freud, volume 2, 1–18. London: The Hogarth Press, 1953–74.

Martínez-Ruiz, Rosaura. "Collective Working-Through of Trauma or Psychoanalysis as a Political Strategy." *Psychoanalysis, Culture, and Society* 25 (2020): 594–611.

Martínez-Ruiz, Rosaura. *Trauma o en busca de la agencia perdida. Una aproximación desde la escucha y lo psicopolítico*. Madrid: Akal, 2025.

Pérez, Juan Diego, "Hacia una (re)vocalización del trauma. Una crítica a Caruth desde la ética de la escucha." *Perífrasis* 9, no. 18 (2018): 117–33.

Richard, Nelly. *Fracturas de la memoria. Arte y pensamiento crítico*. Buenos Aires: Siglo XXI, 2007.

Rottenberg, Elizabeth. "Freud's Other Legacy." *Parrhesia* 21 (2014): 13–22.

Rottenberg, Elizabeth. *For the Love of Psychoanalysis: The Play of Chance in Freud and Derrida*. New York: Fordham University Press, 2019.

Stauffer, Jill. *Ethical Loneliness: The Injustice of Not Being Heard*. New York: Columbia University Press, 2015.

4

Death's Drive in Hegel and Freud

Shannon M. Mussett

While all that lives dies, human beings alone *know* this. What's more, because we are animals, we are anxious about it on a bodily and largely unconscious level as well. G. W. F. Hegel and Sigmund Freud approach the Gordian knot of life and death through the emergence of the organic from the inorganic. Hegel's idealism must contend with the existence of material nature and explain how spirit's negative functions as the opposite of eternal, subjective life, yet also somehow prefigures and sustains it. This leads Hegel into some tricky arguments about life as nature's highest achievement, but only insofar as it is created out of death and is destined for self-sacrifice. Freud's later work considers the emergence of life outside of any kind of teleological purpose so dominant in Hegel's philosophy. And yet, he too tells the story of life emerging from what is dead, destined to return to it by the most expedient pathways. The purposiveness of life's emergence from matter in Hegel stands in contrast with the purposive indifference of life's begrudging emergence in Freud's archaic hypothesis. This leads to a pronounced difference in both on the hopefulness, or lack thereof, regarding death's drive in the workings of life.

Primarily using on Part Two of Hegel's *Encyclopaedia of the Philosophical Sciences: The Philosophy of Nature* (1830) and Freud's *Beyond the Pleasure Principle* (1920), this essay focuses on how the inorganic serves not only as the engine of life but also as the dead core functioning as a mortal coil driving organisms toward inevitable demise. Despite their vastly different frameworks questioning the origin and purpose of life, Hegel and Freud take seriously the notion that life may actually be in the service of something beyond, before, or after itself. To explore this overlap, I address the emergence of the organic from the inorganic, with particular emphasis on the inorganic conceived of as what is dead. Once life appears, the role of animal drive becomes important in the paths taken by organisms, ultimately leading to the human for whom drives are unique. Both theorists conceive of drives as conservative, but Hegel locates the motive force in the genus, where Freud finds it in the individual germ cells. Exploring this shift in focus reveals far-reaching implications on the ultimately optimistic conclusions of the former and the abysmal pessimism—or perhaps realism—of the latter.

Death's Drive in Hegel

Hegel's *Philosophy of Nature* describes the movement from spirit's logical structures as it emerges into the material world in explicitly religious and anti-evolutionary terms. Spirit must *externalize* itself in order to come to know itself in absolute otherness.[1] As abstract mind, it enacts a self-negation, thus transforming into the materiality of nature. It is an act of near total self-annihilation and sacrifice. The unity of mind explodes into nature, entirely lost in the dispersal of matter, utterly alienated from its essence, which is to be subject: an eternally self-sustaining soul. But true, concrete subjectivity requires a return to self, having known itself in and as its other. The *Philosophy of Nature* charts this return as a progressive, nesting movement away from the scattered and irrational chaos of the material world into the inner subjectivity of finite life. Life, particularly animal life, draws increasingly more complicated inorganic matter and chemical operations into itself, forming internal cyclic processes that sustain *and* threaten it.

Repeatedly in the *Zusätze*, Hegel describes the process of natural creation along Christian lines.[2] Matter requires the birth and sacrifice of God's natural son and their combined rebirth into eternal unity: spirit (*Geist*). Of particular interest is how Hegel describes the natural world as both *constituted* and *infected* by the negative. Nature is characterized by apartness (*Außereinander*), infinite separateness (*unendlichen Vereinzelung*), and externality (*Äußerlichkeit*), all of which are versions of the negative, but the negative specifically understood as externality. Externality is best thought of in terms of *separation*: spirit in its inside-out, alienated, dispersed, and negative form. Matter, which pushes against the unity of soul, infuses and contaminates every aspect of the natural world, even as the movement of spirit works to bring the side-by-sidedness of nature into a self-subsistent harmony.

Nature is where spirit must confront finitude, which it does by contesting the negative in the form of what Hegel had decades earlier described as the "Absolute Master." The *Phenomenology* describes spirit through multiple concepts: the universal individual, substance as subject, and pure self-identity in otherness. This wide net of descriptors orbits the central idea that spirit contains within itself the "tremendous power of the negative."[3] This awesome force of separation and negation from the whole is a prodigious and fearful power because it destabilizes and ruptures that which seeks stability and wholeness.[4] Yet, the *Phenomenology* often glides over the surface of death. The fog of idealism suffuses even the most concrete explorations of the natural world, which is why Hegel eventually turns directly to natural philosophy. In the natural, material world, spirit will learn that death is not only omnipresent, but is the necessary, perhaps *sole* driving force behind all life.

Nature is a living whole, composed of circles and cycles that give rise to organisms. Yet, the entire movement is motivated by death and sacrifice.[5] At the conclusion of the *Logic*, Hegel explains that the externalized idea is death, but this death is required for eternal life. The idea must become a living creature destined to be sublated into spirit:

> the Idea *posits* itself as that which it is *in itself*; or what is the same thing, that it returns *into itself* out of its immediacy and externality which is *death*, in order to

> be first *a living creature*, but further to sublate this determinateness also in which it is only Life, and to give itself an existence as Spirit.[6]

Spirit moves out of natural immediacy through a system of determinations, conceived as stages through nature, in which it is "lost" and must "find" itself again. Even as spirit moves through phases wherein it posits its materiality in the most abstract ways (space, time, place, movement, gravity), it is always with one very specific end goal: life, specifically animal life, specifically human life.

Critically, Hegel describes the atemporal origin of material creation as the inner simplicity of mind exploding with centrifugal force into the manifold diversity of nature. Each subsequent developmental stage enacts a centripetal influence toward the subjective unity of the center. Immediate, disembodied mind bursts into matter characterized only by external relationships as opposed to the inner unity of soul. Each stage of nature is a gathering, a pull of materiality toward an ideal center, ultimately resulting in an internally purposive, self-sustaining, *nearly* independent animal organism. It is easy to be taken in by the elegance of Hegel's dialectic, but this story is entirely motivated by the death drive.[7]

Matter (the unity of motion and place) is the essence of the natural world. As externality, it is essentially *de*centered.[8] Its center is outside of itself, moving and forming it in manifold ways as it strives to reach its ideal, but never fully attaining it. True interiority can only be subject, and matter is forever haunted by the soul that motivates it, but which can only reach actualization in human and divine self-consciousness. Soul motivates life, but only in an implicit and unconscious way.[9] Life sublates the earlier stages of natural development into itself, maintaining integrity in the face of the constant pull of externality which seeks to reduce it to inert matter.[10] Most notably, life is both produced and destroyed by inorganic chemical processes.[11] So long as the organism persists, it is sustained by an infinite cycle of mechanical and chemical activity. In this way, the organism touches the infinite through self-preservation, but because of its material finitude, it is only temporarily preserved. Not only is it destined to die, but the inorganic chemical processes fueling it are themselves lifeless. Whether from violence, disease, or age, the chemical process will prevail and retrieve each living entity. This helps to clarify why the chemical process that sustains organisms is also that which threatens and eventually succeeds in destroying them. In sum, Hegel argues that lifeless matter maintains life and ultimately reclaims it; death is both the spark for and terminus of life. Nature's end is in the beginning. But why, then, does life even appear, given that it is produced by and returns to the inorganic? To begin to answer this question, it is necessary to explore the specific constitution of animals.

Living creatures are enmeshed in their environments, which sustain but also threaten destruction. Additionally, animal bodies are not seamless machines. Their parts and organs are in constant friction. Through sensibility, irritability, and reproduction, the animal must posit and overcome divisions within the borders of its body and in its relationship to the external world.[12] This hypothesis brings Hegel to the observation that the practical relationship of the organic and the nonorganic comes together in the animal body's experience of drive or urge (*Trieb*). The organism can never overcome the tension within its bodily borders, as organs and chemical systems sustaining digestion, respiration, and excretion continuously strain against inevitable breakdown. Nor will it ever fully overcome the tension with the external world, insofar as it is reliant upon it for food, shelter, and others of its kind with which to reproduce. The animal is therefore trapped in an internal and external web of materiality that gives rise to it, bolsters it, and ultimately recoups it.

The animal is not wholly unaware of this precarious situation. It *feels* defective; it *feels* itself lacking wholeness. This feeling of absence motivates the urge to overcome it. It experiences "the feeling of *lack* (*Mangle*) and the *urge* (*Trieb*) to get rid of it."[13] What it *feels* is the defect of life manifest in the sensation of being essentially dependent (originally on the environment, but ultimately on the genus).[14] This feeling of lack prods the animal to overcome its displeasure through satisfaction. Put differently, Hegel's animal is motivated by an unconscious drive to negate and sublate the incessantly goading feeling of need. The urge appears as an instinct, which Hegel defines as "purposive activity acting unconsciously (*bewußtlose*)."[15] The use of unconsciousness is telling because it highlights the teleological conception of the animal organism as purposively organized, but the urges that motivate it are entirely unknown as ends.[16] *Trieb*, in Hegel, is specific to the animal. Moving up the ladder of animal development makes this urge increasingly explicit until it becomes something specific to the self-conscious human animal capable of recognizing ends. But this transition does not occur until Hegel's *Anthropology*. The *Philosophy of Nature* presents animal development just up to the cusp of self-awareness (specifically, the awareness of the self as a self).

Need and desire are constantly in tension with the external world—a tension that is as insurmountable as it is sustaining. Thus, the finite creature's life is precarious. The "environment of external contingency contains factors which are almost wholly alien; it exercises a perpetual violence and threat of dangers. Because of this constant state of precarity the animal's life is *insecure*, *anxious*, and *unhappy* (*unsicheres, angstvolles, unglückliches*)."[17] The externality of nature that gives rise to and destroys life mercilessly threatens violence and disorder, causing the animal to be in a nearly constant state of anxiety and unhappiness.

The final stages of *The Philosophy of Nature* involve animal reproduction and demise from violence, disease, and age. At this moment, the genus appears as the motivation and destiny of all individuals. Crucially, individual animals are driven to copulation before they die because they feel a lack in relation to the universal perfection of the genus. The feeling of lack ultimately arises from the failure of the individual to express the perfection of the genus. The eternal, unchanging genus can never be instantiated in the chaos and irrationality of matter. Sex is therefore pursued by the urge (*Trieb*) an individual animal has to copulate in an attempt to mitigate this failure of materialization. Copulation allows the animal "to obtain its self-feeling in the other of its genus . . . to close the genus with itself and bring it into existence."[18] Death thus motivates the entirety of copulation and ultimately, reproduction. Hegel writes, "What the genus brings forth is the procreation of individuals *through the death of other individuals of the same genus*; the individual after reproducing itself as another individual, perishes."[19] Death is the motivation for new living beings *and* their destiny, "insofar as they have no higher destiny."[20] On the one hand, the drive to copulate is conservative as it is motivated by death and the return to it, but on the other, it is progressive in that it serves the interests of the genus and ultimately, the return out of externality and materiality of spirit itself.

Despite the different ways that an organism can meet its end, the ultimate cause of death is the same for every one of them: matter is alienated, finite, and temporal. As such, any entity that comes to be will perish. Hegel writes: "the disparity between its finitude and universality [the individual and the genus] is its *original disease* and the inborn *germ of death*, and the removal of this disparity is itself the accomplishment of this destiny."[21] Thus, a death drive creates and destroys life. Life (as a prefiguration of Freud's Eros) would then be that which unites two individuals into the genus through the negation of their imperfect, material natures. The individual animal wages a temporary and ill-fated war against two equally opposing forces that seek its demise: inorganic nature which gives rise to it and ultimately breaks it apart, and the genus which demands that it reproduce and sacrifice itself. This double relation underscores Hegel's ominous words that "*the goal of Nature is to destroy itself*."[22] Death produces life and destroys it by fulfilling the demands of the genus. Death, as the material processes that sustain animal life, reclaims its temporary loan and reduces the living being to the inorganic. In this way, it assures its role as the absolute master and the emergence of eternal spirit.

Death's Drive in Freud

Freud's death drive also struggles with understanding the urge involved in the paradoxical production and destruction of living creatures. However, Freud rejects any kind of divine teleological framework and the optimism that this resolution promises. One hundred years after Hegel's *Encyclopedia*, Freud added the now notorious final sentence to *Civilization and Its Discontents*. Lamenting the unhappiness and anxiety felt by the species whose domination now threatens global annihilation, he champions "eternal Eros" to assert himself against his adversary, death, adding: "But who can foresee with what success and with what result?"[23] This pessimism suffuses his late work as the emergence and perhaps ultimate dominion of the death drive becomes impossible to ignore in the rapacious destruction wrought by humanity in the twentieth century.[24]

The first thoroughgoing treatment of this destructive drive appears in *Beyond the Pleasure Principle*, which begins with the puzzle posed by the compulsion to repeat painful experiences. Freud discovers that certain dreams and repetitive behaviors point to a force that overrides the pleasure principle. In the economic framework, pleasure is understood as the lowering of unpleasurable tension, a notion indebted to Gustave Fechner's principle of stability.[25] The pleasure principle follows the principle of constancy—seeking to lower excitation or to keep it constant. However, the compulsion to repeat reveals something "more primitive, more elementary, more driven (*angetrieben*) than the pleasure principle which it over-rides."[26] Couching the discussion as "often far-fetched" speculation, Freud nonetheless sets out to explore what could possibly give rise to instances of the compulsion to repeat that do not readily cause pleasure. To do this, he finds himself venturing into the very beginnings and ends of life itself.

Freud describes the simplest living organism as an undifferentiated vesicle of living substance that is somehow receptive to external stimuli. Like the border of the *Pcpt-Cs* system, its surface faces the external world, causing differentiation between the inside of the vesicle and its outward-facing border. Through relentless goading from the environment, a cell's surface eventually develops into a hardened crust (what he calls a "receptive cortical layer"). Freud imagines an environment rife with overwhelming energies that would quickly kill off life without the formation of such a hardened boundary. This crust "becomes to some degree inorganic and thenceforward functions as a special envelope or membrane resistant to stimuli."[27] Deadening the living membrane allows for external stimuli to pass into the cell but with greatly reduced intensity. The dead crust enables life to persist by serving as a protective screen against the threats of environmental destruction. Significantly, Freud suggests that the more highly developed the animal, the more this dead layer *withdraws into the body*, leaving only a fraction behind to function as sense organs amenable to environmental incitements. The inorganic is incorporated into the center of the organism, very much like the inborn germ of death proposed by Hegel. The interiorized dead cortical layer wound into the heart of every organism waits, just as it does in Hegel's mortal seed, to gain mastery over the organism by moving outward from the center.

At the same time, however, the organism experiences internal stimuli against which it has no protection. Because these excitations are felt more acutely than those emanating from the external world, the organism is often positioned to treat internal excitations as coming not from within, but from without.[28] The dead cortical layer is thus largely protected from the external environment but remains defenseless against the onslaught of internal excitations, the drives, which are "the representatives of all the forces originating in the interior of the body and transmitted to the mental apparatus."[29] In this hypothetical tale of the emergence of life from the inorganic landscape of a violent and chaotic Earth, Freud locates a universal attribute of drives; a drive "*is an urge inherent in organic life to restore an earlier state of things* which the living entity has been obliged to abandon under the pressure of external disturbing forces; that is, it is a kind of organic elasticity, or to put it another way, the expression of the inertia inherent in organic life."[30] Rather than functioning as mechanisms of progress and development, drives are essentially conservative, perhaps digressive (even as they necessitate moving forward in order to go backwards). However, unlike Hegel's treatment of drives, Freud proposes that *all* drives tend toward the restoration of an earlier state. Existence thus comes to all organisms (at least originally) from without, with inorganic matter forced into an unwanted, nascent, and temporary life. Life is thus an imposition rather than a fulfillment. What may appear as a drive toward progress is a deceptive sleight of hand to force the organism back through a recapitulation of the pathways it was originally forced to follow into existence. The goal of life thus seeks to restore an earlier, inorganic state. As Freud so succinctly phrases it: "*the aim of all life is death*," the equipoise of inanimate matter.[31] Thus, organisms seek to return to a time before living time. Or, as Catherine Malabou observes, they are driven by "a tendency to go back to a time before death, to *the temporal mode of being of the non-living and of the non-dying*."[32]

Notably, Freud points out that the simpler the life, the quicker the death, "whose direction was determined by the chemical structure of the young life."[33] Just as Hegel proposes that lifeless chemical processes sustain and ultimately reclaim life, so Freud argues that inorganic chemical structures comprise the essence of death in life as well as its final goal. Self-preservation, assertion, and mastery are only component drives serving the organism as it follows its proper path to death. For Freud, all drives are essentially conservative, in which case, *there is no other origin or purpose to life than its emergence from and return to the inorganic*. After his hypothesis concerning the conservative, death-motivated nature of drives, he pauses to anticipate the question anyone familiar with his theories would ask: but what about Eros?

Hegel finds the unification of animals in copulation ultimately serving the teleologically framed demands of the *genus*. Freud, however, focuses on the *germ cells* when questioning if Eros maintains any of its previously held power. The joining of germ cells *seems* to suspend, even overcome death. In unicellular life, cells may neutralize the death drive through unification. And yet, even as Freud describes integration as a neutralization of death, he also calls this unity a kind of "self-sacrifice." Their unity appears to be a sacrifice for a higher good, not unlike Hegel's self-sacrificial nature. For Freud, the sacrifice is in the service of the production of more of the same kind. However, Freud vacillates on this point. Unable to completely abandon the drive toward life, he is conflicted by the fact that reproduction appears to be a lengthening of the path to inevitable death. Ultimately, even life drives are, like death, inherently conservative insofar as they preserve the organism's integrity. There is no progress, only different ways to regress.[34]

Freud concludes that "there is unquestionably *no universal drive towards higher development observable in the animal or plant world*, even though it is undeniable that development does in fact occur."[35] Freud's anti-teleological commitment is most evident when he makes such claims.[36] The drive toward progress and perfection so esteemed by Hegel's spiritual movement is nothing more than repressed drives striving to achieve satisfaction. Organisms "progress" because it is often the only direction available for the release of the drives working tirelessly to express themselves. Ultimately, the absolute master comes to reclaim its chemical loan: "the life process of the individual leads for internal reasons to an abolition of chemical tensions that is to say, to death, whereas union with the living substance of a different individual increases those tensions" which prolongs its life.[37]

Freud ultimately departs from biology in *Beyond the Pleasure Principle*, turning to the story of Aristophanes' androgynes whose arrogant loving unity caused Zeus to violently separate them, thus condemning them to eternally seek reunification with their lost halves. Using this Platonic story, Freud beseeches us to ask, is it possible that

> Living substance at the time of its coming to life was torn apart into small particles, which have ever since endeavored to reunite through the sexual drives? . . . that these splintered fragments of living substance in this way attained a multicellular

> condition and finally transferred the instinct for reuniting, in the most highly concentrated form, to the germ-cells?[38]

But here, amazingly, he breaks off. It's as if the hypothetical paroxysm of life into shards seeking reunification is impossible to think except in mythological terms. Hegel had proposed an initial explosion of scattered matter brought into increasingly purposive and inwardly motivated organic forms. Freud describes a simple cell, torn asunder into smaller particles that seek reconsolidation into a whole. It is certainly a paradoxical thought that at the moment of life's creation it was subject to dissolution. It makes one wonder how life could have ever continued given this improbable situation. It seems that without the guidance of spirit, Freud is left with an origin story that unravels the moment he utters it.

Conclusion

If all life in Freud's conception is dominated by—what may turn out to be—the only actual drive, that means that, similar to Hegel, life is sustained by death. But this also means that any conception of progress into manifold forms of increasingly complicated living expressions is driven by retrograde motion. Progress is fueled by or simply *is* regress. In Hegel, progress is not so disturbingly conceived. Spirit drives toward its own return from material otherness into itself. The end is in the beginning and once spirit ventures on the journey of progressive self-discovery, its attainment is all but guaranteed. Progress is built into the system as it will ultimately move forward in and through human history. However, this progress is tinged with an acute anxiety, an anxiety directly tied to death. Death, that "absolute master" which is always there, even if not foregrounded, is one of—if not *the*—leading enticements toward progress and change. This brings us back to the idea that both Hegel and Freud maintain that death is what creates, fuels, and awaits all life, regardless of whether there is any purpose or redemption to it.

Yet, Hegel's death drive works in the service of the eternal perfection of the genus. If there is a drive akin to the unifying work of Eros in Freud, this would be it. All life, but especially animal life, dies so that spirit can reunite with itself, recovering itself from its alienation in matter. In this way, the eternal spirit overcomes the defect of finitude, which is the inborn seed of death. The dead cortical layer in Freud's organism functions as its own innate mortal coil. And without a God to shepherd this tender emergence to safe harbor, life temporarily maintains itself after birth only by developing a dead protective crust so that it can persist before death comes to reclaim it. But this dead layer sinks ever more into the center of organisms as they develop into more complex forms.

Hegel's emphasis on the eternal perfection of the genus functioning as the goal and provocation of the drive uniting animals in sex allows for the conservative aspect of death in life to bow before the dominant movement toward perfection in spirit. Because nature is the sphere of externality and alienation, death reigns supreme.

However, the result and success of divine unity, spirit returned into itself and once again made complete, justifies and sanctifies material violence and decay. Freud's story, however, finds no justification. The conservative nature of the drives allows him to reject any notion that life contains a drive toward progress on any level: societal, psychological, or biological. This stands in distinction from Hegel's philosophy, which acknowledges a conservative *and* progressive understanding of drives. Yet there exists a peculiar overlap insofar as the conservative bent in both thinkers is evident in the compulsion to repeat. The tendency to repeat experiences and dreams that offer no clear possibility for pleasure in Freud brings him face to face with a destructive drive that motivates all life. There is a tragic compulsion to repeat in Hegel as well, as can be appreciated in the admittedly strange way that the genus forces individuals to come into existence because others have died. And these new generations exist only to be sacrificed themselves. Such a reality, particularly in higher animals, causes constant anxiety and feelings of unfulfillable need.

Freud's attempt to find Eros despite the overwhelming primacy of the death drive leads him to focus on the narrow cellular level where the germ cells *may* temporarily suspend death but which still lead to the performance of life's self-sacrifice in the service of the death drive. Lacking the teleology of spiritual progress, Eros is a shrunken shadow of its former glory. This difference in emphasis helps to explain why Hegel's God is triumphant in redeeming the natural world from its chaos and contingency, bringing humanity up with it into the eternal life of spirit—and why Freud's humanity stands alone at the precipice of self-annihilation, with little to no hope of salvation.

Notes

1 The *Logic* concludes by acknowledging that "the Idea does not merely pass over into life, or as finite cognition allow life to show in it: in its own absolute truth it resolves to let the 'moment' of its particularity, or of the first characterization and other-being, the immediate idea, as its reflected image go forth freely as nature." See G. W. F. Hegel, *Logic*, ed. and trans. J. N. Findlay (Oxford: Oxford University Press, 1975), 296.

2 The *Zusätze* provide a great deal of clarity to what would otherwise be somewhat incomprehensible.

3 G. W. F. Hegel, *The Phenomenology of Spirit*, ed. and trans. Terry Pinkard (Cambridge: Cambridge University Press, 2018), 20. This power, which Hegel attributes to conceptual thinking, is the essence of the pure I. In elaborating what makes up the power of the I, Hegel defines it as "death," or "non-actuality," which is "the most fearful thing of all, and to keep and hold fast to what is dead requires only the greatest force" (20).

4 Spirit is alive; it is the very definition of substance as living. But spirit is alive *only* insofar as it is generated by the power of the negative—the force that constantly rips apart stable forms of thought, society, organic life, and truth itself. This negativity is also the defining feature of the subject. Hegel emphasizes the nature of spirit to linger with the negative, to not shy away from death but to actively confront it and bring it into being. This phenomenon is, in part, where Adrien Johnston finds the force of the split drive. See Adrien Johnston, *Time Driven: Metapsychology and the Splitting of the*

Drive (Evanston: Northwestern University Press, 2005), 322. Slavoj Žižek also shows the versatility of Hegel's use of the negative and death in *Tarrying with the Negative: Kant, Hegel, and the Critique of Ideology* (Durham: Duke University Press, 1993).

5 While dealing almost exclusively with the *Phenomenology*, it is helpful to recall Georges Bataille's discussion in "Hegel, Death and Sacrifice," which emphasizes not so much the way natural death functions in human consciousness, but how human beings make death a celebration, festival, and ultimately a form of pleasure. See Georges Bataille, "Hegel, Death and Sacrifice," trans. Jonathan Strauss. *Yale French Studies* 28 (1990): 9–28.

6 Hegel, *Logic*, 24. Nature's highest level is life, but even this is at the mercy of "unreason and externality, and the living creature is throughout its whole life entangled with other alien existences, whereas in every expression of Spirit there is contained the moment of free, universal self-relation." See G. W. F. Hegel, *Philosophy of Nature: Being Part Two of the Encyclopaedia of the Philosophical Sciences*, trans. A. V. Miller (Oxford: Clarendon Press, 1970), 17. These kinds of observations are why Jon Mills points out that "Hegel has a surprisingly well articulated theory of the unconscious and the psychodynamic processes that govern the structure, function, and operations of the mind." See Jon Mills, *The Unconscious Abyss: Hegel's Anticipation of Psychoanalysis* (Albany: State University of New York Press, 2002), 187. See also Daniel Berthold-Bond, "Hegel, Nietzsche, and Freud on Madness and the Unconscious," *The Journal of Speculative Philosophy* 5, no. 3 (1991): 193–213.

7 In part, I am emphasizing the strange way that Hegel's notion of progress is driven by regress. Life is born from and returns to death not simply by chance but by design. Rebecca Comay's emphasis on resistance in Hegel (and Freud) is helpful here. While Comay focuses on the *Phenomenology*, there is additionally stasis, stalling, and stagnation in the *Philosophy of Nature* as well. See Rebecca Comay, "Resistance and Repetition: Freud and Hegel," *Research in Phenomenology* 45 (2015): 237–66.

8 Hegel, *Philosophy of Nature*, 46.

9 Mills writes in *The Unconscious Abyss* about the ways in which Hegel's notion of the unconscious (*bewußtlos*) underlies all dimensions of human subjectivity.

10 It is worth comparing this idea of preserved stages to Freud, who writes that in animals, "the earlier phases of development are in no sense still preserved; they have been absorbed into the later phases for which they have supplied the material." See Sigmund Freud, *Civilization and Its Discontents*, ed. and trans. James Strachey (New York: W. W. Norton & Co., 1961), 19. There is a similar nesting at work in the development of animals in both authors.

11 Hegel elaborates that through the workings of chemical operations, the "living creature is always exposed to danger, always bears within itself an other, but can endure this contradiction which the inorganic cannot. But life is also the resolving of this contradiction" (Hegel, *Philosophy of Nature*, 274).

12 Despite it being what it is, insofar as it endures contradiction within itself, the animal organism still harbors the beginnings of selfhood that plants lack. Plants lack inwardness, whereas animals have the *feeling* of self. See Hegel, *Philosophy of Nature*, 377.

13 Hegel, *Philosophy of Nature*, 385. See also G. W. F. Hegel, *Hauptwerke: Enzyklopädie der philosophischen Wissenschaften im Grundrisse*, volume 6 (Hamburg: Felix Meiner Verlag, 1999), 358. The organism is beset upon to respond to external stimulation (*Erregtwerdens von Außen*) that takes the form of an object against which the animal braces itself.

14 Hegel has a complicated constellation of terms to capture the animal defect. The *Trieb* is for Hegel, specifically designated as *Instinkt*, which serves as an inner stimulus that relates the animal to various spheres of Nature (Hegel, *Philosophy of Nature*, 388). Impulse (*Trieb*), instinct (*Instinkt*), and need (*Bedürfniß*) are various negations that motivate the animal without the animal having conscious knowledge of how or why. Need (*Bedürfniß*) is specific to the organism and environment but particularized in an infinite variety of ways. Urge (*Trieb*) is the activity of getting rid of the *defect* (*Mangel*) of the need. For its part, negation "is finitude, a lack only for that which is its accomplished sublation, *infinite* self-reference" (Hegel, *Philosophy of Nature*, 385).

15 Hegel, *Philosophy of Nature*, 389.

16 Humans are the best adapted to free themselves from the particularities of the environment and the demands of their urges, but insofar as they are embodied, they can never be fully disentangled from their inner lack and external environmental dependency. Because they are animals, they experience an unending cycle of satisfaction and need that simply cannot be entirely rationalized away. See Hegel, *Philosophy of Nature*, 391.

17 Hegel, *Philosophy of Nature*, 416–17. See also Hegel, *Hauptwerke*, 369.

18 Hegel, *Philosophy of Nature*, 411.

19 Hegel continues that "in the process of the genus, the merely natural being only perishes, for, as such, it does not transcend the natural. But the moments of the process of the genus . . . fall apart and exist as a plurality of particular processes which culminate, in one way or another, in the *death* of the creature." See Hegel, *Philosophy of Nature*, 1970, 410–11; my emphasis.

20 Hegel, *Philosophy of Nature*, 414.

21 Hegel, *Philosophy of Nature*, 441.

22 Hegel, *Philosophy of Nature*, 444; my emphasis. Nathan Gorelick takes up the death drive in Rousseau, emphasizing that he also sees the aim of nature as its own cancellation. This is not coincidental, as Hegel was deeply influenced by Rousseau in both his understanding of nature and education. See Nathan Gorelick, *The Unwritten Enlightenment: Literature Between Ideology and the Unconscious* (Evanston: Northwestern University Press, 2024).

23 Freud, *Civilization and Its Discontents*, 112. It's worth noting the difference between Hegelian animal anxiety, which is the uneasiness produced by the precarity of self-preservation, and Freudian anxiety, which is produced through proximity to one's own desire.

24 I will not take specific issue with the thorny problem of whether the death drive is a separate drive from *Eros*, or whether it is the only drive of which *Eros* is a component, or whether, as Johnston would have it, the name for a feature characteristic of all drives. See Johnston, *Time Driven*. Earlier, Freud explains in *Drives and Their Vicissitudes* (1915) that the drives operate on the frontier between the somatic and mental with provocative temporal implications. As Johnston argues, Freud's drive theory involves a complex temporal dynamic between past, present, and future because "there exists a temporal conflict internal to the very metapsychological structure of each and every drive" (Johnston, *Time Driven*, 146). Mills puts forward the hypothesis that Hegel has a monistic drive and Freud's is bifurcated (Mills, *The Unconscious Abyss*, 73). Whatever the ontological status of the death drive, it exerts a profound and unsettling power in the frustrated, anxious lived experience of human birth, life, and death.

25 See also Sigmund Freud, *The Ego and the Id* (New York: W. W. Norton and Sons, 1960), 46.
26 Freud, *Beyond the Pleasure Principle*, 25. The specific nature of a drive (and what separates it from an animal instinct) is its fourfold form composed of the source, pressure, aim, and object (Johnston, *Time Driven).*
27 Freud, *Beyond the Pleasure Principle*, 30.
28 It is, of course, possible to disrupt this tenuous stability. Trauma overwhelms the barrier and circumvents the pleasure principle.
29 Freud, *Beyond the Pleasure Principle*, 40.
30 Freud, *Beyond the Pleasure Principle*, 43. Catherine Malabou takes issue with Freud's sliding on the function of plasticity and elasticity in this work. She argues that Freud fails to find anything plastic in the death drive; thus, the drive has no form in and of itself. The consequences for Malabou are that Freud's claims to finding something beyond the pleasure principle all fail. See Catherine Malabou, "Plasticity and Elasticity in Freud's 'Beyond the Pleasure Principle,'" *Parallax* 15, no. 2 (2009): 41–52.
31 Freud, *Beyond the Pleasure Principle*, 46. He returns to this in his summary in *Civilization and Its Discontents*, 77–82. Whereas Malabou claims that "Freud articulates the first and unique concept of time in all Western thought in which the very notions of original and end, past, present and future, are merely referred to inorganic matter" (Malabou, "Plasticity and Elasticity in Freud's," 43), Hegel has also presented a number of these possibilities in his natural philosophy. For more on the role of death in life, see Matei Georgescu, "Freud's Theory of the Death Drive," *Review of Contemporary Philosophy* 10 (2011): 228–33; and Havi Carel, *Life and Death in Freud and Heidegger* (Amsterdam: Rodopi, 2006).
32 Malabou, "Plasticity and Elasticity in Freud's," 42.
33 Freud, *Beyond the Pleasure Principle*, 46.
34 This may have something to do with the fact that earlier forms make up later forms because "in the animal kingdom we hold to the view that the most highly developed species have proceeded from the lowest" (Freud, *Civilization and Its Discontents*, 18). As a Darwinian, Freud sees evolution as adaptation rather than a form of biological or spiritual progression.
35 Freud, *Beyond the Pleasure Principle*, 49; my emphasis.
36 Freud often makes it a point to reject any teleological purpose to nature. For example, "it is merely a matter of opinion when we declare that one stage of development is higher than another . . . biology teaches us that higher development in one respect is very frequently balanced or outweighed by involution in another" (Freud, *Beyond the Pleasure Principle*, 50).
37 Freud, *Beyond the Pleasure Principle*, 67.
38 Freud, *Beyond the Pleasure Principle*, 70–1. He repeats the unifying role of Eros in bringing together increasingly far-reaching combinations of dispersed particles in Freud, *Civilization and Its Discontents*, 38. See also his comparison of morality in the super-ego as a product of decomposition analogous to the protista that die from the products of decomposition they have created. See Freud, *The Ego and the Id*, 59. Freud acknowledges how far-fetched some of his ideas are, noting that all the problems would be cleared up if psychological terms could be replaced with physiological or chemical ones.

Works Cited

Bataille, George. "Hegel, Death and Sacrifice," translated by Jonathan Strauss. *Yale French Studies* 28 (1990): 9–28.

Berthold-Bond, Daniel. "Hegel, Niezsche, and Freud on Madness and the Unconsious." *The Journal of Speculative Philosophy* 5, no. 3 (1991): 193–213.

Carel, Havi. *Life and Death in Freud and Heidegger*. Amsterdam: Rodopi, 2006.

Comay, Rebecca. "Resistance and Repetition: Freud and Hegel." *Research in Phenomenology* 45 (2015): 237–66.

Freud, Sigmund. *The Ego and the Id*. New York: W. W. Norton and Sons, 1960.

Freud, Sigmund. *Beyond the Pleasure Principle* (1920). New York: W. W. Norton & Sons, 1961.

Freud, Sigmund. *Civilization and Its Discontents*. Edited and Translated by James Strachey. New York: W. W. Norton & Co., 1961.

Freud, Sigmund. *The Future of an Illusion*. New York: W. W. Norton & Company, 1961.

Georgescu, Matei. "Freud's Theory of the Death Drive." *Review of Contemporary Philosophy* 10 (2011): 228–33.

Gorelick, Nathan. *The Unwritten Enlightenment: Literature Between Ideology and the Unconscious*. Evanston: Northwestern University Press, 2024.

Hegel, G. W. F. *Philosophy of Nature: Being Part Two of the Encyclopaedia of the Philosophical Sciences*. Translated by A. V. Miller. Oxford: Clarendon Press, 1970.

Hegel, G. W. F. *Logic*. Edited and translated by J. N. Findlay. Oxford: Oxford University Press, 1975.

Hegel, G. W. F. *Hauptwerke: Enzklopadie der philosophischen Wissenschaften im Grundrisse*, volume 6. Hamburg: Felix Meiner Verlag, 1999.

Hegel, G. W. F. *The Phenomenology of Spirit*. Edited and translated by Terry Pinkard. Cambridge: Cambridge University Press, 2018.

Johnston, Adrien. *Time Driven: Metapsychology and the Splitting of the Drive*. Evanston: Northwestern University Press, 2005.

Malabou, Catherine. "Plasticity and Elasticity in Freud's 'Beyond the Pleasure Principle.'" *Parallax* 15, no. 2 (2009): 41–52.

Mills, Jon. *The Unconscious Abyss: Hegel's Anticipation of Psychoanalysis*. Albany: State University of New York Press, 2002.

Žižek, Slavoj. *Tarrying with the Negative: Kant, Hegel, and the Critique of Ideology*. Durham: Duke University Press, 1993.

Works Cited

[illegible]

5

Aristotle's Erotic Sublime?

Emanuela Bianchi

What becomes of eros, erotic love, in the thought of Aristotle?[1] Eros, as is well known, is a key philosophical term for Plato, treated richly and generatively in the *Symposium*, *Phaedrus*, and *Lysis*, and animating the discourse more or less explicitly in many other dialogues. Eros is also one of the oldest and most powerfully determinative deities in Hesiod's archaic, eighth-century *Theogony*. Indeed, Eros appears fourth in the genealogy of the gods after Chaos, Gaia, and Tartarus, in the following famous lines:

> First of all Chaos came into being. But then Gaia broad-chested, always the unshakable seat of all the immortals who hold the peaks of snowy Olympus, and dark Tartaros in the recesses of the wide-wayed earth, and Eros, the most beautiful (*kallistos*) among the immortal gods, loosener of limbs (*lusimelēs*), who subdues (*damnatai*—to tame, or seduce) the mind and thoughtful intention (*epiphrona boulēn*) in the chests of all gods and of all men.[2]

In Aristotle, however, eros meets a strange fate. Appearing only sporadically in the ethical, rhetorical, political, and even the logical works, eros in human relations, we learn, is generally best avoided, since it gives rise to all sorts of excessive distress. In fact, as we'll see, there is a relentless polemic mounted against eros throughout Aristotle's corpus, its place in human relations replaced by that more measured, chaste, potentially reciprocal, and beautiful form of love called *philia* or friendship. But this is not the end of the story. There are also other appearances of eros, especially in the cosmological register, perhaps the most resounding and significant of which is that found in Book Lambda, in a strong sense the pinnacle of the narrative of the *Metaphysics*. Here, we learn of the "prime mover," which has the power to move things without being itself moved, and that it does so precisely by *being loved*, *erōmenon*. This passive, or really impassive, being, defined essentially as thought thinking itself, has no matter, no force of its own, no outwardly directed concern or action, but rather it is as the pure "activity" of thought that it becomes the consummate object of desire. Indeed, it is the erotic desire possessed by the celestial spheres *for this thought thinking itself* that provides the source of cosmic motion.

Anyone with even a passing acquaintance with psychoanalysis will be able to name the operation apparently at work here, in which eros is suppressed at the level of human relations and reappears as a generalized force moving the entire cosmos, that is, sublimation. And indeed, it would be possible to halt the analysis here, for this could hardly be more significant insofar as it lights the way toward an understanding of the motion of the cosmos as a whole as fundamentally erotic. In this way, Aristotle neatly dispenses with eros in human affairs, but also finds in it a solution to a fundamental philosophical problem, that of the nature or being of motion, arguably the primary philosophical question for Heidegger and other thinkers. Motion as such is thus newly disclosed as erotic desire. We shall return to the question of sublimation, but before we do so, the question of analysis itself, and in particular the very idea of the *solution of a problem*, will need to be traversed.

In what follows, I would like to trace these threads of Aristotelian eros by other means, by taking a cue from that most vivid, ancient, and pervasive epithet of *eros*, already encountered in the passage from Hesiod, namely *Eros lusimelēs*, Eros the loosener or melter of limbs. The epithet is also found in the lyric poets, Archilochus (Fr. 196), Alcman (Fr. 3, 1+3, 61), and perhaps most famously in Sappho (Fr. 130), and it is applied by the poets to sleep and to death as well as love. It will also reappear in the classical period in Euripidean tragedy, as well as in a host of later Hellenistic poets. Sappho's fragment reads as follows, in Anne Carson's translation: "Eros the melter of limbs (*lusimelēs*) (now again) stirs me—sweetbitter unmanageable creature who steals in." Carson suggests that this bodily melting brought on by eros is profoundly ambivalent—delicious yet threatening: "Alongside melting we might cite metaphors of piercing, crushing, bridling, roasting, stinging, biting, grating, cropping, poisoning, singeing and grinding to a powder, all of which are used of eros by the poets, giving a cumulative impression of intense concern for the integrity and control of one's own body."[3] Aristotle himself does not use *lusimelēs* as a qualifier for *Eros*,[4] and, as we will see, this omission carries some significance. By attending to this absent term, I want to suggest that it is the threat to bodily integrity raised by eros, and the profound anxieties that attend this danger, that will be decisive if we are to shed light on the question of eros's fate in Aristotle's discourse. To assist in this investigation into the Aristotelian ends of eros, then, I will draw on Julia Kristeva's exploration of abjection, which names precisely the terrain of terror and horror that accompanies threats of bodily dissolution. Through careful attention to the vagaries of *lusis* and the verbal form *luō-luesthai* throughout the Aristotelian corpus, it will become clear that the Aristotelian organism and Aristotle's thinking in general might be understood as haunted by eros, as a force at once destructive, disaggregating, and abject, and yet also bearing some relation, yet to be properly clarified, to philosophical analysis and the solution of *aporiai*, via a traversal of the sublime.

To begin thinking through this fate of eros, it is probably prudent to start by separating out its varied registers within philosophical thinking, and here Plato's *Symposium* proves instructive. Following the succession of speeches in this dialogue, we may thus first discern a Phaedrian, Pausanian, or Aristophanic register, in which eros appears as a dynamic between humans, whether of the same or different genders; that is, as a relational force operating in the strictly human sphere, drawing people together and inspiring them to overcome their limitations as singular beings. We may recall Phaedrus's description of the great deeds of valor that are accomplished by lovers in the name of eros,[5] Pausanius' description of Uranian or heavenly love accompanied by virtue,[6] as well as Aristophanes' description of the intense desire that draws one toward one's previously lost other half, whether of the same sex or the opposite sex.[7] (It perhaps should not go unremarked that each of these accounts also has a tragic dimension: one may die for one's lover, virtuous love is always haunted by the specter of vicious or self-gratifying love, and in order for one to have an "other half," one must first have been violently sundered from the being, male or female, with whom one was once united.)

Next comes the doctor Erixymachus's discourse on eros as a cosmological force. Here we find echoes of the Empedoclean cosmic forces, love (*philia*) and strife (*neikos*), that attract and repel the elements and lead to their combination and separation in the formation and destruction of beings. For Erixymachus, however, it is the erotic force alone that encompasses these two opposed forces; eros itself is doubled and internally ambivalent, with a side that attracts, combines, and harmonizes, leading to pleasure, new life, and flourishing in nature, as well as a hubristic side that causes cacophony, plagues, and blights. We have already encountered this duplicity within eros, but for now let us follow the *Symposium*'s lead onward. Agathon's speech reveals eros as a source of divine inspiration, whether of great age and grandeur, or of youth, delicacy, and charm, enchanting and seductive. The Socratic or Diotimean register of eros,[8] in which eros is portrayed as a way of proceeding philosophically toward the being of the forms, as the child of *penia* (poverty) and *poros* (resource, the way through), as an essentially ambivalent mediation between the sensible and the transcendental, reveals perhaps the largest stake of the present inquiry. Kristeva in *Tales of Love* analyzes the Diotima episode as itself an example of movement toward the sublime.[9] But before we equate too quickly this movement of transcendence as sublimity in Plato with the sublimation of eros already noted in Aristotle's text, we should notice two things. First, no one would accuse Aristotle of proceeding erotically in his writing, nor poetically for that matter, nor of fostering eros as a philosophical method. Second, and decisively, there is no explicitly transcendental movement that seeks to arrive at the intelligible by departing from the sensible to be found in Aristotle's thought. Two questions emanating from the *Symposium* therefore emerge. The first is the question of the nature of eros itself as it is transmuted in the thought of Aristotle—is it a singular force, one whose movement is principally combinatory and synthetic? Or is it rather, as Plato sometimes seems to suggest, twofold or internally doubled—both attractive and repulsive, creative and destructive—whether in origin, aim, or being? And second, if Kristeva is right to say that eros is intimately bound up with sublimity or sublimation for Plato, how might we see this playing out, if at all, in the thought of Aristotle?

In the doxography at the start of the *Metaphysics*, where Aristotle reviews previous thinkers on the question of *archai*, first principles or first beginnings, he first considers the early philosophers of nature who propose various elements—water, air, fire, etc.—as *archai*, as well as thinkers like Anaxagoras who propose an infinite number of first principles. Following this, he considers whether the source of motion ought to be considered separately from the matter worked on, or whether a kinetic principle should be understood as simply inhering in a substance, like fire. His conclusion here that motion and matter are indeed separable has quite extraordinary significance, since prior to this, whether in the Presocratics or in Plato's *Timaeus*, the elemental or material realm had not been divested of its internal movement. To this, I would add that it also inaugurates a certain metaphysics of sexual difference, insofar as motion is aligned with form and is active and acting upon (as is the male principle in sexual reproduction), and matter is that which is acted upon (as is the female principle in sexual reproduction).[10] Aristotle, however, is keen to move in this passage to what interests him most of all, namely what causes things to come-to-be qua well-ordered beings rather than as simply haphazard composites. It is here, as we approach for the first time the key question of *individuation*—and this I think is quite telling—that he turns to the figure of Eros. Here is the relevant passage:

> It might be inferred that the first person to consider this question was Hesiod, or indeed anyone else who assumed Love (*erōs*) or Desire (*epithumia*) as a first principle in things; for example, Parmenides. For he says, where he is describing the creation of the universe, "Eros she created first of all the gods . . ." [Parmenides Fr. 13 (Diels)] And Hesiod says, "First of all things was Chaos made, and then/ Broad-bosomed Earth. . . . And Eros the foremost of immortal beings" thus implying that there must be in the world some cause to move things (*kinesei*) and combine them (*sunaxei*).[11]

It is as a very ancient and originary representative of motive force that we find eros, then, at the start of the *Metaphysics*, foreshadowing the central role that we have already noted it will ultimately play in cosmic motion in Book Lambda. But it is not just motion or *kinēsis tout court* that is being proposed here, but also a force of combination or gathering together, *sunaxei*. Looking more closely at Aristotle's imperfect citation of Hesiod, we find that although Gaia's epithet, *eurusternos*, broad-chested, is retained, the famous epithet for Eros, *lusimelēs*, is omitted. We might speculate that this omission serves to intensify Aristotle's case that it is a power of gathering and fusion rather than disaggregation that is decisive here. Also elided in the narrative is the deity Tartarus, who appears in Hesiod after Gaia and before Eros, personification of the deep abyss, site of punishment and torment. Kristeva, writing of Diotima's erotic discourse in the *Symposium*, may provide a clue to this omission when she says that man, in warding off death through symbolic fecundity, which surpasses corporeal, reproductive fecundity, "goes round the feminine, which is his abyss and his night."[12]

Aristotle thus presents Eros here as a purely cohesive and combinatory motile force, a deity who follows on in the *Theogony* from an originary opening, Chaos, which produces a benign broad-breasted Gaia. He then neatly circumvents the abyssal horrors of Tartarus to deliver us an Eros cleansed of its unsettling elements, no longer even the *most beautiful, kallistos* as Hesiod has it, but now the *foremost* (*metaprepei*): the most distinguished or even heroic (I follow Claudia Baracchi's "In Light of Eros" in this reading). He then immediately turns to address the phenomena of disorder and ugliness that are also endemic in the cosmos, citing Empedocles on love and strife (love in this case is *philia* rather than eros), glossing love as the cause of good and strife as the cause of evil. We cannot fail, in the present context, to hear the force of the doubled Freudian drives of *Beyond the Pleasure Principle*: libido and death drive, and indeed in "Analysis Terminable and Interminable" Freud remarks at some length on the Empedoclean provenance of these dual psychic drives.[13] Is it notable that Empedocles, too, suppresses the term "eros," like Aristotle substituting the term *philia*, since he too seems to divest eros of its disturbing ambivalence. Having clearly separated love from strife, Aristotle will, in turn, relate these two opposed forces to two of his own four causes, namely the source of motion (or what Aristotelians call the "efficient cause") on the one hand, and the material cause on the other. *Eros* thus remains here explicitly connected to the source of motion as the positive, good, combinatory force, while the material cause is in this way explicitly connected with strife and evil, dispersion and destruction.

Now, without pretending to finally resolve the sticky problem of whether as a matter of psychoanalytic *fact* there are two opposed drives, or just one drive, a libido that encompasses an aspect that gathers and unifies alongside an aspect that disarticulates and destroys,[14] I want to ask whether, with Kristeva's assistance, we might detect traces of Eros the limb-melter in Aristotle. For Kristeva, unlike Aristotle with his polemic against eros in human relations, recognizes an unsurpassed value in love; she even makes life itself coterminous with love: "If it lives," she writes, "your psyche is in love. If it is not in love, it is dead. 'Death lives a human life,' Hegel said. That is true whenever we are not in love or are not in analysis."[15] But, as we have seen, *Eros lusimelēs* disaggregates the organism and subdues or seduces thought—where in Aristotle is there a place for such a force?

Now Aristotle's teleological thinking is fundamentally grounded in the figure of the organism. His primary phenomenological insight, as I understand it, is that an organism develops from a simple seed into a complex yet unified whole, which when it flourishes is complete in *entelecheia* and active in *energeia*, and comprises a functional system of parts and wholes. Even beyond his extensive biological writings, throughout the corpus he relies on endless analogies with the healthy and flourishing organism, whether he is speaking of proportionate speeches in the *Rhetoric*, political harmony in the *Politics*, moral balance in the *Ethics*, or successful literature in the *Poetics*. The healthy organism, furthermore, is often referenced by Aristotle as a paradigm of anything that lives well, that is, that lives in accordance with the good to which all things in the cosmos tend if unhindered.[16] In this light of the centrality of the organism for his thinking, it is not hard to see why Aristotle might polemicize against *Eros lusimelēs*.

Just to mention a few examples of Aristotle's anti-erotic polemic, we learn in the *Eudemian Ethics* that both love and spiritedness or anger are instances of a *pathos alogiston*, something we undergo beyond *logos* or without reason, since they render one beside oneself (*ekstatikon*).[17] Love, furthermore, is an excessive state of emotion (*huperbolē*) of a kind that is felt by nature toward one rather than for many and therefore exclusive and strife-causing.[18] And love is listed alongside poverty, pain, and sorrow as possible grounds for the cowardly act of suicide.[19] In the *Politics*, a ruling class man's love affair with a friend's *erōmenon* or beloved boy is proffered as a cause of civil unrest. In the *Rhetoric*, eros raises the specter of incest, invoked in a refutation of the assertion that love is always good,[20] and the specter of homosexual incest is also raised in Book II of the *Politics*, in a critique of the obliteration of the family in

Plato's Republic in which we are told that father-son or brother-brother love is an ever-present threat or possibility.[21] A little later in the *Politics*, we find the Aristophanic idea of love in the *Symposium* under fire, in which two lovers, originally one being rent asunder, seek to meet and merge. For Aristotle, this would lead to the obliteration of the personalities: total destruction.[22] Erotic relationships' potential for asymmetry is also problematic in itself for Aristotle, since one party may be looking for what he calls a "pleasurable shared life" while the other may be just instrumentalizing his lover for personal pleasure or gain. In an extraordinary syllogism in the *Prior Analytics*, we are told that in the absence of the ideal situation where you have a lover who desires you and who will actually go to bed with you, it's preferable to have a lover who desires you and won't sleep with you over a lover who will sleep with you without really desiring you. Whatever we think of this judgment, Aristotle's conclusion is that *philia*, or chaste love, is an end in itself, while sex isn't an end in itself at all. Eros is therefore really a subset of *philia* and should just be subsumed into the greater end of friendship, and there, really it meets its end. As he puts it rather pithily in the *Nicomachean Ethics*, "a friendship between two witty people is preferable to the erotic dynamic, which often fades as beauty fades."[23]

And yet beyond the activities of good education and cultivation of character outlined in the *Ethics*, and all his concerns with organismic individuation, Aristotle is not at all concerned with the terrain of individuation covered by psychoanalysis, namely the development of the human subject and the many ordeals the psyche must suffer in order to reach a condition of functionality as it effects its uneven separation from the mother, begins to organize its libidinal life, achieves a sense of its own precarious individuality, or enters into and becomes a subject of language. The Aristotelian individual neither requires nor practices anything remotely akin to psychoanalysis. While appetites, spiritedness, and tendencies to pleasure and excess threaten to lead him astray and *eudaimonia* may not be easily achieved, the elite male (it is always a he) is not structurally prevented from cultivating his *sōphrosunē*, that is his temperance or self-control, and thereby successfully becoming *phronimos*, possessing practical wisdom or prudence. Overall, for the members of the Athenian male elite described by both Plato and Aristotle, such cultivation of the soul is a matter of education in excellence conditioned by aristocratic values of nobility and beauty, and there is little whiff for the Greeks of neuroses, psychoses, or other psychogenic problems. Aristotle, himself the son of a doctor, is surprisingly silent on the subject of mental disorders, and though there are occasional mentions of mania and so on of the sort that may be induced by eros and uncontrolled temper, there is certainly no valorization of the madness brought on by love for its capacity to open us to transcendence and the forms, as we find in Plato's *Phaedrus*.[24] Yet Aristotle also undoubtedly shares with psychoanalysis a primary interest in organismic functionality and in living well, and sees it most ideally manifested in the activities of philosophical contemplation, as well as in the bonds of reciprocal *philia* which subtend his political ideals of rational deliberation and ruling in turns.

The psychoanalytic concept that would seem to provide the clearest analogue with the Aristotelian individual as functional unity is arguably that of the Lacanian imaginary, with its provenance in the mirror stage. In the imaginary's developmental narrative, the visual image of his own body that the infant sees in the mirror stands for the possibility of his coherent being and reflects back a totality and a unity that is quite at odds with his own bodily experience as uncoordinated and uncontrolled; the image thus incites in the infant what Lacan famously calls a "fluttering of jubilant activity."[25] The totality, unity, consolidation, and possibility of control offered by the visual image are primarily phantasmatic, a fiction, with no analogue in the infant's bodily experience, and yet it is a fiction that operates psychically with important developmental consequences for the ego insofar as it provides a proleptic vision of the self as a functional unity. The "imaginary"—the image—has very real consequences. Can, we might then ask, something of the primacy of this visual outline also be found at work in Aristotelian organismic development?

To recap briefly and in broad brushstrokes the development of the Aristotelian organism, or "coming to be by nature" in the animal kingdom, let us recall that three of the four causes—the telos or final cause, the source of motion or "efficient cause," and the form—are identified with one another and transmitted by the father, and opposed to matter, the fourth cause, supplied by the mother. The form—sometimes called *morphē*, shape, that is, an outline that shines forth, and sometimes called *eidos*, form, the root of which is the verb "to see"—is clearly the end process of development for animals as much as humans—the healthy adult horse and adult man represent both the *telos* and *eidos* of the organism in their respective species. Juxtaposing this with Lacan's account of the mirror stage, we find the following from the Second Seminar: "The uncoordinated, incoherent diversity of the primitive fragmentation gains its unity in so far as it is fascinated."[26] And further, "The body in pieces (*corps morcelé*) finds its unity in the image of the other, which is its own anticipated image."[27] Both Aristotle and Lacan share a sense that something visual and topological—*morphē* and *eidos*—are causal in individuation, and both share a sense of a drive within the organism (the same erotic drive found in Book 1 of the *Metaphysics*?) that gathers together, unifies, and individuates. But the experience of primary fragmentation or the specter of a body in pieces, and its corollary of *méconnaisance*, of a fundamentally misrecognized, phantasmatic, futurally displaced subjectivity, is notably missing from Aristotle. Notable here too is the way Lacan names the image of the other and the proto-subject's own specular image—both deceiving—at the heart of this process, while for Aristotle the *eidos* and *telos* are identified together *as the truth* of one's own development: what is good, healthy, well-formed, beautiful. Perhaps we might name what shines forth here as the Apollonian, Nietzsche's heroic *principio individuationis* from *The Birth of Tragedy*, with the shadow of Dionysus and his dispersive, dismembering, dissembling, immersive force quite eclipsed.

In *Tales of Love*, Kristeva tells a dialectical narrative of love and its role in the development of Western subjectivity, at once psychoanalytic, phenomenological, historical, and dialectical. She relates that the subject *fascinated* by its image in the mirror is exemplified by the figure of Narcissus, who is given his first literary treatment in Ovid's *Metamorphoses*, composed in the first decade of the Common Era. The advent of Narcissus, for Kristeva, gives rise for the first time to a new kind of psychic interiority, an "internalization of reflection in order to transform Platonic ideality into speculative internality"[28] that could not have been dreamt of by Aristotle.[29] That for

Narcissus the fascinating object of love turns out to be merely himself is, according to Kristeva, a cause of great anguish, but one that inaugurates a psychic *space* as its own object: "the object of Narcissus *is* psychic space, it is representation itself, fantasy."[30] The risk borne by this new fledgling interiority is twofold: not only does the narcissistic structure form a block to loving another, but it also indicates the presence of "infantilism and perversion on the brim of western internality."[31] Nonetheless, as she also claims, "Platonic dialogism is transformed . . . into a monologue that must indeed be called speculative"—narcissism thus initiates, for Kristeva, the entire subsequent Western tradition of speculative thinking. Here, I would like to follow the sensitive reading of Pleshette DeArmitt in *The Right to Narcissism*, who emphasizes the primacy of this narcissism for Kristeva not only as a closed ipseity but as the condition of possibility of all subsequent genuine love relationships.[32] DeArmitt saw in Kristeva's narcissism the possibility that *all* love of or identification with another is *lined* by narcissism, rather than positing narcissism as an affliction or threat to be necessarily evaded. But if the mirror image opens up for Kristeva the possibility of a genuine love for the other, we also need to attend to what precedes it at the level of corporeity in the infant's experience and being. So to get to the meat, or should I say viscera, of the matter, which we have kept at bay for too long, we will need to consider the infant's uncontrolled and unboundaried body in its precarious separation from the maternal body. This is the terrain of the abyssal, engulfing, visceral, primal relationship with the mother and its role in individuation so vividly described in Kristeva's account of abjection. For Kristeva, the disgust response characteristic of abjection is provoked by a threat to bodily integrity, her famous example being the "skin on the milk" whose filmy insubstantiality revolts and nauseates me, makes me "spit myself out" as I attempt, perhaps vainly, to reestablish wholeness and separateness.[33] This sensation of abjection she relates to the ever-present threat of engulfment by the maternal body (this dripping, feminine trope is familiar to us from texts such as Aeschylus's *Eumenides* up to horror movies such as *Alien*), evoking an abyssal, horrifying, primal dimension of the relationship with the mother. It is the maternal body, I propose, that gives a certain name, place, substantiality, and motivation to that which is suppressed in Aristotle's elision of *eros lusimelēs*.

For Kristeva, following Freud, narcissism or the captivation with one's own image in the mirror emerges as "a third realm supplementing the autoeroticism of the mother-child dyad."[34] Individuation is not therefore just a drama taking place between subject and a captivating specular image, but rather arrives as a necessary interruption of a relationship that too has its pleasures: those of protection, nourishment, warmth, care, touch, sensuousness, rhythm, sonorousness. The qualities here of ordered motility and vocality are also present in her discourse on the *chōra*, the ground of the semiotic that will, for Kristeva, find expression in poetic language, the archaic maternal place or container of the subject. And yet even in the discourse on language, we are told that "the ordering principle of the semiotic *chora* is on the path of destruction, aggressivity, and death."[35] She goes on to say that "For although drives have been described as disunited or contradictory structures, simultaneously 'positive' and 'negative,' this doubling is said to generate a dominant 'destructive wave' that is drive's most characteristic trait: Freud notes that the most instinctual (*plus pulsionnel*) drive is the death drive."[36] The primary bond with the mother is thus both pleasurable and full of aggressivity. In the face of this comes the utmost necessity of violent separation, the need to "reject, ab-ject" the maternal. She writes: "The abject confronts us, . . . and this time within our personal archeology, with our earliest attempts to release the hold of maternal entity even before ex-isting outside of her, thanks to the autonomy of language. It is a violent, clumsy breaking away, with the constant risk of falling back under the sway of a power as securing as it is stifling."[37] "Abjection," she continues, "*is a precondition of narcissism.* It is coexistent with it and causes it to be permanently brittle."[38] The subject forged out of love is necessarily precarious.

Kristeva's dialectical *Tales of Love* proceeds to the later emergence of Christianity, which supplies a loving God as one who loves *first* as an originary ground granting security and guarantee against the threat of abjection posed by the maternal body.[39] But if we stay in antiquity with Aristotle, his divinity, the prime mover, is itself arguably a self-contemplating figure of divine narcissism, entirely impassive (*apathēs*) and uninterested in anything outside itself—a beloved God, but certainly not a God of love capable of granting solace or security. The highest activity of the human organism, therefore, is philosophical contemplation, where, for all too brief moments, it becomes most *like* the divine and enacts the thinking of thought itself. There is a kind of solipsistic communion with divinity here, but, at the same time, in this practice motion comes to a complete halt: the body's materiality is transcended, and eros is, strictly speaking, no longer in operation.

If this wrapping oneself up in one's own thought, or thought wrapped up in itself, represents being's *energeia* and *entelecheia*, its being in act and being at completion, then the process by which the individual achieves such autonomy, that is, his journey of separation from the mother, is of no interest to Aristotle since in the biological works he has already dispensed with her quite neatly. Well over a century before, Apollo in Aeschylus's *Eumenides* defends Orestes' matricide on the grounds that the father is the real parent, while the mother merely safeguards the offspring, as a stranger would a stranger, *xenō xenē*, and is not a real parent at all. Providing an innovative scientific and metaphysical scaffolding for this polemic, Aristotle separates the stuff from which things are made, the matter, from formal, motile, and teleological causes, which means that in sexual reproduction the mother provides the matter as menstrual blood. The mother's contribution is thereby divested of its motility and is now rendered passive, to be acted upon by the sperm, carrier of form and the source of formative motion (recall that this formative motion was attributed to Eros in *Met.*1, discussed earlier).[40] Aristotle's innovation thus radically deactivates the physical, psychical, and ontological power of the maternal body, and its role in the formation and individuation of the human organism, entrapping it within the degraded, presumptively passive placeholder that is "Aristotelian matter." This is, I submit, precisely an act of ab-jection that is far from unique but certainly notable in the history of Western metaphysics for its violence and summary effectiveness.[41]

With the help of Kristeva, then, we can see how the thoroughly masculine world of Aristotelian *paideia* and ethical cultivation—the development of the noble Athenian virtues such as courage, temperance, and friendship; the governing of the well-ordered polis through rational deliberation and ruling in turns; and the motionless activity of philosophical contemplation in which the rational soul emulates the divine—can arise in a way that is relatively free of material and maternal trouble, once the disordering threat of bodily disaggregation, that is, of *eros lusimelēs*, is kept at bay. In the image of the limbs deliquescing and separating from the body; in the physical symptoms of love that render one beside oneself, out of one's mind, and even destroyed in the *ekstatikon*, or in excess of oneself in *huperbolē*; in the possibility of thoroughly merging with another, losing one's bodily boundaries, and the accompanying loss of self in *jouissance*—in this venturing to the very limits of the psyche, we conjure or travel close to the psychical horror of maternal engulfment. To put it bluntly, the maternal-feminine is what eros threatens at any time to reactivate.[42]

Now, while Kristeva's thought in these respects has great explanatory power, it may also be seen to reinscribe misogynous attributions as well as normative heterosexuality at the heart of human development, while treating the body overliterally, threatening essentialism and so on.[43] But it is specifically through the phenomenon of transference love that Kristeva will argue that psychoanalysis is capable of effecting a reorganization in and of the symbolic that provides greater possibilities for movement and connection for the subject, which has the potential to *loosen* the grip of neuroses, anxieties, phobias, threats of psychosis, and other forms of psychical and even political entrapment. In other words, it is precisely through an eros that is capable of presenting the greatest possible psychic threat, that of abject disaggregation, that the possibility of a cure, a solution, an unbinding of knots, is also found.

In closing, I would like, pharmacologically, to draw our attention to the fact that the *lusis* of *lusimelēs* is also the *lusis* of *ana-lusis*, or what we know as analysis. *Lusis*, melting, dissolving, undoing, is also an unknotting, a solving, a solution. Analysis as *ana-lusis* is an intensification and redoubling of that operation, *ana-* being the prefix that signifies up, against, back, or a doing again, analogous to the Latin *re-*. As Derrida points out, this paleonym thus embraces a return to origin, as well as a proleptic, teleological expectation of "solution": "Thus the archeological motif of analysis is doubled by an eschatological movement, as if analysis were the bearer of extreme death and the last word, just as the archeological motif, in view of the originary, is turned toward birth."[44] And, perhaps ironically given what has already been said of Aristotle's own resistance to unbinding, this idea of solution as unbinding is as present for Aristotle as it is for Kristeva. Aristotle puts *lusis* to work throughout his corpus, in the biological works and natural philosophy, in the logical works, in the *Poetics*, and in the *Metaphysics*. In the physical, biological, and medical writings, the middle-passive verb *luesthai* operates to variously signify the dissolving or melting of metals,[45] or the loosening of organs such as the tongue or the neck of the uterus,[46] while in the medical treatises of the Pseudo-Aristotelian *Problemata* it refers to the loosening of the bladder or the bowels,[47] the relieving of fatigue,[48] or the relief of a hangover (by cabbage!).[49] The medical context is a revealing one, since here in particular the valence of *lusis* can be positive or negative depending on the condition—it may signify a freeing or release from some ailment, or on the other hand an unhealthy flux, moving *against* the healthy operations of nature.[50] This destructive sense is found in *De Anima* 2, 12, where it describes an obliteration of the senses by an excess of stimulation precisely along the lines of the account of cacophonous Eros in Eryximachus's speech in the *Symposium*. Aristotle says "concord and tone are destroyed by too violently twanging the strings of a lyre."[51] In the realm of politics, too, we find that *luesthai*, unbinding, refers to the breakdown or dissolution of law,[52] as well as of constitutions and aristocracies.[53] This loosening may be due to internal deviations from justice, external powers, or to incremental relaxations, and here he offers his perhaps timely dictum that "even a small change may cause a revolution."[54] The middle-passive *luesthai* thus operates undecidably in Aristotle's texts, pharmacologically in Derrida's sense, insofar as it may, without final determination, function as both cure and poison. The active sense of the verbal noun, *lusis*, however, seems to shed this ambiguity for Aristotle, conveying instead an entirely positive valence. Moreover, it can hardly bear greater philosophical significance—it denotes not just the denouement of plots, but also the refutation of arguments and the solution of aporias.

Every tragedy, we learn in the *Poetics*, has a binding or complication, *dēsis*, and a *lusis*: an unbinding or denouement (the French word literally means an unknotting). *Lusis* in this context is clearly defined as: "from the beginning of the change to the end,"[55] the change being that from bad to good fortune or from good fortune to bad, that is, the reversal, or *peripeteia*. The *archē* of the *lusis* is coterminous here with the point at which fortunes change. It marks a fulcrum, a point of turning, of instability or perhaps undecidability, but one which will result in a decisive resolution, giving rise, via the affects of pity and fear, to *catharsis* or purgation. The entanglements of a plot, we might say, are disequilibrating, obstructing, while the turn to resolution or denouement returns us to a state of equilibrium, cleansed and purified. So much for the *Poetics*, where both the bodily and symbolic registers of catharsis may easily be discerned. The conception of *lusis* as the solution of an *aporia*, or the refutation of an argument, shares some common ground with the notion of plot, and it is a usage that is endemic throughout the corpus, found in the logical works such as *Sophistical Refutations*, *Topics*, and the *Prior* and *Posterior Analytics*; in the works of natural philosophy such as *De Caelo* and *Physics*; and in the *Metaphysics*. In a 2010 essay, Michel Bastit argues that a prevalent understanding of Aristotle as primarily an aporetic thinker must be supplemented by an understanding of the centrality of *lusis* to his philosophical process. He emphasizes that the "telos of the *aporia* is not *aporia* itself, but it is *euporia* and *lusis*."[56] In Aristotelian fashion, he argues that "*aporia* is methodologically primary, even essential, but the goal of discovery, the solution of the *aporia*, the *lusis*, posterior in the inquiry, is the first in philosophical importance and nature," calling it "an act by which the mind is put into contact with the very thing from which a truth can be predicated."[57] In *Metaphysics* Beta, Aristotle states:

> the later *euporia* is a *lusis* from an earlier state of perplexity, and release (*luein*) is impossible where we do not know the knot (*desmos*). The *aporia* of the mind shows that there is a "knot" in the subject; for in its *aporia* it is in much the same condition as men who are fettered: in both cases it is impossible to make any progress.[58]

The image of Plato's cave here is quite impossible to resist, and it is also in this consideration of the intimate relationship between an *aporia* that must be faced and its *lusis* that we may at last turn to a consideration of eros.

For Aristotle, dialectic alone cannot give rise to *lusis*, since for him it involves simply an exchange of opinions. *Lusis* must come from elsewhere, namely from the very thing under discussion, "below and beyond opinions," as Michel Bastit puts it,[59] or, we might say, by a direct apprehension of the thing, beyond all existing discourse, by one who comes to it having faced the difficulties and is thus properly prepared. Is it in such an encounter with a certain alterity that *eros lusimelēs* might be discerned? A quite extraordinary passage from the *Parts of Animals* may be of assistance. Aristotle writes,

> For though our grasp of celestial things is but slight, nevertheless the pleasure it brings is, by reason of their excellence and worth, greater than that of knowing all things that are here below; just as the pleasure of a fleeting and partial glimpse of the *erōmenon* (the beloved) is greater than that of an accurate view of other things, no matter how numerous or great they are.[60]

Aristotle seems to allow here that the apprehension of celestial things, what we post-Kantians might call sublime things, gives pleasure, and perhaps also the erotic *jouissance* of *lusimelēs*, just as a glimpse of one's beloved might do here on earth. And here, of course, we would need to return to the question of the prime mover as *erōmenon*, the beloved object of erotic desire sublimated into the source of cosmic motion, as a kind of *lusis* in which the source or origin of motion, the *archē kinēseōs*, is transmuted into telos. A momentary and imperceptible shiver in which activity and passivity change places, and which transforms the course of philosophical history. Consider also that other radical Aristotelian innovation, that of the idea of matter as that which underlies all passage from being to not being, which solves the great *aporia* of coming to be, of something coming into being that was not there before. The risk, perhaps, of such a moment of *lusis* or resolution in thought is that beyond what is sublime or transcendent lurks a threat of ab-jection, in this case that of matter and the maternal (recall Derrida's remarks on *analusis* as referring back toward birth, as well as forward toward death), resulting in a foreclosure or closure of the question indexing a flight from difficulty, rather than an incorporation or incarnation of difficulty within speech.

Analysis as *ana-lusis*, as *lusis* always renewed, denouement, catharsis, arrival, solution, thus travels an erotic trajectory that is once abyssal, abject, and sublime. Can we countenance such an abject, abyssal, sublime, erotic alterity within the sober, doggedly antipoetic Aristotelian discourse? Might we yet discern *Eros lusimelēs* lurking in the ineffable moment that intercedes between a problem and its solution, or in the cathartic moment of terror in recognition, encompassing both pleasure and death, where a tragic plot begins to unravel, and where thought is subdued? Such analysis may be perhaps interminable, but never free of the pleasure or *jouissance* that accompanies termination—a dimension, I hope to have shown, that is irreducibly present in love, psychoanalysis, and philosophy alike.

Notes

1 This chapter is a shorter, modified version of an essay originally published as "Aristotle and the Ends of Eros, or Aristotle's Erotic Sublime?" *Research in Phenomenology* 54, no. 3 (2024): 291–321. A Spanish language version appeared as "*Aristóteles y los fines de Eros ¿O el sublime erótico de Aristóteles?,*" in *La Naturaleza in Disputa: Physis y Eros en el pensamiento antigua*, trans. Valeria Campos, Mariana Wadsworth, and Franchesca Rotger (Santiago: Editorial Hueders, 2022). My interest in this question was piqued by Claudia Baracchi's essay, "In Light of Eros," in *Antiquities Beyond Humanism*, ed. Emanuela Bianchi, Sara Brill, and Brooke Holmes (Oxford: Oxford University Press, 2019), where she develops a powerful thesis about ancient eros as beauty, light, luminosity, from which I depart in my emphasis on bodily unbinding. In the essay, I use "eros" uncapitalized, as a cognate of the Greek word ἔρως, love or desire. Especially in a philosophical context, it functions less as the personified deity, Eros, than as a force or drive that plays across multiple registers: divine, human, natural, and cosmic. The ideas herein have been presented at numerous venues and have benefited from the input of many interlocutors, including Claudia Baracchi, Valeria Campos Salvaterra, Chris Cuomo, Sara Brill, Sean Kirkland, Elissa Marder, Noelle McAfee, Paul Allen Miller, Mario Teló, Iván Trujillo, as well as two anonymous peer reviewers—my heartfelt thanks to all. Special thanks to Sara Brill for the invitation to the Collegium Phaenomenologicum, Città di Castello, Italy, as far back as 2018, which set this thinking in motion; to Noelle McAfee for the invitation at the Kristeva Circle's annual meeting at Emory University, Atlanta, GA, 2019, which spurred the turn to Kristeva; and to Jeffrey Di Leo and Paul Allen Miller for the invitation to the Society for Critical Exchange's 2023 Winter Theory Institute at the University of South Carolina, Columbia, SC, on The Death Drive, which served to cast this thinking in a new psychoanalytic light.

2 See Hesiod's *Theogony*, lines 116–22.

3 Anne Carson, *Eros the Bittersweet* (Champaign and London: Dalkey Archive Press, 1998), 40–1.

4 Unless we count a fragment from Plutarch's *Amatorius* in which Aristotle is named as a source for a story about the hero Cleomachus and his bravery on the battlefield inspired by the presence of his *erōmenon*. See Plutarch's *Amatorius*, 761b2. We should note the Phaedrian character of this story and its distinct variance from Aristotle's view of the effects of *erōs* on courage in the ethical treatises.

5 See Plato's *Symposium*, sections 178a–180b.

6 See Plato's *Symposium*, sections 180c–185c.

7 See Plato's *Symposium*, sections 189c–193d.

8 See Plato's *Symposium*, sections 201d ff.

9 She claims that the otherwise homosexual and polymorphous libido investigated by Plato is granted idealization as a result of the feminine "aura surrounding maternal power or wisdom." Julia Kristeva, *Tales of Love*, trans. Leon S. Roudiez (New York: Columbia University Press, 1987), 75. The question of gender is complicated here, since women's bodies are often associated by Plato with what is uncontrolled and appetitive, although Socrates notoriously appropriates feminine roles and capacities at times (see Page duBois, "The Platonic Appropriation of Reproduction," in *Feminist Interpretations of Plato*, ed. Nancy Tuana [University Park: Pennsylvania State University Press, 1994], 139–56). Along these lines, David Halperin has argued that

Diotima's femininity has little to do with actual women, but is rather "a figure by means of which Plato represents the reciprocal and (pro)creative erotics of (male) philosophical intercourse." David Halperin, "Why is Diotima a Woman? Platonic Erôs and the Figuration of Gender," in *Before Sexuality: The Construction of Erotic Experience in the Ancient Greek World*, ed. David M. Halperin, John J. Winkler, and Froma I. Zeitlin (Princeton: Princeton University Press), 1990, 297.

10 See Aristotle's *Generation of Animals*, sections 729a21–32, and further, Emanuela Bianchi, "Matter," in *The Bloomsbury Handbook of 21st-Century Feminist Theory*, ed. Robin Truth Goodman (London and New York: Bloomsbury, 2019), 383–98.

11 See Aristotle's *Metaphysics*, sections 984b24–30.

12 Kristeva, *Tales of Love*, 76.

13 Sigmund Freud, "Beyond the Pleasure Principle" (1920), trans. J Strachey, in *The Standard Edition of the Complete Psychological Works of Sigmund Freud*, volume 18 (London: Hogarth Press, 1955), 1–64; Sigmund Freud, "Analysis Terminable and Interminable," trans. J. Riviere, in *The Standard Edition of the Complete Psychological Works of Sigmund Freud*, volume 33 (London: Hogarth Press, 1964), 209–54, 244–5.

14 This indeed is the argument of Rosaura Martinez Ruiz's remarkable *Eros, Beyond the Death Drive*, trans. Ramsey McGlazer (New York: Fordham University Press, 2021).

15 Kristeva, *Tales of Love*, 15.

16 See Emanuela Bianchi, "Aristotle's Organism, and Ours," in *Contemporary Encounters with Ancient Metaphysics*, ed. Abraham Jacob Greenstine and Ryan J. Johnson (Edinburgh: Edinburgh University Press, 2017), 138–57.

17 See Aristotle's *Eumedian Ethics*, section 1229a20.

18 See Aristotle's *Eumedian Ethics*, section 1157b10.

19 See Aristotle's *Eumedian Ethics*, sections 1116a13–16.

20 See Aristotle's *Rhetoric*, sections 1402b1–4.

21 See Aristotle's *Politics*, sections 1262a33–35.

22 See Aristotle's *Politics*, sections 1262b11–17.

23 See Aristotle's *Nicomachean Ethics*, section 1157a5.

24 Melancholia is described in the spurious *Problemata*, and there are sporadic references to mania elsewhere: for example, in the *Nicomachean Ethics*: "fits of anger (*thymoi*) and sexual desire (*epithymiai aphrodisiōn*) and other such things change (*methistasin*) the body, even causing mania in some persons" (1147a15–17). See Marke Ahonen, *Mental Disorders in Ancient Philosophy* (Cham: Springer, 2014), esp. chapter 4, 69–102.

25 Jacques Lacan, "The Mirror Stage as Formative of the Function of the I as Revealed in Psychoanalytic Experience," in *Écrits*, trans. Alan Sheridan (New York: W.W. Norton, 1977), 5.

26 Jacques Lacan, *The Seminar of Jacques Lacan: Book II: The Ego in Freud's Theory and in the Technique of Psychoanalysis, 1954–1955*, ed. Jacques-Alain Miller, trans. Sylvana Tomaselli (New York: W.W. Norton, 1991), 50.

27 Lacan, *The Seminar of Jacques Lacan*, 54.

28 Kristeva, *Tales of Love*, 115.

29 Jean-Pierre Vernant's argument in "One . . . Two . . . Three: *Erōs*," trans. Deborah Lyons, in *Before Sexuality: The Construction of Erotic Experience in the Ancient Greek World*, ed. Froma I. Zeitlin, et al. (Princeton: Princeton University Press, 1990), 465–78, originally published in France in 1989, follows similar lines, sans Kristeva's dialectical philosophical history.

30 Kristeva, *Tales of Love*, 116.

31 Kristeva, *Tales of Love*, 115.
32 Pleshette DeArmitt, *The Right to Narcissism: A Case for an Im-possible Self-love* (Edinburgh: Edinburgh University Press, 2014).
33 Julia Kristeva, *Powers of Horror: An Essay on Abjection*, trans. Leon Roudiez (New York: Columbia University Press, New York, 1982), 3.
34 Kristeva, *Tales of Love*, 22.
35 Julia Kristeva, *Revolution in Poetic Language*, trans. Margaret Waller (New York: Columbia University Press, 1984), 37.
36 Kristeva, *Revolution in Poetic Language*, 37.
37 Kristeva, *Powers of Horror*, 13.
38 Kristeva, *Powers of Horror*, 13.
39 Kristeva, *Tales of Love*, 111, 139ff.
40 Numerous authors have sought to downplay the passive/active distinction, and thus the demotion of the female contribution to that of passive matter, in Aristotle's account of reproduction by noting that the female residue possesses potentiality for the parts of the embryo and soul, as well as actual nutritive soul (evidenced by unfertilized bird eggs), and is thus already enformed and ensouled. In this lineage, we might include A. L. Peck, "Preface," in Aristotle, *Generation of Animals*, trans. A. L. Peck (Cambridge, MA: Harvard University Press, 1942), v–xxxvii; Daryl Tress, "The Metaphysical Science of Aristotle's Generation of Animals and Its Feminist Critics," *Review of Metaphysics* 46, no. 2 (1992): 307–41; Aryeh Kosman, "Male and Female in Aristotle's *Generation of Animals*," in *Being, Nature, and Life in Aristotle: Essays in Honor of Allan Gotthelf*, ed. James G. Lennox and Robert Bolton (Cambridge: Cambridge University Press, 2010), 147–67; Robert Mayhew, *The Female in Aristotle's Biology: Reason or Rationalization* (Chicago: University of Chicago Press, 2004); Jessica Gelber, "Females in Aristotle's Embryology," in *Aristotle's "Generation of Animals": A Critical Guide*, ed. A. Falcon and D. Lefebvre (Cambridge: Cambridge University Press, 2018), 171–87; Devin Henry, *Aristotle on Form, Matter, and Moving Causes: The Hylomorphic Theory of Substantial Generation* (Cambridge: Cambridge University Press, 2019); Sophia Connell, *Aristotle on Female Animals* (Cambridge: Cambridge University Press, 2016); and Adriel Trott, *The Matter of Form: A Feminist Metaphysics of Generation* (Edinburgh: Edinburgh University Press, 2019), among others. I cannot do justice to the range of arguments offered here in a footnote, and it is certainly true, as these authors variously note, that for Aristotle there is no actually existing thing that is not comprised of both form and matter, and that the hylomorphic stuff that is menstrual blood is of the right kind and possesses appropriate potentials to act as a substratum for an animal, and is thus uniquely suited to its role in mammalian reproduction. Nonetheless, the observable phenomenon of sexual reproduction in the animal kingdom fundamentally anchors Aristotle's metaphysics of form and matter: matter and form as metaphysical causes are paradigmatically separated by sex in generation, so that the latter may *act upon* the former, as a carpenter *acts upon* wood, imparting both motion and form at once, when they reunite in the womb. Aristotelian metaphysics thus finds its primary empirical illustration in sexual reproduction, while the observable, empirical situation provides the evidence that justifies the metaphysical account: a mutually reinforcing deductive-inductive circuit. Aristotle does in fact use in this context the locution "prime matter" (*prōtē hulē*), referring to the menstrual blood (see Aristotle's *Generation of Animals*, section 729a33), which, while not designating a substance that is "matter as such," conveys just how divested of form he intends us to understand the

female contribution to reproduction to be in conjunction with the apportionment of the formal and moving causes to the male. While "prime matter" can, in other contexts, refer to the most immediate or "proximate" matter something is made out of—the bricks for a house, for example—the reasons given above offer grounds for understanding this key instance in a more fundamental, metaphysical sense. See Emanuela Bianchi, *The Feminine Symptom: Aleatory Matter in the Aristotelian Cosmos* (New York: Fordham University Press, 2014), 36ff.

41 For a development of this reading of matter as abject in terms of racial violence in modernity, see Bianchi, "Matter," 392ff.

42 Poetic language also carries this force for Kristeva.

43 See, for example, Judith Butler, *Bodies That Matter* (London: Routledge, 1993), 15–16.

44 Jacques Derrida, *Resistances of Psychoanalysis*, trans. Peggy Kamuf, Pascale-Anne Brault, and Michael Naas (Stanford: Stanford University Press 1998), 20.

45 See Aristotle's *Meteorologica*, section 382b32.

46 See Aristotle's *History of Animals*, sections 492b32, 635a20.

47 See Aristotle's *Problemata*, sections 869a4, 877a32, 884b38.

48 See Aristotle's *Problemata*, sections 863b22.

49 See Aristotle's *Problemata*, sections 873b16.

50 We may be reminded here of Freud's discourse on bound and unbound energy that inhabits his work from the early *Project for a Scientific Psychology*, through *Interpretation of Dreams* and the late *Beyond the Pleasure Principle*. Freud's hydraulic energetics of tension and release within the organism surely ground the notion of the pleasure principle, and yet his efforts to consider the death drive (which also involves a tendency to "quiescence") alongside pleasure in the latter text also reveal the limitations of this model (see esp. 62–4). The "unbinding" indicated by *eros lusimelēs* seems to come closer to the Lacanian notion of *jouissance* and its more intimate connection with what is unbearable.

51 See Aristotle's *Symposium*, section 424a31.

52 See Aristotle's *Politics*, section 1307b11.

53 See Aristotle's *Politics*, sections 1307a–b.

54 See Aristotle's *Politics*, section 1307b4.

55 See Aristotle's *Poetics*, section 1455b28.

56 Michel Bastit, "Réhabilitation d'une Notion Aristotélicienne Negligée: la 'Lysis,'" *Méthexis* 23 (2010): 105; my translation.

57 Bastit, "Réhabilitation d'une Notion Aristotélicienne Negligée," 105; my translation.

58 See Aristotle's *Metaphysics*, sections 995a28–33.

59 Bastit, "Réhabilitation d'une Notion Aristotélicienne Negligée," 105; my translation.

60 See Aristotle's *Parts of* Animals, sections 644b32–645a1.

Works Cited

Ahonen, Marke. *Mental Disorders in Ancient Philosophy*. Cham: Springer, 2014.

Baracchi, Claudia. "In Light of Eros." In *Antiquities Beyond Humanism*, edited by Emanuela Bianchi, Sara Brill, and Brooke Holmes, 287–304. Oxford: Oxford University Press, 2019.

Bastit, Michel. "Réhabilitation d'une Notion Aristotélicienne Negligée: la 'Lysis.'" *Méthexis* 23 (2010): 103–11.

Bianchi, Emanuela. *The Feminine Symptom: Aleatory Matter in the Aristotelian Cosmos.* New York: Fordham University Press, 2014.
Bianchi, Emanuela. "Aristotle's Organism, and Ours." In *Contemporary Encounters with Ancient Metaphysics*, edited by Abraham Jacob Greenstine and Ryan J. Johnson, 138–57. Edinburgh: Edinburgh University Press, 2017.
Bianchi, Emanuela. "Matter." In *The Bloomsbury Handbook of 21st-Century Feminist Theory*, edited by Robin Truth Goodman, 383–98. London and New York: Bloomsbury, 2019.
Butler, Judith. *Bodies That Matter.* London: Routledge, 1993.
Carson, Anne. *Eros the Bittersweet.* Champaign and London: Dalkey Archive Press, 1998.
Carson, Anne. *If Not, Winter: Fragments of Sappho.* New York: Knopf, 2002.
Connell, Sophia. *Aristotle on Female Animals.* Cambridge: Cambridge University Press, 2016.
DeArmitt, Pleshette. *The Right to Narcissism: A Case for an Im-possible Self-love.* Edinburgh: Edinburgh University Press, 2014.
Derrida, Jacques. *Resistances of Psychoanalysis.* Translated by Peggy Kamuf, Pascale-Anne Brault, and Michael Naas. Stanford: Stanford University Press, 1998.
duBois, Page. "The Platonic Appropriation of Reproduction." In *Feminist Interpretations of Plato*, edited by Nancy Tuana, 139–56. University Park: Pennsylvania State University Press, 1994.
Freud, Sigmund. "Beyond the Pleasure Principle" (1920), translated by J Strachey. In *The Standard Edition of the Complete Psychological Works of Sigmund Freud*, volume 18, 1–64. London: Hogarth Press, 1955.
Freud, Sigmund. "Analysis Terminable and Interminable," translated by J. Riviere. In *The Standard Edition of the Complete Psychological Works of Sigmund Freud*, volume 33, 209–54. London: Hogarth Press, 1964.
Gelber, Jessica. "Females in Aristotle's Embryology." In *Aristotle's "Generation of Animals": A Critical Guide*, edited by Andrea Falcon and David Lefebvre, 171–87. London: Cambridge University Press, 2018.
Halperin, David. "Why is Diotima a Woman? Platonic Erōs and the Figuration of Gender." In *Before Sexuality: The Construction of Erotic Experience in the Ancient Greek World*, edited by David M. Halperin, John J. Winkler, and Froma I. Zeitlin, 257–308. Princeton: Princeton University Press, 1990.
Henry, Devin. *Aristotle on Form, Matter, and Moving Causes: The Hylomorphic Theory of Substantial Generation.* Cambridge: Cambridge University Press, 2019.
Kosman, Aryeh. "Male and Female in Aristotle's Generation of Animals." In *Being, Nature, and Life in Aristotle: Essays in Honor of Allan Gotthelf*, edited by James G. Lennox and Robert Bolton, 147–67. Cambridge: Cambridge University Press, 2010.
Kristeva, Julia. *Powers of Horror: An Essay on Abjection.* Translated by Leon Roudiez. New York: Columbia University Press, 1982.
Kristeva, Julia. *Revolution in Poetic Language.* Translated by Margaret Waller. New York: Columbia University Press, 1984.
Kristeva, Julia. *Tales of Love.* Translated by Leon S. Roudiez. New York: Columbia University Press, 1987.
Lacan, Jacques. "The Mirror Stage as Formative of the Function of the I as Revealed in Psychoanalytic Experience." In *Écrits*, translated by Alan Sheridan, 1–7. New York: W.W. Norton, 1977.
Lacan, Jacques. *The Seminar of Jacques Lacan: Book II: The Ego in Freud's Theory and in the Technique of Psychoanalysis, 1954–1955.* Edited by Jacques-Alain Miller. Translated by Sylvana Tomaselli. New York: W.W. Norton, 1991.

Mayhew, Robert. *The Female in Aristotle's Biology: Reason or Rationalization*. Chicago: University of Chicago Press, 2004.
Peck, A.L. "Preface." In *Generation of Animals*, translated by A. L. Peck, v–xxxvii. Cambridge: Harvard University Press, 1942.
Ruiz, Rosaura Martinez. *Eros, Beyond the Death Drive*. Translated by Ramsey McGlazer. New York: Fordham University Press, 2021.
Tress, Daryl. "The Metaphysical Science of Aristotle's Generation of Animals and Its Feminist Critics." *Review of Metaphysics* 46, no. 2 (1992): 307–41.
Trott, Adriel. *The Matter of Form: A Feminist Metaphysics of Generation*. Edinburgh: Edinburgh University Press, 2019.
Vernant, Jean-Pierre. "One . . . Two . . . Three: *Erōs*," translated by Deborah Lyons. In *Before Sexuality: The Construction of Erotic Experience in the Ancient Greek World*, edited by Froma I. Zeitlin, et al., 465–78. Princeton: Princeton University Press, 1990.

Part II

Poetics of the Death Drive—Literary Connections

6

Moral Masochism, Sexuality, and the Death Drive

Freud and Late James

David Greven

Emblematic of the antisocial thesis at the center of some prominent queer theory positions, Lee Edelman's much-discussed book *No Future: Queer Theory and the Death Drive* (Duke University Press, 2004), as its subtitle suggests, claimed Freud's concept as inherently and utilitarianly queer. The death drive embodies societal homophobia and its constant associations of homosexuality and death, the idea that queerness is anti-family, antilife. But as Edelman deploys the concept, the death drive is also queerness's assaultive counter-mirror against homophobia. If society denounces us as antilife, we should, instead of challenging this idea, resolutely embody it, holding up the parodistic mirror to society and its faith and deep investment in fantasies of reproductive futurity, embodied in the figure of the Child, the chief object of protective regard and zealous fascination.

Much of this argument has become so familiar that few readers of this chapter will need the précis I just provided. That said, I believe that part of the power of Edelman's thesis is that it can be so neatly summarized. I emphasize that this summarizability is only a part of his thesis's continued hold on academic audiences because I do not want to diminish or underestimate its critical sway. That said, his argument is also something of a blunt tool, with the ability to flatten whatever it touches. In an effort to imagine other possibilities for the usefulness of Freud's concept, to say nothing of queer theory itself, I propose that we reconsider the death drive, not solely by any means, as a diagnostic instrument for societal views of sexuality.

For Edelman, the death drive indicates both a homophobically regarded queerness and mobilizes a queer response that takes a defiant, derisive form. For Freud and Henry James, early queer theorists, the death drive illuminates what we can call sexual modernity, a break from the Victorian obsession with decorum, which prohibited direct expression of sexual content, a period of new articulation about sexual identities, and from the Foucauldian standpoint that has shaped our understanding of sexual history, a period that began to insist on sexuality *as* identity. The nineteenth century suppressed sexuality as discourse on the one hand. On the other hand, it *became* discourse, a public topic across a wide range of social discussions. It was through rhetorical means, debates in medical and literary texts, in lyceum halls and in mass-market periodicals, that sexuality was brought to bear upon the modern subject and became the modern subject. As Jay Cocks observes, "The simultaneous negation and incitement of sexuality resulted in part from a paradox at the heart of liberalism which formed around the contradictory need to represent public affairs and at the same time control the nature of knowledge."[1] Michel Foucault's well-known debunking of Freud's "repressive hypothesis" aimed to demonstrate that, far from being silenced, the sexual was actively deployed in and incited Victorian-era discursive practice.[2] Literature animated these deep tensions and contradictions. Henry James's work charts the difficulties of becoming sexually modern, exploring female sexual autonomy and the limits placed on it in novels such as *The Bostonians* (1886) and *The Portrait of a Lady* (1881). In the late James, questions of gender identity cede, in their earnestly focused intensity, to matters of the sexual, the sexual as index to the self, the sexual as a divisive and disturbing but also socially organizing force. In focusing on overlaps between James and Freud, and in naming them early queer theorists, I am pursuing a new approach to several interrelated questions regarding the political uses of queer theory, on the one hand, and the question of nineteenth-century sexual history, on the other hand, which is to say the long nineteenth century as it encompasses the early twentieth century leading into Modernism.[3] Edelman's *No Future* and its recent follow-up *Bad Education: Why Queer Theory Teaches Us Nothing* (Duke University Press, 2023) constitute a pronounced, resolute stance in queer theory. Edelman's use of Freud politicizes his theory of the death drive as the foundation of the antisocial thesis that has been central to queer theory thought since the 1990s, as indicated by Leo Bersani's book *Homos* (Harvard University Press, 1996), which establishes a genealogy of queer negativity—the antisocial position—from the writings of Jean Genet forward, a negativity that counters positive images of the family, marriage, social ties, and sexual intimacy with images of nullity and estrangement. Edelman uses Bersani's work as a springboard for his own theory linking the antisocial position to a defiant queer embrace of the death drive.

One of the most notable aspects of the reception of Edelman's work, which has been a wide-ranging one, to be sure, generating a great deal of often contentious discussion, especially from feminist and trans critics, is that in many ways it has come to be seen as *the* queer theory position. Much the same can be said for similarly intransigent queer theory positions, such as D. A. Miller's Foucauldian critique of works ranging from *Middlemarch* to *Brokeback Mountain* and Michael Warner's hostile critique of Freud's theories of narcissism, metonymic of a Foucauldian queer theory opposition to psychoanalysis, and Warner's celebration of "world-making" homosexual cruising and anonymous sex. My effort here is not primarily to dissent from these views (even though in some instances I do) but to establish that they are, indeed, views—positions taken by notable and distinctive critics, not some kind of communal logic or dogma that defines queer theory, even if frequently taken as such.

To offer a counterexample of the kind of thinking possible when we consider the death drive for queer purposes, the Freudian film scholar Robin Wood, in his *Sexual*

Politics and Narrative Film, covers similar terrain, a political use of the Freudian death drive for antihomophobic purposes among other goals. Revisiting the Freudian cultural commentator Norman O. Brown's *Life Against Death*, Wood glosses Brown's thesis: "the human race . . . has been a battleground for a continuously developing and shifting struggle between the forces for Life (creativity, freedom, spontaneous impulse, joy, love unconstrained by rules or limits) and Death (repression, denial, punishment, prohibition, authoritarianism, mechanization, possessiveness, greed, money values)." For Wood, the most horrifying aspect of Brown's argument is that the Death force robs us of "the incalculable, unpredictable vastness of human potential."[4]

Wood's book was published in 1998. His return to Brown, and by extension to Freud and the question of Life versus Death forces, is eerily prescient of the post-September 11, Trump-era global calamities we face. It is difficult not to feel that we live in the clutches of death, caught within the ever-spinning gears of the death drive. As Wood writes:

> The Death forces are easier to identify than the Life because they have crystallized into organizations and institutions: religion, at the point where it hardens into dogma; nationalism, at the point where it becomes imperialism; government, at the point where it becomes authoritarian or privileges one group above others—in short, everything that sets nation against nation, class against class, person against person, promoting hostility and competition instead of cooperation.[5]

Wood was an ostensibly heterosexual man who came out in the 1970s and became a vocally gay and feminist critic, politicizing his work in new ways. Unlike contemporary queer theorists, Wood sees a struggle between Life and Death forces and views that struggle as dramatized in Freud's writings.

I include Wood in this discussion for two reasons. First, as a critic working in two fields, nineteenth-century Americanist literary studies and Film Studies, I have learned from Wood's work and consider it a vital influence, especially his treatments of gender, sexuality, and representation in his books *Hitchcock's Films Revisited* (New York: Columbia University Press, 2002) and *Hollywood from Vietnam to Reagan* (Columbia University Press, 1986; expanded edition, 2003). Second, Wood, who has written from investments in both Freud and Henry James (he wrote a BFI Film Classics volume on the film adaptation of *The Wings of the Dove*), represents a political and queer (though he would use the term gay and lesbian) and feminist use of Freudian theory that has been overlooked in the wake of the Edelman-Bersani antisocial theory approach. Wood represents Gay Liberation theory's critique of patriarchy and misogyny and support of queer life while also insisting on overlaps between gay and feminist concerns. While I do not share many of his critical stances or concur with all of his assessments, I nevertheless recognize in Wood an attempt to speak for queer concerns without submitting to the Death forces—without resorting to an antisocial position. My analysis of James and Freud stems from a desire for engagement with the intermeshed experience of artistic creativity and social critique, to begin with, and to learn from their insights into the role that sexuality plays in both.

James and Freud

Freud is a theorist of sexuality for whom sexuality eschews the normalizing stability with which it is frequently associated in conventional, mainstream popular psychology; for whom sexuality is enigmatic and vexing, a force that disturbs culture, society, and self.[6] I see many of the same qualities in Henry James's galvanizing work.

Henry James and Freud are rarely discussed as contemporaries, but they were. James died at seventy-two in London in 1916. Freud's work had begun to be translated into English in the first decade of the twentieth century. G. G. Meynell summarizes:

> Freud was born on 6 May 1856. His psychological work, which followed studies in conventional neurology, began to appear from the late 1880s. His first three books, *Studies in Hysteria* (with Josef Breuer), *The Interpretation of Dreams* and *The Psychopathology of Everyday Life*, were published in German in 1895, 1900 and 190I. The *Studies* was the first book to appear in English (1909), some fourteen years after the German original, and was translated by the celebrated American psychiatrist, A A Brill (1874–1948), with Freud's permission.[7]

One earlier critic suggestively argues that James's knowledge of Freud may date to the late nineteenth century, informing James's famous 1898 ghost story *The Turn of the Screw*.[8]

James's famous brother, the psychologist William James, and Freud met one another in a noteworthy encounter in 1909.[9] Whether Freud directly influenced Henry James is a topic for a discrete discussion. Here, my intention is to frame James and Freud as leading theorists of a new sexual modernity, characterized by an unprecedented explicitness about sexual matters. As two prominent theorists of modern sexuality, they each associated this new development with death and nullity. Unlike Edelman, Leo Bersani, and other queer theorists who have championed the antisocial thesis,[10] James and Freud viewed the relationship between sexuality and death as dynamic and unpredictable, an ongoing battle.[11] And this battle can be summarized as a contest between Life and Death forces, rather than the politically prescriptive injunctions of Edelman's argument.

My argument is that "Late James," a period of James's greatest achievement or most alienating aesthetic difficulty, depending on which Jamesian one asks, is also the most Freudian James. The three novels that constitute "Late James" and "The Major Phase" all revolve around the question of illicit sexuality. The first of the three novels was *The Ambassadors* (1903). Here, a middle-aged American named Lambert Strether journeys to Paris at the behest of his fiancée, the wealthy New England widow Mrs. Newsome, who financially supports the New England publication that Strether edits. She enlists Strether to convince her son Chad Newsome, an affluent young man who has been floating around Europe for too long, to return to New England and claim his rightful position as scion. Chad, Strether discovers, has been having an affair with a middle-aged French woman, Madame de Vionnet (though her daughter initially seems to be Chad's *inamorata*). Though ostensibly Mrs. Newsome's "ambassador," Strether ends up captivated by Chad's European and sexual adventurism and famously encourages Chad's friend, "little Bilham," to "Live all you can." In an ironic turn of events, Chad resolves to return to New England to reclaim his social position while Strether struggles with his newfound excitement over European possibilities, finally deciding by the end of the novel that he, too, will return home.

The Wings of the Dove, the second of this series of novels, was published in 1902, although it was written before *The Ambassadors*. Milly Theale is a wealthy young heiress with a fatal illness. Kate Croy, an impecunious young woman commanded by her well-off aunt to marry someone prestigious and rich, loves the far-from-wealthy journalist Merton Densher. Learning of Milly's illness, Kate devises a plan for Merton to woo Milly and, once they are married, inherit her money, thereby allowing Merton and Kate to live most comfortably after Milly dies. In his final novel, *The Golden Bowl* (1904), James transforms a study of adultery with four principal characters into a meditation on consciousness that occurs through seismographic observations of every nuanced thought on the part of his heroine of sorts, Maggie Verver, as she contemplates her Italian husband Amerigo's adulterous affair with an impecunious American woman named Charlotte Stant. I will return to *The Golden Bowl* centrally below.

What unites James and Freud is their understanding of modern sexuality as an arena where Life and Death forces vie for power, dominance, and victory. Emblematic of the strange confluence of death in life, the young, dying heroine of *The Wings of the Dove*, Milly Theale, who is as close to a figure of immaculate goodness as we can find in James's fiction, stares at a Bronzino portrait hung in the English country house she is visiting. She has this reaction to it:

> Perhaps it was her tears that made it just then so strange and fair—as wonderful as he had said: the face of a young woman, all splendidly drawn, down to the hands, and splendidly dressed; a face almost livid in hue, yet handsome in sadness and crowned with a mass of hair, rolled back and high, that must, before fading with time, have had a family resemblance to her own. The lady in question, at all events, with her slightly Michael-angel-esque squareness, her eyes of other days, her full lips, her long neck, her recorded jewels, her brocaded and wasted reds, was a very great personage—only unaccompanied by a joy. And she was dead, dead, dead. Milly recognized her exactly in words that had nothing to do with her. "I shall never be better than this."[12]

That the figure of youthful beauty, Milly, or the portrait's subject, is also a figure of "dead, dead, dead" affect summarizes James's position in this novel. What Kate Croy and her lover Densher want is the opportunity to have their love and eat its financial resplendence too, through the marriage of Densher and Milly, who will in death make him and his lover rich in life. But as Kate and Densher discover, in pursuing this life-affirming resplendence, they meet with death—certainly, the death of their relationship. At Densher's assurance, after Milly has died knowing of the lovers' plot, to Kate that he will marry her, she responds, ending things between them, "We shall never be again as we were!"[13] Kate challenges her now irrevocably altered, now rejected lover at the end of the novel. Their diabolical scheme has soured their erotic and emotional connection at once.

James, Hawthorne, and Sexuality

Henry James's interest in Nathaniel Hawthorne and the older author's influence on the latter's work have been frequently discussed.[14] Hawthorne, as I have argued elsewhere, is the Freudian author par excellence.[15] Hawthorne, along with Edgar Allan Poe, anticipates many important Freudian concepts, especially the uncanny (represented by the titular object of the tale "The Minister's Black Veil") and the importance of dreams (occurring throughout Hawthorne's work, which often destabilizes borders between dream and reality, as in his tale of a seemingly pious young Puritan newlywed who ventures into the forest at night to participate in a Satanic ritual, "Young Goodman Brown"). What particularly interests me here is these authors' shared interest in sex and the death drive. James's late work, especially *The Golden Bowl* and *The Wings of the Dove*, links sexual experience and an inexorable movement toward death that prefigures Freud's theories of the death drive, elaborated in his cultural or, as Freud called them, "metapsychological" texts and Lacan's reworking of Freud. Specifically, the idea of sex as unspeakable in *The Golden Bowl* and as a means to a seemingly certain end (financial stability) in *The Wings of the Dove* denatures sex and sexuality in a manner that evokes the death drive's movement toward the cessation of pleasure and an embrace of inorganic nothingness. Late James reflects his enduring preoccupation with Hawthorne's schemas, particularly in his last published novels *The Blithedale Romance* (1852) and *The Marble Faun* (1860) and their similar linkages between sex and the death drive. I argue that James discovers his own preoccupations mirrored back to him in Hawthorne's image and offers narratives of unpleasurable and deadened sexual relationships as a means of registering the impossibility of union with his literary precursor while thematizing and enacting this very union.

In the main, Hawthorne's novels figure sexuality not as a liberating but instead a constrictive force. The veil that drapes the central figure of the Veiled Lady in *The Blithedale Romance* functions as a death shroud that anticipates the premature death of the heroine, whereas *The Marble Faun* depicts female sexuality as embattled, constricted, and the object of a stalker, known as the Model, first encountered in catacombs. James arguably begins his mature work with his analysis of Isabel Archer's relationship to sexuality and marriage in his 1880 *The Portrait of a Lady*. The late novels, however, subject the very idea of sexuality and marriage to a critical, even withering scrutiny. What James revises, in such a way as to signal profound shifts in both his artistic style and the discursive permutations of sexuality in the era we refer to as "Late James," is Hawthorne's depiction of sexuality as aftermath. In James, the dread of sexuality is not its aftermath but its very possibility, the idea that it may have occurred or that it will occur. In his 1850 masterpiece *The Scarlet Letter*, Hawthorne painstakingly tracks the aftershocks of the adulterous sexual relationship between the married woman Hester Prynne and the young minister Arthur Dimmesdale. Hester's English husband, the much older physician Roger Chillingworth, rejoins Hester in Boston once her shame has been publicly exposed along with her newborn child Pearl, conceived as a result of her affair with the minister. In sharp contrast, James creates, in *The Golden Bowl*, a narrative that revolves around not a sexual act, but the idea that the sexual act may or may not have occurred. As Maggie Verver contemplates whether her husband and her friend Charlotte have had an affair, the novel itself hovers over Maggie's uncertainty and obsessive brooding on the question, the question itself becoming far more vexed and fascinating than the reality of the act that may or may not have been consummated.

Part of the controversy over the Late James is that, for some critics, the circumlocution-heavy, obsessive pondering over small details—over seemingly inconsequential plot points and character interactions—and the merger of a heavily abstracted style with a maddeningly small-bore set of tensions and worries among the characters constitute a world of aesthetic force overpowering minor events. "I wonder if Henry James expected us to sympathize," writes P. D. James,

> with Maggie Verver and her father, the millionaire American who first uses his money to buy a suitable husband for his daughter in the person of the Prince, and then, when her marriage results in his loneliness, buys a suitable wife for himself in the person of her husband's ex-lover. This is to suggest that writers occasionally don't know what or whom they have created, which is surely a nonsense.[16]

Following her line of reasoning, let us acknowledge James's intentionality in creating at the very least highly ambiguous characters in Maggie and Adam Verver.

The Ververs are an immensely rich pair, a father and daughter who collect art pieces around the world. Adam Verver wants to populate the museum of the so-called American City with art objects procured during their travels. The Ververs find two particularly choice "works of art," the Italian Prince Amerigo, fine-looking but impoverished, and the American Charlotte Stant, who, like many of James's characters, is an expatriate living in Europe and, like Amerigo, short of funds. Unbeknownst to the Ververs, Amerigo and Charlotte have had a preexisting relationship, one that they rekindle and consummate while married to Maggie and Adam, respectively. Fanny Assingham is a mutual friend of these four main characters.

Before Amerigo's marriage to Maggie, he and Charlotte visit an antiques shop where she shops for a wedding present for Maggie. They consider the titular golden bowl, but Amerigo decides against it because it contains a hidden flaw. Later, Maggie persuades her father, lonely after his daughter has married, to marry Charlotte. Given Adam's and Maddie's intense closeness, which some have read as incestuous, his decision to marry Charlotte primarily reflects his love for his daughter and desire to accommodate her wishes. The second half of the novel focuses on Maggie's attempts to grapple with her increasingly certain knowledge of her husband and Charlotte's affairs. Maggie obsessively broods over the possibility of Amerigo and Charlotte's affair, in this intensive focus doubled by Fanny, always hashing out the possibilities of these intrigues with her husband Bob, albeit constantly assuring him that nothing untoward will ever occur, largely through Fanny's seemingly benevolent negotiation of these relations and her preventative measures. As Hugh Stevens argues,

> *The Golden Bowl* is James's most passionate novel. In it the question is the sexual question—in its most mundane form, "are the Prince and Charlotte having an affair?" Fanny and Bob ("the Colonel") Assingham, James's two *ficelles*, pose that question repetitively, and augment the erotic tension of the novel by subjecting it to the fervid curiosity of the voyeur—a voyeurism which is theirs and that of the reader.[17]

Stevens's reference to voyeurism allows us to consider another crucial link between James and Hawthorne. A recurring theme throughout Hawthorne's work, the theme of scopophobia, the fear of looking, powerfully informs such narrative sequences as Hester Prynne's public humiliation when, released from prison and holding her adulterously conceived, newborn child Pearl in her arms, she stands on a scaffold before a cruelly contemptuous crowd largely composed of vindictive other women. James locates in *The Golden Bowl*'s last scene a recognition that, in contemporary parlance, we might describe—to the unhappy Maggie, regarding her husband's newfound appreciation of her—as, "He sees you." Having conspired with her father to bring Charlotte, accompanied by her husband, to America and therefore away from Amerigo, Maggie must now take up the demands of her marriage anew, possibly as a fresh start for both herself and Amerigo, who now has reason to appreciate Maggie's self-sacrificing strength and may finally become a properly devoted husband to her. The final moments of *The Golden Bowl* show us Maggie being embraced by Amerigo, who announces, "I see nothing but *you*." He says this while facing her and holding her by the shoulders. But she cannot continue to look him in the face even as their bodies press against one another. "And the truth of it"—"it" being his declaration that he sees only her—"had, with this force . . . so strangely lighted his eyes that, as for pity and dread of them, she buried her own in his breast."[18] My language for describing this scene has been deliberately qualifying and conditional. Some critics have read this final encounter between the married pair as one of healing recognition and a new beginning. For example, James D. Hart summarizes the emotional stakes thusly: "The Prince understands that, by losing his mistress, he has gained a new depth of character and a wife whose value he has only begun to appreciate. The process of 'conversion,' which began with the smashing of the golden bowl, is thus completed."[19] Hart refers to the moment when the vexingly meddlesome Fanny Assingham smashes the golden bowl that Maggie has discovered and purchased as proof of her husband's and Charlotte's affair.

I find it chiefly an expression of an impasse on Maggie's part, one that implies that Amerigo may only see her literally, as the person in front of him, but not yet really recognize her personhood nor her status as an authentic object of his desire. Maggie buries her face in his breast so that she does not have to return his look—either because she recognizes it as a counterfeit one and does not want to return a similarly inauthentic meeting of the eyes, or because the emotional intensity of it is too much to bear.

Stevens focuses more lengthily on the overlaps between Maggie and sexological and Freudian writings on masochism, including the female masochist. "By comparing Freud to Krafft-Ebing, Havelock Ellis, and G. Stanley Hall, we can see to what extent Freud was escaping the nineteenth-century biologism of the sexologists."[20] Other prominent scholars of Henry James, such as David McWhirter, have also discussed overlaps between Freud's account of masochism and James's depiction of Maggie Verver. McWhirter, in particular, has discussed the theme of "moral masochism" in reference to these overlaps. In dialogue with Stevens and McWhirter, I now turn to Freud's theorization of moral masochism as a component of the death drive. I then consider the death drive as "early queer theory"—as an account of the relationships among sexuality, moral prohibition, and a culture of surveillance that James and Freud treated as central to their cultural moment and thematic concerns. Of particular salience, both James and Freud see sexuality as a site of struggle, and the death drive and sexuality as enmeshed within the larger conflict between Death and Life forces.

Moral Masochism and the Death Drive

In his 1924 essay "The Economic Problem of Masochism," Freud stages a battle between Life and Death forces and assigns the libido, the Life force, the role of subjugator of the death instinct, right down to the cellular level: "In (multicellular) organisms,"

> the libido meets the instinct of death, or destruction, which is dominant in them and which seeks to disintegrate the cellular organism and to conduct each separate unicellular organism [composing it] into a state of inorganic stability. . . . The libido has the task of making this destroying instinct innocuous, and it fulfills the task by diverting that instinct to a great extent outwards . . . towards objects in the external world. The instinct is then called the destructive instinct, the instinct for mastery, or the will to power.[21]

The libido, or Life force, primordially wages a war against Death forces. The libido, as Freud argues in "On Narcissism," accounts for primary narcissism, not a perversion, but our universal human desire to live: "the libidinal complement to the egoism of the instinct of self-preservation, a measure of which may justifiably be attributed to every living creature."[22] Masochism, on the other hand, corresponds to the death drive, "primal sadism" being "identical with masochism." After this primal sadism has been projected outwards, "a residuum" of it remains, which is the "erotogenic masochism proper," "a component of the libido" that "still has the self as its object." That outwardly projected primal sadism "can once more be introjected," and if this occurs, "a secondary masochism is produced, which is added to the original masochism."[23] Masochism is the "introjection" of sadistic and destructive forces. In later life, libidinal failure against Death forces, our capitulation to the death drive, constitutes secondary masochism.

Freud establishes three forms of masochism: erotogenic, feminine, and moral. Erotogenic masochism is "pleasure in pain," and it undergirds the other two forms. Feminine masochism is "most accessible to our observation and least problematical." It places the subject "in a characteristically female situation," "being castrated, or copulated with, or giving birth to a baby." Castration, being blinded, and a sense of guilt all resonate in feminine masochism, which is "entirely based on the primary, erotogenic masochism, on pleasure in pain." The sense of guilt leads us to the third type, moral masochism.[24]

Moral masochism is "chiefly remarkable for having loosened its connection with what we recognize as sexuality." Here, the "restriction" that "masochistic sufferings" emanate from "the loved person" and "shall be endured at his command" is "dropped." Now, it is "suffering itself" that matters. Whether this suffering "is decreed by someone who is loved or by someone who is indifferent" matters not at all. This phenomenon might easily lead us to leave "the libido out of account," to assume that the destructive instinct turns inward again and attacks the self. And yet there must be some meaning in the fact that we continue to see a "connection between this norm of behavior and erotism" and that we continue to call these "self-injurers masochists."[25]

David McWhirter identifies moral masochism as a Freudian concept that illuminates James's work. "Observing that the superego's sadism 'becomes for the most part glaringly conscious,' while 'the masochistic trend of the ego remains as a rule concealed from the subject,' Freud is led to a radical conclusion about the moral masochist's 'unconscious sense of guilt.'" McWhirter cites Freud's language: "through moral masochism morality becomes sexualized once more, the Oedipus complex is revived and the way is opened for a regression from morality to the Oedipus complex."[26] The guilt that unconsciously impels the moral masochist is a "need for punishment at the hands of a parental power." The wish "to be beaten by the father stands very close to the other wish, to have a passive (feminine) sexual relation to him."[27] Freud elaborates on this fantasy in his 1919 essay, "A Child is Being Beaten," beginning with female masochism and extrapolating male masochism from the feminine example. (Hugh Stevens also discusses this paper in relation to *The Golden Bowl*.)

Noting that the super-ego's sadism and the ego's masochism "supplement each other," Freud posits that it is the "suppression of an instinct" that leads to guilt, and "a person's conscience becomes more severe and more sensitive the more he refrains from aggression against others." The danger of moral masochism is that "it originates from the death instinct and corresponds to the part of that instinct which has escaped being turned outwards as an instinct of destruction." Here's the clincher, however. Since "it has an erotic component, even the subject's destruction of himself cannot take place without libidinal satisfaction."[28]

Freud's essay amply evinces his continuing power to provoke. His findings are useful to us on several levels. The self-directed torment of James's characters such as John Marcher in his 1903 novella "The Beast in the Jungle" and Maggie Verver in *The Golden Bowl* can be read as being erotically charged even in their fanatical display of self-policing and self-renunciation. At the very least, Freud sheds light on these moral masochists' unwavering commitments to their apparent self-abnegation.

Becoming Sexually Modern

James, who has for several years now been treated as a queer author, responded to the question of new sexual taxonomies by focusing on sexuality as a death force, especially in its enmeshment with the forces of capital. The moral masochism that binds the late novels as they each grapple with the realities of sexuality as either fettered by financial necessities or procured through financial freedom suggests that sexuality was emerging as a privileged site of cultural, social, and individualized negotiations of selfhood, autonomy, and romantic and marital relationships. The late novels therefore engage with and anticipate Freud's later elaborations of a sexually charged desire to undermine the psyche, whether one's own or that of a rival or an entire social order, anticipating many of the major turns of contemporary queer theory, such as Edelman's fiery thesis in *No Future* and Leo Bersani's concept of self-shattering. This is to suggest that James and Freud, if they did not begin it, vigorously pursued a dialogue still articulated within the debates of queer theory.

What characterizes Modernism, writes Peter Faulkner, is "an acute awareness of the problems of art, an unremitting self-consciousness."[29] Modernist artists knowingly conspire to construct the movement. Modernism strove to dismantle entrenched forms, to revivify and transmute the canon by destroying it. Defying the traditional realism of the nineteenth century, Modernism pointedly critiqued the experience of reading by critiquing even the most experienced reader's reading. Hence, the portentous and pointedly inscrutable mysteries of Eliot's famous 1922 poem *The Waste Land*, with the explanatory notes in the back that Eliot's publisher demanded, and Joyce's 1920 *Ulysses* and its relentless shape-shifting, indexing the canon while blasting it to smithereens. Eliot's poem and Joyce's novel are impenetrable without some knowledge of the literary history that precedes them. And yet they refuse to allow that history to claim or shape them. "Reading *The Waste Land*, then, is in part reading about reading in the twentieth century. [The poem provides] a set of instructions on how to read in the twentieth century."[30]

The self-consciousness of Modernism finds an allegorical register in Maggie Verver's endless preoccupation with her husband's affair with Charlotte Stant, which becomes a preoccupation with the idea of the sexual itself. Whether one agrees with Foucauldian theories of sexuality as compulsory, and whether Foucault himself agreed with the idea that sexuality was the key to the self, these late nineteenth-century notions take literary form in the preoccupation with sexual norms, morality, transgressions, and betrayals of the kind Maggie fears have been committed by others and against her. Her masochistic agony as she broods over what the illicit pair may or may not have done sexually emerges as her compensation for loss, her version of participating in matters of the sexual. Which is to say, Amerigo and Charlotte have sexual relations, and Maggie mulls over these relations in ways that cause her pleasure and harm. Sexuality in late James becomes the chief hermeneutical subject, something to be brooded over and interpreted endlessly, causing pleasure and pain on multiple layers at once.

Late James comes close to suggesting that Freud's idea that what we want more than anything else is to return to a state of inorganic nothingness is another way of saying that what we want is escape from the sexual, from its ability to fixate us and for its distinctive quality of embodying personal bonds and libidinal transgressions at once. Sexuality has a grim and unsettling quality in late James, emerging as a force that impels desire and self-sabotaging effort without offering refuge or solutions (*The Wings of the Dove*) or a maddening event that enraptures and suffocates (*The Golden*

Bowl). Instead of decoding literary references deliberately embedded in the text (which is not to say that James is *not* an intertextual author, by any means), the reader of late James enters a realm in which sex and sexuality are inscrutable, forever subject to interpretation and discernment.

Notes

1 H. G. Cocks, *Nameless Offenses: Homosexual Desire in the Nineteenth Century* (London: I. B. Tauris, 2003), 5. For an exploration of nineteenth-century sexual and gender histories, see David Greven, *Gender Protest and Same-Sex Desire in Antebellum American Literature* (New York: Routledge, 2016).

2 See Michel Foucault, "The Repressive Hypothesis," in *The History of Sexuality, Volume I*, trans. Robert Hurley (New York: Vintage Books, 1990), 15–50.

3 Focusing on such topics as the aesthetic, sensuality, nonhuman/inhuman/animal relationships, and, especially, temporality, post-2000s queer scholarship has moved beyond what we can call "the thesis": Michel Foucault's contention in *The History of Sexuality*, volume 1, that the "homosexual became a species" in the 1860s, with the term for heterosexual not emerging until the 1880s. Consequently, the late nineteenth century is the decisive period in which modern sexuality, through new terminologies in medical and criminal discourse, emerged along with the identities and subjectivities not only tethered to but also created because of them. For example, Peter Coviello's book *Tomorrow's Parties* problematizes and rethinks nineteenth-century American literature's relationship to the thesis, yet, like many works in the field, never relinquishes his fidelity to it. A 1914 letter from Henry James to Annie Fields (the longtime companion of the great realist author Sarah Orne Jewett) provides a foundation for the readings to follow in that, for Coviello, James alludes to a sense of loss that both he and Fields (and the now-dead Jewett) share. This loss is the period of more free-floating, less categorized and categorizable affectional and sexual feeling before the Oscar Wilde trials and the burst of new sexual taxonomies produced the more recognizable present dominated by the hetero/homo divide and its strictures. See Peter M. Coviello, *Tomorrow's Parties: Sex and the Untimely in Nineteenth-Century America* (New York: New York University Press, 2013).

4 Robin Wood, *Sexual Politics and Narrative Film Hollywood and Beyond* (New York: Columbia University Press, 1998), 73.

5 Wood, *Sexual Politics*, 74.

6 Brilliant queer uses of Freud have been made by Leo Bersani, especially in his *The Freudian Body: Psychoanalysis and Art* (New York: Columbia University Press, 1986); Jonathan Dollimore, especially in his *Sexual Dissidence: Augustine to Wilde, Freud to Foucault* (New York: Oxford University Press, 1991); and Henry Abelove in his essay "Freud, Male Homosexuality, and the Americans," in *Deep Gossip* (Minneapolis: The University of Minnesota Press, 2003), 1–20.

7 G. G. Meynell, "Freud Translated: An Historical and Bibliographical Note," *Journal of the Royal Society of Medicine* 74 (1981): 306.

8 Discussing James's famous ghost story, *The Turn of the Screw*, Oscar Cargill wrote in 1956 of this connection: "While most critics would concede that an author of genius could in his characterizations anticipate a later scientific elucidation of behavior, none has held that James in his study of the governess combined the perceptions of genius

with actual technical knowledge. The date of the story, 1898, seems too early, save for the remote possibility that there might be something relevant in that early joint publication of Doctors Breuer and Freud-*Studien über Hysterie* in 1895. But indeed here is included a case of the greatest relevancy, one which supplies more important elements than Archbishop Benson's anecdote, 'The Case of Miss Lucy R.'" Oscar Cargill, "Henry James as Freudian Pioneer," *Chicago Review* 10, no. 2 (Summer 1956): 21.

9 According to Levi Asher, their 1909 meeting was an unusually charged one. William James, one of the first Americans to promote the field of psychology in the United States, published his innovative study *The Principles of Psychology* in 1890. His work attracted a great deal of attention, and he "began to reach a larger audience with his speeches and writings on philosophy, religion, and the nature of truth." Asher describes the meeting of these pioneers: "Freud and James met once, in 1909, at a gathering of psychologists at Clark University in Worcester, Massachusetts. Several other soon-to-be-notable psychologists, including Carl Jung, Alfred Adler, and Ernest Jones, had arrived with Freud. (Some, notably Jung, would later break with him, but at the time they formed his loyal entourage.) Freud was clearly the star attraction at the conference, and it was to hear him speak that James, by this time an elderly eminence, fourteen years older than Freud and in failing health, made the short trip to Worcester from Boston. According to all accounts, Freud and James were eager to meet each other. The two men ended their brief encounter by strolling alone together to a train station, and a dramatic scene unfolded: James, suffering from heart problems, suddenly felt an attack of angina pectoris coming on and asked Freud to walk ahead alone so he could gather himself. This appears to have ended their chance for a deeper conversation, and later accounts of the meeting by both men hint at an undefined tension underlying the friendly meeting." See Levi Asher, "When William Met Sigmund (Guest Post by Levi Asher)," *The Second Pass*, August 26, 2010, http://thesecondpass.com/?p=6447. My thanks to the eminent Henry James scholar Julie Rivkin for alerting me to Asher's account.

10 The "anti-social" turn in queer theory, as it has been called by Jack Halberstam and others, reached an early level of sophisticated articulation in Leo Bersani's 1995 study *Homos*. With Jean Genet's novel *Funeral Rites* providing the template, Bersani developed a theory of anti-relationality as a queer response to demands for "healthy," affirming forms of sexuality, always already understood as heterosexual. Most notably, Bersani develops a theory of "self-shattering jouissance," the ecstatic submission of the submissive partner in homosexual sex to the dominant one. Bersani argues that gay/queer fantasy manifests an identification with oppressive straight culture, as evinced by the gay male sexual ardor for fascist and other kinds of authoritarian masculinities.

11 I should add that, as much as I dissent from some of his positions, such as the self-shattering radicalism of the passive partner in gay male sexual intercourse, I am indebted to Bersani's work, especially his deeply stimulating study *The Freudian Body*.

12 Henry James and Peter Brooks, *The Wings of the Dove* (New York: Oxford World's Classics, 2009), 157.

13 James and Brooks, *The Wings of the Dove*, 509.

14 See, for example, Dan McCall, *Citizens of Somewhere Else: Nathaniel Hawthorne and Henry James* (Ithaca: Cornell University Press, 1999); David Greven, "The Homoerotics of James' Hawthorne: Race, Aesthetics, and American Masculinity," *American Literary Realism* 46, no. 2 (2014): 137–57.

15 David Greven, *The Fragility of Manhood: Hawthorne, Freud, and the Politics of Gender* (Columbus: Ohio State University Press, 2012).
16 P. D. James, *Time to be in Earnest: A Fragment of Autobiography* (New York: Knopf, 2010), 38.
17 Hugh Stevens, *Henry James and Sexuality* (Cambridge; New York: Cambridge University Press, 1998), 46.
18 Henry James and Virginia Llewellyn Smith, *The Golden Bowl* (New York: Oxford World's Classics, 2009), 567.
19 James D. Hart and Phillip Leininger. "Golden Bowl, The," in *The Oxford Companion to American Literature* (Oxford: Oxford University Press, 1995), 250.
20 Stevens, *Henry James and Sexuality*, 52.
21 Sigmund Freud, "The Economic Problem of Masochism," in *The Standard Edition of the Complete Psychological Works of Sigmund Freud*, volume 19 (London: Hogarth Press, 1961), 163. With "the will to power," Freud echoes Nietzsche's famous phrase and theory. The overlaps and divergences between Freud and his philosophical precursor demand a discrete analysis. Paul-Laurent Assoun, in his impressive study *Freud and Nietzsche*, observes, "we notice a remarkable functional homology between Will to Power and Libido." In Nietzsche, "every instinct becomes in the last instance a specific articulation of the Will to Power. Likewise for Freud, every drive activity comes back to consummate the libido." Assoun reminds us, however, that these are two distinct concepts: "a principle of domination, on the one hand, and one of pleasure, on the other." Paul-Laurent Assoun, *Freud and Nietzsche*, trans. Richard L. Collier Jr. (New York: Continuum, 2002), 91–2. Topics to be explored beyond this chapter are Henry James's investments in his authorial power and overlaps between his work and Nietzschean theory. See, respectively, Mark Seltzer, *Henry James and the Art of Power* (Ithaca: Cornell University Press, 1984); Stephen Donadio, *Nietzsche, Henry James, and the Artistic Will* (New York: Oxford University Press, 1978).
22 Sigmund Freud, "On Narcissism: An Introduction," in *The Standard Edition of the Complete Psychological Works of Sigmund Freud*, volume 14 (London: Hogarth Press, 1961), 73.
23 Freud, "The Economic Problem of Masochism," 164.
24 Freud, "The Economic Problem of Masochism," 162.
25 Freud, "The Economic Problem of Masochism," 165.
26 Freud, "The Economic Problem of Masochism," 169. David McWhirter, "Restaging the Hurt: Henry James and the Artist as Masochist," *Texas Studies in Literature and Language* 33, no. 4 (1991): 481.
27 Freud, "The Economic Problem of Masochism," 169.
28 Freud, "The Economic Problem of Masochism," 170.
29 Peter Faulkner, *Modernism* (London: Methuen & Co., 1977), 19.
30 Jewel Spears Brooker and Joseph Bentley, *Reading The Waste Land: Modernism and the Limits of Interpretation* (Amherst: University of Massachusetts Press, 1990), 33.

Works Cited

Abelove, Henry. "Freud, Male Homosexuality, and the Americans." In *Deep Gossip*, 1–20. Minneapolis: The University of Minnesota Press, 2003.

Asher, Levi. "When William Met Sigmund (Guest Post by Levi Asher)." *The Second Pass*. August 26, 2010. http://thesecondpass.com/?p=6447.
Assoun, Paul-Laurent. *Freud and Nietzsche*. Translated by Richard L. Collier Jr. New York: Continuum, 2002.
Bersani, Leo. *The Freudian Body: Psychoanalysis and Art*. New York: Columbia University Press, 1986.
Bersani, Leo. *Homos*. Cambridge, MA: Harvard University Press, 1995.
Brooker, Jewel Spears, and Joseph Bentley. *Reading The Waste Land: Modernism and the Limits of Interpretation*. Amherst: University of Massachusetts Press, 1990.
Cargill, Oscar. "Henry James as Freudian Pioneer." *Chicago Review* 10, no. 2 (1956): 13–29.
Cocks, H. G. *Nameless Offences: Homosexual Desire in the Nineteenth Century*. London and New York: I.B. Tauris, 2003.
Coviello, Peter M. *Tomorrow's Parties: Sex and the Untimely in Nineteenth-Century America*. New York: New York University Press, 2013.
Dollimore, Jonathan. *Sexual Dissidence*. Second edition. Oxford: Oxford University Press, 2018.
Edelman, Lee. *No Future: Queer Theory and the Death Drive*. Durham: Duke University Press, 2004.
Edelman, Lee. *Bad Education: Why Queer Theory Teaches Us Nothing*. Durham: Duke University Press, 2022.
Faulkner, Peter. *Modernism*. London: Methuen & Co., 1977.
Freud, Sigmund. "On Narcissism: An Introduction." In *The Standard Edition of the Complete Psychological Works of Sigmund Freud*, volume 14, 67–102. London: Hogarth Press, 1961.
Freud, Sigmund. "The Economic Problem of Masochism." In *The Standard Edition of the Complete Psychological Works of Sigmund Freud*, volume 19, 157–70. London: Hogarth Press, 1961.
Foucault, Michel. "The Repressive Hypothesis." In *The History of Sexuality, Volume I*, translated by Robert Hurley, 15–50. New York: Vintage Books, 1990.
Greven, David. "The Homoerotics of James' Hawthorne: Race, Aesthetics, and American Masculinity." *American Literary Realism* 46, no. 2 (2014): 137–57.
Greven, David. *Gender Protest and Same-Sex Desire in Antebellum American Literature*. New York: Routledge, 2016.
Halberstam, Jack. "The Anti-Social Turn in Queer Studies." *Graduate Journal of Social Science* 5, no. 2 (2008): 140–56.
Hart, James D., and Phillip Leininger. "Golden Bowl, The." In *The Oxford Companion to American Literature*. Oxford: Oxford University Press, 1995.
James, Henry, and Peter Brooks. *The Wings of the Dove*. Oxford and New York: Oxford University Press, 1984.
James, Henry, and Virginia Llewellyn Smith. *The Golden Bowl*. Oxford and New York: Oxford University Press, 2009.
James, P. D. *Time to be in Earnest: A Fragment of Autobiography*. New York: Knopf, 2010.
McCall, Dan. *Citizens of Somewhere Else: Nathaniel Hawthorne and Henry James*. Ithaca: Cornell University Press, 1999.
McWhirter, David. "Restaging the Hurt: Henry James and the Artist as Masochist." *Texas Studies in Literature and Language* 33, no. 4 (1991): 464–91.
Meynell, G. G. "Freud Translated: An Historical and Bibliographical Note." *Journal of the Royal Society of Medicine* 74, no. 4 (1981): 306–9.
Seltzer, Mark. *Henry James and the Art of Power*. Ithaca: Cornell University Press, 1984.

Stevens, Hugh. *Henry James and Sexuality*. Cambridge and New York: Cambridge University Press, 1998.

Warner, Michael. “Homo-Narcissism; or, Heterosexuality.” In *Engendering Men*, edited by Michael Cadden and Joseph A Boone, 192–208. New York: Routledge, 1990.

Warner, Michael. *The Trouble with Normal: Sex, Politics, and the Ethics of Queer Life*. New York: Free Press, 1999.

Wood, Robin. *Sexual Politics and Narrative Film Hollywood and Beyond*. New York: Columbia University Press, 1998.

7

Elegy, Queerness, and the Lacanian Death Drive

Sara H. Lindheim

This chapter seeks to trace the narrativization of the death drive in a collection of six Latin elegiac poems written at the end of the first century BCE.[1] We shall also explore how the drive's insistent presence in the poetry, always only partially acknowledged at best, haunts the scholarship about the collection, my own included. I had just written a chapter about queer temporalities in the six poems in Tibullus' second book of elegies,[2] and yet, like a moth to the flame, I kept returning in my mind to my earlier reading. Lacan warns in Seminar II that "to draw the rabbit out of the hat, you always have to have put it in beforehand."[3] At the risk of seeming intellectually inconstant, I want to circle back to my interpretation because it is increasingly clear to me that, when I came face to face with the text's narrativization of the death drive, like so many other readers, I reached into the hat and pulled out a reparative reading from a predetermined set of defensive fantasies against the dissolution of personal and collective identities in the face of the Real.

In this chapter, I pair Tibullus Book 2 with Lee Edelman's queer, Lacanian death drive.[4] The results will alter how we think about the genre of Latin love elegy in general and the scholarly reception of Tibullus Book 2 in particular. I suggest that these six Tibullan elegies, regularly maligned in and marginalized from discussions of Latin love elegy, are more radical and disruptive to their contemporary Augustan sociopolitical order than any other text we possess from the period, including the notoriously subversive Ovid. Further, and interrelatedly, the nihilistic disruption to the self and the social order that the text lays bare explains why and how readers turn away from it. At the end we will ask what alternatives the opposite impulse—leaning into and embracing the death drive—offers not only to a reader of Tibullus but also, by extension, to any subject operating within the Symbolic structures by which a society conceptualizes totalizing meaning. And here we will look beyond Edelman for other, alternative (yet still Lacanian-inspired) solutions.

First, a few brief preliminaries. Defining the genre of Latin elegy generally invites complicated and highly nuanced explanations, and I propose to simplify to what will prove essential for the purposes of this argument.[5] The poetry itself consists of first-person subjective narrative, the "I" almost exclusively a male lover-poet, whose primary story is an erotic one. He, a Roman citizen, noble and equestrian in rank, pursues a mistress, whom he often describes as all-powerful. The liaison he seeks with her, however, never encompasses legitimate marriage; she herself is not an eligible partner, either because she already has a spouse or because she already belongs to another man in some other proprietary arrangement. In addition, the elegiac lover-poet's tale adheres strongly to neither linear nor teleological momentum. There does exist, however, a broad narrative commitment to an overarching story, even if this impulse to narrativize stems primarily from the reader's desire to string fragments together into something coherent. The lover-poet desires a *puella* (girl), pursues her, sometimes celebrates erotic success, more often does not, but constantly fantasizes about the elusive possibility of erotic fulfillment. Elegy tells a tale of subjectivity and desire;[6] we should not be terribly surprised then that the death drive makes an appearance.

As a genre, Latin elegy has a very circumscribed lifespan. It comes into existence, flourishes, and then disappears over a period of about seventy years, a period that saw the end of the Roman Republic as well as the rise and establishment of Augustus, who ultimately became the first Roman emperor. It is a tumultuous moment of profound political, social, and cultural transformation. And yet, precisely because of the upheaval, Augustus leans hard into presenting his regime as a restoration of a traditional Roman way of life, tapping into cherished cultural ideals about a "good Roman life" for Roman, male, citizens. Augustus trumpets a program of return to traditional *mores*, which stresses, among other things, the absolute imbrication of individual desire and duty to the state. The "good life" foregrounds piety, complete devotion to public duty in political, military, social, and religious spheres, along with simplicity and restraint in individual consumption. The Augustan program culminates in moral legislations that underscore the importance of family, imposing legal requirements for marriage, for the procreation of children, and, in the same vein, outlawing adultery.

As we turn to Tibullus Book 2, we shall see that the male lover-poet bumps up against normative fantasies of the Roman, male, citizen good life. Indeed, this is true of all elegy. But Tibullus Book 2 does so more urgently, more explicitly, more radically than its generic bedfellows, and to such an extent that readers almost uniformly condemn the darkness of the poetic vision. We will trace how darkness becomes the core takeaway of Tibullus' second collection of elegies with the help of Lee Edelman's argument for queerness as an anti-futural negation of any sociopolitical order, or, as the embodiment of the death drive. I will suggest that the unabashed nakedness of the death drive that the text reveals forms the core of what readers experience as most unpalatable. Readers have found it difficult, if not impossible, to gaze in such an unobstructed fashion at the drive, at the irruption of the Real, and seek instead a defense in fantasy. Conversely, we will embrace the destructive energies of the Real, encounter negativity, and consider the creative potential that emerges.

Tibullus Book 2 contains six elegies that divide evenly into two halves: on the one hand, three poems about Rome and Roman values, with an emphasis on religious rites and ceremonies; on the other, three poems about the lover-poet and his *puella* (girl). The Roman poems offer up a stable and coherent fantasy of the Roman good life, singing the praises of rustic simplicity, the proper devotion to the gods, and family that passes genetic, material, and cultural inheritance from generation to generation. The opening two poems highlight steady, linear chronological narrative progression and unproblematic continuity while enshrining heteroreproductive family values. Poem 2.1 invites the reader to a rustic religious festival, honoring Bacchus and Ceres, gods who prop up a triumphalist narrative of progress and civilization unfolding through time. In the distant past, men dwelled in fields or caves and dined on acorns. With the passage of time and divine assistance, men learned to build houses, cultivate the land to produce food, and drink wine. Other creature comforts followed soon after. Every year contemporary Romans reenact the ritual celebration, annually reproducing a rite "handed down to them from ancestors from an earlier time."[7] The elegy emphasizes inheritance from one generation to another, the passage of time, and the handing down of tradition from one set of family members to the next.

The poet summons his patron, Messalla, to the festivities, and in the process, he emphatically centers the importance of ancestral kinship and inheritance. Tibullus praises Messalla's recent victory over the Aquitanians, for which he was awarded a triumph. Specifically, the poet notes that Messalla's victory and public celebration cast "glorious light on his unshaven ancestors."[8] Here conquest rather than ritual represents the act that links generations. In traditional Roman terms, the ancestors watch over their future descendants, judging their actions, expecting in death to bask in the glorious light of descendants who re-produce in the present and the future the illustrious past deeds of their ancestors. Messalla brings honor to his ancestors by walking in their footsteps; like many in his great patrician family, he achieves military success for Rome. The adjective "unshaven" emphasizes a long continuous chronological span of distinction for this family; sources contemporary with Tibullus tell us that shaving became the default practice for Roman men about three hundred years before the time of the poem.[9]

Poem 2 adds another layer to the fantasy of the "good Roman life." Continuity, progression, and generations within families resurface, as does ritual, but this time we confront ritual on the scale of the private individual. The elegy commemorates Cornutus' birthday, again, like the festival for Bacchus and Ceres in poem 1, a recurring, annual, family-centered celebration. And indeed, Tibullus underscores the significance of family when he imagines his friend's sole birthday wish as the desire for "the faithful love of a wife."[10] With a subtle sleight of hand, Tibullus extends the ask: "let Love bring golden bonds of marriage"[11] and lest we gloss over the choice of the word "bonds," he continues: "the kind of bonds that last forever, until sluggish old age brings wrinkles and dyes hair grey."[12] The couple's faithful love leads to children and grandchildren. We end on the perfect heteronormative familial fantasy of reproductive futurism.

The fifth poem in the book closes out the first group of poems we have been considering. It is perhaps worth noting that even the scholars who remain unfavorable in their reception of the collection often mark out poem 2.5 as an exception worthy of serious consideration and praise.[13] Again the poet summons us to a religious ceremony during which Messalla's son becomes a priest charged with the care of the Sibylline books. But mention of the Sibyl pushes the poet toward national poetry, more specifically toward a narrative about Rome, and he embarks on a sweeping tale of Rome's history from its beginning until the poetic present. His tale highlights fathers and pious, warrior sons as well as glory continuing through time. We begin with

Aeneas escaping a burning Troy with his father, who will ultimately die before Aeneas becomes Rome's earliest founder at Lavinium. Aeneas' proto-Roman line continues with his son Ascanius, until Mars fathers Romulus, who will become the founder of the actual city of Rome. We see a city grow from humble, but morally upright origins of rustic simplicity and piety to the hub of a quasi-unbounded empire, sanctioned by divine destiny and still undergirded by the same earlier moral principles. The emphasis remains on generational inheritance, on great sons following in the footsteps of their great fathers. We finish with a vignette of a simple rustic festival, an annual celebration of the city's birthday. We witness the countryside overflowing with agricultural produce thanks to divine blessings in return for rustic piety, a shepherd who leaps over lighted bales of hay to ensure fertility. And then, sure enough, images of family continuity follow; the shepherd's wife gives birth to a child who playfully grabs his father's ears, and grandfathers appear to protect their grandsons and speak baby talk with them. The poet then concludes with a form of ring composition. He must continue his poetic career in order to be able to celebrate the future deeds of Messalla's son "when he will drive conquered towns before his chariot as war plunder."[14] As his father brought glory to his ancestors (as we saw in poem 1), so the final Roman poem closes with the son replicating the illustrious conquests of his father, who himself followed in the footsteps of his glorious ancestors.

So far we have been tracing the Roman (Lacanian) Symbolic sustained by collective fantasies of the good life that center on heteronormative families, simple rustic piety, coherent chronologically linear narratives that tie citizens to the progression of history and of the city of Rome itself. These fantasies require an adherence to what queer theorist Lee Edelman has called reproductive futurism, a belief in a sustaining framework that must reproduce itself or be reproduced into the future, continuity thus conferring coherence and stability on present reality. Such a fantasy, Edelman writes, "presumes a reality guaranteed, not threatened, by time, sustained by the certainty that a 'course of events' is bound to continue in due course long after we are gone."[15] It also means that we must ignore the moments in which the Real intrudes, when the fictional nature of the structures of the Symbolic and the subject within it come to light. For example, if we return to the poems we have been considering, we can see an overarching exultation in forward chronological momentum and progression. But we should simultaneously note that focusing solely on the linear narrative demands obfuscating the insistence on an equally strong sense of cyclic recurrence and repetition of the status quo into the future as descendants attempt to reenact the roles of their forefathers, whether they replicate (community or individual) rituals or expansionist, imperial military conquest.

If we can paper over the circuit of repetition at the heart of the Roman Symbolic, the other poems in Tibullus Book 2, the elegies about the lover-poet's relationship with his *puella*, however, render it impossible to turn a blind eye to repetition and a foreclosure of futurity. Through the structural construction of Book 2, with its two distinct halves, Tibullus explicitly represents his relationship with Nemesis as separate from, or as an alternative narrative to, the poems about the Roman good life. (And yes, the beloved's name in Tibullus' turbulent, dark love affair is Nemesis, surely not a casual instance of signification and a point to which we will return.) For the most part, the two different halves do not overtly come into contact, but two brief moments of intersection highlight a dramatic contrast. We first learn of the poet-lover's affair with Nemesis in elegy 2.3, which follows directly on the birthday poem for Cornutus. Tibullus establishes a clear link between the two poems by addressing 2.3 to this same Cornutus. But while poem 2.2 centers on legal marriage founded on faithful love and engendering a long line of frequently reproducing offspring, Tibullus summons Cornutus in this new poem to witness a very different sort of love embodied in the poet-lover's relationship with Nemesis. Indeed, the lover-poet never intimates that legitimate marriage or family is an option; moreover, he even offers to sell his ancestral property, thus cutting rather than underscoring familial ties, if Nemesis just says the word.[16] A second striking juxtaposition arises in poem 2.5, the poem that features Rome's grand historical narrative. As the elegy reaches its conclusion, the poet seemingly distances himself from the very poetry extolling Roman virtues and values that he currently is engaged in writing with a brief moment of self-reflection: "I continuously sing about Nemesis, without whom no verse of mine can find the proper words or the right meter."[17] In opposition to the linear and diachronically developing story of Rome, the song of Tibullus and Nemesis features an iterative playback loop.

And yet, if we burrow into this relationship with Nemesis, we discover that the erotic narrative does not remain separate from the Roman good life. In fact, time and time again the governing fictions of the political social order, "the Roman good life," represent precisely what turns out to be impossible or untenable for Tibullus with Nemesis. Rather than setting out distinct, separate parameters for their relationship, the lover-poet instead constructs their narrative so that it negates what he has just presented as the Roman Symbolic. The countryside, earlier a place of rustic simplicity and family values, now morphs into a locus of physically demanding work, enslavement, and pain in which the ideals of family and inheritance fly out the window. In poem 2.3, Nemesis has relocated, at least in Tibullus' imagination, to a country villa. The lover-poet dreams of following her, but only for the chance of catching a glimpse. Just to see her, however, he imagines for himself a life of harsh manual labor. He fantasizes about trailing a plow, suffering sunburn and blisters in elegy 2.3, images which quickly devolve into enduring enslavement and corporeal punishment while working the fields at the end of 2.3 and the opening of 2.4. Rather than biological reproduction or inheritance of ancestral possessions and traits handed down from one generation to the next, we now discover the lover-poet volunteering to sell his family home for money to grant him access to Nemesis, and conversely, exposing Nemesis' new lover as a formerly enslaved barbarian who has purchased her love, a self-made man with wealth he accumulated himself rather than obtained through inheritance.[18] Moreover, in a shocking moment, the lover-poet attempts to plead his case with Nemesis by appealing to her younger sister, who surely, he insists, would offer familial support to their union. But she turns out only to haunt the poem peripherally, a ghost of a young person who suffered a premature and violent end by falling from an open window. The only child even vaguely associated with the Nemesis-Tibullus relationship is a dead one.

Furthermore, the values that earlier seemed paramount, of morally upright and pious existence based on an ideal of having just enough, now also begin to inspire resistance. From one side of his mouth, the lover-poet clings to rustic simplicity. He claims that he longs for nothing more than country feasts and earthenware vessels; he maligns marble-clad homes in the city or many tracts of land in the country, obtained by the loot amassed by warriors and merchants.[19] At the same time, however, despite a long diatribe against the acquisition of riches in poem 2.3, he also promises to pursue them in order that, he announces, "my Nemesis may drip with luxury items, and may advance through the city, a sight to see in the gifts I have procured for her."[20] As country life fades away, the poet-lover and Nemesis appear firmly planted in the city; she rejoices in see-through garments, vibrant with expensive foreign dyes and woven through with gold. Poem 2.4 soon adds exotic, foreign, luxurious gems, emeralds and pearls, to the mix. To acquire the necessary precious gifts, the lover-poet no longer maintains his reverence for the gods. He will amass his imaginary wealth "by means of slaughter and crime"[21] in poem 2.4, perhaps even through the impious acts of stealing sacred objects from the temples of the goddess Venus, whom he holds responsible for his new found criminality.[22] In poem 2.3, again directly defying formerly celebrated piety, he curses both Ceres and Bacchus,[23] gods central to the rustic good life in poem 2.1.

The lover-poet's self-representation refuses to accommodate itself to the Symbolic fantasy of the Roman good life that he sets out in Book 2 of his elegies. He systematically seeks out a mode of enjoyment that turns its back on community, both by opposing notions of communal good and by refusing to participate in its futural continuity. When we examine the overarching narrative of Tibullus' relationship with Nemesis, we discover quite literally that nothing happens—the narrative has no forward momentum at all. Even when we thread together all the fragments of the story as they emerge over the elegies of Book 2, we notice that each fragment is actually a replica of the first. In poem 2.3, we learn that Nemesis has moved house; she and her new lover have moved to the countryside. The lover-poet seems abandoned in the city, left to rant and rail about the fortune he does not possess that might grant him access to Nemesis. When the next poem opens, he occupies the same position, on the outside looking in, unable to obtain the exotic luxury items that might persuade her to open the door to him. He remains there for the entirety of poem 2.4, and then presumably during the interlude of poem 2.5 about Rome. When the final poem, elegy 2.6, begins, the lover-poet appears to be precisely where we left him in 2.4, on Nemesis' doorstep staring in vain at the locked doors of her house. While other men leave behind unsuccessful affairs and pursue more "manly" or socially acceptable occupations as soldiers or poets of more elevated genres than love poetry, the lover-poet can do no more than constantly retrace his steps. "How often I swore," he confesses, "that I would never return to her threshold. Whenever I have duly sworn, nevertheless my foot returns of its own accord."[24] Tibullus ends poem 2.6 exactly in the spot he seems to have occupied for the entirety of their affair, suspended on Nemesis' threshold, unable to gain entry yet equally incapable of moving too far away from the door, he and their relationship stuck in a stuttering, iterative time loop.

The lover-poet's refusal of the coherent fiction made up of the various elements that constitute the fantasy unity of the Roman good life plays out in the text as compulsive and ultimately meaningless narrative repetition. It lacks all teleological impetus. If we turn back for a moment to elegy 2.5, the poem about the founding of Rome, we notice that while the lover-poet devotes very little space to his relationship, he does offer some significant details. The god Cupid has pierced the lover-poet with a well-chosen arrow. The lover-poet confesses, "I have lain wounded for a year (or, in an alternatively possible translation, for a very long time) and I indulge in the sickness since the pain itself is pleasurable." "I continuously sing Nemesis," [25] he concludes. We should note two things: when the lover-poet briefly summarizes his relationship with Nemesis, he conceives of time's unfolding movement not as a linear, diachronic progression, but rather as a repetitive loop. He confesses that he sings about Nemesis *usque*, continuously or over and over again, and he lies wounded, suspended in time, getting neither better nor worse for a year (or longer). Moreover, he announces that the relationship brings him intense suffering, yet he makes no effort to combat this pain. On the contrary, he confesses that he rather likes it; the pain itself, he notes, is pleasurable.

Indeed, if we look back again at the various moments in his iterative narrative of Nemesis, we discover a frequent intersection of repetitive pleasure with pain. As the lover-poet describes the riches he does not possess but must acquire to have access to Nemesis, he reveals both a sharp distaste for them and his anguish at the means he will ultimately have to deploy in his effort to obtain them. Loot, the lover-poet repeatedly asserts, finds itself ineluctably intertwined with "many evils,"[26] and amassing loot requires that the collector brave blood, slaughter, and death on the battlefield or perilous voyages by sea.[27] In poem 2.4, he must set aside ethical ideals and indulge in crime and sacrilege to acquire riches.[28] Nevertheless, he cannot pass over in silence the aesthetic pleasure these riches arouse in him. He lingers over loving descriptions of green emeralds, shining pearls, snow-white garments with brilliant red and purple dye, and see-through silk with golden stripes in poems 2.3 and 2.4. More conventionally bringing together pleasure and pain, the lover-poet revels in the imagined chains and whippings that will inevitably accompany his enslavement to his mistress both at the end of poem 2.3 and at the beginning of poem 2.4, as well as the blisters and the sunburn his enslaved body will suffer because of intense manual labor in the fields (2.3). He brings poem 2.4 to its conclusion with an abject offer to consume a large quantity of poison, but only if he can enjoy the pleasure of drinking the deadly concoction under the calm, watchful eye of Nemesis.

As we consider the empty repetition of experiences in which the pleasure arises with and from iterated suffering, we must openly acknowledge that the erotic relationship of Tibullus and Nemesis, which founders on the shoals of "the good Roman life," narrativizes the entwined Lacanian notions of *jouissance* and the death drive. The lover-poet himself stands in the role of an Edelmanian queer figure, anti-futural, resisting the stable construction of self and social order, thus embodying the remainder of the Real internal to the Symbolic, revealing the subject's constitution by, and attachment to, varieties of being undone. But before we allow our Roman text of the first century BCE fully to embrace the death drive and queer negativity, we need to grapple with one more passage that emerges near the beginning of the final elegy. "How often I swore that I would never return to her threshold. Whenever I have duly sworn, my foot itself returns of its own accord,"[29] the lover-poet laments and accuses Love of instantiating endless torture. But then he pivots:

Now I would have put an end to my sufferings, but credulous
hope cherishes life and always says that tomorrow will be better.
Hope nourishes farmers, hope entrusts to plowed furrows
seeds, in order that the field return them with great interest.
This hope entices birds in a net and fish on the rod,
when bait in front has concealed the slender hooks.
Hope even brings solace to the man bound with strong restraint;
his thighs make iron resound, but he sings amidst his labor.
Hope promises me that Nemesis will be compliant, but she herself says no.
Woe is me![30]

Does hope (*spes*) put a spring in the lover-poet's literal and metrical step (*pes*) on the very threshold of suicide? Can we read this as a moment of pure optimism—a last-ditch gesture to opt back into a fantasy of social order with coherence, stability, and futurity? Can we imagine hope for Tibullus and Nemesis, and if so, in what temporal register, the present or the future? If we read hope more negatively in this passage, why do we discount the lover-poet's seeming turn to hope? And here we move to consider how the death drive we now see at the core of Tibullus Book 2 in fact provides the key to unpacking different readers' responses to the text.

At precisely this point in my earlier interpretation of these poems, I turned away from the death drive.[31] Grabbing onto José Esteban Muñoz's theory of queer futurity,[32] I argued that Tibullus' hope intersected with the form of utopian hope that Muñoz holds out as the key to a future that breaks with the present and escapes the heteronormative script. The lover-poet's "credulous hope" is only potential; in other words, maybe one day in the future the seed will grow, but maybe not, and maybe one day the fish will get the bait and not the hook, but maybe not. For Muñoz too, the "there and then" might one day be different from the "here and now." But this solution, in fact, emerges as a direct response to the death drive. It rests on a utopian decision to elide the iterative mess in the present and put one's faith instead in the possibility of a different, better future yet to come. Surely a fantasy.

If we refuse this turn to futurity and remain in the present, we find ourselves face to face with an optimism that may not, on closer examination, remain so optimistic. The ancient Greco-Roman notion of hope, interpreters point out, is not a positive one. On the contrary, a quick glance at Greek and Roman literary and philosophical texts reveals that hope appears unreasonable, deceptive, or, at best, unrealized.[33] In this passage, hope receives the modifier "credulous," indicating that those who espouse it can do so only because they refuse to foresee all the inevitable consequences. Hope veils over the unattainability of what is desired: the fish and the bird most likely will not manage to escape death, while the farmer will always need, year after year, more seeds to grow in the furrows. By the same token, the lover-poet implies that if only he can have Nemesis, life will be good. But here at last we need to confront the significance of the name Nemesis, a name that strikingly stands apart from the usual names (Delia, Cynthia, Corinna) associated with the elegiac beloved that often reference poetry.[34] What can it possibly mean to love Nemesis? Nemesis recalls through her name the powerful goddess of retribution, and as such, she eternally promises future punishment for an action that occurred in the past.[35] But in the present moment, she remains suspended, insistent, and eternally looping. By conferring the name Nemesis on his beloved, the lover-poet ensures that his object choice looks very much like the death drive itself, never occupying the present, thereby holding out the promise of nothing more than endless circulation and repetition.

And indeed, for many readers, Nemesis becomes the focal point for their profound dislike of Tibullus Book 2. Rarely does one find such unrelentingly misogynistic and heteronormative narratives underwriting analyses. We hear over and over again of a tortured affair with the cruel Nemesis, a heartless and rapacious mistress who drives poor Tibullus to abandon his cherished ideals of idyllic country life.[36] On the other side of the same coin, we discover a very early reception of Tibullus in Ovid's own elegiac poetry. Written only a decade or two after Tibullus, Ovid composes a poem in which he elaborately imagines Tibullus' funeral, seemingly "correcting" Nemesis' behavior in the process. In a stunning about-face, Nemesis emerges from the Ovidian reimagination as the veritable instantiation of the loving elegiac mistress, professing her deep love for Tibullus as she weeps over his pyre and reminisces about holding his hand as he took his dying breath.[37] And yet, whether scholars render her abject or Ovid idealizes her, the response to the death drive, to the radical exposure of a riven subject in the face of the Real's *jouissance*, in both cases is to cast it off from the normative and locate it elsewhere. Tibullus' Nemesis, somewhat paradoxically, because she, unlike Edelman's examples, is a woman and not a queer man, becomes what Edelman calls the "sinthomosexual," the character positioned, by readers, by the poet, to represent the narcissistic, the antisocial, and all that refuses futurity; in short, the embodiment of the death drive who preserves the continuity of the fantasy of reproductive futurism for everyone else.[38]

No wonder readers consistently malign this text. But let us conclude otherwise, by purposefully considering a different response to the death drive at the heart of this text. What happens if we, as readers, embrace the death drive rather than turn somersaults to marginalize it, or to deny it outright? If we focus our attention on Nemesis, Penelope Deutscher's productive reading of the omission of women from Edelman's category of the sinthomosexual serves to move us in a new direction.[39] The fantasy of reproductive futurism requires ideal mothers, responsible life-givers to sustain it. And indeed, the elegies that feature the Symbolic fantasy of the Roman good life (2.1, 2.2., 2.5) are littered with just such women (like Cornutus' wife or the shepherd's pregnant spouse[40]) who serve to provide offspring, thus ensuring that the future replicates and continues the past. But the fantasy of the ideal mother also requires its opposite: the vilified mother, irresponsible, unintelligible, who poses a threat to our collective futures. The ideal woman's behavior sustains and preserves the Symbolic order whereas the female sinthohomosexual stands in the way of the Symbolic's flourishing, disrupting normativity, but offering no intelligible alternative solution. The reader easily slots Nemesis into this latter role: a cipher for anxiety, even fear, over a woman who seems to choose not to participate in reproductive futurism in any way and whose desires and intentions remain inscrutable, all the while holding out no viable substitute. Let us step back to consider that it is the *discourse* around reproduction, the Symbolic's heteronormative fantasy that offers to women only a choice of two dichotomous options: subjectivized or desubjectivized, idealized or vilified. This recognition opens up a tantalizing possibility to imagine a woman's antisocial choice in more nuanced and multiple ways than simply as the negative pole of a binary position.

Or we could focus on the lover-poet. First, we must disengage him from his disingenuous claim that "Hope promises Nemesis will be compliant but she herself says no."[41] It is the lover-poet, as we have seen, who says no to the future, to the social order and its reproductive futurism. He himself embodies the death drive, wholeheartedly embracing negativity, refusing the fantasy of the social and political order. The lover-poet of Tibullus Book 2 becomes a subject not as desire but as drive, manifesting the presence of the death drive disconcertingly at the heart of the Symbolic. The text represents the most radical pushback against the Augustan social and political order—in fact, against any sociopolitical fantasy of the good life—of all our extant elegies.[42] We are left with the death drive's aesthetic and political disruption. But then, what do we do?

Tibullus Book 2 never gets tied up in a neat package with a bow. Indeed, many scholars complain about the work's unfinished state, surely interrupted by the author's untimely death.[43] And yet, this too bespeaks a turning away from the death drive. The Tibullan text offers us nothing redemptive to cling to in the end, suggesting perhaps an Edelmanian embrace of a radical politics of refusal. The lover-poet embodies the *jouissance* of the Real, the death drive that disrupts symbolically viable subjectivity. The ball is in the reader's court. Do we celebrate the rebelliousness of the destructive posture, try to bear the unbearable, bestow upon queerness this wholly impossible position? Or do we turn again to Lacanian thought, pursuing, as Mari Ruti suggests, the possibility of his link between the death drive and creativity,[44] where Lacan suggests that the death drive "challenges everything that exists" and is "a will to make a fresh start from zero, a will to begin again."[45] If *jouissance* and the death drive dwell at the heart of the Symbolic, the Real that irrupts, then does this not point to a fleeting rather than a permanent state of affairs? And what if the destruction of the carefully constructed fantasy edifice of the subject in the Symbolic, its disengagement from the discourse of the Other, makes room for something creative, like Lacan's artisan-potter who fashions a spectacular vase around and out of a void, *ex nihilo*?[46] Ruti suggests that the "no" the subject utters to the heteronormative fantasies of the Symbolic should not be a celebrated end point, but rather opens up a possibility for revitalization, for the emergence of the defiant queer subject who embraces rather than denies their own riven-ness, the *jouissance* at the heart of subjectivity. That defiant queer subject in turn adopts an ethical position toward others not based on imaginary identification but instead on acceptance that others, like the self, are also riven by the Real in their own unique ways. Perhaps then Tibullus Book 2 opens up a potential space for a radical ethical call fundamentally to reimagine encounters between self and other, inviting them to be antinormative but not antisocial, to bear more traces of the Real, to sit more acceptingly with the individual inscrutability of the fragmented and decentered subject.

Notes

1 My thanks to Jeffrey Di Leo, Allen Miller, and all the participants in the Winter Theory Institute's Death Drive Conference, and as always to Mario Telò and Helen Morales for reading and discussion.

2 Sara Lindheim, "Queerly Beloved: Nemesis, *Credula Spes*, and Queer Temporalities in Tibullus Book 2," in *The Routledge Handbook of Classics and Queer Theory*, ed. Ella Haselswerdt, Sara H. Lindheim, and Kirk Ormand (London and New York: Routledge, 2024).

3 Jacques Lacan, *The Ego in Freud's Theory and in the Technique of Psychoanalysis, 1954–1955: The Seminar of Jacques Lacan, Book II*, trans. Sylvana Tomaselli (New York: Norton, 1991), 61.

4 See Lee Edelman, *No Future: Queer Theory and the Death Drive* (Durham: Duke University Press, 2004) and *Bad Education: Why Queer Theory Teaches Us Nothing* (Durham: Duke University Press, 2022). On the death drive and its development in Lacanian thought, the significant texts are: Jacques Lacan, *The Four Fundamental Concepts of Psychoanalysis: The Seminar of Jacques Lacan, Book XI*, trans. Alan Sheridan (New York: Norton, 1981); *The Ego in Freud's Theory and in the Technique of Psychoanalysis, 1954–1955: The Seminar of Jacques Lacan, Book II*, trans. Sylvana Tomaselli (New York: Norton, 1991); *The Ethics of Psychoanalysis, 1959–1960: The Seminar of Jacques Lacan, Book VII*, trans. Dennis Porter (New York: Norton, 1992); *On Feminine Sexuality, the Limits of Love and Knowledge, 1972–1973: The Seminar of Jacques Lacan, Book XX*, trans. Bruce Fink (New York: Norton, 1999); *Écrits*, trans. Bruce Fink (New York: Norton, 2006).

5 Thea Thorsen, "Introduction: Latin Love Elegy," in *The Cambridge Companion to Latin Love Elegy*, ed. Thea Thorsen (Cambridge: Cambridge University Press, 2013), 1–20, provides an overview.

6 See, for example, Micaela Janan, *The Politics of Desire: Propertius IV* (Berkeley: The University of California Press, 2001) and Paul Allen Miller, *Subjecting Verses: Latin Love Elegy and the Emergence of the Real* (Princeton: Princeton University Press, 2004).

7 Tibullus 2.1.2: *ritus . . . a prisco traditus . . . avo*. The translations are mine.

8 Tibullus 2.1.34: *magna intonsis gloria . . . avis*.

9 Robert Maltby, *Tibullus: Elegies. Text, Introduction and Commentary* (Cambridge: Francis Cairns Publications, 2002) ad loc. cites Varro, *De Re Rustica* 2.11.10 and Pliny, *Natural History* 7.211.

10 Tibullus 2.2.11: *uxoris fidos . . . amores*.

11 Tibullus 2.2.18: *flavaque coniugio vincula portet Amor*.

12 Tibullus 2.2.19–20: *vincula quae maneant semper, dum tarda senectus / inducat rugas inficiatque comas*.

13 Paul Murgatroyd, *Tibullus: Elegies II* (Oxford: Oxford University Press, 1994), 165–8 praises the elegy as "an extremely learned poem. . . [a] national elegy to mirror Virgil's national epic . . . an ambitious and pioneering elegy . . . a monumental and intricate composition . . . a novel departure for Tibullus . . . *it is especially surprising after the amatory 2.3 and 2.4 (whose somewhat hysterical conclusion is succeeded by the calm, dignified, and reverential opening here)*" (my emphasis).

14 Tibullus 2.5.115–16: *cum praemia belli / ante suos currus oppida victa feret*.

15 Edelman, *No Future*, 34.

16 Tibullus 2.4.53–54.
17 Tibullus 2.5.111–12: *usque cano Nemesim, sine qua versus mihi nullus / verba potest iustos aut reperire pedes.*
18 Tibullus 2.4.53–54 and 2.3.59–60, respectively.
19 Tibullus 2.3.47ff.
20 Tibullus 2.3.51–52: *ut mea luxuria Nemesis fluat utque per urbem / incedat donis conspicienda meis.*
21 Tibullus 2.4.21: *per caedem et facinus.*
22 Tibullus 2.4.23–25.
23 Tibullus 2.3.67–70.
24 Tibullus 2.6.13–14: *iuravi quotiens rediturum ad limina numquam! / cum bene iuravi, pes tamen ipse redit.*
25 Tibullus 2.5.109–11: *et mihi praecipue iaceo qui saucius annum / et faveo morbo cum iuvat ipse dolor. / usque cano Nemesim.* Murgatroyd *Tibullus; Elegies II*, *ad loc.* notes that *saucius* means "suffering pain because of love" and suggests that *annum* can "denote an actual year (more or less) or just = *longum tempus* ['a long period of time']."
26 Tibullus 2.3.36: *multis . . . malis.*
27 Tibullus 2.3.37–40.
28 Tibullus 2.4.21ff.
29 See note 24, above.
30 Tibullus 2.6.19–28:

iam mala finissem leto, sed credula vitam
Spes fovet et fore cras semper ait melius.
Spes alit agricolas, Spes sulcis credit aratis
semina quae magno faenore reddat ager.
haec laqueo volucres haec captat harundine pisces
cum tenues hamos abdidit ante cibus.
Spes etiam valida solatur compede vinctum:
crura sonant ferro, sed canit inter opus.
Spes facilem Nemesim spondet mihi, sed negat illa:
ei mihi.

31 Lindheim, "Queerly Beloved," 161–3.
32 José Esteban Muñoz, *Cruising Utopia: The Then and There of Queer Futurity* (New York: New York University Press, 2019).
33 For a discussion with bibliography, see Laurel Fulkerson, "*Credula Spes*: Tibullan Hope and the Future of Elegy," in *Intratextuality and Latin Literature*, ed. Steven Harrison, Stavros Frangoulidis, and Theodore Papanghelis (Berlin: De Gruyter, 2018), 55–66.
34 Maria Wyke first suggested that the elegiac mistress metaphorically embodies the poetry itself. See her collected essays in *The Roman Mistress: Ancient and Modern Representations* (Oxford: Oxford University Press, 2002), which sparked much productive discussion.
35 Emma Stafford, "Tibullus' Nemesis: Divine Retribution and the Poet," in *What's in a Name?: The Significance of Proper Names in Classical Latin Literature*, ed. Joan Booth, Robert Maltby, and Frédérique Biville (Swansea: Classical Press of Wales, 2006), 33–48, offers a less negative view.
36 The introductory materials to the Nemesis poems (2.3, 2.4, 2.6) in the commentaries of Maltby, *Tibullus: Elegies*, and Murgatroyd, *Tibullus: Elegies II* provide nice examples of inveighing against the darkness of Book 2. That this continues to be the

prevailing view can be seen in the recent overview of Tibullan scholarship by Erika Zimmermann Damer, "Introduction: Recent Work on Tibullus," *The Classical World* 107, no. 4 (2014): 445.

37 See Ovid, *Amores* 3.9.

38 See Edelman, *No Future*.

39 Penelope Deutscher, *Foucault's Futures: A Critique of Reproductive Reason* (New York: Columbia University Press, 2017).

40 Tibullus 2.2.21–22 and 2.5.89–94, respectively.

41 Tibullus 2.6.27.

42 This position opposes the more accepted scholarly opinion that Tibullus was less engaged with Augustus and his regime than his contemporary elegiac poets. For example, Maltby, *Tibullus: Elegies*, 53–5; Parshia Lee-Stecum, "Tibullus in the First Place," in *The Cambridge Companion to Latin Love Elegy*, ed. Thea Thorsen (Cambridge: Cambridge University Press, 2013), 80. There are, of course, exceptions to this view; for example, Miller, *Subjecting Verses*.

43 See Fulkerson, "*Credula Spes*," 61–2.

44 See Mari Ruti, *The Ethics of Opting Out: Queer Theory's Defiant Subjects* (New York: Columbia University Press, 2017), especially 87–168.

45 Lacan, *The Ethics of Psychoanalysis*, 212.

46 Lacan, *The Ethics of Psychoanalysis*, 120–1.

Works Cited

Deutscher, Penelope. *Foucault's Futures: A Critique of Reproductive Reason*. New York: Columbia University Press, 2017.

Edelman, Lee. *No Future: Queer Theory and the Death Drive*. Durham: Duke University Press, 2004.

Edelman, Lee. *Bad Education: Why Queer Theory Teaches Us Nothing*. Durham: Duke University Press, 2022.

Fulkerson, Laurel. "*Credula Spes*: Tibullan Hope and the Future of Elegy." In *Intratextuality and Latin Literature*, edited by Steven Harrison, Stavros Frangoulidis, and Theodore Papanghelis, 55–66. Berlin: De Gruyter, 2018.

Janan, Micaela. *The Politics of Desire: Propertius IV*. Berkeley: The University of California Press, 2001.

Lacan, Jacques. *The Four Fundamental Concepts of Psychoanalysis: The Seminar of Jacques Lacan, Book XI*. Translated by Alan Sheridan. New York: Norton, 1981.

Lacan, Jacques. *The Ego in Freud's Theory and in the Technique of Psychoanalysis, 1954–1955: The Seminar of Jacques Lacan, Book II*. Translated by Sylvana Tomaselli. New York: Norton, 1991.

Lacan, Jacques. *The Ethics of Psychoanalysis, 1959–1960: The Seminar of Jacques Lacan, Book VII*. Translated by Dennis Porter. New York: Norton, 1992.

Lacan, Jacques. *On Feminine Sexuality, the Limits of Love and Knowledge, 1972–1973: The Seminar of Jacques Lacan, Book XX*. Translated by Bruce Fink. New York: Norton, 1999.

Lacan, Jacques. *Écrits*. Translated by Bruce Fink. New York: Norton, 2006.

Lee-Stecum, Parshia. "Tibullus in the First Place." In *The Cambridge Companion to Latin Love Elegy*, edited by Thea Thorsen, 68–82. Cambridge: Cambridge University Press, 2013.

Lindheim, Sara H. "Queerly Beloved: Nemesis, *Credula Spes*, and Queer Temporalities in Tibullus Book 2." In *The Routledge Handbook of Classics and Queer Theory*, edited by Ella Haselswerdt, Sara H. Lindheim and Kirk Ormand, 153–65. London and New York: Routledge, 2024.

Maltby, Robert. *Tibullus: Elegies. Text, Introduction and Commentary*. Cambridge: Francis Cairns Publications, 2002.

Miller, Paul Allen. *Subjecting Verses: Latin Love Elegy and the Emergence of the Real*. Princeton: Princeton University Press, 2004.

Muñoz, José Esteban. *Cruising Utopia: The Then and There of Queer Futurity*. New York: New York University Press, 2019.

Murgatroyd, Paul. *Tibullus: Elegies II*. Oxford: Oxford University Press, 1994.

Ruti, Mari. *The Ethics of Opting Out: Queer Theory's Defiant Subjects*. New York: Columbia University Press, 2017.

Stafford, Emma. "Tibullus' Nemesis: Divine Retribution and the Poet." In *What's in a Name?: The Significance of Proper Names in Classical Latin Literature*, edited by Joan Booth, Robert Maltby and Frédérique Biville, 33–48. Swansea: Classical Press of Wales, 2006.

Thorsen, Thea. "Introduction: Latin Love Elegy." In *The Cambridge Companion to Latin Love Elegy*, edited by Thea Thorsen, 1–20. Cambridge: Cambridge University Press, 2013.

Wyke, Maria. *The Roman Mistress: Ancient and Modern Representations*. Oxford: Oxford University Press, 2002.

Zimmerman Damer, Erika. "Introduction: Recent Work on Tibullus." *The Classical World* 107, no. 4 (2014): 443–50.

8

Reading beyond the Death Drive

Living Phantasms

Daniel T. O'Hara

During the Christmas to New Year's period, I watched *The Banshees of Inisherin* several times. It is a film starring Colin Farrell and Brendan Gleeson. It is written, directed, and produced by Martin McDonagh. Beautifully shot by Ben Davis, a cinematographer of extraordinary genius, it is set on one of the Aran Islands off the coast of Ireland. The film was meant for me as a treat to myself since I loved "In Bruges." That great film, more ha-ha funny than "Banshees," but still mordant, had brought the same stars and director together for the first time. Given that my wife and granddaughter (who live with us) both had Covid-19 and were taking Paxlovid for free, things could have been worse—a phrase that could be the tagline for this latest film. Definitely, I needed a break. As I thought about it between samplings of the film, it seemed to me the perfect embodiment of the death drive at work.

The Colin Farrell character is a tiresome Irish type of man who prefers speaking to his donkey rather than to his sister and prefers, most of all, hanging out with his lifelong pal, Brendan Gleeson's character. Estragon and Vladimir of Beckett's *Waiting for Godot* immediately came to mind, among other dramatic ancestors, including some minor characters in John Millington Synge's classic Abbey Theater drama *The Playboy of the Western World*, which sparked a famous Dublin riot. As you can see, we Irish are on good terms with the death drive's penchant for destruction and especially self-destruction.

One day Gleeson tells Farrell, as nicely as possible at first, that he no longer wants to be friends with him, and that it is not Farrell's fault, except for his repetitive brainless nattering all day long, but his own, that is, Gleeson's fault. An accomplished fiddler, Gleeson wants at last to complete an original tune of his own and hopes to do so while performing snippets of it while playing at night with the group he belongs to at the one pub on the island. And now all day he spends his time composing in his ramshackle house not far from Farrell's own.

Gleeson warns Farrell (who is now pestering him all the time with all the why's and wherefores and self-exonerations) that he would rather lose the fingers on his left hand than fail to complete his one song. Sure enough, as Farrell insists on seeking reasons for this drastic change in his friend, Gleeson, in two incredible scenes, cuts off his little finger first and throws it against Farrell's door; and then, after Farrell continues to haunt Gleeson with wanting explanations and making amends and acting like nothing is wrong, our fiddler of Inisherin cuts off the remaining fingers of the left hand, including the thumb, which Farrell's beloved donkey eats by chance when Farrell is late getting home one day after Gleeson had thrown these remaining digits against the door again. The donkey has choked to death on the thumb, going the way of all flesh. A victim of this phallus substitute, as Lacan might say.

What follows is that this self-destructive display of aggression gives rise to a full-out war between the two old friends, increasing in intensity each step of the way. In the end, Farrell's sister has taken a job as a librarian on the mainland, despite it being 1923 at the height of the Irish Civil War—periodically the viewer has seen the battles with cannon puffs signaling the worst at a picturesque distance—and the village police officer has been totally exposed as an abuser of his apparently autistic son, who gives up all hope when Farrell's sister sails off, right before which she had made it clear to him that they have no future together, ever.

In short, *The Banshees of Inisherin* displays the death drive in a number of strong ways. While there is an ancient neighbor woman who dresses like the stage representation of a Banshee, we are meant to see the two friends in the end as taking on that role even more than she does: by the film's final scene, with distant cannon puffs across the long bay, they have become the steadfastly opposing, stone-still omens of universal death. If director Martin McDonagh is suffering from a fatal illness, I would not be surprised. Of course, the good news is that my wife and granddaughter have completely recovered, and I have found a memorable way to open my essay, all the while basking in the stark phantasms of my ancestral legacy.

André Green's *The Work of the Negative* is my guide to how best to think now about the Freudian death drive.[1] As we know, the compulsion to repeat is experienced by returning war veterans, so that they return repeatedly in their dreams to the traumatic incident that shocked and scarred them. Their dreams, contrary to Freud's founding psychoanalytic insight in *The Interpretation of Dreams* (1900), do not provide any obvious wish fulfillment but only underscore more and more intently the traumatic experiences that their roles in the First World War caused them to suffer.

The death drive, as originally proposed in Freud's *Beyond the Pleasure Principle* (1920), is inspired by this new clinical phenomenon. Despite Freud's reflection on the famous *Fort/Da* game his grandson invents to master the scenes of interruptions in his mother's presence, throwing a cotton reel over the edge of his crib, saying what sounds like the German word for "gone" (*Fort*) and reeling it back up into his hand, saying what sounds like "there" (*Da*), this playful imitation and reversal of his painful experiences of the absent mother just may indeed master his minor trauma, but nothing similar can be found by Freud in the clinical experience of the war veterans. This admission interrupts the facile application of this *Fort/Da* game to this new clinical experience's devastation of the first elaboration of psychoanalytic theory under the measure of the pleasure principle. No longer will psychic conflict for Freud be divided between the unconscious demand for pleasure at all costs and the self-preservative defenses of the ego or species. Now the psychoanalytic topography will consist of the newly conceived conflict between the life drives (including both erotic and self-preservative tendencies) and the death drive (for which the end of all life is death, each in one's own way). Green argues that this gloomy conclusion actually satisfies what he terms death narcissism, that is, it creates the phantasm of heroic, albeit tragic, defeat.[2]

For Green, the defenses of turning-around-upon-the-self and the reversal into the opposite—primary defenses of the ego, which result from death narcissism, the ego's perverse masochistic love of itself as suffering—exhibit what we can know via clinical experience (and its artistic elaborations) of the death drive. The mother-in-law who always ascends the imaginary cross when anything does not accord with her sense of rightness is a perfect common example. Similarly, what Green names "negative hallucination" appears many times in such experiences of defenses gone wild and crazy.

Negative hallucination is that phenomenon in which the analysand cannot remember not only a particular experience but even the moment in which the blankness of memory is first discovered in analysis by the analyst. The analysand goes double blank, with a blank desertion that is seen in the mind's eye at best as a gap, a void, radiating a pale light, perhaps. Green calls this experience that of blank or white psychosis, a spot of the ego necrotized or mortified, as it were, entirely out of existence in conscious memory, so much so any trace of that layered experience is gone, save in the unconscious mind.[3] Negative transference and other expressions of negation, including the defense of sublimation, are defined by Green as instances of the psyche putting the death drive to work, even as the life drive puts its defenses, especially its self-preservative ego defenses, to work.

We can see what Green means, I think, by briefly analyzing an early poem by Ezra Pound.

"Histrion"
No man hath dared to write this thing as yet,
And yet I know, how that the souls of all men great
At times pass through us,
And we are melted into them, and are not
Save reflexions of their souls.
Thus am I Dante for a space and am
One François Villon, ballad-lord and thief
Or am such holy ones I may not write,
Lest blasphemy be writ against my name;
This for an instant and the flame is gone.
'Tis as in midmost us there glows a sphere
Translucent, molten gold, that is the "I"
And into this some form projects itself:
Christus, or John, or eke the Florentine;
And as the clear space is not if a form's
Imposed thereon,
So cease we from all being for the time,
And these, the Masters of the Soul, live on.[4]

"Histrion" first appears in Pound's second volume of poems, *A Quinzaine for This Yule* (1908). We should probably understand it easiest if we read the last stanza first. For it envisions the Soul as "a sphere/Translucent, molten gold."[5] The human "I" is a round glowing empty container into which "some form projects itself." This form may be Dante, "Villon, Christus, or John, or . . . the Florentine,"[6] presumably, this is Dante again. The cost of what Keats calls such negative capability of being open to one or another form's self-projection is that human beings, especially poets, "cease . . . from all being for the time"[7] of this mutual melting. This momentary "little death" results in the rebirth of all great figures from human history, especially those souls that were the most creative, imaginative, and filled with genius. "This for the instant and the flame is gone."[8]

Of course, this vision is that of "Histrion," which in Greek means actor. Pound, a disciple of Browning and with an embrace of tradition as wide as Whitman's—think the dramatic monologues written on double espressos all day long while running through the streets of London—is here as in the wings of the stage, announcing to whoever may be in the audience that he is the poetic medium of world history. If we remember *The Cantos* to come, this fits as a self-prophecy, perhaps, all too well. His own Soul is a spherical but glowing, empty vessel, filled repeatedly by molten golden light, inseminated by one Form, as he says, after another by the Masters of the Soul, not surprisingly, given the time, all males.

Here we have what in the psychoanalytic clinic could be seen as the bits and pieces of psychosis that the combination of Freud (death drive and the economy of investment), Klein (the good/bad object of the mother), Lacan (foreclosure), Winnicott (transitional objects and playing with reality), and Bion (linking and de-linking, binding, and unbinding), which Green assembles to aid him in his work of the negative. It would surely delight him. It would also be hard to distinguish the gleeful tone and slightly archaic diction deployed here; is it early Pound or Green spoofing us all? The Imagist, Vorticist, Modernist extraordinaire is still five years off for Pound. What Green could pick out is that negative hallucination of the Soul, the Dead Mother container like the spherical crystal ball of the occult mystic, the passive positioning of the speaker, whose life is being led not by him but by phantasms of past lives of genius, poetic fathers that Histrion enjoys giving new life to via the process of his self-abnegating creative work. The death drive is sublimated into this mad lyric vision of psychic masochism in imaginary overdrive.

Green calls such a vision when arising in the clinic, that is, in the transference/countertransference relationship of free associative analysis between analysand and analyst, "the dead mother." In "Histrion," she is reduced to the figure, the phantasm, of the empty but repeatedly lit-up sphere. For Green, she is the ultimate containment figure, the bad enough mother whose original maternal care had been at least good enough and perhaps even better, but for some contingency of life—loss of another child, abandonment by the father—turns sour on childcare and living children and so instills depression into the new child. The dead mother is the Muse of Death-in-Life that Green sees as the hardly Beatrice guide to every modern would-be Dante. What the analyst, after winning the analysand's at least minimal cooperation, must do is "the work of the negative," a Hegelian phrase Green discusses at length in his book of this title.[9]

> The work of the negative . . . will concern itself with the relation to the object caught in the cross-fire of the destructive drives . . . and the life or love drives. The work of the negative thus comes down to one question: how, faced with the destruction which threatens everything, can a way be found for desire to live and love? And reciprocally, how should we interpret the results of the work of the negative which inhabits this fundamental conflict, i.e. the dilemma which we are caught in, between the anvil of absolute satisfaction, to which omnipotence and masochism bear witness, and the hammer of renunciation, for which sublimation is a possible outcome? Beyond this conflict, looms detachment, a step towards the [absolute] disinvestment which is supposed to free one from all dependence on anyone or anything, so as to be able to encounter oneself at the price of murdering the other person.[10]

And, given today's world of many travesties of the master-slave dialectic, we know Green must silently add to himself, "and the price of murdering oneself."

And to round off, for now, this reading of Pound, I cite a famous final admission in fragmentary form from *Canto 116*, summing up the failure of his fifty-year-plus effort to compose a truly modern epic:

> I have brought the great ball of crystal;
> who can lift it?
> Can you enter the great acorn of light?
> But the beauty is not the madness
> Tho' my errors and wrecks live about me.
> And I am not a demigod,
> I cannot make it cohere.
> If love be not in the house there is nothing[11]

Near the last scene in *The Banshees of Inisherin*, we see the policeman's abused autistic son, in his late teens, floating face-up in the salt pond between Gleeson's and Farrell's makeshift cabins, the echoes of the relentless waters pressing in on our ears.

A return to *Beyond the Pleasure Principle*'s most famous passages, about Freud's grandson inventing his "*Fort/Da*" game of symbolizing the absence and return of the mother, is at last sharply pertinent. For the game has a less specific reference than Sophia, Freud's daughter, her mother Martha's favorite. Sophia died on January 20, 1920, from complications of the rabid, so-called Spanish flu epidemic, and *Beyond the Pleasure Principle* was published later in 1920. There remains a dispute about whether Freud composed this massively self-revising work directly in the baleful event's light.

Naturally, Freud would identify with his grandson in the connection of any lost love object. But what I find even more relevant is that the game, "an intellectual acquisition," as Freud suggests, "a great cultural achievement," as he in fact spells out, means that the boy has acquired not just a rudimentary sense of words, of language, but that he has acquired the power of symbolization. Such power is not merely a simple one-to-one allegory, because the game of throwing a spool tied with string into his curtained-off cot in the parents' room and then retrieving it from where he stands beside it, making sounds remarkably like the German words for "gone" (*Fort*) and "There" (*Da*), is potentially applicable to any and all who can envision themselves in the position of the one who goes away (and may return or not), the one who is left there, at first bereft, and that same one who then invents and plays the game and/or observes its imaginary results.[12]

This grandson is ultimately put by his own creation into the positions of mourner, lost one, and the mortal god of the entire show. Grandpop Freud is the analytic observer, so he can identify with the occupant of any position, or perhaps with all in wild positional montage. As we know from what follows in *Beyond the Pleasure Principle*, however, Freud's theoretical aim is to revise his first topography of Pre-conscious, Conscious, and Unconscious into Super-ego, Ego, and Id. But for us on this occasion, we need only recognize that not only does repetition-compulsion express the death drive, but so too does sublimation in its deployment of diversion of the drives and their reembodiment in symbolic objects, a matter of binding and unbinding, of investment and disinvestment that puts the psyche at the service of life and death drives alike. This child's play makes the investment/disinvestment and binding/unbinding of sexual aims from the absent object now rebind with the emerging ego. Such psychic interplay gives rise to the ego ideal of the super-ego once it fully forms, thanks to sublimation's diversion and redirection of the basic drives from radical conflict to graduated semi-satisfaction, a new cultural/civilizational achievement and object. All such psychic objects—complexly metapsychological or simply speculative—are art, of course, not-so-pure imaginative fabrication, what I see as living phantasms. As Green's earlier discussion suggests, they fit best in his sublimely bizarre category of "negative hallucination."

Here is how Green says this psychic defense works. There is a severely denied unconscious memory and an intolerable, provoking perception. As they struggle, they marshal both the sexual drive energy to release the wishful memory trace and the death drive energy to focus attention upon the perception. As the perception loses ground, it whitens out, Green says, leaving the space of the perception to be filled by the upwelling dream-like memory. So, rather than a day dream, an abolished perception and a newly activated phantasm produce the negative hallucination. "The unbearable perception is 'irreconcilable' (to us an old expression of Freud's) with the unconscious representation and, rather than the latter disappearing, it is the perception which is invalidated. The space which has been liberated by the negative hallucination is occupied, through projection, by the unconscious representation in a form which cannot easily be defined."[13]

This is because the unconscious representation takes on "the attributes of perception," which incorporates an effect "that 'whitens' whatever presents itself to the mind."[14] For Green, this defensive process is what he claims "Freud qualifies as 'pulling away' from what is perceived. Between external reality which presses against internal reality, and internal reality which refuses to give way, the psychical apparatus has decided in favour of the latter, to the point of giving it credence accorded to perceptions, as if the latter had done away with censorship."[15] Green concludes this dense passage in this way: "Thus negative hallucination is the process by which the ego can break off or interrupt its relations to reality."[16] This process, then, is "carried out thanks to a withdrawal of investment, or in more extreme circumstances by a disinvestment."[17] Phantasms are perceived as external objects as they play host to otherwise unconscious memories of experience and earlier wish-fulfillment dream images. Under the rule of negative hallucination, blank-faced perceptions haunt the mind as much, if not more than repressed fantasies. If we return to Pound's "Histrion," that so casually put line, "This for an instant, and the flame is gone," may be now taken more like a threat than a promise.

We can see Green himself come to a similar conclusion in his extended analysis of Gerard De Nerval's *Aurelia* (1855), his version of Dante's *La Vita Nuova*, later in *The Work of the Negative*. *Aurelia* is the two-part work published in different issues of the *Revue de Paris*, in between which Nerval commits suicide, hanging himself after many years of a repeating cycle of treatment for madness— institutionalization, release, and more episodes of a nomadic, even homeless life. "Aurelia" tells the story of the narrator's quest, based on Nerval's, to come to terms with both the loss of his own mother and that of his original beloved, who is presented in the mold of Dante's Beatrice or Petrarch's Laura. This idealized muse of visionary romance (based on the actress Jenny Colon) becomes the expression, one of several in this semi-autobiographical narrative, that stands in for the Eternal Feminine of Goethe's *Faust*, Goddess Isis, and other ancient or occult figures including the Gnostic Sophia.

The following passage from *Aurelia* inspires Green, as we shall see:

> I thought I had ended up in some vast charnel house where the history of the world was scrawled in blood [on my walls]. The giant body of a woman stood painted before my eyes, except that she had been hacked apart as if by a sabre; on the other walls, more women of various races, their bodies growing ever more pronounced, loomed forth in a bloody tangle of limbs and heads, extending from empresses and queens down to the humblest of peasants. The history of every crime was written here, and it was enough to direct one's gaze to a given place in order to see some tragic scene taking shape. This, I said to myself, is what happens when power is bestowed upon men. Bit by bit, they have destroyed the archetype of beauty and cut it up into a thousand pieces, progressively sapping the races of mankind of their strength and perfection. . . . And in fact, on a thread of shadow slanting through the latticed door I saw the descending generations of future races.[18]

Nerval was born in Germany in 1808 as Gerard Labrunie to a father who was an army doctor and a young mother who accompanied him. She died when Nerval was two and a half years old. Growing up with relatives in the Valois, Nerval eventually changed his name, spending his life trying to come to terms with his conflicted emotions over what Green has named "the dead mother complex," in which longing, loss, rage, and narcissistic masochism afflict the person so circumstanced. The latter is the assumption of superiority based upon the strength and quality of one's suffering. Only a great one would suffer so.

Based on Green's placement of sublimation within the category of the negative—along with disavowal or foreclosure, negation, repression, and negative hallucination—he draws the following conclusions from his reading of *Aurelia*, Nerval's visionary romance of his own madness:

> [Nothing] permits us to believe that [sublimation's diversion and redirection of psychic energies are] sufficient to protect the subject from psychical catastrophes. . . . [T]he setting-up of a good internal object was a prerequisite for establishing the [transitional] intermediate area of experience. In fact, the transitional field functions as a formation [in lieu of a transitional object], affected by influences from both the inside and the outside, trying to anchor the ego by interesting it in this kind of production so as to give the deployment of illusion some moorings which can serve as an obstacle and filter against the most impaired defenses. Thus, from the point of view of sublimation, Nerval' s endeavor [in "Aurelia"] cannot be judged either in terms of failure or in terms of success with respect to his conflictual psychical organization [centered by "the dead mother"]. It has simply been a means of waiting and hoping, while trying to transform dream into delusion, as if to exorcise the pain which it brought with it; and delusion into dream, as if he hoped that, thanks to this appropriation, he would make contact again with himself. It is for us, to whom this sublimation is offered, that Aurelia can act as a love object, furthered by the activity of the objectalising function.[19]

Green goes further, much further, in saying then: "Moreover, the text puts us in a privileged position to recognize in it the movements of a work of the negative in terms of the mechanisms we have already analyzed."[20] Writing then, and through or in writing, "there are sufficiently convincing traces of the resumption of a work of the negative which succeeds in finding its coherence in and through writing."[21]

Green means that Nerval's writing in *Aurelia* is as much the reader's transitional love object as it is the author's. The text itself mothers its readers, who live out in their reading experiences, personal and professional, its previously absent life. The dead mother lives, no matter what has happened to Nerval or will happen to his readers, living out his phantasms:

> Writing has the effect, by constructing its own space, of creating its object: the work. More than any other, it requires that we emphasize the transitional status of such a creation. It is impossible to determine a criterion in it which enables to decide whether it refers to an existing reality—or one which has really existed—or whether the reality in question is a psychical reality drawn exclusively from the author's inner world without his losing control over it.[22]

This conclusion allows Green to add a supplemental corollary that transforms the literary work into a love object of the reader's as well. "[Nerval] has managed to make the work [as such] sufficient unto itself so that the question of its relation to reality does not arise."[23] Finally, Green goes even further in his conclusions by asserting the following:

> The beauty of the work lies not only in the superb use of language and an unflinching honesty which renounces all concessions to decorum, but also in the stamp which marks the forehead of someone who, having made a descent into hell, managed to come back amongst us for a while, simply to converse with us about it before continuing on his lonely way. Thus, the idea that artistic creation is motivated by the desire for reparation and counters the destructiveness of the psychotic process is illustrated here.[24]

The author (in this case, Nerval) creates via his work of the negative an imaginative textual object. It becomes the reader's living phantasm. Nerval can potentially become so for himself. Should he be capable and willing to recognize all of this potentiality, he can replace the dead mother complex within himself with revisionary love. In this way, Green would show how the work of the negative harnesses the life and death drives in the service of the progress of love.

Nerval had his version of such a perspective: "None the less, it seemed to me that [the crescent moon] was the sanctuary of my sister souls, and I saw it populated by wistful shades, destined one day [when full] to be reborn on earth."[25] Of course, we know that Nerval lost this vision in the end, hanging himself.

I want to conclude on a different note by presenting the final scene of Saul Bellow's last novel of ideas and personality, *Ravelstein* (2000). Abe Ravelstein is closely based on Allan Bloom, whose 1987 unlikely bestseller *The Closing of the American Mind* made him suddenly rich enough to indulge every desire for fine clothes and fancy dishes and so much more. Abe is a larger-than-life intellectual and Jewish Falstaff, exploiting the culture wars of the time—in fact, leading the battles of the Neo-Conservatives against the Neo-Liberals—even as his HIV status unfolds. Abe is both in an intimate loving relationship with a younger Chinese-American man and enjoys to the hilt the Paris street boys. While espousing Platonic Eros, he is as much an Alcibiades grown old. So passionate is Abe that when he handles things, even before getting sick, his hands shake with the powerful energies he must manage in his large frame. Standing, as we learn, 6 feet 6 inches tall, Abe's huge bald head becomes a talisman of strength, reminiscent for me of Pound's "Histrion."

The narrator, based on Bellow, is a writer but of lesser achievement, who we only know as "Chick," as in "boychick," the Yiddish slang diminutive for a callow if promising young man. Ironically, "Chick" is only somewhat younger than his best friend "Abe." The story of this roman à clef and novel of ideas is that as the narrator retells the final days of Abe, Chick flashes back to familiar and new scenes of Abe and presents progressively more chilling scenes of his own near-final days. Chick's horrific hallucinations after Abe's memorial service, as he suffers from food poisoning from a red-snapper dinner with Janis on their vacation in St. Martin, deserve their own essay. While the novel is not broken into chapters, it is divided into three large parts, not quite like Gaul. In the first, we see Abe in all his glory and wonder why Chick is even named. In the second, as Chick is left by his latest wife Vela for a stage Don Juan and he falls in love with Rosamund, Chick and his fate take over most of the novel's attention. The third part of *Ravelstein* has the reader dividing attention between Abe and Chick's fates, even though we already know the former is dead and the latter lives, thanks to his new wife's loving care. The reader even enjoys the spectacle of a new birth, as Chick at eighty-four and Janis a half-century younger have a new baby before the novel ends. What keeps this fictionalized memoir from simple sentimentality is that Bellow was accused of "outing" Bloom, whose role as the intellectual leader of the Reagan/Bush era cultural conservatives suffers now from hypocrisy on a grand scale—in America, you cannot have your Socratic gadfly die from the gay plague. And Bellow, as Chick does in the narrative, repeatedly claims Abe/Allan had insisted that he write him up, warts and all.[26]

The final scene in the novel consists of a last flashback before Ravelstein gets too sick to go out and Chick has succumbed (or submitted?) to his final wife's saintly care. For me, it points to an extravagant vision of what the writer, indeed any artist, truly falls for, forever:

> Ravelstein, dressing to go out, is talking to me, and I go back and forth with him while trying to hear what he is saying. The music is pouring from his hi-fi—the many planes of his bare, bald head go before me in the corridor between his living room and his monumental master bedroom. He stops before his pier-glass—no wall of mirrors here—and puts in the heavy gold cufflinks, buttons up the Jermyn Street Kisser & Asser striped shirt—American Trustworthy laundry-and-cleaners deliver his shirts puffed out with tissue paper. He winds up his tie lifting the collar that crackles with starch. He makes a luxurious knot. The unsteady fingers, long, ill-coordinated, nervous to the point of decadence, make a double lap. Ravelstein likes a big tie-knot—after all, he is a large man. Then he sits down on the beautifully cured fleeces of his bed and puts on the Poulsen and Skone tan Wellington boots. His left foot is several sizes smaller than the right but there is no limp. He smokes, of course, he is always smoking, and tilts the head away from the smoke while he knots and pulls the knot into place. The cast and orchestra are pouring out the *Italian Maiden in Algiers*. This is dressing music, accessory or mood music, but Ravelstein takes a Nietzschean view, favorable to comedy and bandstands. Better Bizet and *Carmen* than Wagner and the *Ring*. . . .
>
> He loses himself in sublime music, a music in which ideas are dissolved, reflecting these ideas in the form of feeling. He carries them down into the street with him. There's an early snow on the tall shrubs, the same shrubs filled with a huge flock of parrots—the ones that escaped from cages and now build their nest sacks in the back alleys. They are feeding on the red berries. Ravelstein looks at me, laughing with pleasure and astonishment, gesturing because he can't be heard in all the bird-noise.
>
> You don't easily give up a creature like Ravelstein to death.[27]

Whichever it be—"Banshees," "Histrion," *Aurelia*, Freud, Green, or Ravelstein—Bellow/Chick is right on target here.

Notes

1 André Green, *The Work of the Negative*, trans. Andrew Weller (London and New York: Free Association Books, 1999). Two invaluable books of commentary on Green are Gregorio Kohan, ed., *The Dead Mother: The Work of André Green* (London and New York: Routledge, 1999) and Rossella Valdre, *Psychoanalytic Reflections on the Freudian Death Drive* (London and New York: Routledge, 2019).
2 See André Green, *Life Narcissism, Death Narcissism*, trans. Andrew Weller (London: Free Association Books, 2001).
3 See Rossella Valdre, *On Sublimation: A Path to the Destiny of Desire, Theory, and Treatment* (London and New York: Routledge, 2014).
4 Ezra Pound, *A Quinzaine for This Yule* (London: Pollock and Co., 1908), 26.
5 Pound, *A Quinzaine for This Yule*, 26.
6 Pound, *A Quinzaine for This Yule*, 26.
7 Pound, *A Quinzaine for This Yule*, 26.
8 Pound, *A Quinzaine for This Yule*, 26.
9 See Green, *The Work of the Negative*, 1–49.
10 Green, *The Work of the Negative*, 185.
11 Ezra Pound, *The Cantos of Ezra Pound* (New York: New Directions, 1995), 816.
12 Salman Akhtar and Mary Kay O'Neil, eds., *On Freud's "Beyond the Pleasure Principle"* (London and New York: Karnak Books, 2011), 21.
13 Green, *The Work of the Negative*, 171.
14 Green, *The Work of the Negative*, 171.
15 Green, *The Work of the Negative*, 171.
16 Green, *The Work of the Negative*, 171.
17 Green, *The Work of the Negative*, 171.
18 Gerard De Nerval, *Selected Writings*, trans. Richard Sieburth (London: Penguin Books, 1999), 310.
19 Green, *The Work of the Negative*, 250.
20 Green, *The Work of the Negative*, 250.
21 Green, *The Work of the Negative*, 250.
22 Green, *The Work of the Negative*, 250.
23 Green, *The Work of the Negative*, 250.
24 Green, *The Work of the Negative*, 251.
25 Green, *The Work of the Negative*, 308.
26 See Saul Bellow, *Ravelstein* (New York: Viking/Penguin, 2000). A helpful recent study is Leah Garrett, "The Late Bellow: *Ravelstein* and the Novel of Ideas," in *The Cambridge Companion to Saul Bellow*, ed. Victoria Aarons (Cambridge and New York: Cambridge University Press, 2017), 171–82.
27 Bellow, *Ravelstein*, 231–3.

Works Cited

Akhtar, Salman, and Mary Kay O'Neil, eds. *On Freud's "Beyond the Pleasure Principle."* London and New York: Karnak Books, 2011.

Bellow, Saul. *Ravelstein*. New York: Viking/Penguin, 2000.

De Nerval, Gerard. *Selected Writings*. Translated by Richard Sieburth. London: Penguin Books, 1999.

Garrett, Leah. "The Late Bellow: *Ravelstein* and the Novel of Ideas." In *The Cambridge Companion to Saul Bellow*, edited by Victoria Aarons, 171–82. Cambridge and New York: Cambridge University Press, 2017.

Green, Andre. *The Work of the Negative*. Translated by Andrew Weller. London and New York: Free Association Books, 1999.

Green, André. *Life Narcissism, Death Narcissism*. Translated by Andrew Weller. London: Free Association Books, 2001.

Kohan, Gregorio, ed. *The Dead Mother: The Work of Andre Green*. London and New York: Routledge, 1999.

Pound, Ezra. *A Quinzaine for This Yule*. London: Pollock and Co., 1908.

Pound, Ezra. *The Cantos of Ezra Pound* (1925). New York: New Directions, 1995.

Valdre, Rossella. *On Sublimation: A Path to the Destiny of Desire, Theory, and Treatment*. London and New York: Routledge, 2014.

Valdre, Rossella. *Psychoanalytic Reflections on the Freudian Death Drive*. London and New York: Routledge, 2019.

9

Death—Automation—Language

Adriana Michele Campos Johnson

For my mother, with a shattered heart.

In grappling with the death drive, Freud engages in what he calls "speculation, often far-fetched speculation."[1] "Let us picture," he says, "a living organism in its most simplified possible form as an undifferentiated vesicle of a substance that is susceptible to stimulation."[2] This vesicle, a "little fragment of living substance,"[3] is already halfway to the "earlier state of things"[4] toward which the conservative instincts pull life back, as if by "daemonic power,"[5] already halfway on the circuitous road of return toward the "inanimate things [that] existed before living ones."[6] Its outermost surface, for example, is imagined as ceasing "to have the structure proper to living matter, [it] becomes to some degree inorganic and thenceforward functions as a special envelope or membrane resistant to stimuli."[7] Freud stages here a micro literary scene, an example to ground and give form to his "metapsychological" speculations. But it is the wrong form if we believe Catherine Malabou. Freud, she says, does not ultimately "succeed in characterizing the proper—temporal—form of the death drive."[8] His attempts to figure the imbrication of death and life, an intermediary state or simultaneity of life and death as seen in this scene, remain partial and limited, always subordinated to life, she says, and thus bound to Eros.[9] She is thinking more specifically of his location of the death instinct in sadism, a literary derivation, but the inorganic envelope in the scene cited above is also there in function of the need to protect the vesicle from the overpowering stimulation that would kill it outright.[10] There is no autonomous form of the death drive, one that is not bound to sexuality/life/love and so, "[w]ithout phenomena or representatives," the death drive "remains essentially unenvisagable."[11] The compulsion to repeat, the tendency to inertia, the drive to return to or restore a previous inanimate existence all indicate processes of disaggregation of form, much like elastic material returns to its initial form and loses the memory of the deformations it has undergone.[12] What Freud fails to imagine, she argues, is the *form-giving* capacity of destruction, a phenomenon that becomes clear in the injury and damage wrought by brain lesions, wounds unlike the cases of trauma considered by Freud. Malabou starts from the ontology of the accident[13] and proposes the negative plasticity that makes its appearance in these new wounded as figuring the death drive: "The deserted identities of cerebrality, living figures of death, emerge precisely as representatives of the tendency to annihilation and destruction that psychoanalysis has always failed to bring to light."[14]

I take my cue from Malabou in this chapter to probe the intersection of various figurations of the death drive—points of overlap, splitting, abutment, diversion—as well as the form of the difficulties in doing so. I shuttle between a poetics grounding theoretical texts and the theorization that drives fiction, trying to feel for the potential plasticity amid the stickiness of form. On the one hand, Jonathan Beller's *The Message is Murder: Substrates of Computational Capital* gives us a poetics of the deadening of life and the concomitant spread of the inorganic, inanimate structures that are the "life of nonlife" that is capitalism. On the other hand, China Mieville's sci-fi novel *Embassytown* turns on a poetics of the breakdown, the cut, as well as the unexpected plasticity and becoming life of infrastructure. Both texts—one theoretical, one fictional—center on language and its associated processes, the infrastructure of messages, communication, information, but also fabulation.[15] Both figure language as the medium of a death drive. How can we read their speculative propositions alongside Malabou's contention that it is plasticity—after writing—that should function as the new motor scheme of our times? What might plasticity bring to bear upon the contemporary transformations and wounds we live-die through? What is living and what is dead in language? Amid automaticity and abstraction, what possibilities are there for plasticity—modes of change that are not transcendental but are nonetheless change? Whether it has no future is another question, one bound, as I understand it, to the entanglement of the graphic and structures of temporality.

One

The fable on language that is China Mieville's *Embassytown* is set in something like a colonial outpost on a planet on the edge of known/unknown space. The alien hosts of the planet, the Ariekei, are unusual in the diegetic world of the novel for speaking not a language but rather Language (with a capital L). There are several peculiarities to Language. The first is that it is double-voiced. The Ariekei (or Hosts) have two mouths and can only hear, or process as Language, that which is spoken to them with two voices, simultaneously, by a single mind—or what is perceived as a single mind. In the world of the novel, this presents years of incommunication until humans breed Ambassadors in the form of twinned clones, doppels, who are interconnected and learn to simultaneously perform the double-voiced language, simulating enough of a shared mind that Hosts can understand. Until then—after then—even the exact reproduction of the sounds by one person (or by machines) is simply "empty barks"[16] to Hosts: humans who are not Ambassadors are perceived by the Ariekei as "speechless amputated half-things"[17] or simply as "meat belongings of Ambassadors."[18] The second peculiarity is that, for the Ariekei, Language is the manifestation of thought itself, described at one point like dropping stones from their mouths: it is not representational and does not signify. A consequence of this—the third peculiarity—is that every utterance is necessarily true in Language. Ariekei cannot say things that are false; they cannot lie just as—as it were—the humans cannot consciously think what is unthought. There is also no polysemy, no what-if, when Hosts speak. They are, however, able to grasp when Ambassadors lie in their language (saying "this door is blue" when it is not). This giddying impossible intoxicates the Ariekei, making them lie-drunk. In the wake of this possibility, some institute a Festival of Lies, striving to *almost* utter untruths as much as they are able. But the plot of the novel follows the falling apart of the world of Embassytown when a new Ambassador pair (who are not cloned twins) arrives on the planet and speaks: while the new pair are close enough to speak Language they are not quite sufficiently enmeshed: when they speak, therefore, Language sounds broken or fractured to the Ariekei. A unity that is both there and not there. Like a hallucination.

The Ariekei call these voicings the god-drug (using something like a compound expression). They mainline this contradiction, and addiction spreads in pandemic fashion through their world. The infection is textually manifest above all through the quasi-living infrastructures that constitute Ariekei cities: they have herds of houses, factories that graze, bridges that mature from cells in order to link up city regions, and stations that "twitch" their antennas. Under the spell of the addiction, the walls sweat, the houses grow expectant ears, the architecture quivers gluttonously, and medical tech goes feral, all shaking in withdrawal when the god-drug isn't heard. Bred to be immortal, the biorigging begins to break down and die.

The Ariekei are enormous and strong, and the human inhabitants of the small colonial outpost are almost utterly dependent on them, among other things, for biorigging that allows them to breathe. But the god-drug renders the alien hosts helpless, subject to a "walking death." A faction of Ariekei becomes so desperate at this subjection that they rip out their fanwings, the organs with which they hear, apparently condemning themselves to live thus without language, trapped in soundless solipsism. These languageless Ariekei become a destructive horde, "an unsociety of psychopaths,"[19] seeking to similarly mutilate (castrate) their afflicted brethren by ripping off *their* fanwings, effectively muting, blinding, and deafening those that manage to survive the trauma. The enraged horde also attacks the infrastructure and the humans, striving to wipe out Embassytown. The humans call them "the Surdae" (the deaf), a term that is then said to be *misprisioned* into "the Absurd."

Mieville presents us with a world in the throes of a doubled death drive occasioned by the breakdown of a language that is not really a language, a doubling which to some extent maps onto what Malabou described as two seemingly contradictory characteristics of Freud's death drive: on the one hand, the expression of inertia or elasticity (the restoration of an earlier inanimate state), and on the other the manifestation of aggression or destruction (generally toward objects in the external world). On the one hand, the Ariekei drugged by the fracture in Language: zombie-like they are passive, disengaged, inert, compelled only to repeat, over and over, the intoxication they experience under the impossible voicing of Language. On the other hand, against this mindlessness, the self-mutilation of the Surd. The attempt perhaps to acquire immunity against this fracture through its transposition onto their own body, leads to a new wounded, one that is both deaf and absurd after the cut: a willed languagelessness and drive to destruction, but one that is not beyond love or hatred.

Two

Like so many books of philosophy or theory, Jonathan Beller's *The Message is Murder: Substrates of Computational Capital* is assembled on the back of a poetics. Beller generally updates Marx's gothic imaginary for a sci-fi one, but one scene that is key to his title is taken from Borges's "The Garden of Forking Paths," where the narrator Yu Tsun kills a person named Stephen Albert simply in order to communicate to German intelligence that the English town *Albert* needs to be bombed. Thus: "The treatment of Albert, killed for the accident of his name with the express aim of targeting a military strike, concisely demonstrates that the medium is the message and the message is murder."[20] Beller's book tracks this *becoming information* of life in the generalized warlike situation that is the advance of capitalism. The drive behind this process—as his title indicates—is more properly a murderous one since capitalism is already inanimate, machine-like: "the very image of nonbeing, the very life of nonlife, the spitting image of death."[21]

In Beller's story, the transmitted message stands in for media writ large. Underpinning his narrative is the inexorable transformation of language (communication) through machinic prostheses: key moments are the printing press, cinema (what he calls visual infrastructures for attentional production), and current media forms organized through computation, data, digitization, and information. Insofar as such media converge today with the tech industry, Beller follows Marx's analysis of the machinery of industrial capitalism as both (1) dead labor (the product of previous labor) soaking up living labor and (2) acquiring a momentum of its own, becoming an automaton: "a lifeless mechanism which is independent of workers, who are incorporated into it as its living appendages."[22] Media-machines therefore function according to an extractivist logic, absorbing our visual, linguistic, and cognitive capacities only to then reformat and automate them, a metabolic process that transforms "bloodlife" (borrowing from Mieville) into automated life. In the process, communicative and representational forms are reduced and instrumentalized: "From the emergence of print as an economic exploit forward, the denaturing of 'natural' language into code was a long time coming."[23] Such capacities are also, finally, put to work for capital: rather than mediating, therefore, the media serve primarily as instruments of production.[24] The reframing of intellectual and cognitive capacities under the matrix of production extends the figure of the "general intellect," which Marx employed to index machines and railroads as the "alienated output of socialized human knowledge and collective labor," "organs of the human brain, created by the human hand; the power of knowledge, objectified." [25] Like a collectively generated exoskeleton, once out there, railroads and machines figured as forms of transindividual connectivity. If Beller stresses that today's social-media is to be written with a hyphen, it is because "social" is not just an adjective qualifying some media. Instead, a new compound is formed by technologies that seek to effectively become the very infrastructure of social articulations and transindividual communication for the purpose of value extraction and production. Much like the withdrawal from perception of railroad tracks, once laid down, this infrastructure functions off-screen: there is an "unthought and largely unthinkable history of computational praxis that materially underpins current thought, knowledge and computation,"[26] and that Beller will tag as the "computational unconscious." Beller's text ceaselessly narrates, therefore, the colonization of language, communication, and thought by semiotics, informatic, and computation.[27] If language, turned into a medium for the master-code of the capital-automaton, "surrenders its powers of fabulation,"[28] Beller's theorizing strives to "outmaneuver the programmed logistics of the sign." "What type of poetry can disrupt all that?" he wonders.[29] Sentences like the following one, which condense and coordinate multiple elements of a plot that might very well produce a shock of (dys)recognition worthy of most sci-fi, need to be read as partial responses to that question: "Utterance, positioned as standing reserve by ambient computation, . . . scripted in advance, generative like much of metabolism itself of swathes of data and meta-data for capture, is largely programmed for capitalist harvest."[30]

Before proceeding, it is important to note that there is not one but two forms of killing taking place in Beller's account. First, as noted so far, to the extent that information is "a dialectical advance of the calculus of the value-form," it also advances the becoming-abstract of the life-world. Abstraction kills in general as it de-qualifies everything that comes into its purview, removing, for example, a chicken from its web of living connections and rendering it a number, advancing what we might call death #1, the "wholesale production of nonbeing."[31] To return to the story, the transmission of critical data in the word "Albert" overcodes and overrides whatever living body may be attached to the name. Second, however, crucial to Beller's argument is the fact that capitalism (and the media that is its current medium) distributes death differentially: our current digital culture, digital culture 2, he argues, had earlier iterations in slavery, plantations, colonialism, and industrial capitalism (think of the statistical calculations involved in slave-holding ships). Beller links what Ruth Gilmore famously calls the "group-differentiated vulnerability to premature death" to the calculus of computational capital (where one sees the automation rather than abatement of racism). Thus, the murderous system is "built atop a deadly disavowal and oftentimes denial of black life and the life of numerous (and fungible) others."[32] So contemporary media kills both because it extracts life, generating out of the sedimentation of dead labor the machinery of fixed capital, the computational unconscious, but also because it distributes death differentially (death #2). Either way, there is no way out: we are all possessed and dispossessed in the process, and when not killed, rendered zombie by the machines.

Beller briefly cites an image from another China Mieville novel, *Perdido Street Station*, as an example of the inter-facialization of power in ghoulish forms, the "splicing of machines and brains into the same circuit."[33] He is reminded, he says early in his book, of "the AI prosthetic composed of an old white man/corpse with a cable plugged into his open skull."[34] The old white man/corpse in question is the organic interface of an enormous construct, a vast automated skeleton composed of cast-off pieces and stolen engines, said to be born of random power, virus, and chance, "powered without the intervention of human design" and "without a cerebellum."[35] As Beller would have it, the self-generated machine intellect claims that "I am the data bank" and that "its sustenance is information";[36] media forms constitute the infrastructure through which it gathers information: "I have spread my senses. My cables grow longer and reach further. I receive information from cameras fixed around the dump. My cables connect to them now like disembodied nerves."[37] What Beller calls the "spectral I of information,"[38] the subject as a grammatical function generated by the movement of the signifying chain, is embodied through fiction in the anthropoid construct giant. However, its spectrality is carried forward in the curious detail that it cannot synthesize its own voice but must borrow one in order to intercede with what it calls *bloodlife*. Hence the need for the brainless corpse, deployed like a flesh puppet for its quivering, trembling, hissing voice. While Borges's story usefully stages a form of the subsumption of life into data transmission, it is the undead puppet and its relationship to the machine intellect that exemplifies the more material cyborg imaginary that suffuses Beller's argument. It also gives shape to the subordination of "the human" under what Beller describes as "the new and astonishing agency of financialized intelligent machines."[39] While the need to transmit information oriented the plot in Borges's story, agency there was still located in human form. But it is capital and its machinations that occupy the place of vitality and agency in Beller's work: our planet and bodies play host "to the virulent, material intelligence of computational capital."[40] Meanwhile vectors of a deadening spread and burrow into "the embattled AI that is us."[41] Devoid of its own life, Mieville's avatar, nude and horrifically thin, its skin slowly submitting to gangrene, is deployed as a figure for Beller's argument that "man" or "humanity" was ever just a ruse or an icon, "the subjective presentation of the universal value-form of capital" at a particular historical junction, at one time a useful technology for the operating system of racial capitalism, but now just an obsolescent platform. The cable running into the corpse's open skull figures the extension of digital operations into what used to be called "the self"[42] (now undead) so that human behaviors are revealed to be just a computational effect, "a program of sorts . . . churning in the background, iterating complexity along rule-bound lines."[43] Beller continues the scene: "Those of us who perceive that vital aspects of our extended being are enslaved, othered, black, see the master, whether embodied, machinic, affective, spatial, proprietary, algorithmic or whatever, as an alien presence, a body-snatcher. We strain ourselves to warn each other, 'Get out!'"[44]

The flesh puppet is, however, only a singular instance in *Perdido Street Station*, one among a multiplicity of forms that populate a novel. Indeed, the novel's title centers it precisely on the intersection of five train lines at the heart of a city teeming with competing but partial projects of power. Both *Embassytown* and *Perdido Street Station* take place in a sci-fi version of a colonial contact zone traversed by alterity. While the construct in *Perdido Street Station* is worshipped as a God-machine by some of the inhabitants of the city, the protagonists view it with horror as a "calculating intelligence that will try [to] . . . *maximize* itself . . . [and] kill—to increase its own power."[45] They put to use the construct's capacity to calculate, its lack of unconsciousness and dreams, and its cabled, articulated body in order to fend off another enemy and then destroy it. If Mieville's novels take us to worlds marked by what one might describe as processes of formal subsumption in Marxist terms, Beller's book, on the other hand, stages a world of real subsumption where there is only what he calls elsewhere the "included excluded" that are forests and people as well as sectors of our mind. Rather than ask what there may be beyond the pleasure principle, Beller flips the question and asks "[i] s there anymore anywhere a beyond number?"[46]

Three

The man-corpse with the cable cleaved into his skull can also pivot us back to what Malabou calls the "living figures of death."[47] While Beller's book centers on the spread of the violent agency of computational capital, where the damage left behind crops up through the literary images or metaphors that populate his book, in *The New Wounded*, Malabou starts her thinking from the experience of living on or surviving injury: an *overlife (from survival—sur-vivre)*. The microliterary scenes that ground Malabou's thought are neurological case studies of brain lesions. The injury wrought on the brain by Alzheimer's or strokes exceeds the Freudian paradigm because, among other things, what falls out of memory does so through forces other than repression. What is experienced is a fundamental cut or rupture to the self: "where the psyche breaks off, on the side of a leap out of the meshwork and continuity that holds it together."[48] Like the hole opened up in the skull of the man-corpse, the wounds in her argument are the product of accidents that befall from the outside and that cannot be anticipated by the self. The metamorphosis, the form after the cut, cannot therefore be traced back to or made sense of in terms of a previous story. While her central preoccupation is the ontology of the accident, not the death drive per se, it necessarily reframes Freud's speculations on the matter. The undead puppet—we might say—is radically discontinuous from the person he was before but still a form of life, of death in life, and it is this form that Malabou exhorts us to think seriously as something other than just a breakdown of a previous form. The overlife of the new wounded is marked by detachment, indifference, neutrality, or coolness but even if they are "psyches deserted by pleasure . . . they remain psyches,"[49] Malabou insists. Ever attuned to the question of form, Malabou proposes Beckett's "theater of absence" as one possible model for a narrativity that might stage such a destructive metamorphosis: "Its rhetoric comprises figures of interruption, pauses, caesuras—the blank spaces that emerge when the network of connections is shredded or when the circulation of energy is paralyzed. . . . [T]he theater of exhausted identity . . . is the possible born after the exhaustion of all possibles."[50]

In a sense, Malabou starts thinking where Beller's argument stops. Although Malabou and Beller push off in opposite directions from the cut in the skull (she would think about the form of overlife we might associate with the animated corpse while Beller dwells on the construct behind the puppet), they overlap where Malabou scales up from concrete cases of brain lesions to make an argument for a more generalized contemporary condition. For Malabou, the "new wounded" are representative of new ways of being in the world, a generalized coolness that is the product of a globalized form of trauma: "the posttraumatic state is a gaping wound that appears on all the battlefields of contemporary society."[51] This trauma is both political and natural, mixing or collapsing the distinction between the two. It is political because the symptoms of such trauma appear even when brains haven't suffered an organic lesion like an aneurysm, yet it "assumes the face of nature" insofar as it appears as anonymous as a natural catastrophe. "The distinction between organic traumas and political traumas becomes blurred precisely because of the type of event that gives rise to them—a brutal event, without signification, that tends to efface its intentionality in order to appear as a blow inflicted upon any possible hermeneutics in general."[52] This insistence on the senselessness of this trauma is one of the key places of her diversion from Freud. The effect of blows or catastrophes that fall seemingly out of nowhere and appear to lack a responsible instance or author leads to what she calls a spreading war on sense, the blow on any possible hermeneutics ("The enemy, today, is hermeneutics," she writes).

What Beller calls the "included excluded" also depends on a cut: the hole in the skull makes the cable's connection possible. But Beller doesn't think the cut itself, particularly the cut as the effect of an accident. Instead, Beller assigns a quasi-cause to the effacement of sense in the empty and alternately viral or machinic agency that is capital: its logic "is to use meaning for the purposes of accumulation and dispossession beyond all possible meaning."[53] Meaning/sense is subsumed as an instance within a larger process that drives blindly, automatically, toward accumulation and dispossession. A large part of this process is, as we saw earlier, off-screen or unconscious so that what appears might as well take on the anonymous face of what is natural or given: if the media-machines reproduce inequality, he writes, it does so "under the guise of a value-neutrality that tends to render their exploitative operations unconscious even if many of the resultant effects do not remain in the unthought or the unfelt."[54] Beller's text is also littered with figures of wounding that are the effects of such operations: "historically specific incarnations"[55] of a crisis brought about by the "shattering of traditional life-forms and the imposition of new forms of life (and of statistically distributed death)."[56] The wounds in question are the end point of a vector of deadening driven by processes of subsumption, abstraction, and expropriation, the "proliferation of metrics of extraction to linguistic, psychic, neuronal and metabolic levels" such that "every attack surface of the body and cerebellum is exploited."[57] If subjects are indifferent it is because they are: "posited, interpellated, fragmented, dis-/re-/al-located . . . and functionalized"[58] by machinic calculations and processes that are themselves "content indifferent." Indifference is assigned to a cause, therefore, but is not itself a stand-alone form. And Beller's examples of psychological suffering include afflictions that are not, like strokes, outside a psychoanalytic paradigm: burnout, depression, autism, OCD, ADD, sociopathology, schizophrenia. To understand such deadening as accidental, the blow of chance, would be precisely an effect of capitalist alienation; it would be a blindness to the cable burrowing into our brains and flesh, and the self-propelled automaton behind it.

My point is that out of the bricolage drafted here between Malabou, Beller, and Mieville (form smashed against form), there appears to be no room in Beller's diegetic world for what Malabou calls the accident, a break that would be senseless, a negative plasticity. While Beller calls for rethinking "from the ground up" the interface and bios within a digital domain, this is a domain closed off from the unforeseen, firmly bounded by this ground and a digital outer edge. That which is not subordinated to calculation is figured as the "incalculable remainder."[59] What escapes the automaticity, abstraction, and deadening of capital is called "intellection, engaged in active self-decolonization."[60] We are given the possibility that there exist subaltern spaces of insurrectionary ground, breakaway voices, the fugitive poetry of objects,[61] but such imagery remains bound to reiterations. "The only cure for psychosis is revolution."[62] On the one hand Beller's writing is rich, imaginative, and provocative. But on the other, what are we then not able to envisage?[63]

Four

If the AI prosthetic figures a possible end point in Beller's argument, the completion or consummation of some program, seen from Malabou's argument, the open skull also figures the cut, the break of psychic continuity, a negative plasticity. Beyond the "beyond of the pleasure principle," beyond the death drive lies, she says, a new materialism (in the brain itself) that is radically open to accidents that might destroy it. There is an openness in Malabou's thinking that echoes the breach represented by cerebral lesions and an attempt to stay with how this might be made to mean. While the accident is traumatic or negative in these clinical cases, she also thinks of positive forms of plasticity elsewhere, citing, for example, Althusser's late essay on a new materialism of the encounter as one forerunner and contrasting the openness to possibility and new forms in biology to the logic of conformity, reproduction, and the "sociological heaviness" of cultural and social processes.[64] The articulation of political discourse on bodies is always partial, she writes,

> for it cannot absorb everything that the structure of the living being is able to burst open by showing the possibilities of a reversal in the order of generations, a complexification in the notion of heritage, a calling into question of filiation, a new relation to death and the irreversibility of time, through which emerges a new experience of finitude.[65]

Our thinking is outpaced, outflanked, not only by the machinic logic of information and the calculations of capital, but also by other processes at work through us.

When Malabou proposes the concept of plasticity as the "the dominant formal motif of interpretation and the most productive exegetical and heuristic tool" for our times,[66] she is making the case that it supersedes and follows writing which, in its expanded definition, functioned as the motor-schema of thought for much of the twentieth century. As such, it relates not only to inscription more generally but also to code and program, the concept so central to Beller's plotting of the becoming information of language: "it is the concept of program—which is obviously also a concept in the field of cybernetics—that culminates and which completes the constitution of the graphic scheme as the motor scheme of thought."[67] If the motor-schema of writing saturates Beller's text, I have brushed his poetics up against Mieville's to track the surfacing of plasticity there where it might not yet be a concept, not yet a clear gathering place, but something more like a touchstone for processes we can't fully articulate.

Reduced to code, there is no room for language to ever be double-voiced in Beller's text. *Embassytown*, on the other hand, ends up with an unexpected transformation of Language that we might call epigenetic.[68] The figure of the ghoulish flesh puppet is a site of unproblematic transmission. But in *Embassytown*, this translation is precisely what is interrupted, language thickened or stretched out speculatively so it forms instead into a membrane or surface. From speaking with similes, some of the Ariekei learn to speak in metaphors and thus to speak truth lying. They learn to say something like "the city's a heart . . . and in that heart and a city were sutured a third thing, a heartish city, and cities are heart-stained, and hearts are city-stained too."[69] Once the Ariekei learn metaphor, the god-drug no longer affects them. With the opening to polysemy, to new kinds of double-voicedness, futurity becomes once again indeterminate in the novel. Those that are fanwingless learn to signify in more minimal ways: pointing, gesturing, scratching in the earth, a process led by an Ariekei that is nicknamed, of all things, Theuth. A fall into writing, a new extension that follows an amputation, the emergence of a new unforeseen surface, or a new kind of technology. Undoubtedly there is a messianism at play in the end of *Embassytown*, a "coefficient of positivity of . . . world-reconstruction."[70] *Embassytown* rewrites an early colonial moment and ends with a return to the dangerous glory days of homo diaspora. The inhabitants of the colonial enclave of *Embassytown* shake off the shackles of the power to which they were beholden and realign themselves in a new human-alien compound, positioning themselves for new forms of exploration and dispersion into the alternate fold in space called the *immer* which looms just beyond the planet: "just beyond our planet's shores will be, people will say, El Dorado immer lands."[71]

Yet something else happens in the form of the living infrastructures that spread throughout the novel, in the figuration of an animated technology that is not even a subplot but forms a backdrop of the novel. "Freud is looking for a kind of form [for the death drive] that would be neither architectural nor organic. And it is also clear that he fails on this point," says Malabou.[72] The Ariekei biorigging, curiously, is both architectural and organic, but also somewhere between the animate and inanimate. Mieville makes literal the metaphors used to speak of cities as organisms (infrastructures as arteries): in the cities of the Ariekei, brickwork becomes biology unlike the bloodless tech of humans. In fact, the novel lightly suggests a contrast between this biorigging and the automaton Ehrul, who is the human version of "live" machines. Ehrul is always described as "resembling" rather than "being": she looks/acts human, speaks, and has emotions. But the biorigging does not resemble the Ariekei, is not their doppelganger, and yet is connected to them. It manifests a kind of assemblage (heartish cities) but as forms/formations of animate/inanimate life and not as signification: "Walls and ceilings moved with ratcheting mechanical life like the offspring of chains and crabs."[73] The novel pushes through an imaginary of doublings, couplings, horizontal proliferations but also perhaps of something like what Malabou calls the materialism of the brain. The biorigging is a compound, doubled like the language itself, but also like antagonyms or autoantonyms, things simultaneously joined and separated: bound, cleave, enjoin, rent.

Heterogeneity exists in *Embassytown*, cuts but also membranes, other sides where what is incommensurable or impossible to imagine (*the immer*) runs alongside the known world (underlying or overlying it). In its diegetic world, in this theorizing which takes place in poetics, language and what it means to speak are not infrastructure running in the background, like the pipes of a machinic construct, but defamiliarized, enlivened, turned into the pivot of difference, the site of rupture but also of just change.

Notes

1 Sigmund Freud, *Beyond the Pleasure Principle* (New York: W. W. Norton & Company, 1989), 26.
2 Freud, *Beyond the Pleasure Principle*, 28.
3 Freud, *Beyond the Pleasure Principle*, 30.
4 Freud, *Beyond the Pleasure Principle*, 43.
5 Freud, *Beyond the Pleasure Principle*, 43.
6 Freud, *Beyond the Pleasure Principle*, 46.
7 Freud, *Beyond the Pleasure Principle*, 30.
8 Catherine Malabou, "Plasticity and Elasticity in *Beyond the Pleasure Principle*," in *Plasticity: The Promise of Explosion*, ed. Tyler Williams (Edinburgh: Edinburgh University Press, 2022), 281.
9 Catherine Malabou, "Toward a Plasticity of the Compulsion to Repeat," in *The New Wounded* (New York: Fordham University Press, 2012), 189–202.
10 Catherine Malabou, *The New Wounded* (New York: Fordham University Press, 2012), 282.
11 Malabou, *The New Wounded*, 190.
12 Malabou, *The New Wounded*, 177.
13 Also the title of one of her books, Catherine Malabou, *The Ontology of the Accident: An Essay on Destructive Plasticity* (New York: Polity, 2012).
14 Malabou, *The Ontology of the Accident*, 209.
15 Although I don't engage directly with it, lurking behind this essay is Lacan's association of the death drive with language and the symbolic. In Seminar XVII he writes, "What forced this notion [the death drive] upon him [Freud] was the development of an experience, analytic experience, insofar as it has the structure of discourse. For don't forget that one does not invent the death drive by considering people's behavior./We have the death drive here. We have it here, where something is taking place between what you and what I am saying." Jacques Lacan, *The Other Side of Psychoanalysis: the Seminar of Jacques Lacan*, book 17, ed. Jacques-Alain Miller (New York: W.W. Norton & Company, 2007), 16.
16 China Mieville, *Embassytown* (New York: Ballantine Books, 2011), 55.
17 Mieville, *Embassytown*, 85.
18 Mieville, *Embassytown*, 172.
19 Mieville, *Embassytown*, 274.
20 Jonathan Beller, *The Message is Murder: Substrates of Computational Capital* (London: Pluto Press, 2018), 34.
21 Beller, *The Message is Murder*, 152.
22 Karl Marx, *Capital Volume One* (1867; New York: Vintage Books, 1977), 548.
23 Beller, *The Message is Murder*, 52.
24 Beller, *The Message is Murder*, 3.

25 Karl Marx, *Grundrisse: Foundations of the Critique of Political Economy*, trans. Martin Nicolaus (London: Penguin Books, 1993), 706.
26 Beller, *The Message is Murder*, 44.
27 Beller, *The Message is Murder*, 23.
28 Beller, *The Message is Murder*, 27.
29 Beller, *The Message is Murder*, 23.
30 Beller, *The Message is Murder*, 24.
31 Beller, *The Message is Murder*, 157.
32 Beller, *The Message is Murder*, 15.
33 Beller, *The Message is Murder*, 84.
34 Beller, *The Message is Murder*, 5.
35 China Mieville, *Perdido Street Station* (New York: Ballantine Books, 2000), 396.
36 Mieville, *Perdido Street Station*, 401.
37 Mieville, *Perdido Street Station*, 401.
38 Beller, *The Message is Murder*, 91.
39 Beller, *The Message is Murder*, 7.
40 Beller, *The Message is Murder*, 9.
41 Beller, *The Message is Murder*, 26.
42 Beller, *The Message is Murder*, 42.
43 Beller, *The Message is Murder*, 46.
44 Beller, *The Message is Murder*, 6.
45 Mieville, *Perdido Street Station*, 546.
46 Beller, *The Message is Murder*, 33.
47 Malabou, *The New Wounded*, 198.
48 Malabou, *The New Wounded*, 198.
49 Malabou, *The New Wounded*, 197.
50 Malabou, *The New Wounded*, 55.
51 Malabou, *The New Wounded*, 161.
52 Malabou, *The New Wounded*, 214.
53 Beller, *The Message is Murder*, 12.
54 Beller, *The Message is Murder*, 4.
55 Beller, *The Message is Murder*, 117.
56 Beller, *The Message is Murder*, 115.
57 Beller, *The Message is Murder*, 95.
58 Beller, *The Message is Murder*, 54.
59 Beller, *The Message is Murder*, 33.
60 Beller, *The Message is Murder*, 81.
61 Beller, *The Message is Murder*, 152.
62 Beller, *The Message is Murder*, 157.
63 In his sharp reading of the Communist Manifesto, Mieville writes that the model of Marx and Engels "is predicated simply on the plasticity of humanity" (*On the Communist Manifesto: A Spectre Haunting* [Chicago: Haymarket Books, 2022], 99) and also that: "The strongest weapon against revolution . . . [is] not any claim that the world in which we live is good enough, but that capitalist-realist common sense that it's impossible, even laughable, to struggle or hope for change. The tenacity of such a view is in part . . . at a base level, because it's so difficult to think beyond the reality in which one has been creative, lives and thinks now. The yearned-for social rupture would be a Rubicon towards a repurposing of social reality itself. Conditioned as we are by *existing* reality, we cannot prefigure or simply 'imagine' such radical alterity. As

such, it's beyond our ken—we can only yearn for it, strain for it, glimpse some sense of betterness out of the corner of the eye" (Mieville, *On the Communist Manifesto*, 84).

64 Catherine Malabou, "Whither Materialism? Althusser/Darwin," in *Plasticity: The Promise of Explosion*, ed. Tyler Williams (Edinburgh: Edinburgh University Press, 2022), 210.

65 Catherine Malabou, "One Life Only: Biological Resistance, Political Resistance," in *Plasticity: The Promise of Explosion*, ed. Tyler Williams (Edinburgh: Edinburgh University Press, 2022), 235.

66 Catherine Malabou, *Plasticity at the Dusk of Writing: Dialectic, Destruction, Deconstruction* (New York: Columbia University Press, 2010), 57.

67 Malabou, *Plasticity at the Dusk of Writing*, 57–8.

68 Malabou writes of epigenesis as a second genesis, one that takes place after engendering. See Catherine Malabou, "Epigenesis of the Text: New Paths in Biology and Hermeneutics," in *Plasticity: The Promise of Explosion*, ed. Tyler Williams (Edinburgh: Edinburgh University Press, 2022), 159. Epigentic reading, she writes, would be a way of "making the epigenesis of a text appear, of finding the precise point of contact between times in a text, of exhibiting a surface which is not pre-programmed—a surface contact from which a form has to emerge; in other terms, a synapse" (Malabou, "Epigenesis of the Text," 161).

69 Mieville, *Embassytown*, 312.

70 Malabou, *The New Wounded*, 188.

71 Mieville, *Embassytown*, 344–5.

72 Malabou, *Plasticity at the Dusk of Writing*, 280.

73 Mieville, *Embassytown*, 82. Malabou calls for imagining "something between the animate and the inanimate, something that is not animal but that has none of the inertia of stone either. The inanimal? A between, or an instance that in no way resembles any intermediary." See Malabou, *Ontology of the Accident*, 70.

Works Cited

Freud, Sigmund. *Beyond the Pleasure Principle*. New York: W. W. Norton & Company, 1989.

Lacan, Jacques. *The Other Side of Psychoanalysis: the Seminar of Jacques Lacan*, book 17, edited by Jacques-Alain Miller. New York: W.W. Norton & Company, 2007.

Malabou, Catherine. *Plasticity at the Dusk of Writing: Dialectic, Destruction, Deconstruction*. New York: Columbia University Press, 2010.

Malabou, Catherine. *The Ontology of the Accident: An Essay on Destructive Plasticity*. New York: Polity, 2012.

Malabou, Catherine. "Toward a Plasticity of the Compulsion to Repeat." In *The New Wounded*, 189–202. New York: Fordham University Press, 2012.

Malabou, Catherine. "Epigenesis of the Text: New Paths in Biology and Hermeneutics." In *Plasticity: The Promise of Explosion*, edited by Tyler Williams, 157–66. Edinburgh: Edinburgh University Press, 2022.

Malabou, Catherine. "One Life Only: Biological Resistance, Political Resistance." In *Plasticity: The Promise of Explosion*, edited by Tyler Williams, 227–36. Edinburgh: Edinburgh University Press, 2022.

Malabou, Catherine. "Plasticity and Elasticity in *Beyond the Pleasure Principle*." In *Plasticity: The Promise of Explosion*, edited by Tyler Williams, 275–86. Edinburgh: Edinburgh University Press, 2022.
Malabou, Catherine. "Whither Materialism? Althusser/Darwin." In *Plasticity: The Promise of Explosion*, edited by Tyler Williams, 203–14. Edinburgh: Edinburgh University Press, 2022.
Marx, Karl. *Capital Volume One* (1867). New York: Vintage Books, 1977.
Marx, Karl. *Grundrisse: Foundations of the Critique of Political Economy*. Translated by Martin Nicolaus. London: Penguin Books, 1993.
Mieville, China. *Perdido Street Station*. New York: Ballantine Books, 2000.
Mieville, China. *Embassytown*, New York: Ballantine Books, 2011.
Mieville, China. *On the Communist Manifesto: A Spectre Haunting*. Chicago: Haymarket Books, 2022.

10

Antigone's Gaza

Mario Telò

How do we interpret the force of the death drive in the current moment—dominated by the destruction of besieged Gaza; by famine and disease, slaughter and environmental catastrophe; by death that is both slow and sudden, chronic and acute, ordinary and extraordinary? An article in the Palestine issue of the journal *Parapraxis* is titled "Persecution Terminable and Interminable"[1]—an allusion to Freud's "Analysis Terminable and Interminable" (1937) glossed by the phrase "Zionism's circuit of retributory violence." The mix of complicity and indifference shown by most Western countries, as well as the surge of police violence against campus protests, makes one think of another Freudian intervention, *Civilization and Its Discontents* (1930), where "what he had called an 'unconquerable part of human nature' in *Beyond the Pleasure Principle* ten years earlier . . . takes on a new form as Freud develops a dualistic metaphysics, counterposing Eros, the force that creates ever more complex human bonds, to Thanatos, the force that breaks them down."[2] In *Civilization and Its Discontents*, we famously read:

> The fateful question for the human species seems to me to be whether and to what extent their cultural development will succeed in mastering the disturbance of their communal life by the human instinct of aggression and self-destruction. . . . Men have gained control over the forces of nature to such an extent that with their help they would have no difficulty in exterminating one another to the last man.[3]

Here the return to the inorganic at the center of the theorization of the death drive in *Beyond the Pleasure Principle* morphs into an impetus toward apocalyptic destruction, into a scenario of technologically engineered global genocide, which entails in each of its iterations a denial of participation in "the human species." In Freud, the extinction of "the human species" or of "civilization"—presented here with appropriate scare quotes—never partakes of the negative redemption attached to the notion of Symbolic collapse (and to the temporal register of repetition) in the Lacanian tradition, most recently emblematized by Afropessimism.[4] Lacan's Antigone embodies this collapse, as her catabatic suicide refuses the inescapable normativity inscribed in the very experience of living as such, of existing in and through language.[5] Yet, as Judith Butler has shown, Antigone can also be read, against Lacan, as the articulation of the possibility of alternative modes of being, of political counterimaginaries within a social order that grounds humanity in the ostensibly insurmountable givens of heteronormativity, colonialism, and racialized capitalism.[6]

How does our view of Antigone, Lacan's death-driven heroine, change in light of Gaza's apocalyptic destruction and the political dissent materialized in the cave-like tents of pro-Palestine, Antigonean protests on American campuses? I intend to offer a provisional answer by juxtaposing moments of Sophocles' play with the overdetermined collapse in Gaza, a target of the "instinct of aggression and self-destruction" that, for Freud, makes and unmakes the human. I am particularly interested in elemental and environmental marginality and opacity, in the cave, the tunnel, and the dust stirred up by the auto-immunitarian, fundamentally death-driven violence of the nation-state, whether perpetrated by Creon or Israel.[7] Animated by the fantasy of reappropriating ancestral land, of reconstituting a lost wholeness, the foundational project of Israel is arguably grounded in what Derrida calls *archive fever*, a different death-driven impetus, which could be said to mobilize Antigone's connection with the inorganic cave, a wish to reconnect with her father/brother, with the familial origin that turns nonexistence into existence, or brings nonlife (in)to life.[8] One could also advance the argument, in light of the semantic duality of *archê* as both "power" and "origin," that every exercise of state power, every nomological foundation, is fatally enmeshed with a rushing toward the ultimate beginning, that is, what precedes symbolization. The psychic motion of the Lacanian Antigone, her familial and political orientation toward the Real of death, may, in fact, trope, through displacement, the disavowed self-destructive instinct of the state as it apparently protects its integrity by suppressing dissent—the irruptions of disagreement that aggravate its illusory pursuit of immunity and self-possession.

My juxtapositional exercise begins with a consideration of the relation between "tragic madness" and the political psychology of gaslighting, which informs the ever-expanding McCarthyist attempts to shut down protest against Israel's actions in Gaza, even as indictments from the International Criminal Court are pending (at the time of writing). On March 3, 2024, Judith Butler made this statement, which triggered a backlash and various efforts at censorship:

> It is historically correct to say that the uprising of October 7 was an act of armed resistance; it is not a terrorist attack and it is not an antisemitic attack; it was an attack against Israelis. It was, for me, anguishing, it was terrible; however, I would be very *foolish* if I then decided that the only violence in the scene was the violence done to Israeli people. The violence done to Palestinians has been happening for decades. This was an uprising that comes from a state of subjugation and against a violent state apparatus.[9]

When Butler uses the word "foolish" to describe a position that views October 7 apart from the background of Israel's well-documented practices of necropolitical oppression, they are pushing against a particular form of censorship, the "gaslighting" that goes along with the philo-Zionist narrative imposed by the conservative and neoliberal governments of the United States and most European countries. In this regime of gaslighting, according to which the killing of tens of thousands of people, the starvation of many more, and the destruction of Gaza are held to be legitimate, albeit regrettable, expressions of Israel's right to defend itself, anyone who rejects such thinking is held to be unreasonable, crazy, or *foolish*. "[Even if you knew my prohibition], you still dared to violate these laws?"[10] Creon asks Antigone. After being called "foolish" by Ismene[11] and the Chorus,[12] Antigone closes off her response to Creon by saying, "If you think now that what I do is *foolish*, I am basically accused of *foolishness* by a *fool*."[13] Antigone is "foolish" because she sacrifices her life by refusing to perform the negative speech act, the denial of her unauthorized act of burial, that would place her in compliance with the self-serving ideology of the nation-state, which it assimilates to the reality principle, to a self-evident truth that one must be foolish, if not psychotic, to resist. In an article published in *Pittsburgh City Paper* on January 17, "Elected Officials Are Gaslighting Us about Their Support for Israel," Kirby Jayes writes:

> This is what I mean when I say I am going crazy every day. *No* matter how high the public support for a ceasefire, *no* matter how explicitly genocidal the rhetoric of Israeli officials, *no* matter how obvious it becomes that the IDF is targeting civilians, journalists, and health workers . . . the message received from my elected officials is the same. . . . I go a little crazy every day because we are all trapped in an electoral busy box. . . . Trying to move the wheel of history is a crazy-making task. That is not to say it is a foolish goal.

Here and in Antigone's denied denial of her responsibility—"And I say I did it, and I do not deny having done it" (*kai phêmi drasai kouk aparnoumai to mê*)[14]—the sequence of three negatives tracks the rhetorical and affective motion of a refusal to comply with gaslighting, to become complicit in it, an opposition to a counterfeit reality principle ("no, no, no!"), which ancient and modern Creons disingenuously dismiss as a psychotic vocalization. In Patrick Hamilton's 1938 play *Gas Light*, from which the term originates, a man "slowly, methodically, and deliberately aims to steal his wife's fortune by *isolating* her and questioning her sanity."[15] Isolating Antigone in a dark cave, a uterine space, Creon also "hystericizes" her, institutionalizes her, as though in a Foucauldian psychiatric clinic. Yet gaslighting is also a manifestation of the gaslighter's own paranoia, his own subjection to the "hystericization of discourse"[16] in the very act of violently hystericizing the other, his (quasi-)psychotic, death-driven circling around the same defensive tropes and the "overstatement of harm as a justification of cruelty."[17] The omnipotence of the Law, the nation-state's securitarian obligations toward its citizens under terrorist attack—obsessively, jouissantly inflected, these tropes reveal the impotent *mania*, the auto-immunitarian frenzy of a state invested in gaslighting, constituting (and undercutting) itself through self-identification with the psychiatric prison, a state positing as an ideal-ego a mental police force that preempts any fractures of the cognitively given, any emergence of spaces of social unintelligibility.[18]

The hystericization of Antigone goes along with her animalization, which resonates with the many statements by Israeli authorities dehumanizing Palestinians—first and foremost, the disturbing words of Defense Minister Yoav Gallant as he announced a "complete siege" of Gaza after October 7: "We are fighting human animals, and we are acting accordingly." As I reread the words of Creon claiming to have seen Antigone "rabidly raging (*lussôsan*) inside the palace, without being in control of her mind,"[19] that is, behaving like a canine Fury, or enraged dog, I stumble upon the headline of a blog post for *The Times of Israel*, "Rabid Dogs," which cites a psychiatrist's opinion that "the next generation of Palestinians will be a very murderous population full of anger and hatred." The image activated in both cases is that of a guest "generously" welcomed *inside* one's house, though, in the case of Creon, it was appropriated by a lateral heir and, in the case of Israel, built through settler colonialism by alleged natives. This construction of the unmarried Antigone or the (now) landless Palestinian as a disloyal canine guest, plotting the destruction of its human master while being compassionately fed and taken care of, betrays the gaslighter's own melancholic incorporation of an enraging loss. We can identify this loss with the gaslighter's disavowed animality—the abjected ontology that does not agree to be abandoned inside but manifests itself in the sadomasochistic antics of the master, in his rabid, impossible desire for a pure, fully de-animalized humanity.[20] This de-animalized humanity—a fantasized lost purity, an impossible past—is the *objet petit a* that generates the sadist's death drive, his efforts to "break the veil of the present, to break the surface of the Other's body in an effort to penetrate the insistent facticity of the temporal present," which is conceived as the hindrance to "recovery and reparation of the past."[21] The bestiary haunting Creon's house (his mind) also includes a viper, Ismene—discovered to be Antigone's ally or double. As he puts it, addressing her, "Having infiltrated my house, you were secretly drinking up my lifeblood."[22] These lines acquire particular resonance in light of an incident involving Ahed Tamimi, a Palestinian activist arrested for "inciting terrorism" in November 2023. Tamimi had received media attention in 2012 when, at the age of eleven, she confronted an Israeli soldier in the occupied West Bank, asking to release her younger brother (!). Three years later, she was caught on video biting a soldier who was holding down a Palestinian boy, and in 2017 she slapped two soldiers who were about to burst into her house. (In 2019, her brother was arrested again, and we see her on video again, confronting the arresters.)[23] In November 2023, Fox News triumphantly reported on the arrest "by the IDF for allegedly inciting terrorism" of this "Palestinian woman whom liberal media compared to Rosa Parks." In "a social media post allegedly from her social media account," Tamimi was accused of having written: "Our message to the herd of settlers, we are waiting for you in all the West Bank cities from Hebron to Jenin—we will slaughter you and you will say what Hitler did to you was a joke, *we will drink your blood* and eat your skulls, come on, we are waiting for you." According to Tamimi's mother, "the account had been hacked—a common occurrence for the fiery activist," as the Associated Press reported.[24] On the other hand, this language, which the IDF attributed to Tamimi, does illuminate a projective impetus also evident in Creon's words, the enraged terror of which he is the autoimmunitarian enforcer materialized in the heavily consonantal word for viper (*echidna*),[25] like thickened gore. The pertinence of Creon's imagery to the Palestinian struggle is not limited to the figure of reptilian displacement ("Palestinian viper," the name given to Israel's national snake, evokes the settler-colonial project of draining snake-ridden swamps).[26] The metaphorical force of "drinking up lifeblood" extends to the thirst and dehydration that became an emergency in Gaza only a few weeks into the current conflagration,[27] an extreme expression of Israel's aquapolitics, its "biopolitical water warfare" waged through "the expropriation of Palestinian rivers and aquifers but also through Israel's targeted destruction of wells and sewer systems."[28]

Dehydration leads us to a reflection on Creon's necropolitical limitation of food. As I am writing (on April 14, 2024), the US Agency for International Development has acknowledged that "parts of Gaza are experiencing famine." As Omar Shakir, Israel and Palestine director at Human Rights Watch, declared on April 9, "The Israeli government's use of starvation as a weapon of war has proven deadly for children at Gaza."[29] Similarly to Yoav Gallant, whose "complete siege" of Gaza meant "no electricity, no food, no fuel," Major General Ghassan Alian said: "There will be no electricity and no water; there will only be destruction"—language that evokes Freud's notion of Thanatos. The goal, in the words of Israeli analyst Giora Eiland, a retired IDF general, would be "to create conditions where life in Gaza becomes unsustainable." Creon's plan for Antigone—to "hide her alive in a rocky cave, supplying *as much* food *as* is necessary to avoid pollution, so that the whole city may avoid contamination"[30]—casts immurement or entombment as a necropolitical technology of slow death, not unlike Israel's system of calorie regulation, a "'starvation diet' to keep Palestinians barely alive," which was in force prior to October 7.[31] Like *tosouton hoson* ("as much . . . as") in Creon's words, the "barely" in "barely alive" encapsulates the thin gap between the infliction of death and the "right to maim," the phrase used by Jasbir Puar to characterize Israeli necropolitics, a stategy, like Creon's, of killing without killing, of stretching death durationally, repetitiously yoking colonizer and colonized to the same death-driven temporality.[32] As the flow of humanitarian aid is slowed down or blocked from getting into Gaza, the full control of borders is extended to the borders of subjugated bodies. Stomachs are closed off through starvation, while mouths are also shut through censorship, the idea that "only speech that defends injustice is defensible."[33] Yet the pairing of carefully curated starvation with siege—the entombment of Antigone—encloses Creon too; it does not shut him down but imparts a tautological, repetitious, autoimmunitarian structure to his words ("avoid pollution . . . avoid contamination"), as though his tongue were folding back on itself in the absence of a way out, in the absence of a path to immunity. At the same time, the language of Antigone's impending encryptment hints at a fear of the outside, the heterogeneity threatening the state's imagined wholeness. A phobia of ingestion is encrypted in Creon's psyche.

Using *Antigone* to read our predicaments means heeding not only uncanny resonances, but also the formal ways in which tragedy might manifest necropolitics working against itself, caught in a self-sabotaging mechanism, which we can call a manifestation of the death drive. In the remainder of my discussion, I will focus on two figures, dust and the cave, suggestive of the conflated genocide and ecocide in the siege of Gaza.

The smoky vortex of bombarded Gaza induces us to rethink *Antigone*'s ecological imagery, aerial and earthly. "I'll tell you," the Guard says in the play, "*someone* just now departed after having buried the corpse of Polynices, sprinkling on its skin thirsty dust and performing all the rites."[34] The mysterious agent ("someone") is an indefinite subject aligned with the dust in its impersonality, coopted into its negative, deindividuated ontology. In the Guard's account, dust empowers the earth by liquefying it, making it borderless, unbound, in a quasi-return to prehuman ancestrality, pre-Symbolic life, resistant to the partitioning, the delimitation, that creates the very idea of "land." Creon's terroristic decree can be connected through a folk etymology with Latin *terra* ("land"), which Salar Mameni employs, since (neo)colonialism's "terrorism" is, in part, a war on the earth.[35] Not simply "hard and dry," Gaia is in an enjambed position (*stuphlos de gê/kai chersos*),[36] opening itself to syntactical continuation, moving from one edge to another, from the end of one line—the same position where feminine "dust" (*konis*)[37] is located—to the beginning of another. This dust coalesces into the whirlwind (*tuphôs*)[38] that, in the same report of the Guard, threatens a burial of the upper world.[39] In our own day, a thick whirlwind occupies the Gazan sky, materializing the threat uttered by an Israeli policeman to a journalist: "We will turn Gaza into dust." Seeing the faces of Palestinian children covered in dust, enveloped in a thick layer of toxic gray, weighed down by matter, like Antigone as she touches, absorbs, and almost merges with the dirt sedimented on her brother's body, we perceive the entanglement with dirt, with the apparent pollution of the nonhuman that is disavowed—and violently displaced—by Creon and other state-authorized enforcers of the right to kill or to maim. The kin or the inside of the organic and the human, the inorganic, the destination of the Freudian death drive, is downgraded to the outside, a self-distancing other, in humanistic illusions, just as, in *Beyond the Pleasure Principle*, the death drive, which constitutively haunts the pleasure principle, stage-managing the life instinct itself, is seen by structuralist, dichotomizing readings as the opposite of that instinct. The dense clouds produced by Israeli bombardment expand beyond their target, beyond ecocide—or genocide. As we read in a news report: "Conditions in Gaza continue to worsen, raising the risk of the emergence of bacteria and viruses that cause intestinal and digestive tract, respiratory and skin diseases, as well as others. . . . The air is filling up with toxic substances and heavy metals as a result of substantial bombing."[40] Such a whirlwind is, we might say, like Antigone's whirlwind, bound to confound the nation-state's immunitarian disavowal through an elemental concentration of life-as-death or life-in-death (or lifedeath),[41] a shared exposure to loss and extinction.

In *Antigone*, this life-in-death materializes as a returning whirlwind that spreads decomposed flesh, as we can infer from Tiresias's account of his failed sacrifice, which conjures a plague.[42] As Mark Griffith explains, "The offerings . . . should have flared up in the flames, but instead the fuel merely smouldered as 'embers' . . . , while the fat from the meat oozed onto them and 'smoked and sputtered' . . . and the gall-bladders (*cholai*)[43] burst messily into the air."[44] Recalcitrant animal flesh, contrary to human plans, explodes into a toxic elementality, gaseous as well as liquid, which transforms the earlier whirlwind (*tuphôs*), unmistakably evoked by the "sputtering" (*etuphe*)[45] ooze, into a tempest of bile, an outburst of environmental rage, almost acid rain (*katarrueis*),[46] which nourishes and is nourished by the effluvia of Polynices' remains brought to the city's altars by other animals, birds and dogs.[47] In Gaza, as we read in a report in Al Jazeera, "the destruction has a smell. The stench of burned and rotting flesh of the bodies lying under the rubble is unavoidable, bringing with it health risks and more trauma."[48] As Middle East Eye reported in January:

> In Gaza, you don't only see death; you smell it, you breathe it. You feel how death feels with all your senses and then how it smells, only to watch with horror and disbelief as stray dogs feast on the decomposed fragments of bodies of those you knew and loved.
>
> . . . The dogs, facing starvation like all of Gaza's inhabitants, smell the decaying bodies, crawl deep into the ruins and emerge with body parts in their mouths.[49]

At the end of his speech, Tiresias warns Creon not to goad the dead man,[50] not to overkill him by subjecting him to animal ingestion. The destruction of Palestinian lives—programmatically cast as non-grievable non-lives in the genocidal language of Israeli authorities and media figures—exposes a fundamental contradiction comparable to the illogic of overkilling, one that resembles the fixation of the Lacanian death drive, the futile game of inflicting death on the dead.[51] If Palestinian lives are not lives to begin with, there should be no need to devitalize them or annihilate them. Speaking of this particular necropolitical dynamic, a lethally unequal distribution of (in)animacy, Butler says:

> There is a disavowal of the violence but also a disavowal of the life as a living creature of any kind. The fact that [Palestinians] have to be killed, according to this logic, means that they are alive. You don't kill non-living creatures, because they are already dead. There is something animate about them, but whatever it is that is animate is [seen as] murderous or potentially so.[52]

This is the same paradox imposed on animal lives, which are cast as not fully lives and then subjected to forms of (over)killing. The morbid inversion of the human/animal hierarchy in Thebes and Gaza presages an inversion of victimizer and victim brought about by unbound environmental rage, an atmospheric manifestation of unwitting self-destruction. Valorizing the psychoanalytic potential of "surplus," something that "either spills or escapes capture"—language reminiscent of Lee Edelman's characterization of the death drive[53]—Adam HajYahia has observed that "surplus is the Palestinian rockets fired back at Israel's settlements, made out of the unexploded Israeli munition that reaches Gaza." The surplus suddenly breaking the bounds of the repressed also takes the shape of "the recycled material waste of exploded airstrikes repurposed to build low-tech guerrilla weaponry."[54] The animal eating the human—a taboo reversal of the customary direction of the zoopolitics targeting Antigone or the Palestinians as figurations of the nonhuman or inhuman[55]—is an instance of the surplus's capacity for fracture, for creating moments "when the violently enforced architecture of repression, also designed to keep the Zionist psyche contented, crumbles."[56]

Gaza's (and Thebes') underground plays a prominent role in figuring what HajYahia calls "Palestinian radical expenditure of (liberatory) psychic and physical matter that rearranges the machinations of repression."[57] Speaking of Gaza's subterranean landscape, he observes:

> During Israel's military occupation and settlement within Gaza that lasted until 2005, the IDF built tunnels below residential neighborhoods to spy on, and

> neutralize Palestinian resistance fighters. These same tunnels were abandoned when Israel was pushed out of Gaza, and re-activated and expanded by Palestinians.[58]

From this perspective, the tunnels might be cast as channeling the rebellious impetus of a geopower depleted by settler colonialism, which would connect it with the imagery of Blackness as an underground, what Sylvia Wynter calls "underlife." (Frantz Fanon famously speaks of an insurrection as a "descent into real hell," where an authentic upheaval can be born.)[59] This subterranean upheaval—with the potential to destroy "life above," that is, in "*this*" or "*our* world," intended as the cosmos subjugated to the white logic of possession—is a form of the death drive, a movement toward formlessness and extinction, that threatens the death residing in the status quo, of the settler colonialism responsible for the spatial division of "above" and "below," for the establishment of the very notion of "land." In *Antigone*, the whirlwind imagistically morphs into the spiral of her underground descent, of her journey to her cavernous tomb. While Antigone is dragged away by guards, her attachment to the possession of loss—"I have no bed (*a-lektron*)," "I have no husband (*an-umenaion*)," "I have no part in wedding or filial sustenance"[60]—reclaims the dispossession foisted upon her by the biopolitical state, which will itself be thrown downward, as Creon's change of heart will force him to face the "underlife."[61] The Gazan tunnels can be juxtaposed with the site of Creon's downward journey, as described by the Messenger, a journey that takes him through narrow passageways, labyrinthine corridors, and chasms, geological features intimated by formal effects, all leading to the cavernous crypt.[62]

In a radio interview, Tzipi Hotovely, the Israeli ambassador to the UK, declared: "One of the things we exposed to the world after getting into the areas in Gaza [was] all those tunnels and [the] underground metro city that Hamas has built. . . . We realized . . . every school, every mosque, every second house, has . . . access to [a] tunnel." When the host suggested that she was making "an argument for destroying the whole of Gaza, every single building in it," Hotovely replied, "Do you have another solution?" Destroying the underground where the threatening outside is supposed to reside blends genocide with ecocide; it blends an attack cast as self-defense with the destruction of the land, the dismantling of the surface that sustains life. The media accounts of these tunnels have the quality of phantasms—to use a concept of Jean Laplanche that Butler has most recently employed to analyze the global right-wing panic around gender.[63] As Reuters put it: "Beneath the warscape of Gaza City lies a vast network of tunnels . . . a warren of interconnecting passages that stretches below Gaza's streets, extending for hundreds of miles into almost every area of the enclave."[64] A tragic horror and dread, like what we find in Sophocles' Messenger speech, feeds a panic machine that works in the narrow intervals between fantasy and the reality principle. While the sky is shaken by explosive whirlwinds, the underground is depicted as a threatening opacity, a blinding (and thus Oedipal) Blackness, which shakes the aspiration to possess instrinsic to visual intelligibility with a seismic force, what we can call an Antigonean earthquake, the counterpart of the whirlwind. In the verbal texture of *Antigone*, the seismic movement that uproots an edifice by divine will (584) converges with the rebellious swaying of heads in Creon's paranoid fantasies of disobedience to the yoke of his absolute rule.[65]

Poet Ahmad Ibsais envisions Palestinian soil's growing rage, plotting revenge against colonialist geontopower:[66]

> The land is plotting its revenge
> It must,
> but not against the child
> who walks through it gently[67]

Let us return to the images of the dusty faces of Palestinian children seeking shelter in the midst of unrelenting bombardment, and of one Palestinian girl in particular, who, through Niobe, brings us back to Lacan's discussion of Antigone and the death drive in *The Ethics of Psychoanalysis*. The grayness of the dust almost blends a Palestinian girl (Figure 10.1) into the ground where she still stands and into the wall behind her—infrastructure doomed to become rubble. This Antigone shades into Niobe, the mother-turned-motherless, transmuted into an ever-weeping stone, with whom Antigone compares herself in Sophocles' play:[68]

> I have heard that the Phrygian stranger, the daughter of Tantalus, died *most miserably* (*l-ugrotatan*) by high Sipylus, she whom stony growth tamed like tight ivy, and rains and snow, as men say, never leave her *as she melts away* (*takomenan*), and she wets ridges under her *all-crying* (*pan-klautois*) brows. The god lays me to rest *most similarly* (*homoiotatan*) to her.

Figure 10.1 A Palestinian girl covered in dirt and dust is rescued from a collapsed home following an Israeli air strike in Rafah, on Saturday, November 11, 2023. Photo by Ismael Mohamad/UPI. Alamy.

Commenting on this passage, Lacan observes: "When Antigone depicts herself as a Niobe becoming petrified, what is she identifying with, if it isn't that inanimate condition in which Freud taught us to recognize the form in which the death instinct is manifested?"[69] Yet a different reading—of the Sophoclean passage and of the death drive—is suggested by the current ecocide in Gaza, the no-longer habitable strip of land precariously inhabited by countless Antigones and Niobes stripped of the right to grieve and be grieved. Regarding just one of the innumerable wrenching videos circulating in the course of this war, Hatem Al-Bazian writes of the anguished woman swinging an oversize handbag: "She went to get food for Her family and came back to find all her family and kids killed by an Israeli bombing attack."[70] Speaking of Niobe in Gaza, I cannot pass over Banksy's Niobe mural, painted in Gaza in 2015 (Figure 10.2). In another photograph of the mural, a Palestinian woman (a mother?), whose face is not revealed, stops in front of it, performing her affinity with Niobe in the very act of looking at her, mirroring herself, even though her face remains invisible, in the aggrieved, fasting ancient mother enveloped by ruins. According to UNRWA (The UN Relief and Works Agency for Palestine Refugees in the Near East), "The destruction across the Gaza Strip has created nearly 23 million tons of debris. It will take years to clear the rubble." In Al Jazeera, Mohammed Mhawish writes: "I see children combing through the ruins for their dolls, teens for their schoolbooks, their parents for food[,] and the elderly sift through the debris for their belongings and for missing sons, daughters and grandchildren."[71] The ruins in the picture are, in a sense, fragmented or pulverized replicas of frozen Niobe herself—a crying stone, a screaming rock—extending their own contradictory ontology, their broken, wounded, and wounding solidity to the nation-state that produced the ruins. But Niobe's liquefaction, the impossible "surplus" of her solidity, the intimate life in the apparent death of her stoniness, redirects the whirlwind, metamorphosing it into a flood. We can say, citing the words of Ben Ware in "The Death Drive at the

Figure 10.2 Banksy, Niobe Mural. Photographed by Mohammed Saber/EPA/Shutterstock.

End of the World," that this flooding surplus is "the excess of life, what is in life more than life itself." It is "a life that sets itself against life, that carries death at its core; but it is a *life* nevertheless."[72] As indicated by the resonance of the participle *takomenan* ("as [Niobe] melts away")[73] with Tiresias's description of the "melting" of sacrificial entrails (*etêketo*),[74] tears and rain also mix with the ooze of immolated nonhumans (literal and figurative), enabling this expansive, if repressed, countermovement of life-as-death to engulf besieging infrastructures and the besiegers themselves. The feminine superlatives opening and closing Antigones's song, *lugrotatan* and *homoiotatan*—the former conjuring double liquidity through the adjective *hugros* ("humid") and its supplemental lambda (*l-ugrotatan*)—present a pentasyllabic expansiveness that enacts the flooding signposted by *pan-klautois* ("all-crying"), life carrying "death at its core," accelerating the law's autoimmunitarian reckoning, the dissolution of its self-styled solidity.[75]

Paralyzed by a law that institutes itself, that deceptively identifies itself with justice by punishing her, by fabricating her guilt—as both Walter Benjamin and Butler have illustrated—Niobe grieves, or, differently put, she is allowed to make her offspring grievable only by relocating into the inhuman realm, into the rocky ontology that, in fact, corresponds to the cave, the despised underground where Antigone is imprisoned.[76] In the picture of the Banksy Niobe, the rubble is an accumulation of dust, which solidifies the tears endlessly shed by her and Antigone.[77] The elemental cycle of dust mimics that of water, as Michael Marder has argued—and in the diction of Antigone's transgressive gesture, a granular pouring segues into, and replicates or continues, an aqueous one.[78] Niobe's tears are difficult to separate from the whirlwind, from the dust storm that casts Antigone's protest as an elemental response to the state's contempt for the earth, its own form of ecocide. Discussing Benjamin's treatment of Niobe in "Towards a Critique of Violence," Butler, in 2012, observed: "One hears, time and again in Israeli public discourse, that a single Israeli life is worth more than countless Palestinian lives. Yet only when such obscene calculations definitively fail, and all populations are deemed grievable, will the principle of social and political equality start to govern."[79] A dusty tempest, a storm of tears collects the grievous liquidity shed on the ground as Antigonean, Niobean persistence—homologous to the "insistence" that the Lacanian tradition attributes to the death drive, which resists the Symbolic's destructive project, its investment in the preservation of the world as we know it. A deindividuated life in common emerges from the diffused burden of loss, the accumulated deaths, the pooling tears. The rage of this deindividuated life, in turn, brings the underground upward and the nation-state's contemptuous aboveness downward. This elemental deindividuated life folds the dehumanizing logic of countless or uncounted lives into a commons or undercommons of undulations, of ruptures, which insist (i.e., remain in and on) even as ancient and modern Creons want to imagine that, after catastrophe, there will be no trace of loss.[80]

Notes

1 David Markus, "Persecution Terminable and Interminable," Palestine Issue: From the River to the Sea, *Parapraxis*, accessed November 28, 2024, https://www.parapraxismagazine.com/articles/persecution-terminable.

2 Judith P. Butler, *Antigone's Claim: Kinship between Life and Death* (New York: Columbia University Press, 2000), 151.
3 Sigmund Freud, "Civilization and Its Discontents" (1930), in *The Standard Edition of the Complete Psychological Works of Sigmund Freud*, trans. James Strachey, volume 21 (London: The Hogarth Press, 1955), 145.
4 On the collapse of the Symbolic, see, for example, Slavoj Žižek, *The Sublime Object of Ideology* (London: Verso, 1989), 71. On extinction, see esp. Ben Ware, "The Death Drive at the End of the World" *e-flux* 134 (2023), https://www.e-flux.com/journal/134/525929/the-death-drive-at-the-end-of-the-world/ and Steven Swarbrick and Jean-Thomas Tremblay, *Negative Life: The Cinema of Extinction* (Evanston: Northwestern University Press, 2024); on extinction and Afropessimism, see Axelle Karera, "Blackness and the Pitfalls of Anthropocene Ethics," *Critical Philosophy of Race* 7, no. 1 (2019): 32–56.
5 Jacques Lacan, *The Seminar of Jacques Lacan: The Ethics of Psychoanalysis (Book VII)*, ed. Jacques-Alain Miller (New York: Norton, 1992), 280, 282. Antigone illustrates that "there is no ethical act . . . without taking the risk of . . . a momentatry suspension of the big Other, of the socio-symbolic network that guarantees the subject's identity," as noted by Slavoj Žižek, *The Ticklish Subject* (London: Verso, 1999), 263–4.
6 See Butler, *Antigone's Claim*; and Mario Telò, *Reading Greek Tragedy with Judith Butler* (London: Bloomsbury, 2024), chapter 1. See also Andrés Fabián Henao Castro, *Antigone in the Americas* (Albany: State University of New York Press, 2021).
7 On the death drive and political autoimmunity, see Jacques Derrida, "Autoimmunity: Real and Symbolic Suicides," in *Philosophy in a Time of Terror*, ed. Giovanna Borradori (Chicago: University of Chicago Press, 2003), 85–136 and "Deconstructing Terrorism," in *Philosophy in a Time of Terror*, ed. Giovanna Borradori (Chicago: University of Chicago Press, 2003), 137–72.
8 Jacques Derrida, *Archive Fever: A Freudian Impression*, trans. Eric Prenowitz (Chicago: University of Chicago Press, 1996). On Zionist fever, see Gil Anidjar, "*Mal de Sionisme* (Zionist Fever)," in *Living Together: Jacques Derrida's Communities of Violence and Peace*, ed. Elizabeth Weber (New York: Fordham University Press, 2012), 45–58.
9 Judith P. Butler, "Judith Butler—Contre l'antisémitisme et pour la paix révolutionnaire en Palestine," *Paroles D'Honneur*, March 7, 2024, video, 2:02:12, https://www.youtube.com/watch?v=rlQNBJOq-0E.
10 See Sophocles' *Antigone*, line 449.
11 See Sophocles' *Antigone*, line 99.
12 See Sophocles' *Antigone*, lines 381–3.
13 See Sophocles' *Antigone*, lines 469–70.
14 See Sophocles' *Antigone*, line 443.
15 Yasmeen Abu-Laban and Abigail B. Bakan, "Anti-Palestinian Racism and Racial Gaslighting," *The Political Quarterly* 93, no. 3 (2022): 509.
16 On the "hystericization of discourse," see Jacques Lacan, *The Seminar of Jacques Lacan: The Other Side of Psychoanalysis (Book XVII)*, trans. Russell Grigg (New York: Norton, 2007), 33.
17 Sarah Schulman, *Conflict Is Not Abuse* (Vancouver: Arsenal Pulp Press, 2016), 190.
18 On Antigone's challenges to intelligibility, see Butler, *Antigone's Claim*, 23–4.
19 See Sophocles' *Antigone*, lines 491–2.
20 On the masochistic violence intrinsic to the anthropocentric hierarchy between human and nonhuman animals, see Judith P. Butler, "Companion Thinking: A Response" *NLH* 51, no. 4 (2020b): 687–94.

21 Judith P. Butler, "The Pleasures of Repetition," in *Pleasure beyond the Pleasure Principle*, ed. Robert A. Glick and Stanley Bone (New Haven: Yale University Press, 1990), 274–5.

22 See Sophocles' *Antigone*, lines 531–2.

23 See "After Going Viral for Slapping an Israeli Soldier, Ahed Tamimi Shares Her Story," *MSNBC*, September 21, 2022, https://www.msnbc.com/the-mehdi-hasan-show/watch/after-going-viral-for-slapping-an-israeli-soldier-ahed-tamimi-shares-her-story-148985413804 and Bethan McKernan and Sufian Taha, "Activist Ahed Tamimi among 50 Jailed Palestinians Listed for Release by Israel," *The Guardian*, November 28, 2023, https://www.theguardian.com/world/2023/nov/28/ahed-tamimi-release-israel-hamas-ceasefire-deal-jailed-palestinians. Tamimi's memoir is entitled *They Called Me a Lioness*: Ahed Tamimi and Dena Takruri, *They Called Me a Lioness: A Palestinian Girl's Fight for Freedom* (New York: One World, 2022).

24 See Hannah Grossman, "Palestinian Woman whom Liberal Media Compared to Rosa Parks is Accused of Threatening to Drink Jews' Blood and Eat Their Skulls," *Fox News*, November 10, 2023, https://nypost.com/2023/11/10/news/palestinian-rosa-parks-hailed-by-media-as-hero-accused-of-sharing-hitlerian-threat-to-drink-jews-blood/ and Julia Frankel, "The Family of a Palestinian Activist Jailed for Incitement Says Young Woman's Account Was Hacked," *Associated Press*, November 8, 2023, https://apnews.com/article/palestinians-israel-ahed-tamimi-west-bank-raids-8833619f1924676a9b7dbd053b2fa3ba.

25 See Sophocles' *Antigone*, line 531.

26 See Mario Telò, *The Late Animal: Edward Said, Classicism, and the Limits of Humanism* (Oxford: Oxford University Press, forthcoming).

27 See "Gaza is Dying of Thirst," *Action Contre la Faim*, October 27, 2023, https://www.actioncontrelafaim.org/en/press/gaza-is-dying-of-thirst/.

28 Joseph Pugliese, *Biopolitics of the More-Than-Human* (Durham: Duke University Press, 2020), 93.

29 Human Rights Watch, "Gaza: Israel's Imposed Starvation Deadly for Children," *Informed Comment*, April 14, 2024, https://www.juancole.com/2024/04/israels-starvation-children.html.

30 See Sophocles' *Antigone*, lines 774–6.

31 Pugliese, *Biopolitics*, 61. See, for example, Sana Noor Haq and Rosa Rahimi, "'We Are Dying Slowly:' Palestinians Are Eating Grass and Drinking Polluted Water as Famine Looms Across Gaza," *CNN*, February 1, 2024, https://www.cnn.com/2024/01/30/middleeast/famine-looms-in-gaza-israel-war-intl/index.html.

32 See Jasbir Puar, *The Right to Maim: Debility, Capacity, Disability* (Durham: Duke University Press, 2017).

33 See Judith P. Butler, *Who's Afraid of Gender?* (New York: Farrar, Straus, and Giroux, 2024).

34 See Sophocles' *Antigone*, lines 245–7.

35 Salar Mameni, *Terracene: A Crude Aesthetics* (Durham: Duke University Press, 2023). The distinction between "earth" and "land" corresponds to what Elizabeth A. Povinelli, *Geontologies: A Requiem to Late Liberalism* (Durham: Duke University Press, 2018) calls "geopower" and "geontopower," respectively.

36 See Sophocles' *Antigone*, lines 250–1.

37 See Sophocles' *Antigone*, line 256.

38 See Sophocles' *Antigone*, line 418.

39 See Mario Telò, *Greek Tragedy in a Global Crisis* (London: Bloomsbury, 2023), 109–25.

40 Ido Efrati, "Spread of Disease in Gaza Endangers the Hostages Held by Hamas, and Will Soon Even Risk Israel," *Haaretz*, December 13, 2023, https://www.haaretz.com/israel-news/2023-12-13/ty-article/.premium/morbidity-in-gaza-endangers-the-hostages-and-possibly-israel/0000018c-5fe1-d6f9-afbc-5febf3e60000.
41 On lifedeath, see Jacques Derrida, *Life Death*, ed. Pascale-Anne Brault and Peggy Kamuf (Chicago: University of Chicago Press, 2020).
42 See Sophocles' *Antigone*, lines 1007–11.
43 See Sophocles' *Antigone*, line 1010.
44 Mark Griffith, ed., *Sophocles: Antigone* (Cambridge: Cambridge University Press, 1999), 299.
45 See Sophocles' *Antigone*, line 1009.
46 See Sophocles' *Antigone*, line 1010.
47 See Sophocles' *Antigone*, lines 1016–18.
48 See Mohammed R. Mhawish, "Gaza's Morning Ritual: Searching under Rubble for Dolls, Books, Loved Ones," *Al Jazeera*, January 19, 2024, https://www.aljazeera.com/features/2024/1/19/the-scale-of-destruction-is-unimaginable.
49 See Mohammed al-Hajjar, "In Gaza, You Don't Only See Death. You Smell It. You Breathe It," *Middle East Eye*, January 14, 2024, https://www.middleeasteye.net/opinion/gaza-dont-only-see-death-smell-breathe-it.
50 See Sophocles' *Antigone*, lines 1029–30.
51 See Slavoj Žižek, *Looking Awry* (Cambridge: MIT Press, 1991), 5–6, on the myth of Sisyphus as an enactment of the death drive's futile rhythm. Alenka Zupančič, *Let Them Rot: Antigone's Parallax* (New York: Fordham University Press, 2023), 13, reads Teiresias's account as the "obscene" description of a cannibalistic feast. As she adds, "it is Creon who is the first . . . to push the limit of the symbolic law (*What use to kill the dead a second time?)*."
52 In Telò, *Reading Greek Tragedy*, 164.
53 See, for example, Lee Edelman, *No Future: Queer Theory and the Death Drive* (Durham: Duke University Press, 2004), 9: "As the inarticulable surplus that dismantles the subject from within, the death drive names what the queer . . . is called forth to figure: the negativity opposed to every form of social viability"; see also *Bad Education: Why Queer Theory Teaches Us Nothing* (Durham: Duke University Press, 2023), 86: "the unreadable surplus of the signifier" is "the zero degree of (il)legibility that constitutes the drive." See also Žižek, *The Sublime Object*, 69 and Zupančič, *Let Them Rot*, 25.
54 Adam Hajyahia, "The Principle of Return: The Repressed Ruptures of Zionist Time," Palestine Issue: From the River to the Sea, *Parapraxis*, accessed November 28, 2024, https://www.parapraxismagazine.com/articles/the-principle-of-return#_ftn12.
55 Here I intend "zoopolitics" in the sense developed for the analysis of Israeli necropolitics by Pugliese, *Biopolitics* 52, who defines the "zoopolitical space" as the one "in which the colonized can be both quartered and executed, like nonhuman animals, in acts of noncriminal putting to death."
56 Hajyahia, "The Principle of Return."
57 Hajyahia, "The Principle of Return."
58 Hajyahia, "The Principle of Return."
59 See Sylvia Wynter, "Sambos and Minstrels," *Social Text* 1 (1979): 149–56 and Frantz Fanon, *Black Skin, White Masks* (New York: Grove Press, 1967), 8.
60 See Sophocles' *Antigone*, lines 917–18.
61 Telò, *Greek Tragedy*, 117–19.

62 Telò, *Greek Tragedy*, 120–1.
63 See Butler, *Who's Afraid*.
64 Adolfo Arranz, et al., "Inside the Tunnels of Gaza: The Scale, and the Sophistication, of Hamas' Tunnel Network," *Reuters*, December 31, 2023, https://www.reuters.com/graphics/ISRAEL-PALESTINIANS/GAZA-TUNNELS/gkvldmzorvb/.
65 See Sophocles' *Antigone*, lines 291–2.
66 See note 27.
67 Ahmad Ibsaid, "Angry Soil: Poem on Palestine," *State of Siege*, April 7, 2024, https://ahmadibsais.substack.com/p/angry-soil.
68 See Sophocles' *Antigone*, lines 823–33
69 Lacan, *The Ethics*, 281.
70 Hatem Al-Bazian (@hatembazian), "She Went to Get Food for Her Family and Came Back to Find All Her Family and Kids Killed by an Israeli Bombing Attack!" Instagram video, March 18, 2024, https://www.instagram.com/hatembazian/reel/C4qNb0RAaE4/.
71 See Mhawish, "Gaza's Morning Ritual."
72 See Ware, "The Death Drive." According to Zupančič, *Let Them Rot*, 25, Antigone embodies the paradox whereby "to say death, you have to make it 'symbolically alive,' alive in the symbolic." Shall we say that, in a complementary fashion, Niobe brings life into the Real of death? For Elissa Marder, "Anti Antigone." *Diacritics* 49, no. 2 (2021): 20, Antigone is "still (un)born: born still dead."
73 See Sophocles' *Antigone*, line 828.
74 See Sophocles' *Antigone*, line 1008.
75 Commenting on the sequence of adjectives with alphas privative in Sophocles' *Antigone*, lines 847, 867, 876, and 881, Rebecca Comay, "*Nihil est in imagine vivum*," in *Niobes: Antiquity, Modernity, Critical Theory*, eds. Mario Telò and Andrew Benjamin (Columbus: Ohio State University Press, 2024), 41 observes that "the *torrent* of negatives keeps beating through," my emphasis.
76 On Benjamin's Niobe, see esp. Mathura Umachandran, "Niobe between Benjamin and Arendt—and Beyond," in *Niobes: Antiquity, Modernity, Critical Theory*, ed. Mario Telò and Andrew Benjamin (Columbus: Ohio State University Press, 2024), 195–207.
77 Victoria Rimell, "Philosophers' Stone: Enduring Niobe," in *Niobes: Antiquity, Modernity, Critical Theory*, ed. Mario Telò and Andrew Benjamin (Columbus: Ohio State University Press, 2024), 76, notes that "in the two-minute video accompanying the work on his website . . . Banksy seems to awaken the voice of enraged, sarcastic Niobe in Ovid's *Metamorphoses*, who dares to speak to power by mocking those who worship gods in some desperate act of self-abasement in order to avoid the violence of tyrannical divine whim."
78 See Michael Marder, *Dust* (London: Bloomsbury, 2016), 5; and Sophocles' *Antigone*, lines 429–31.
79 Judith P. Butler, *Parting Ways: Jewishness and the Critique of Zionism* (New York: Columbia University Press, 2012), 21.
80 Conceived in the context of an event organized by Judith Butler for the Centre Pompidou in April 2024, "Comment vivre maintenant?," this paper was delivered on the panel "Antigone pour le présent" on April 25. The event was haunted by the demand by some members of Emmanuel Macron's Renaissance party to have the program canceled by the minister of culture because of Butler's pro-Palestinian position—in particular, a characterization of Hamas's attack on October 7 as an "act of armed resistance." Butler removed their name from the program and decided "not

to participate formally," not to appear onstage, but to remain in the depths of the auditorium, ostensibly silent, a listener rather a speaker.

Works Cited

Abu-Laban, Yasmeen, and Abigail B. Bakan. "Anti-Palestinian Racism and Racial Gaslighting." *The Political Quarterly* 93, no. 3 (2022): 508–16.

"After Going Viral for Slapping an Israeli Soldier, Ahed Tamimi Shares Her Story." *MSNBC*, September 21, 2022. https://www.msnbc.com/the-mehdi-hasan-show/watch/after-going-viral-for-slapping-an-israeli-soldier-ahed-tamimi-shares-her-story-148985413804.

Al-Bazian, Hatem (@hatembazian). "She Went to Get Food for Her Family and Came Back to Find All Her Family and Kids Killed by an Israeli Bombing Attack!" Instagram video, March 18, 2024. https://www.instagram.com/hatembazian/reel/C4qNb0RAaE4/.

al-Hajjar, Mohammed. "In Gaza, You Don't Only See Death. You Smell It. You Breathe It." *Middle East Eye*, January 14, 2024. https://www.middleeasteye.net/opinion/gaza-dont-only-see-death-smell-breathe-it.

Anidjar, Gil. "*Mal de Sionisme* (Zionist Fever)." In *Living Together: Jacques Derrida's Communities of Violence and Peace*, edited by Elizabeth Weber, 45–58. New York: Fordham University Press, 2012.

Arranz, Adolfo, et al. "Inside the Tunnels of Gaza: The Scale, and the Sophistication, of Hamas' Tunnel Network." *Reuters*, December 31, 2023. https://www.reuters.com/graphics/ISRAEL-PALESTINIANS/GAZA-TUNNELS/gkvldmzorvb/.

Benjamin, Walter. "Critique of Violence" (1921). In *Reflections: Essays, Aphorisms, Autobiographical Writings*, edited by Peter Demetz, 291–316. New York: Schocken Books, 1986.

Butler, Judith P. "The Pleasures of Repetition." In *Pleasure beyond the Pleasure Principle*, edited by Robert A. Glick and Stanley Bone, 259–75. New Haven: Yale University Press, 1990.

Butler, Judith P. *Antigone's Claim*. New York: Columbia University Press, 2000.

Butler, Judith P. *Parting Ways*. New York: Columbia University Press, 2012.

Butler, Judith P. "Companion Thinking: A Response." *NLH* 51, no. 4 (2020): 687–94.

Butler, Judith P. *The Force of Non-Violence*. London: Verso, 2020.

Butler, Judith P. "Judith Butler - Contre l'antisémitisme et pour la paix révolutionnaire en Palestine." *Paroles D'Honneur*, March 7, 2024. Video, 2:02:12. https://www.youtube.com/watch?v=rlQNBJOq-0E.

Butler, Judith P. *Who's Afraid of Gender?* New York: Farrar, Straus, and Giroux, 2024.

Comay, Rebecca. "*Nihil est in imagine vivum.*" In *Niobes: Antiquity, Modernity, Critical Theory*, edited by Mario Telò and Andrew Benjamin, 36–53. Columbus: Ohio State University Press, 2024.

Derrida, Jacques. *Archive Fever: A Freudian Impression*. Edited by Eric Prenowitz. Chicago: University of Chicago Press, 1996.

Derrida, Jacques. "Autoimmunity: Real and Symbolic Suicides." In *Philosophy in a Time of Terror*, edited by Giovanna Borradori, 85–136. Chicago: University of Chicago Press, 2003.

Derrida, Jacques. "Deconstructing Terrorism." In *Philosophy in a Time of Terror*, edited by Giovanna Borradori, 137–72. Chicago: University of Chicago Press, 2003.

Derrida, Jacques. *Life Death*. Edited by Pascale-Anne Brault and Peggy Kamuf. Chicago: University of Chicago Press, 2020.

Edelman, Lee. *No Future*. Durham: Duke University Press, 2004.

Edelman, Lee. *Bad Education*. Durham: Duke University Press, 2023.

Efrati, Ido. "Spread of Disease in Gaza Endangers the Hostages Held by Hamas, and Will Soon Even Risk Israel." *Haaretz*, December 13, 2023. https://www.haaretz.com/israel-news/2023-12-13/ty-article/.premium/morbidity-in-gaza-endangers-the-hostages-and-possibly-israel/0000018c-5fe1-d6f9-afbc-5febf3e60000.

Esmeir, Samera. "The End of the Colonial Government." In *From the River to the Sea*, edited by Sai Englert, Michal Schatz, and Rosie Warren, 110–20. London: Verso, 2023.

Fanon, Frantz. *Black Skin, White Masks*. New York: Grove Press, 1967.

Frankel, Julia. "The Family of a Palestinian Activist Jailed for Incitement Says Young Woman's Account Was Hacked." *Associated Press*, November 8, 2023. https://apnews.com/article/palestinians-israel-ahed-tamimi-west-bank-raids-8833619f1924676a9b7dbd053b2fa3ba.

Freud, Sigmund. "Beyond the Pleasure Principle" (1920). In *The Standard Edition of the Complete Psychological Works of Sigmund Freud*, translated by James Strachey, volume 18, 1–64. London: The Hogarth Press, 1955.

Freud, Sigmund. "Civilization and Its Discontents" (1930). In *The Standard Edition of the Complete Psychological Works of Sigmund Freud*, translated by James Strachey, volume 21, 64–145. London: The Hogarth Press, 1955.

"Gaza is Dying of Thirst." *Action Contre la Faim*, October 27, 2023. https://www.actioncontrelafaim.org/en/press/gaza-is-dying-of-thirst/.

Griffith, Mark, ed. *Sophocles: Antigone*. Cambridge: Cambridge University Press, 1999.

Grossman, Hannah. "Palestinian Woman Whom Liberal Media Compared to Rosa Parks Is Accused of Threatening to Drink Jews' Blood and Eat Their Skulls." *Fox News*, November 10, 2023. https://nypost.com/2023/11/10/news/palestinian-rosa-parks-hailed-by-media-as-hero-accused-of-sharing-hitlerian-threat-to-drink-jews-blood/.

Hajyahia, Adam. "The Principle of Return: The Repressed Ruptures of Zionist Time," Palestine Issue: From the River to the Sea. *Parapraxis*. Accessed November 28, 2024. https://www.parapraxismagazine.com/articles/the-principle-of-return#_ftn12.

Haq, Sana Noor, and Rosa Rahimi. "'We Are Dying Slowly:' Palestinians Are Eating Grass and Drinking Polluted Water as Famine Looms Across Gaza." *CNN*, February 1, 2024. https://www.cnn.com/2024/01/30/middleeast/famine-looms-in-gaza-israel-war-intl/index.html.

Henao Castro, Andrés Fabián. *Antigone in the Americas*. Albany: State University of New York Press, 2021.

Human Rights Watch. "Gaza: Israel's Imposed Starvation Deadly for Children." *Informed Comment*, April 14, 2024. https://www.juancole.com/2024/04/israels-starvation-children.html.

Ibsaid, Ahmad. "Angry Soil: Poem on Palestine." *State of Siege*, April 7, 2024. https://ahmadibsais.substack.com/p/angry-soil.

Karera, Axelle. "Blackness and the Pitfalls of Anthropocene Ethics." *Critical Philosophy of Race* 7, no. 1 (2019): 32–56.

Lacan, Jacques. *The Seminar of Jacques Lacan: The Ethics of Psychoanalysis (Book VII)*. Edited by Jacques Alain Miller. New York: Norton, 1992.

Lacan, Jacques. *The Seminar of Jacques Lacan: The Other Side of Psychoanalysis (Book XVII)*. Translated by Russell Grigg. New York: Norton, 2007.

Mameni, Salar. *Terracene*. Durham: Duke University Press, 2023.

Marder, Elissa. "Anti Antigone." *Diacritics* 49, no. 2 (2021): 13–22.
Marder, Michael. *Dust.* London: Bloomsbury, 2016.
Markus, David. "Persecution Terminable and Interminable." Palestine Issue: From the River to the Sea. *Parapraxis.* Accessed November 28, 2024. https://www.parapraxismagazine.com/articles/persecution-terminable.
McKernan, Bethan, and Sufian Taha. "Activist Ahed Tamimi among 50 Jailed Palestinians Listed for Release by Israel." *The Guardian*, November 28, 2023. https://www.theguardian.com/world/2023/nov/28/ahed-tamimi-release-israel-hamas-ceasefire-deal-jailed-palestinians.
Mhawish, Mohammed R. "Gaza's Morning Ritual: Searching under Rubble for Dolls, Books, Loved Ones." *Al Jazeera*, January 19, 2024. https://www.aljazeera.com/features/2024/1/19/the-scale-of-destruction-is-unimaginable.
Povinelli, Elizabeth A. *Geontologies.* Durham: Duke University Press, 2018.
Puar, Jasbir. *The Right to Maim.* Durham: Duke University Press, 2017.
Pugliese, Joseph. *Biopolitics of the More-Than-Human.* Durham: Duke University Press, 2020.
Rimell, Victoria. "Philosophers' Stone: Enduring Niobe." In *Niobes: Antiquity, Modernity, Critical Theory*, edited by Mario Telò and Andrew Benjamin, 69–84. Columbus: Ohio State University Press, 2024.
Schulman, Sarah. *Conflict Is Not Abuse.* Vancouver: Arsenal Pulp Press, 2016.
Swarbrick, Steven, and Jean-Thomas Tremblay. *Negative Life.* Evanston: Northwestern University Press, 2024.
Tamimi, Ahed, and Dena Takruri. *They Called Me a Lioness: A Palestinian Girl's Fight for Freedom.* New York: One World, 2022.
Telò, Mario. *Greek Tragedy in a Global Crisis.* London: Bloomsbury, 2023.
Telò, Mario. *Reading Greek Tragedy with Judith Butler.* London: Bloomsbury, 2024.
Telò, Mario. *The Late Animal: Edward Said, Classicism, and the Limits of Humanism.* Oxford: Oxford University Press, forthcoming.
Umachandran, Mathura. "Niobe between Benjamin and Arendt—and Beyond." In *Niobes: Antiquity, Modernity, Critical Theory*, edited by Mario Telò and Andrew Benjamin, 195–207. Columbus: Ohio State University Press, 2024.
Ware, Ben. "The Death Drive at the End of the World." *e-flux* 134 (2023). https://www.e-flux.com/journal/134/525929/the-death-drive-at-the-end-of-the-world/
Wynter, Sylvia. "Sambos and Minstrels." *Social Text* 1 (1979): 149–56.
Žižek, Slavoj. *The Sublime Object of Ideology.* London: Verso, 1989.
Žižek, Slavoj. *Looking Awry.* Cambridge, MA: MIT Press, 1991.
Žižek, Slavoj. *The Ticklish Subject.* London: Verso, 1999.
Zupančič, Alenka. *Let Them Rot: Antigone's Parallax.* New York: Fordham University Press, 2023.

Part III

Critique of the Death Drive—Theoretical Confrontations

11

The Queer Life of Auto-repugnancy in Freud

Penelope Deutscher

The critique of reproductive futurism may have sometimes been understood as staking a position against reproduction, but its caution is concerned, rather, with the phantasmatic role that is assigned to children. Lee Edelman's *No Future*[1] offers an acute analysis of the use of the child because it is made into the "icon and promise of meaning"[2] against which is opposed a figure of obstruction that is taken to be antagonistic to the interests attributed to the child (continuity, the projection of self into the future, social meaning). The sinthomosexual—whose drives include a curiously motivated interest in impeding the happy ends (marriage, childraising, resolved narratives, anticipated futures) conventionally associated with social meaning and reproductive futurism—is one of the terms used for this figure of obstruction in *No Future*, and the figure is reprised in *Bad Education*.[3]

Those queer figures in *No Future* include some of film's representations of women whose obsessions, as depicted in *Leave Her to Heaven* and *Rebecca*, range from machinating the death of an adolescent ward, to inducing a miscarriage by throwing oneself down a staircase, killing oneself to provoke a spouse's murder charge, to a housekeeper's obstruction of her employer's new wife and efforts to produce the latter's suicide. As also shown in *No Future*, these figures of obstruction are most visibly found in the religious right's homophobic depictions of same-sex unions as if they amounted to impediments to national or natural futures, and of queer adults as capable of deviating children from the path toward eventual heterosexual union they might otherwise follow. In short, through the depiction of a range of such figures as impeding such futures, the possibilities of self-continuity and forward projection are rendered as if these are thwarted outcomes that would otherwise have unfolded. As Edelman recapitulates, *No Future* asserted

> that social relations, which imagine an end to their structural antagonism in a tomorrow ceaselessly deferred, invoke the future as the guarantee of meaning's realization. Such a future, . . . compels us [to] take our social value from our various relations to *it* and to make ourselves, in whatever way, the guardians of *its* future.[4]

Since children appear within such a project as "as ifs" (imaginary projections of what would have been possible if not for the figure of impediment) whose effect is generated by obstruction and the illusory temporal form of the "if not for," what elides scrutiny in this psychic mechanism is the "if not for"'s actual realizability: it conceals the impossibility of the permanently deferred realization of social meaning, identity, or persistence of selfhood. To that end, as Edelman continues, "A class of persons must therefore emerge to materialize the *danger* to that future."[5]

Politically, this can produce forms of political violence against that class of persons. Psychically, it can produce a kind of selfhood that projects its possibility into the future through its repudiation of a countering incoherence, discontinuity, and absence of meaning theoretically associated with the Real. In terms of its valence in works such as *No Future*, then, the "child" to which Edelman refers is an operator of this suturing function, a projection of an impossible self-continuity.

So, whereas theories of queerness[6] are primarily associated with sexuality studies, here queerness is a more specific operator: playing a structural role (as seeming obstruction, making it seem as if that which is deemed impeded would otherwise be possible), in an omnipresent negotiation that must otherwise take place with impossibility within a sexual relation, relation to meaning, or relation to life.

Meanwhile, since the queer theory that is relevant here pinpoints the suturing figures of obstruction that generate the meaning of what they seem to impede, the charged satisfactions in which it has been particularly interested are those forms of *jouissance* illustrated in *No Future*, the reverberating energy of intense attachment to, or specific enjoyment taken by the sinthomosexual in what thwarts social legibility—impeding the happy ends of others, particularly those associated with life, futurity, continuity, unions, and their flourishing children. So, to such obstructive figures as *Leave Her to Heaven*'s Ellen Berent, *North by Northwest*'s Leonard, and eponymous destructive visitants of *The Birds*, *Bad Education* adds the murderous visitants of Haneke's *Funny Games*, who go further still by drawing attention to the suturing role of narrative's very conventions.

The projected impediment that sutures together the projection of those ends is a position that may be filled by a putatively obstructive person, creature, or another form of forceful antagonism to life. Such an account can also concern the "forces of nature"—for which *No Future* suggested the mysterious attacks of *The Birds*, impeding the putative interests of life, new heterosexual bonds, and happy ends.

Resistance to Life

Just as the argument of *No Future* concerns the role assigned to children without amounting to taking a position for or against them, Edelman's analyses of theories within natural history and biology that, in various ways, have resituated death at the heart of life are not positions adopted for or against life. Instead, the question is, again, how have phantasmatic prospects of continuity been sutured by certain accounts of, or relationships to, life? Where life is seen as seeking its own continuity, it may seem as if it is impeded or interrupted by death, disease, or resistance to life as binary opposites. By contrast, some theorists of *Lebenskraft* have situated resistance to life—decomposition, disease, morbidity, the nonliving, and the pathological—as integral to life. Even so, Edelman points out they may still interpret pathology in a particular way, as a condition of possibility—for example, so as to argue that there can be no life without its own pathology. This speaks to the seemingly subtle, but significant, difference of emphasis between seeing life as in a state of constant decomposition or as made possible by that decomposition. For this reason, life might still be deemed ideological insofar as these accounts presuppose the principle of life's preservation (even where, more radically, this is an account of persistence paradoxically accomplished by factors resistant to life). One analogy is homeostasis, suggesting a possible view of life as incessantly having to adjust to changing internal and external circumstances so as to maintain its constancy. Such an account could, as Edelman points out, potentially emphasize that an organism is constantly becoming other. But if that becoming other is instead interpreted as essential to an organism's persistence of identity—however paradoxically—Edelman suggests we look again, so as to identify, here also, an interpretation of nature as "speak[ing] in the voice of doxa when life is represented as the regulatory maintenance or constancy of what is."[7]

Thus, whether the point of reference is homophobic or pro-life accounts producing the phantasmatic child impeded by sinthomosexuals and abortions, or theories that project a continuity of life accomplished either despite, or because of, the forces deemed death, disease, pathology, or resistance, and despite the seemingly different politics, both a phantasmatic child and an ideological life, on this account:

> Induc[e] the imperative of promoting and protecting a phantasmatic construct: the salubrious integrity of an order of existence threatened by something foreign and external.[8]

Thus, here too, one can speak of a suturing effect. We track the flexibility of the term queerness connecting these contexts of application as we find that this ideological life of natural history and biology is characterized as: "[k]eep[ing] its distance from queerness."[9]

Notwithstanding the breadth with which the term is used, in this analysis queerness has a recognizable structural form, within which the critical diagnosis of the "if not for" is indispensable. The continuity of life or of futurity is projected as what could be *if not for* the figure (occupied by a range of placeholders) situated as an obstacle. Moreover, it is the reference to the seeming obstacle that generates the phantasmatic meaning (all the more so since the latter never arrives) of what this "obstruction" is taken to impede.

How, then, might that form bear on Freud's "Beyond the Pleasure Principle"? This will also amount to the question: How to read Freud? This question particularly arises given that, in "Beyond the Pleasure Principle," Freud offers multiple inflections of the death drive, and, by the lights of this discussion, some with more queer potential than others.

This range includes Freud's cross-referencing in "Pleasure Principle" of the death drive to theories of life developed by early thinkers in natural history and biology. The heterogeneous meaning and function he attributes to the death drive are further seen in his analogies to the reproduction of both monocellular and complex biological entities.[10]

Freud and Life's *Streben*

As is well-known, Freud confronted the death drive as a puzzle, first, because it suggested that some psychic mechanisms and strivings were inconsistent with the pleasure principle.[11] The puzzle also arises in light of his speculations about parallels with the impetuses of nonconscious organic life. Freud construes life (at once individually, sub-, and supra-individually) in terms of a striving, or outward-directed urge (for which he uses the terms *Streben* and *Trachten*) that has single cellular, collective, and species-oriented dimensions, but in terms that are also analogized with early psychic development. One version of this application coalesces into a reproductive teleology, although it also bears a more promising surplus to the latter.

Thus, Freud refers to the neonate's object cathexes prior to ego formation, and so to the oral stage, in which the "act of obtaining erotic mastery over an object coincides with that object's destruction," and then to a stage of eventual libidinal maturity at which "extraordinarily strong" drives seek to "bring about sexual union."[12] Where, at this stage, he refers to life drives [*Lebenstrieben*],[13] the micro (the sub-individual) has come to encompass both the individual and the supra-individual, as if they can all share the same organic aim. At this point in "Beyond the Pleasure Principle," the death drive manifests as attempted possession or domination of a gratifying object. Thus, we are further told that it can enter into "the service of the sexual function,"[14] thereby becoming, in adult sexual encounters, a desire for "erotic mastery" of the other. As Freud offers this account, we could ask why individual psychic life is being referred to aims that are understood to be collective (most literally the purported interests of a species), in this case in the guise of transindividual species-based interest in reproduction. A heavily figurative dimension within this account is allowing a "sexual function" [*Sexualfunktion*] in individuals to be characterized as if it expressed the reproductive interests of the species:[15]

> During the oral stage of organization of the libido, the act of obtaining erotic mastery over an object coincides with that object's destruction; later, the sadistic instinct separates off, and finally, at the stage of genital primacy, it takes on, *for the purposes of reproduction*, the function of overpowering the sexual object to the extent necessary for carrying out the sexual act. (Emphasis mine)[16]

We can ask what secures this figurative dimension, what it is intended to secure, and also, what legitimates these oscillations in scale? Given their general anonymity, to what are we supposed to attribute the aim [*Zweck*] of the micro and macro, given that species-wide reproductive interest and individual reproductive interest are depicted as if they are parallel or enfolding each other, merely operating on different scales? Understood collectively, this *Streben* is attributed to all human existence and to existence more generally. But Freud anthropomorphizes it with the force and urgency also attributed to the urge to reproduce in (some) individual humans. It is as if "life" generally has the kind of urge, striving (*Streben*) toward and interest in reproduction manifested by some adult humans who strongly desire parenthood. So, for all that Freud borrows analogies from biology to produce this account, he also relies on the ability to reverse the direction of the analogy.

One might expect a general critique of reproductive futurism to focus on this reproductive dimension within Freud's account of the death drive. But Edelman also invites us to consider the heterogeneity with which Freud's uses of biology presuppose life's aim of self-preservation. Insofar as "Beyond the Pleasure Principle" oscillates in this regard also, it establishes the resources for a less preservative form of critique.

The Paradox of the Death Drive

For that reason, Edelman finds in "Pleasure Principle's" account of the death drive a less obvious means of engaging the queer potential of Freud's work. Multiple interpretations have been provoked by the famous ambiguity in Freud's account of the relationship between the pleasure principle and the death drive. Moreover, Edelman has found in them examples of more (or less) suturing forms of critique,[17] as suggested in his response to the accounts of Geoffrey Bennington and Elizabeth Grosz.

On the one hand, Freud characterizes the rudimentary impulses of living entities in terms of a surging forward that is also a striving for their own continuity, a striving that also involves incorporation of, or attachment to, objects in their vicinity. On the other, his account of the death drive points to a mysterious and seemingly contradictory impetus toward stasis, annihilation, self-annihilation. The impetus toward satisfaction by a libidinally cathected object blurs with the pursuit of resolution or stilling of its stimulation. Thus, a pursuit that seems expressive of a pleasure principle can also manifest as an impulse toward annihilation: either by satisfying and satiating the excitation's friction; or by erasing the object causing the latter; or by quelling an excitation that can be indistinguishably external and internal. While these impetuses can be characterized as if they are mysteriously opposed in their aims, the latter can also be depicted as overlapping: as when (according to Freud) the death drive infuses eros with aggressivity, or when the pleasure principle's temporary satiation is indistinguishably the realization of an impetus to extinguish an excitation that, in both senses, also provides satisfaction.

And, just as Freud's account of the death drive oscillates in this (and other) senses, it does so also when it plays a role in his reference to the natural sciences in discussing the putative aims of life and reproduction. On the one hand, we will find here the interests of self-continuity and reproduction associated with life's *Streben*: we will find the teleology of persistence. But on the other hand, another, arguably more promising account in "Beyond the Pleasure Principle" is seen when Freud's references to the natural history and biology of his day also seem to indicate a concurrent potential for redefining life in terms of an auto-repugnancy whose friction would be that of an original heterogeneity. Since, as such, it would, impossibly, seek to depart from itself, this would force a rethinking of what it might mean to return to itself.

Freud's Analogies

These multiple resources sometimes gave rise to Freud's drawing a further analogy between inorganic life and the psychic in terms of their relationship to milieux that are too simplistically seen as external. Freud describes a pressure of excitation exerted on an entity that can be resistant to the responsive modification thereby forced on it by its interaction with its milieu, with the result that sometimes, the only changes that take place, and/or are preserved, are those that it cannot withstand.[18] That might seem to suppose that rudimentary organic entities attempt to preserve themselves *against* an external pressure that forces reaction or change. But if we look within this material for its countercurrent, we can construe also this life as emerging from, or *as*, a self-repugnant auto-irritation.[19] What might otherwise be imagined as its most original form is nothing but its own heterogeneity. As a matter of how to read Freud, this returns us to the malleable direction of analogy on which he relies when he turns to biology.

On the one hand, Freud can characterize, as he does in "Group Psychology and the Analysis of the Ego," the neonate as an antagonism of forces, adding its impulses toward stasis to those of connectivity and growth.[20] As a rudimentary *Ich-trieb*, it is also described as resisting some excesses of stimuli—as in Freud's example of the newborn that has only just begun to distinguish its boundaries from those of its milieu and from those of the objects in that milieu, and whose low tolerance to these concurrently "internal" and "external" environmental stimulations[21] might manifest in its long sleep periods and intermittent rejection of the objects to which it also attaches.[22] In "Pleasure Principle," Freud suggests an analogy with the emergence of organic forms of life, in that "the coming to life of inanimate matter [seeks] to restore the inanimate state."[23] As he sees this, both could be expressive of an original impetus of resistance, repudiation, or regression that accompanies and counterbalances the impetus to connect, bind, appropriate, persist, expand, or proliferate. While this analogical relation between a seeking ("*Wollen*") that is ascribed to a "coming [in]to life" and to ego formation[24] is complex, to the extent that it is seen as original, what could the impulse to regression mean? His reference to a newborn concerns an entity that has just begun to distinguish its boundaries from those of its milieu and those of objects in that milieu and might be better described as dissolved in, or as enveloping, its environment—delineating itself only subsequently. Thus, the resistance of a neonate's rudimentary *Ich-trieb* could be seen both as different from and also *as* the (putatively "external") stimulus to which it emerges as responsive.

Freud does observe at one point that the "attributes [*Eigenschaften*] of life" must have emerged in inanimate matter given that "inanimate things existed before living ones."[25] But because he characterizes simple forms of biological life[26] (if assumed to be an emergent animacy) as bearing an irritation: an impulse to quell or appease stimulation, one could, at the limit, characterize this as an original self-irritation, as if life's emergence would be a self-differentiating force to alleviate the irritation that is its own existence.[27] This blurring of internal and external also bears on the ambiguity between the pursuits of a pleasure principle and those of the death drive. The relief of appeasement in the wake of excitation (that pressure to seek relief) is also thinkable in terms of the drive toward stasis since an absence of irritation or stimulation would also amount to an absence of being.[28] In a sense, the origin of primordial life on this account is not inanimacy nor stasis but the death drive.

If for Freud, then, there is a speculative parallel between psychic and biological life, it concerns the seeming paradox of referring to the emergence of life out of inanimacy, given that rudimentary life, *as* that very emergence, would, on this account, be self-repugnant. The most primordial animacy would be, from the outset, that life which "endeavo[rs] to cancel itself out,"[29] analogized with a psychic life or consciousness that, as psychic animacy, would also be expressive of a rudimentary death drive. Since it can be formulated by Freud in terms of the tension [*Spannung*] that seeks not to be ["*nach unserer Annahme rühren die Ich-triebe von der Belebung der unbelebten Materie*"], Freud likens the rudimentary states of the psychic and organic as follows:

> The tension which then arose in what had hitherto been an inanimate substance endeavored to cancel itself out. In this way the first drive came into being: to return to the inanimate state.[30]

Despite this reference, Freud's own account offers further resources for reconsidering this reference to an inanimate state out of which animacy would emerge. An ambiguity resides in both of the terms analogized by Freud: the life thematized in the life sciences and rudimentary psychic life. The development of both is described as arising from interaction with a countering force,[31] yet both can also be described, according to the elements offered by this account, as not "originally" distinguishable from that countering force: it is, if anything, the force positioned as "countering" (excitation, irritation, repugnancy) that could be considered original. In other words, Freud offers the resources for contesting the references (also to be found in his work) of an original entity (organic or psychic) somehow emerging from inanimacy and reacting to heterogeneous externalities. In light of a primordial absence of established internal-external boundaries between organism and environment, a primordial organism (whether the single-cellular life to which he refers in "Pleasure Principle," or the rudimentary "*Ich-trieb*") could also be seen as always already its own self-irritation, an original heterogeneity to "itself."[32]

Edelman and Freud

Connecting these reserves to the ambiguity concerning the extent to which we should see eros, the pleasure principle, and the death drive as opposing each other's interests, we recall Edelman's attention to how such ambiguities can lead to two alternative readings of Freud's death drive. According to one version, eros would seek constancy in the form of binding, organization, and order, and as such would be resisted by the death drive, as an impetus to nothingness or inanimacy in lieu of unity. Here, the death drive would be understood as the pursuit of a return of the organism, or of psychic life, to a former state. When, for contrast, Edelman points to Elizabeth Grosz's interest in the parallel between the death drive (construed as seeking to alleviate excitation) and the constancy principle for which Fechner was a point of reference for Freud,[33] he suggests seeing the ambiguity between interpretations of the death drive (such as those of Grosz and Geoffrey Bennington[34]) as demonstrating the "inconsistency of the constancy principle"[35] in Freud's work. Consistent with that suggestion, and with Edelman's interest in redefining the pursuit of "constancy" as recognizing that life must be a perpetual inconstancy, Freud's account also depicts life as already its own principle of heterogeneity. To these ends, Edelman himself points to the version of life *as* aversion to life that is elaborated in the sections on Bichat in Foucault's *Birth of the Clinic*:

> In the wake of Bichat, Foucault announces, life no longer derives from an ontologically specific vital principle; it names, instead, a resistance to what inhabits it *from the outset.*[36]

Again, Edelman indicates the suturing principle salient to admitting (or excluding) an account of life as never not having been inhabited by resistance to life. Importantly, there are different ways of construing this point. Whereas one variant would depict self-antagonism as a "condition of possibility" of life, and while this does situate heterogeneity at the heart of life, the language of condition of possibility could still presuppose the telos of life's persistence and survival. Having made this point, Edelman suggests that this variation loses the radicality with which life is understood as heterogeneous to itself. I have argued that a version corresponding more closely to that radicality (particularly in light of Edelman's interest in the role of the organic in "Beyond the Pleasure Principle"[37]) can be derived from a surplus embedded in Freud's analogical use of the life sciences. This is to amplify the account of life's relation to death as paradoxical: to see Freud's "Pleasure Principle" as also suggesting life's friction in relation to itself, a life that (to suggest a counter-anthropomorphization) just can't stand itself. Rather than seeing death as anterior to life in the sense of inanimacy preceding animacy, this would be to see death as the principle of resistance (death would be the animacy organizing life). Death's principle of resistance would not arrive in a secondary time to oppose the interests of a more original life. Rather, intolerability would come first, in relation to which the seeming binary of life and death would later be articulated, as if separate, and as if the latter were secondary to, and interrupted the former. Rather than seeing life as "made possible" by auto-repugnancy, the alternative would be to see auto-repugnancy (a principle of heterogeneity) emerging *as* life: to put this another way again, life would already be, on this version, its own negativity. Animation is depicted as immediately intolerant of its excitation, but without a life, or an ego, *prior* to that excitation and that intolerability. This means that so-called primordial life (or, since Freud considers these in parallel, a primordial *Ich-trieb*) would be described in terms more paradoxical than those of an entity's stimulation by milieu. Rather, the friction or auto-repugnancy of rudimentary organic life and of rudimentary psychic life[38] would be a more promising resource reserved within Freud's analogical references to the life sciences, particularly when compared to the best-known alternative in "Beyond the Pleasure Principle": the idea that organic entities seek a return to stasis or the inert as an original state somehow anterior to being or animacy.

To take this further, once the organic and psychic are analogized in this way, rudimentary "life itself" (a paradoxical formulation) would, therefore, be "misidentifying" itself to the extent that it resists a stimulation that it registers as foreign interruption. For the death drive can be defined in these redoubled and opposed terms: as a drive to stasis whose very effort (as if against a foreign principle) would be a structural misrecognition of its own auto-repugnant form. To return to one's anterior state is not to return to a state of nonbeing. There is no thoroughly inert state that is original to an entity's animacy.

This could be seen as a further context in which the critical resources within Freud's speculative biology-psyche analogies profit from the flexible reversibility of their application. To consider the implications of Edelman's intervention, the "active effort" in life that exists *as if* its principle is that of continuity might (amplifying the potential of this reversibility in Freud) even be thought of as the biological or energetic equivalent of suturing: a life whose most rudimentary form would already consist of an impetus of repudiation of intolerability. This is to reconsider the resources of the biological life on which Freud draws as a reference in "Pleasure Principle," also as a means of amplifying Edelman's reference to

> the inconsistency that Freud discovers at the core of the constancy principle, which turns it against itself, [as having] everything to do with disruption for which the death drive tries to account: a disruption of the "constancy" or "norm" of "what is" that exposes the active effort involved in making what is seem continuous.[39]

Thus, when the queerness Edelman understands in structural terms[40] is re-parsed within this material, it allows a reconstrual of the principle that would otherwise present as a binary, where the principle otherwise understood as the foreignness of death would convert into a paradoxical account of life as never not an auto-repugnancy whose principle of heterogeneity cannot be displaced as if it were an external intrusion against which life could be defended. That resource is consistent with Edelman's reconsideration of the Freudian analogies between psychic life and the constancy principle (reinterpreted as the perpetual heterogeneity of inconstancy, the necessary, reiterating, self-interruption of self-adjustment):

> The resistance, the stance of againstness, by which life stands opposed to death, thus pits life against life as well. It interprets life as the differentiation both of and from itself and so as the constant queerness, the non-self identity or discontinuity, to which the pursuit of constancy leads.[41]

A further question: assuming that, as suggested here, its best application is seen when it illustrates life's auto-repugnant form, how might this Freudian bank of analogical borrowings from natural science further clarify the amplitude given by Edelman to the term queer? Could it offer a means of reconsidering a much-debated preference expressed in *Bad Education* for construing negativity in terms of queerness?[42]

Structural Queerness (Is Not) Substituability

This has been a fraught dialogue because of Edelman's foregrounding of the term queer has also been set against seemingly alternative theories of negativity, including a number of Afro-pessimist concepts discussed in *Bad Education*. For example, it can seem as if *Bad Education* is offering an answering view to Wilderson's account of ontological negativity: that there is, for the singular ontological destruction of Blackness, no analogy.[43] Edelman might seem to be directly responding when he comments that "Black persons, despite the history that places them inextricably in relation to slavery are not . . . the singular or exclusive embodiments of ontological exclusion."[44] Clearly, these positions are different, but they can also—misleadingly—appear with the seeming proximity of oppositional points situated on the same terrain: as if Edelman and Wilderson meant the same thing by "ontological exclusion," respectively favoring a theorization of Blackness or queerness in its terms:

> without denying other (mis)namings of exclusion, I primarily refer to queerness as the catachresis of this nothing, of this ontological negation.[45]

But Blackness and queerness are not alternative embodiments of ontological negativity, at least in the sense that these arguments do not concern the same negativity. That is apparent from passages in which Wilderson speaks to the singularity of Blackness's ontological destruction,[46] and in which Edelman speaks to his reasons for thinking radical negativity with the term queerness.[47] For the former, this is a matter of understanding that Blackness emerged historically *as* an ontological destruction. For the latter, signifying life is founded on the exclusion of *ab-sens* as intolerable, an ab-sens for which "queerness, woman, Blackness, and trans*" belong to a longer list of terms that can stand in for, and obscure its intolerability. Thus while Wilderson and Edelman would not necessarily disagree in seeing "queerness, woman, Blackness, and trans*" as catachreses, those seeming social identities stand in for different structures of impossibility. Wilderson argues that historical violence produced Blackness as an impossibility of Being and social meaning, a catastrophe that is obscured by the identity and meanings of social exclusion that seem to offer Blackness the possibility of eventual inclusion. When Edelman points out that "Blackness, woman, trans*, incest, and sex" can all be the "catachreses of ab-sens," he understands that ab-sens to be general, for all that it has, historically, been "posited and positivized in those made to embody nothing."[48] These are not alternatives to each other because the former indicates a catastrophe in terms of which Blackness emerges, and the latter a universal impossibility or radical intolerability without which there would not be subjectivation.[49]

Moreover, because Edelman is a theorist of the sinthomosexual: while both discuss catachresis, that term is situated within a different structural understanding of the impossibility for which terms of identity stand in. If the sinthomosexual is the suturing figure of the "if not for" that generates a phantasmatic identity as if precluded or lost, for Edelman, that suturing again obscures and stands in for an absence of meaning that pertains to all and is intolerable to all—hence his suggestion at one point: "we are all sinthomosexuals."[50]

That these are not alternative positions concerning the same ontological negation, but noncomparable positions which are best understood as *not* taking alternative positions concerning the same problem, is all the clearer if we turn to the reasons why Edelman prefers the term queerness:

> All are rooted in the ontological antagonism that structures the logic of sense by which we are divided into being: divided between the subject of desire and of the subject of the drive, where the former consigns the latter to the status of what is not.[51]

For Wilderson, to see Blackness in terms of realized or realizable identity would be to misrecognize the degree of ontological catastrophe in terms of which Blackness has been produced. For Edelman, it would be the projection of an identity occluding ab-sens. While the difference in their priorities of analysis is consequential, Edelman's view that subjectivation is founded on the exclusion of *ab-sens* is not necessarily excluded by these alternative positions concerning ontological negation.

This is further seen if we turn to the further reasons proposed by Edelman for preferring the term queer, which assumes (at least) three senses in Edelman's work.[52] First, he does not refer to queer as a positive identity,[53] but rather as a mobile, open-ended term, and as the most eligible for indicating the strange drive toward the satisfactions that "seems to threaten a world."[54] Second, it stands in for a world-threatening enjoyment that can potentially be attributed (he reminds) to any "persons, objects, acts" as a catachresis for "the negativity of ab-sens."[55] Third, and in particular, we have seen the argument that, catachrestically, the negativity deemed threatening to the world's "unity, comprehension, or identity" is displaced onto "*queerness, woman, Blackness, trans**" as if the latter are the forces of harm, anti-meaning, or antilife, or disruption of the natural, a displacement generating the impression that "unity, comprehension, or identity" would be possible if not for these figures of againstness.[56]

Life

Why, from this perspective, is it important that within Edelman's project, life can also belong to this series? It further clarifies why Edelman and Wilderson are not presenting alternative positions on a shared conceptual terrain concerning negativity. Insofar as life appears within the open-ended series to which he refers, Edelman can still foreground the suturing function of the "if not for" that stands in the place of an intolerable absence of meaning. The ideology of life stands in for an (impossible) encounter with that intolerability, as do other catachrestic figures he mentions, including those associated with "againstness." By contrast, for Wilderson, Blackness specifically has undergone or been produced as an ontological catastrophe. Its radical negativity is not to be confused with a realizable idea of its coming into meaning or potentially accomplishing meaningful survival, because—for Wilderson—that optimism would underestimate the degree of Black catastrophe. And while both Wilderson and Edelman can refer to Blackness as the catachresis for a division that "structures the logic of sense,"[57] for Wilderson the latter's catastrophe (Blackness as absence of sense, meaning and value) is sutured by construing Blackness as an identity of againstness. For Edelman, there is an infinite number of catachreses of againstness for the unbearability of radical negation and ab-sens, the radical impossibility of a more general absence of meaning and value[58]—an infinite number to which "life" belongs.

In consequence, just as there are (at least) three meanings of queer, there are—as figured within this discussion—at least three meanings of life: ideological, catachrestic, and those associated with phantasmastic obstruction. Perhaps this is more obviously true of death, but life, too, can stand in for the out-of-joint drive toward strange satisfactions in excess of the good.[59]

Edelman clarifies that ideological life can be differentiated from biological life that in "Again and Against" is reconstrued as "queer life." It is analogous to the structural role of the sinthomosexual in that it coordinates two elements: (1) a deployment of the structure of the "if not for" which constructs a phantasmatic possibility of survival, and (2) its construction of the figures that stand in the way of that possible survival, through which they also become objects of violence.

Negativities

Wilderson speaks to the making of Blackness as the antithesis of life and ontology, and it is true that in *No Future*, Edelman describes the antilife associations of queerness.[60] Why, I have asked, aren't these parallel positions? To engage that question is to return to the range of figures of antilife in *No Future*, spanning sinthomosexuals, gay families, aborting women, and birds, and to a core element in Edelman's account of ontological negativity: its analysis of the suturing function effected by figures constructed as impediments to the "if not for." They appear to stand in for what is (putatively) being impeded, and is in fact being generated as an effect. Here, by obscuring the general and intolerable, the *if not for*'s suturing figures stand in the way of (effectively acting as a denial of, and projecting the phantasmatic possibility of) the continuity that is erroneously projected as if it were a lost possibility. An ideological life defended as if from threats construed as heterogeneous, an ideological life that, as such:

> keeps its distance from queerness, the death drive, and the repetitive "composition and decomposition" informing biological life.[61]

Life as auto-resistance becomes the equivalent of ontological negativity. The phantasmatic life that keeps its distance from queerness keeps its distance from an intolerable void of identity. This fundamental heterogeneity is a rudimentary auto-repulsion, and it generates the phantastic projection of a life (as identity, survivable, continuity, positivity) that stands in for auto-repugnancy.

Notes

1 Lee Edelman, *No Future: Queer Theory and the Death Drive* (Durham and London: Duke University Press, 2004).
2 As *No Future's* argument is summarized in Lee Edelman, *Bad Education: Why Queer Theory Teaches Us Nothing* (Durham: Duke University Press, 2023), 47.
3 Edelman, *Bad Education*, 47.
4 Edelman, *Bad Education*, 46–7.
5 Edelman, *Bad Education*, 47. Making the point even clearer, while it is true that children (represented as vulnerable, in need of protection from forces of contamination depicted as if exterior threats to be defended against) are often used as the figures of that imperiled future, it is no less true that some children are also represented as imperiling figures, or as both imperiled and imperiling. Examples can be seen in contemporary radical right-wing politics adopting both anti-immigration and anti-trans activism.
6 See Edelman, *Bad Education*, 171.
7 Lee Edelman, "Afterword: Again and Against," in *Against Life*, ed. Alastair Hunt and Stephanie Youngblood (Evanston: Northwestern University Press, 2016), 270.
8 Edelman, "Afterword," 271.
9 Edelman, "Afterword," 271.
10 In addition to drawing on other points of reference ranging from ancient Greek philosophy and myth to the revisitation of past trauma by war casualties.
11 As discussed below, particularly its confrontation with the reproduction of monocellular and multicellular organisms, and the difference between the asexual and sexual reproduction of elementary organisms.
12 Sigmund Freud, "Beyond the Pleasure Principle" (1920), in *The Standard Edition of the Complete Psychological Works of Sigmund Freud*, ed. James Strachey, volume 18 (London: Macmillan/Hogarth Press, 1955), 56–7; translation modified. In German, "*die außerordentlich heftigen Triebe, welche die geschlechtliche Vereinigung herbeiführen wollen*."
13 Freud, "Beyond the Pleasure Principle," 57.
14 Freud, "Beyond the Pleasure Principle," 54. In German, "*Ein Todestrieb . . . tritt dann in den Dienst der Sexualfunktion*."

15 Freud's "Civilization and its Discontents" also depicts the sex and reproduction he associates with the family unit as serving the ends of "*die Kultur*," translated as "civilization."

16 Freud, "Beyond the Pleasure Principle," 54; my emphasis. In German, "*Im oralen Organisationsstadium der Libido fällt die Liebesbemächtigung noch mit der Vernichtung des Objekts zusammen, später trennt sich der sadistische Trieb ab und endlich übernimmt er auf der Stufe des Genitalprimats zum Zwecke der Fortpflanzung die Funktion, das Sexualobjekt so weit zu bewältigen, als es die Ausführung des Geschlechtsaktes erfordert.*"

17 Similarly, see the attention he gives, arguably from a similar perspective, to Foucault's interpretation of Bichat, Edelman, "Afterword," 269.

18 Freud, "Beyond the Pleasure Principle," 38–9.

19 A longer account of life as self-repugnancy as one of the currents within "Beyond the Pleasure Principle" is offered in Penelope Deutscher, "Auto Repugnancy: In-between Freud's 'Pleasure Principle,'" *Psychoanalysis, Culture & Society* 25, no. 4 (2020): 518–36.

20 Sigmund Freud, "Group Psychology and the Analysis of the Ego" (1921), in *The Standard Edition of the Complete Psychological Works of Sigmund Freud*, ed. James Strachey, volume 18 (London: Macmillan/Hogarth Press, 1955), 130. In German: "*nach unserer Annahme rühren die Ich-triebe von der Belebung der unbelebten Materie her und wollen die Unbelebtheit wieder herstellen.*"

21 In German: "*nach unserer Annahme rühren die Ich-triebe von der Belebung der unbelebten Materie her und wollen die Unbelebtheit wieder herstellen.*"

22 Freud, "Group Psychology," 130, so that an "*absolut selbstgenügsamen Narzißmus zur Wahrnehmung einer veränderlichen Außenwelt und zum Beginn der Objektfindung gemacht, und damit ist verknüpft, daß wir den neuen Zustand nicht dauernd ertragen, daß wir ihn periodisch rückgängig machen und im Schlaf zum früheren Zustand der Reizlosigkeit und Objektvermeidung zurückkehren.*"

23 Freud, "Beyond the Pleasure Principle," 44.

24 This would, arguably, also be to attribute a kind of self-repugnancy to the ego's aim of "restoring" inanimacy, an impulse of restoration that would amount to equally rudimentary structure of misrecognition of the state that might count as restoration.

25 Freud, "Beyond the Pleasure Principle," 38. In German, "*Das Leblose war früher da als das Lebende.*" Making a point of avoiding speculation about how this could have occurred, he begins with the fact of this emergence and the vehicle of that preposition, "in": "The properties of life were at some time evoked in inanimate matter through the action of some force that remains incomprehensible." See Freud, "Beyond the Pleasure Principle," 38; translation modified. In German, "*Irgend einmal wurden in unbelebter Materie durch eine noch ganz unvorstellbare Krafteinwirkung die Eigenschaften des Lebenden erweckt.*"

26 As discussed in Deutscher, "Auto-Repugnancy."

27 Again, what complicates the account of psychic forces as seeking to relieve the pressure of an excitation perceived as heterogeneous, or as emanating from surroundings, is that, on this account, the boundaries between milieu and primordial human conscious embodiment are not clearly defined. For Freud, the excitation in question is therefore as much "internal," as response to the "external."

28 For Derrida (also a point of reference in *Bad Education*), this would also be the (impossible) absence of *différance*.

29 Freud, "Beyond the Pleasure Principle," 38. The translation from the German, "*trachtete danach, sich abzugleichen*," suggested by Strachey.

30 Freud, "Beyond the Pleasure Principle," 38; translation modified. In German, "*Die damals entstandene Spannung in dem vorhin unbelebten Stoff trachtete danach, sich abzugleichen; es war der erste Trieb gegeben, der, zum Leblosen zurückzukehren.*" As argued in Deutscher, "Auto-Repugnancy," the parallel relies on supposing the repetition of this specific force of self-repugnant striving ["*Trachten*"] in both organic and psychic life, such that the former may perhaps have been a forerunner similar to that which later gave rise to the development of consciousness in a particular stratum of living matter. In German, "*Vielleicht war es ein Vorgang vorbildlich ähnlich jenem anderen, der in einer gewissen Schicht der lebenden Materie später das Bewußtsein entstehen ließ.*"

31 Freud discusses the effect of external stimuli on rudimentary organisms, sometimes as imposed [*aufgezwungene*] by environments and retained and communicated to next generations. See Freud, "Beyond the Pleasure Principle," 38. And yet, even in his accounts suggesting a parallel between protozoa and "erster Trieb," animacy is also an irritation whose alleviation is just as immediately sought. Note that much of Freud's modeling (from single-celled organisms to psyches whose ego-libido is likened to pseudopodia extending libidinal catheses toward objects) characterizes reactions to exterior stimuli whose excitation prompts the impetus to alleviation or abatement, impetuses taken to accord with the death drive and the pleasure principle. But Freud's analogy also undermines the modeling of resistance to exterior change by what would erroneously be depicted as a discretely delineated entity, once that reactive entity would already be, in its most original form, its own self-irritation. Conceptually, this impacts the modeling of aversion to change ascribed to the death drive and the reference to animation emerging from the inanimate. In these primordial moments of animate life, the friction of animacy on the one hand or of rudimentary consciousness or psychic life on the other—this animation would not be distinguishable from its resistance to this animation. The result might be a more conceptually interesting (and paradoxical) original self-repulsion. See Sigmund Freud, "On Narcissism" (1914), in *The Standard Edition of the Complete Psychological Works of Sigmund Freud*, ed. James Strachey (London: Hogarth Press, 1966), 75–6.

32 If one sees that heterogeneity as original, one would need to problematize the status of this term "itself." This is also significant insofar as Freud's interest in suggesting parallels with the life sciences also suggests to him an understanding of the death drive as a return to a state of anterior inanimacy. But in just one of the many paradoxical dimensions in "Beyond the Pleasure Principle," Freud's speculative reference to an effort toward self-cancellation or inanimacy would need revision as misrecognition (whether psychic, organic, or philosophical) of rudimentary auto-repugnancy.

33 In other words, while Freud does hypothesize that the death drive would be analogous to Fechner's "tendency towards stability" (discussed in the first section of "Beyond the Pleasure Principle"), in so doing, Edelman argues that he also "destabilizes the stability of that concept and produces inconsistency in the very principle of constancy. Constancy, after all, comes to signify for Freud both the absolute discharge, the reduction to zero, of neuronal stimulation, and the retention of the necessary quantum of stimulus to achieve such a stable state; it underlies both the desire for inertia and the energetics of homeostatic regulation. In the first of these functions, it serves . . . as the basis for the pleasure principle; in the second it . . . also pertains, and at the same time, to the death drive that Freud explicitly places *beyond* the pleasure principle." See Edelman, "Afterword," 270.

34 Edelman discusses those suggested in Geoffrey Bennington, *Lyotard: Writing the Event* (New York: Columbia University Press, 1988) and in Elizabeth Grosz, *Volatile Bodies: Toward a Corporeal Feminism* (Bloomington: Indiana University Press, 1994), and for a further variation, see Catherine Malabou's interrogation of the differentiation between eros and the death drive given that the pleasure principle's pursuit of relief from irritation blurs with the impulse of the death drive. See Catherine Malabou, "Plasticity and Elasticity in Freud's 'Beyond the Pleasure Principle,'" *Diacritics* 37, no. 4 (2007): 78–85; and for the most extensive discussion of this problematic, see Jacques Derrida, *Life Death (The Seminars of Jacques Derrida)*, eds. Pascale-Anne Brault and Peggy Kamuf, trans. Michael Naas (Chicago: University of Chicago Press, 2023).

35 Edelman, "Afterword," 271.

36 Edelman, "Afterword," 269. One way of putting this is: with Bichat one could think of morbidity as constituting and defining life, not befalling it; one could think of life as pathological, as inherently morbid—an idea that can extend this concept of pathological life as an explanation of death and disease. There isn't a life that one would preserve from the pathological because there is no life except as pathological.

37 See Edelman, "Afterword," and in *Bad Education*, the brief reference to this dimension of Freud: "Freud sees the death drive as an unconscious wish to return to a preorganic state not threatened by energic stimulation and so not requiring a reserve of energy to regulate the conscious and unconscious systems" (Edelman, *Bad Education*, 105).

38 While not drawing this outcome from Freud's reference to rudimentary organic life, Edelman does—in generating from "Pleasure Principle's resources a reference to organic life as differentiation that would be "constant queerness"—suggest a similar aim for thinking through the resources of this text." See Edelman, "Afterword," 271.

39 Edelman, "Afterword," 271.

40 For his explicit comments in this regard ("*Bad Education* argues for a structural understanding of queerness," see the prefatory comments in Edelman, *Bad Education*, ix).

41 Edelman, "Afterword," 271.

42 Edelman, *Bad Education*, 19.

43 See Frank Wilderson, *Red, White, and Black: Cinema and the Structure of U.S. Antagonisms* (Durham: Duke University Press, 2010), 10 14, 33. On this, see also Elizabeth Weed, *Reading the Impossible: Sexual Difference, Critique, and the Stamp of History* (New York: Fordham University Press, 2024). Wilderson argues that the difference between the slave, on the one hand, and the Palestinian, the Native American, or the subject of settler colonialism, on the other, is that the latter suffer dispossession of territorial sovereignty, while the former loses "being," and see footnote 19 and 20 in Weed, *Reading the Impossible*.

44 Edelman, *Bad Education*, 19.

45 Edelman, *Bad Education*, 19.

46 Remembering that Wilderson's argument concerns an absolute negativity that is beyond comparison but nonetheless thinkable in terms of degrees of destruction—just in the sense that Wilderson compares it to genocide that could destroy peoples grotesquely, but not necessarily by obliterating identity or community.

47 Edelman, *Bad Education*, 19; Wilderson, *Red, White, and Black*, 10, 14, 33.

48 Edelman, *Bad Education*, xviii.

49 Edelman has pointed to a closer parallel in the argument provided by Jared Sexton, for whom racial Blackness approximates "that which disturbs every claim or formation of identity and difference as such," Edelman, *Bad Education*, 20–1. Also

included within this constellation of thought is Calvin Warren, who speaks to the double ontological obliteration of Blackness and queerness, as Edelman indicates, "Warren like Wilderson, links Blackness as ontological impossibility to the foreclosure from subjectivity of those who embody it catachrestically." See Edelman, *Bad Education*, 24 (discussing Calvin Warren, "Onticide: Afropessimism, Queer Theory, and Ethics," *Ill Will*, November 18, 2014, https://illwill.com/onticide-afropessimism-queer-theory-and-ethics).

50 Edelman, *Bad Education*, 47.
51 Edelman, *Bad Education*, 19.
52 This does differentiate Wilderson's and Edelman's references to Blackness, even as two accounts of radical negativity whose impossibility with which they structure worlds.
53 Edelman, *Bad Education*, 20.
54 Edelman, *Bad Education*, 20.
55 Edelman, *Bad Education*, 20.
56 A fourth sense is their becoming the objects of quotidian, social, and political violence.
57 Edelman, *Bad Education*, 19.
58 Edelman, *Bad Education*, 19.
59 On this argument, there are "infinitely mobile" catachreses for intolerable, nonnormative enjoyments that, on Edelman's account, "may follow from *any* attribute, including, among others, race, gender, gender expression, sexuality, ethnicity, caste, class, religion, mental or physical ability, marital status, and educational background, the list could go on forever." See Edelman, *Bad Education*, 19.
60 Wilderson, *Red, White and Black*, 23 and see Edelman, *No Future*, 16, 91.
61 Edelman, "Afterword," 271.

Works Cited

Bennington, Geoffrey. *Lyotard: Writing the Event*. New York: Columbia University Press, 1988.

Derrida, Jacques. *Life Death (The Seminars of Jacques Derrida)*. Edited by Pascale-Anne Brault and Peggy Kamuf. Translated by Michael Naas. Chicago: University of Chicago Press, 2023.

Deutscher, Penelope. "Auto Repugnancy: In-between Freud's 'Pleasure Principle.'" *Psychoanalysis, Culture & Society* 25, no. 4 (2020): 518–36.

Edelman, Lee. *No Future: Queer Theory and the Death Drive*. Durham and London: Duke University Press, 2004.

Edelman, Lee. "Afterword: Again and Against." In *Against Life*, edited by Alastair Hunt and Stephanie Youngblood, 269–74. Evanston: Northwestern University Press, 2016.

Edelman, Lee. *Bad Education: Why Queer Theory Teaches Us Nothing*. Durham: Duke University Press, 2023.

Freud, Sigmund. "Beyond the Pleasure Principle" (1920). In *The Standard Edition of the Complete Psychological Works of Sigmund Freud*, edited by James Strachey, volume 18, 7–64. London: Macmillan/Hogarth Press, 1955.

Freud, Sigmund. "Group Psychology and the Analysis of the Ego" (1921). In *The Standard Edition of the Complete Psychological Works of Sigmund Freud*, edited by James Strachey, volume 18, 69–144. London: Macmillan/Hogarth Press, 1955.

Freud, Sigmund. "On Narcissism." In *The Standard Edition of the Complete Psychological Works of Sigmund Freud*, edited by James Strachey, 67–102. London: Hogarth Press, 1966.

Grosz, Elizabeth. *Volatile Bodies: Toward a Corporeal Feminism*. Bloomington: Indiana University Press, 1994.

Malabou, Catherine. "Plasticity and Elasticity in Freud's 'Beyond the Pleasure Principle.'" *Diacritics* 37, no. 4 (2007): 78–85.

Warren, Calvin. "Onticide: Afropessimism, Queer Theory, and Ethics." *Ill Will*. November 18, 2014. https://illwill.com/onticide-afropessimism-queer-theory-and-ethics.

Weed, Elizabeth. *Reading the Impossible: Sexual Difference, Critique, and the Stamp of History*. New York: Fordham University Press, 2024.

Wilderson, Frank. *Red, White, and Black: Cinema and the Structure of U.S. Antagonisms*. Durham: Duke University Press, 2010.

12

Labor and Desire

Peter Hitchcock

J'aime mieux avoir eu la peau de nos patronnes que leur avoir laissé la nôtre.

—Christine Papin[1]

Poor Sisyphus was much happier in accepting his fateful labor, and we might say that the rock he pushed was death driven rather than muscled. Few consider, however, the labor in decision, the labor of decision as well as labor's decision. Here I am primarily interested not in the content of struggle, nor necessarily in the individual's consciousness of their fate, neither in the purely symbolic function of the drive, nor in the paradox of being toward death as its own mighty and justly revered philosophical reward (even as I necessarily reflect on all of these elements). The problem of the wanton and insistent discovery of psychoanalysis in the commodity chapter of *Capital*, the fetish of the fetish, or bourgeois aesthetics on the march, is that proletarian investment in the commodity begins in a displacement of desire that does not yet interrogate the logic of desire in proletarian being itself, which, after all, does not exist in having things, even nice things that you are told are nice, but persists in a horizon of socialization that pivots precisely on the death of that very subject. This is a death drive, an objective fiction of class I will argue, with an altogether different dimensionality than the revelation of a hidden content in the form. The desire of labor is not to make proletarians (even large families in modernization were largely a gamble on labor power in numbers). There is, of course, a deeply significant discourse about labor and reproduction, especially in relation to gendered divisions of labor and the wage. It is the capitalist, however, who desires proletarians, assemblages of labor power primed for extraction and accumulation. The proletarian cannot completely disavow this interpellation, for it is, after all, often tied to certain basic elements of existence: food, water, shelter, and so on, which are not simply nominalist irregularities. Yet it is important to accentuate that the proletarian does not desire proletarians, for the latter as subject exists only as the sign of subjugation and immiseration. The point of proletarian subjectivity is its destruction, its historical negation. This is the essence of its real abstraction, which is blind to any other purpose, to borrow from Lacan. We are familiar with Sabina Spielrein's theorization of the death drive, "Destruction as the

Cause of Coming Into Being" ("Die Destruktion als Ursache des Werdens"[2]) but the death drive for the proletarian within the capital/labor relation is closer to "destruction as the cause of overcoming becoming" (Zerstörung als Ursache der Überwindung des Werdens). Freud often used death drive in the plural, but for the bourgeoisie as a class, Thanatos is singular and absolute. The only drive greater than their own is proletarian, and capital, as capital—not as individual psychology—will not cease to make it.

Desire here, like the drive, is a materialist injunction, not a biological function. My title obviously invokes Paula Rabinowitz's classic book on working-class feminist writing of the 1930s in the United States, and I share her theorization of a kind of figuration of class/gender in writing for radical political change.[3] Desire in her project becomes a space of regendering the history of literary radicalism, tracing a force both internal to the subject and one that writes the body and attempts to shape its socialization. For the most part, Rabinowitz uses desire as wish or want, but it is not necessarily isomorphic with a subject's consciousness or even self-consciousness in general. The desiring woman in Rabinowitz's critique is easily misread either through objectification or through a categorical paradigm that registers the woman worker, for instance, only as an integer of commodity circulation. This, however, is not the limit case of desire either in Rabinowitz's case studies nor indeed in the relation of labor and capital. I will refer back to *Labor and Desire*, but I want to take something of the edge of desire to identify simultaneously a set of tensions in the theorization of the psychic pulsions of desire while beginning to reconfigure the problem of labor and desire in a specific syntax of image. I will take the position that in capitalism qua capital this is the only way the death drive can "appear." The liberation of labor desire does not care if you do not like parties or state apparatuses (which does not mean it wants them). It does not care if you are able or not to track its rhizomatic function, mischievous signifiers, or semiotic transversality, all of which are defensible but not exactly the point. The symptoms are never less than decisive (and I will soon provide some rather stark examples), but the axis of labor desire is only liberated through a certain death, which is its drive and an affirmation of eros beyond the historical materialization of the labor/capital nexus. Perhaps this is a desire that escapes, paradoxically, its philosophical perquisites, or at least those that mark a distinct historical rupture, like the upheavals of 1968. It often appears, therefore, as something that it is not. It cannot insist that anti-capitalism be anti-Leninism or that it must be a desire that does not seize power or the state. It must fight capital without such distinction, correction, or purification. The desire in class war is not a vanity project or a virtue-laden checklist. It is not motivated by reflexively dismissing the dismal Descartes, although it might pause to consider further his automaton, Francine. It might perform dialectically, yet need not name its process so. The liberation of labor desire is not an event in Paris, like the Commune, even when it trembles with *jouissance* (which will remain immanent to its event). Lacan took Freud seriously enough to reconceptualize his schema. If this is not yet the liberation of labor desire, it relays a provocative pattern in its becoming. But could it unite the workers? Only at the expense of proletarian being. And the violence in that must be externalized, displaced, and devastating. For labor as relation, the drive is involuted. The aim is not preservation, but abject abnegation. Small wonder anti-capitalist revolution is a hard sell when the promise of victory is predicated on loss.

To win is to lose oneself. Where will the new irruption of desire come from, Deleuze and Guattari famously ask[4] and, while I cannot agree with their response (why must we choose between Fidel and Felix?), it is the necessity for a response within current contingencies that keeps alive the basic sentiment. Desire must be free of capital.

Of course, one must qualify this righteous slogan (the meming if not the naming of change is a practiced art, but praxis may be something else again). Robert Reich, who unlike Wilhelm Reich seems generally unperturbed by muscular armor, might argue that if capitalism was so bad why has it been around so long?[5] Surely desire, like love, is free enough under the sign of capital that capitalism inexorably endures, like fossil fuels and the *Fast and Furious* franchise? Modes of production are historical and confront constitutive limits—nobody now believes vassals and serfs should harbor obligations in produce, tithes, or taxes to some effete aristocracy or royal figureheads, yet medieval land practices persist, so that a royal family, for instance, might be the technical "owner" of 6.75 billion acres of land, or that a major religion might harbor 177 million acres on the same principle. Modes of production die, but not in an instant and not under conditions of their own choosing. To say that desire must be free of capital is also a measure of its agency within processes of liberation and a recognition that its experience will also be transformed, even if the time of delinking and the measure of the moment of freedom can only be conjectured (like utopia, its promise is much disputed). Desire free from capital must be identical with revolution if by the latter we mean the transformation of a specific mode of production. For the same reason, however, its force is rendered abstract precisely by the specificity of the time of change. At what point can one claim a liberation in desire if capitalism does not die but fades? It is difficult to conceptualize such an architectonic of aphanisis as a sociopolitical dynamic. Does proletarianization need to reduce to zero before desire transforms, or are signs of this desire, more or less classic "symptoms," cognizable in capitalism's decline as new orders of socialization struggle to be born?

Because neither Freud nor Lacan set out to theorize or to transform the material conditions of socialization, they need not articulate the full extent of desire's dimensionality (this is, by the way, a distinct advantage in Deleuze and Guattari's approach by contrast). It is not just a question of scaling up from the individual (the self, the identity, the authenticating yet paradoxical urge to say "I am") for social change can always let go of individualism rather than the individual as such (the singularity of AI is in part only a discovery of this difference in the recalibration "beyond" the subject). The challenge rests in discerning the precarious yet positive grammar of desire seemingly caught between "What does the object want?" (redolent in some versions of O3 or new materialist manifestations of objecthood) and "What does the subject want?" when not mediated or overdetermined by commodity desire. The questions are insufficient if they do not simultaneously take up desire as more than want, or desire as unrecuperable in a subject/object binary. Beyond scale, therefore, one must address the splitting-off of proletarian as concept, for instance, from proletarian as an agglomeration of appropriate signs. Labor as relation congeals in subject form but is ultimately not reducible to it, even as here the figuration is a determinate referential reflex. For the same reason, one does not see the death drive; one witnesses it.

To come to terms with proletarian agon as death driven, we can only think of the death drive as itself a negation of Freudian theorization. First, as both Deleuze and Lacan pointedly argue, the putative difference of Eros and Thanatos offers a false opposition in the logic of each. Deleuze will take the position that the death drive is not about destruction so much as repetition, a compulsion of a different kind than that countenanced by Freud.[6] It is not that which makes Eros true, but it pursues its own degree of affirmation. Lacan also highlights the role of repetition, although whereas for Deleuze repetition disguises itself in the death drive (but never from the philosopher, of course!), for Lacan, it ceaselessly deconstructs the opposition of life and death via a projection of indestructible life.[7] We are certainly in the realm of fantasy here, but whether this extends to Lacan's imagination of a false organ, the infamous Lamella, the reader must decide. The dialectical tension between abstract desire and desire for abstraction is not resolved in the relation of Lacan's organ without organs to Deleuze's body without organs, yet the status of materialization, of desire and more, is worth further comment. The drive permits Deleuze to think of repetition as the base; not as pathological, but as prime. For Lacan, the drive does have a negativity, just not one that originates in normative codes of death and destruction. Lacan and Deleuze both privilege the death drive, but in a way that says "not Freud." *Trieb* becomes repetition, or in Lacan, pulsion. These, of course, are not direct translations but are closer to what we might think of as the difference of difference. For Deleuze, the death drive is a space of negativity, not negation as such, which as a principle is the possibility of affirmation. Rather than a lack or void, it is something of a fulcrum or organizing idea that exists in its recognition. If we think of this in terms of desire, it is not want but a force around which drives in general can be articulated.

Yet to approach the death drive dialectically, as Lacan does with desire, suggests that even in affirmation, or in Freud, preservation, the absence of death is never yet absent from its inscription in desire. Rather than some pervert's peregrination, it describes something of a proletarian reversal, one grounded, albeit phantasmatically, in ontological overcoming. Of course, what might take the form of a case study of an individual psyche does not necessarily obtain at the level of class, even metonymically, although the procedural promise of lack is common to both. At this level, the proletariat desires that substance from which it has been alienated in its objective conditions. In effect, its subjectivity is produced by a certain substancelessness, a volatile division spun between money and capital. The wage returns to the worker a token of subjectivity, a reward in equivalence for its alienated approximation. The prize is disposable income even as the worker knows there is so much more that is disposable and disposed of across such transactions. At this level, the proletarian lives not just in contradiction, but in paradox. On the plus side, this short circuit in desire enables the repeated possibility of *jouissance*; on the negative side, its being-towards-death is a violent joy, an ache of *destrudo*. Surely, however, we are not saying that capital works like language, as in Lacan's notion of the unconscious being like a language, to produce a structural lack? If this lack is overdetermined, would this imply that the proletarian, as subject, is actually capital's *petit objet a*? It cannot possibly be this object and yet might be an embodiment of drive, as that which threatens all that is ontological in capitalism's "I."

Violent joy is neither a formula nor a wayward symptom. It might productively be thought of as a proletarian pulsion at the edge of loss, at the edge of repetition bleached of compulsion. There are several ways in which it is a madness of subjectivation, a frenzy (between *die Raserai* and *der Rausch*, between madness and ecstasy). For Marx, madness does not reside in labor desire and, for the purposes of his critique of political economy, neither does it rest in the proletariat qua subject (as we know, the worker is not the subject of *Das Kapital* and when Marx is in need of personification, it is the capitalist who duly appears). Interestingly, in the *Grundrisse*, madness is ascribed to money. Why? Money offers a perpetual passage between use and exchange value where its commodity form, say currency, belies its dual nature, within and without circulation. What it seems to express is not what it says, and the tenor of its existence Marx calls "a moment"—the baleful concreteness of a time that is "determinant of the practical life of peoples." Capitalists talk of "mad money" as a lucrative investment opportunity; for Marx, the madness rests in the social life it predicates. Money, like the Federal Reserve, is imperfect, and anyone who thinks it can automatically mesh the incommensurability of simultaneous yet uneven production cycles is not a little unstable themselves. Capital circulation produces abstract spaces that are functionally dead—much has been written about the proliferation of zombies and specters in the voids of MCM.[8] The madness of money qua capital is that its increase is not satiation. Wealth for the capitalist is not a number but a drive. Violent joy neither expresses it nor negates it. But if the madness of money is malevolent, and especially when it comes to value, is it enough to return happy opprobrium?

Bernie Sanders argues that it is ok to be angry about capitalism.[9] It is a sad comment on the weight of American conformism that this acknowledgment, senatorial in its incitement, even needs repeating. Still, it is a tribute to Sanders's political perspicacity that he identifies why workers are right to be mad about the madness they confront:

> Workers have a right to be angry because, despite huge increases in productivity, their wages have been stagnant for fifty years. They are angry because they lost good-paying jobs when their companies shut down and moved to China. They are angry because they are working for starvation wages and the federal minimum wage has not been raised since 2009.[10]

To be fair to China, a company like Apple is an equal opportunity value extractor, and it can find price points just as easily in other places of the Global South—most recently India. The difficulty is whether the feeling of anger is felt *by* a class or *as* a class. The protests for racial justice after the brutal murder of George Floyd were spontaneous, widespread, and deeply purposeful, all this against a backdrop in the United States of pandemic restrictions and white anomie. There is good cause for intersectional organization and solidarity, and Sanders's book is obviously appealing to that possibility, especially since racial capitalism is not simply a dimension of socialization but intrinsic to a logic of exploitation and prejudice. On one level, Sanders is urging the Democratic Party to, at the very least, recognize anger as a set of genuine and actionable social grievances. On another level, Sanders wants to counter contemporary Republican populism, but here the emotional register alters: Republican expertise,

Sanders goes on to argue, rests in the manipulation of "working-class frustration."[11] Obviously, this is a rhetorical conceit because great swathes of the Republican Party have framed the problems as immigrant communities, communities of color, LGBTQ communities, liberal teachers who indoctrinate, and rampant discrimination against white men. The dilemma for Sanders in his argument is not the identification of ideological fabrication but the feelings the Republicans seek to tap. Such appeals are not to the righteous anger intimated above but to a kind of mild irritation based on wild assertions and wanton misrecognition. It is not clear that the class constituents of anger and frustration settle so easily across party lines, particularly when the answer to Republican racist appeals is a Democratic reminder to the US working class that they are right to be angry their jobs are in China. To read Sanders's support of anger about capitalism across the contradictory terrain of contemporary American politics is to witness a dissimulation between the political articulation of putative class psychology and the filaments of desire in the labor/capital relation.

Does the death drive provide a relay across this disjunction? Can it address in any way the manifestation of proletarian pulsion wrought by class division with all of its indeterminacy and fracture? It can shed light on the conceptual difficulty (and indeed, recent US history), but only if we pose class war as a resolute and continuing archetype of resistance (a consistency akin to the way *Das Kapital* pivots on a model of real abstraction), forms of struggle that contingently embody a certain immanence of the death drive—not just a sacrifice *to*, but a sacrifice *from*. A dialectic of dissonance is symptomatic rather than emblematic, and the death drive from this perspective becomes something of a materialist heuristic, a way to read class war by other means. So even though death is not actually the drive in the death drive, it nevertheless remains proximate for the proletariat when articulating desire within the concrete materiality of labor *bios*, a particular way of living the capitalist Real.

Marx (in contrast to Lacan and Deleuze) writes about death's proximity to labor/capital relations a great deal in *Capital*, for accumulation requires so much death to maintain circulation. As Marx puts it, matter-of-factly,

> The owner of labor-power is mortal. If then his appearance in the market is to be continuous, and the continuous transformation of money into capital assumes this, the seller of labor-power must perpetuate himself "in the way that every living individual perpetuates himself, by procreation." The labor-power withdrawn from the market by wear and tear, and by death, must be continually replaced by, at the very least, an equal amount of fresh labor-power.[12]

Of course, what might come to supplement this loss is not absolute as labor power given the dynamism of economic relations as a whole. Historically, as Marx notes, those who lord over the means of production saw death as a sign labor power was used up and were none-too-concerned they were the reason for it ("The recognized form of overwork here is forced labor until death."[13]—Marx notes laconically, then refers the reader to Diodorus Siculus and ancient lore). Marx then takes us on a tour of industries where death is a metric of production (life expectancy among potters and miners, for instance, where the desire for value extraction takes life and/or physically reshapes the body (potters are stunted in growth, age prematurely, and embody "*dégénérescence*"[14]). The *objet a* of the capitalist is a kind of grotesquery, a body *with* organs forced to betray itself. Then there is the report remarked upon by Marx from London newspapers in 1863 under the heading, "Death from simple over-work." A twenty-year-old milliner, Mary Anne Walkley, collapsed and died after working a twenty-six-hour shift in a business that regularly required thirty-hour shifts to maintain respectable London ladies in their finery. This Freudian urge for preservation through fashion (class status) is a death drive that inconveniently produces the death of others (for which the coroner had to provide a shorthand: "apoplexy"[15]). In the fiction Rabinowitz reads, this death remains proximate and is interrelated with the labor of working-class women's reproductive power and maternity as a memory interlaced with class consciousness. Rabinowitz's analyses critically engage how the body of labor is reconfigured not just before capital demands but in the contradictory desires of women and men workers produced by the labor itself and the place of work. These do not produce a typology or a positivist category, say "woman worker" or "heterosexual worker," both because of sex/gender dynamism but also because work, under any mode of production, is not unilaterally determinant even if demonstrably operative. Death only features in this consideration of labor and desire because it cancels through or internally structures the logic of labor and capital in relation.

There is a madness, which here I am reading as a kind of frenzy of desire in displacement, that Lacan ascribes to a breakdown between language and speech, seemingly a "subject in a language devoid of dialectic."[16] It would take much more space than here to interrogate the role of language in the proletarian desire sketched so far. In the brief examples below, the labor/capital relation is a reimagined collocation of "symptoms, inhibition, and anxiety" in the constitutive economy of the different *classes* (rather than "neuroses" in Lacan's understanding[17]). Again, there is no formula for the path of *méconnaissance* in proletarian desire, some pathology of precision, but the more the sublation of self is rendered obtuse, the more it feeds a *destrudo* of the other. The desire enacted is not a pretense, but its performance in relation to proletarian subjectivity is almost pretending to pretend; thus, perhaps paradoxically, a dialectic of the drive in the capital/labor relation that represses historical meaning (the irruption of violent joy often appears anachronistic). In a recent work, I have explored this refraction of an Other in terms of paranoid style, by specifically addressing Lacan's early essays on paranoia that include his analysis of the Papin sisters' case, a case that remains relevant here.[18] In Le Mans, 1933, two maidservant siblings, Christine and Lea Papin, suddenly turned on their employer, Mme. Lancelin, and her daughter, Genevieve, and beat them to death using a hammer, knife, and pewter jug.[19] The eyes of their victims were torn out while they were still alive, and at least one of the victims had their legs mutilated. When the police and Mme. Lancelin's husband finally got into the house, they found the sisters upstairs in bed together. In his analysis, Lacan claims part of their psychosis was the malady of being two, a twin delirium, and his elaboration of paranoia only begins to touch on the public interest in the case, not just because of the extreme brutality of the murders but because of implied and phobic questions of both lesbian incest and trans desire (in another life, says Christine, I would have been the husband of my sister). The prosecution claims the sisters are sane and responsible for their actions; the defense suggests there is a third character present—the two sisters together (the malady to which Lacan refers). The epigraph above from Christine was what she told the officers at the scene ("I'd rather have had our bosses' skin than for them to have had ours."[20]). It was an act of self-defense, an act indeed of class vengeance. There is a lot to the Papins' biography and its interpretation that must be left aside, but here proletarian desire, however theorized, is not being thought of as consistently verifiable, as either holding the hammer or as sitting in bed afterward. The Papin case is for many a fantastic exception (remarkably, one of the policemen on the case was called Deleuze). Beyond Lacan's prompt for the mirror stage, I am thinking of the shattered glass, the disjecta membra (the fragments), the tain (the ground of reflection), and the parerga (the framing logic)—these "mirrorations" of a historical compulsion, a death instinct that drives scenes of abject carnivalization and the passionately grotesque. Yes, the fetish is a symptom of the Papins' commodified subjectivation (as their only friends, the Papins bought clothes to dress for each other), but as indicated, there are other elements to their alienation and disaffection (none of which by themselves necessitate the removal of eyes and the performance of disfigurement). I am not saying the Papins murder and mutilate merely because they could not sublate themselves or their worker selves. I would argue, however, and this thought lingers in Lacan's theorization of the death drive, that as proletarianized labor, the Papins achieve in the other what they cannot achieve as a class in themselves and as themselves in a class.

The French Left press of the time, including *L'Humanité*, portrayed the sisters as victims of exploitation and servitude; the Right-wing press played on ruling class fear and anxiety—workers in general were dangerously unstable. Simone de Beauvoir, who was an avid reader of the popular journal *Détective*, which reported the murders under the headline "Les Brebis Enragée" ("the angry sheep"), called the crime a "rebellion"[21] against subjugation. The prosecution described the sisters as savages and wild beasts and argued they should be treated as such: "they are aggressive, vicious dogs."[22] If we are to believe Freud, such aggression is obstinately human, to which he adds the phrase, *Homo homini lupus* [Man is a wolf to man]. The Real of the case is sensitively dependent on context, and the social frame of the time was mediated by socioeconomic crisis. The jury took forty minutes to reach a verdict (one book claims just four) and the sentence called for Christine to be guillotined in the town square and Lea to receive ten years of hard labor (the latter, for some, no different from the life she lived; Christine's sentence was eventually commuted to a life of hard labor). Christine starved herself to death (adjudged to be a case of *vesanic cachexia*) in 1937; Lea was assumed to have died in 1982 but for many years she worked under an assumed name and, incredibly, as a maid! She was discovered alive in 2000 but died the following year. The cultural casebook on the crime has steadily grown and includes documentary films, feature-length fiction films, and "based on" treatments, articles, histories, and biographies. This is not just a genealogy of paranoia but a compendium of disputed material instantiations (Lacan uses the word motifs) of social dysfunction and what remains to be done. Here the desire works as *fait divers*, sometimes sensational but always everyday.

In addition to reading Lacan on paranoia, Bong Joon-ho studies the Papin case as he develops his film, *Parasite* (the Korean film, *The Housemaid*, is also an inspiration—

in addition, he may have seen the adaptation of the Papin case, *Murderous Maids*). Alongside the paranoid style, does Bong's film project this sense of proletarian desire, a desire displaced in what, to borrow from Lacan, we can call *imagos* of the fragmented body.[23] The desire for sublation itself has no body but is materially manifest in images of one as such (a basic concept at the heart of cinematic sorcery). How does Bong figure labor desire as also, as in the Papins' case, a scene of violent paroxysm? One key sequence in *Parasite* occurs during young Da-song's birthday party. Briefly, Geun-sae, a former servant who has been hiding in the Parks' house bunker to avoid loan sharks, emerges to avenge his wife's death. His wife dies as a result of a fight with the working-class Kim family over who should be the better parasite living off the wealthy Parks (Bong's film also makes it clear the Parks are living off their servants, which is another lesson from the Papins on the logic of social division and the production of parasitism). Entering the party, Geun-sae attacks Ki-jung, the Kims' daughter, stabbing her in the chest. Mayhem ensues, Da-song faints, and Geun-sae runs to confront Chung-sook, Ki-jung's mother. Even though it is Ki-jung who is bleeding to death, Da-song's mother orders Ki-taek, Ki-jung's father and driver for the Parks, to bring the car around so they can take Da-song to the hospital. Da-song's father, Dong-ik, demands the car keys from Ki-taek. He throws them, but they land on the grass and are immediately covered by Geun-sae's body following a blow from Chung-sook. The melodrama is frantic (almost hysterical, but troubling the designation), as Bong's editing emphasizes, but particular shots stand out. As Dong-ik goes to retrieve the keys, he briefly pulls back, affronted by the smell of Geun-sae (this perception of dirty workers is repeated several times in the film as a form of bourgeois distaste for poor hygiene—or the overdetermined hygiene of the poor). Bong accentuates the absurdity of class difference by having the dying Geun-sae blurt out to Dong-ik (in English) "Respect!" Seeing Dong-ik's revulsion, and considering all that has happened and is happening to his family in the present, Ki-taek picks up the knife and, rather than finish off Geun-sae, stabs Dong-ik in the chest. Bong dwells on Ki-taek's face in close-up. The ambivalence of his expression is wonderfully conceived. Is this a dream? Should he feel remorse? Should he try to rationalize this act of murder? What will happen now to what remains of his family? Is not the solution to class war regular showers and perfumed soap?

While it is relatively easy to see working-class revenge as a counter to the fantastic projections of contemporary South Korean bourgeois economics, with the expensively arrayed spaces of the Parks' house as its calculated theater, there is no simple relay between what we are suggesting is a proletarian pulsion and spontaneous violence. For his part, Lacan begins his analysis of the dialectics of desire by stating, "The praxis that we call psychoanalysis is constituted by a structure"[24] but quickly adds that situating the subject in this way is never less than ambiguous in relation to knowledge (the complex graph of desire he formulates in the approach only intensifies the sense of instability across its structure). The film reveals a subject and structure; its mise-en-scène is indeed the desiring subject, but while Lacan remembers well the Papins and the prolepsis of paranoia, in his essay on dialectics he notes "a radical questioning of social bases" is broader than the analytic he offers.[25] Evenso, the dialectics of desire mediate the sequence described above and its relation to an *enoncé* on labor and capital in contemporary South Korea. There is more to the scene than we can address here (is "Respect!" an appeal to class compromise?), but between Ki-taek's expression as Dong-ik holds his nose and his look after Dong-ik has been summarily dispatched, an allegory of class desire is at stake. Ostensibly, this might seem to follow a standard dialectic of thesis, antithesis, synthesis, one that precipitates an almost literal death of the bourgeois Subject. Not so. Bong's nuanced reading of Lacan on the Papins maintains the ambiguity of structure pondered by Lacan's later work. Bong's film is replete with fantasy and a kind of meta-subjectivity where actors are playing roles in which role-playing is key. Both the bourgeois and proletarian subjects prey on one another through class demands that cannot be met within their structure. While one of the posters for the film probably refers to the parasite as eyeless (at least as a worm), the covered eyes of the characters in the image also symbolize barred Subjects and Others (beings of nonbeing), enmeshed in social antinomy—witnesses who do not see. Ki-taek's expressions are a passage of the act and signify a kind of class (un) consciousness, a desire to attenuate class contradiction without synthesis or knowledge of its sublation. We might say, in Althusserian fashion, Ki-taek's murder of Dong-ik is an imaginary resolution of a real contradiction. Symptomatically, there is closure, but the end of the film underlines a certain inertia in the class structure displayed (Ki-taek now lives in hiding in the basement). The violence, instant and profound, is an enunciation of desire, but not one that in itself can complete a Subject. It may be labor's decision (the decision in labor as relation, as the pulsion of desire), but its dialectical demand is rendered as a kind of madness and grotesquery, a paradox of catharsis without guarantee.

Labor desire in *Parasite*, through violence and non-resolution, signifies something of an almost Subject, the barred Subject who demands what seems unattainable and exists on the cusp of structural nothingness. In the death throes of neoliberalism, a global "my market, my self," there are many examples of contemporary cinema that have attempted to figure workers caught in such moments of violent decision. These are not revenge tragedies because the perceived wrong is ultimately less personal but systemic. Yet such tales of contradictory becoming attempt to visualize a violence that provides individual not social solace. Nevertheless, moments of labor frenzy offer desire's decision as a shock of inequity. Even if films that take up this challenge do not constitute a genre, they still image and problematize the rationalization of class hierarchy under capitalism. The house in *Parasite* is less a space of negotiation but one allied to the maintenance of division, the assigned place where workers work. The irruption of violence at the Parks' home makes it *unheimlich* and barely recognizable as a home. Irreconcilability does not always mean death (there is also acquiescence and compromise), but fundamentally, labor must overreach its prescriptions and proscriptions. This is the madness of its reason.

However, just as Lacan's graph of desire is crisscrossed by a structural ambiguity between consciousness and the unconscious, so even violent decisions can deracinate what might otherwise seem to be praxis in the becoming of labor. For instance, in Ramin Bahrani's film *The White Tiger* (2021—based on the 2008 novel of the same name by Aravind Adiga), an allegory of labor defeating capital in the poor overcoming the rich is subject to radical dissemblance, so that knowledge of neoliberal nostrums under globalization ultimately validates an arc of cynical aspiration. Young Balram, the central character, is not happy with village life. His cunning and basic opportunism allow him to reach Delhi as, like Ki-taek, a driver to a wealthy family, in this case the Storks (Bahrani shows that much of their money is based on corruption). Eventually, Balram finds out that Ashok, his boss, is going to hire a replacement driver (the problem of disposability we invoked earlier), so while driving Ashok to deliver yet another bribe, Balram becomes the titular "white tiger," a rarity in the sense that in this situation he is the servant willing to dispatch the master. After slitting Ashok's throat with a broken bottle, Balram drives off and the viewer, positioned as passenger, watches as Balram screams, then screams again. But what might be a cathartic triumph is then followed by Balram glancing at a bag in the car stuffed with bribe money and then giggling. The relationship of the subject to the signifier as one of subjection is complicated in and as desire via labor's political unconscious. In a dialectical reversal, what this scene figures is both brutal frenzy and yet a rational reclamation of money's power. Balram not only gets away with murder (in part, he claims, because he looks like everyone else—like money, he is a universal equivalent) but he also assumes the name and practices of his victim. Balram escapes to Bangalore and becomes an arbiter of transnational capital named Ashok. Given his experiences, Balram is of course an enlightened and empathetic neoliberal ("I don't treat my drivers like servants"), but in a final close-up he speaks both directly to the viewer and to his implied interlocutor (the story as a whole is a fantastic autobiography addressed to the former premier of China and consummate neoliberal Wen Jiabao). Balram/Ashok declares, "I've switched sides. I've made it. I've broken out of the coop." The vectors of labor desire constellate both fantasies of proletarian paroxysm and determinate modes of cynical realism.

Like the murderous Papins, there is a signifying slippage between the stark viciousness of murder and the symptomatic irruption of the murderous, a concomitant sacrifice of a self. Neither Bong nor Bahrani declaratively endorse the right of the proletarian to kill the capitalist, even when a validation is provided at the level of character. The close-up shots are of a killer who has in some sense already been condemned in an antinomy of desire. The look in these moments is not wholly of the body that wears it. But desire of this kind, caught in the contradictions of labor and capital, remains a cinematic challenge, and one is not surprised it is compulsively displaced onto the representation of a wronged individual taking matters into their own hands: an exceptional derangement that is visually interesting because it is presented as pathologically unique. Between the absolute violence of the moment and the relation in which it is recuperated, the death drive here floats within a visual economy overdetermined by the inequities of social division. In Ridley Scott's *Blade Runner* (1982), an adaptation of Philip K. Dick's sci-fi classic, *Do Androids Dream of Electric Sheep?*, the labor/capital relation is built into notional extensions of the cyborg, the imago of a technological sublime. The cyborg Batty, a basic combat model, goes to see Tyrell, who heads the company that made him, to discuss labor disposability (a four-year lifespan, shorter even than a potter). "It's not often one gets to meet one's maker," quips Batty, shortly before gouging out Tyrell's eyes, as if the sense of sight itself were at stake in class war.

Jia Zhangke's anthology film from 2013, *A Touch of Sin*, offers a series of micronarratives drawn from recent Chinese history and features stories of capitalist modernization already alluded to in *The White Tiger*. Dahai is an unofficial worker representative at a local mine that has been privatized and is now owned by the uber-wealthy Jiao who, among other skills, is embezzling funds from the mine and the miners. Dahai has already been beaten up and hospitalized by Jiao's thugs for his protests, and Jia's version of a standard revenge rampage follows. In one scene, Dahai goes to confront Jiao about social injustice and waits for him in the back of Jiao's Maserati. "How can we fix this?" asks Jiao before Dahai shoots him in the head and gets blood all over the leather seats. In close-up, Dahai contemplates what he has done; then he breaks into a smile. Jia's film is much more than this moment of glory satisfaction, but he asks difficult questions about what modernization has come to mean for workers when desire is mediated by a crass accumulation axiom.

Proletarian desire need not be spectacular; indeed, it can be silent, mute, and submerged. It lends itself to resistance rituals, workplace sabotage, absenteeism, theft, tardiness, and is directly related to complex discourses around abuse. Its most obvious manifestations are neither in acts of killing nor in submission, but in the strike, the march, the occupation, the slowdown, community solidarity, and/or unionization. Why then comment on these otherwise wanton acts of aggression and bloody violence? If the death drive, from Lacan's theorization to now, is less about death itself than it is a collocation of drives and symptoms, why emphasize proletarian pulsion as murderous mayhem? In part, it permits us to think about a stark representational problem in labor desire, an instinct caught between impulsion and compulsion. It is not a coincidence cinema returns to these moments of madness (other recent examples would include *Triangle of Sadness* and *Saltburn*) not just because the logic of violence is so easy to visualize, but because the revelation of desire struggles mightily to contain the consequences that norms and prohibitions would otherwise preempt. This is a précis of a political and aesthetic problem, the coding of the Other for which completing a Subject must in some sense end it. In the brief examples mentioned, at the moment of murder, in the capture of frenzy, as if almost habitual, it would be wrong to think intense violence is only dutifully or rightfully intentioned. What is glimpsed is rather a disassociated alienation, something of the psychological automatism Deleuze elsewhere ascribes to the masses before the image movement of cinema.[26] The pulsion here is not in fact in the act of killing the bourgeois, of, for instance, taking sight from that which surveils through the scopophiliac imaginary of capitalist command. What is visualized is a displaced *destrudo*, violent in content but often absent/present in form. It is not the sublimation ascribed to sublation but is its detournement, whose *Grund* is rather a potential sublimation of the self—the proletarian, *not* the capitalist, effaced. Is extreme violence posed as a false agency in contrast to some pure figure of transformation like the fully conscious revolutionary? No. There is a constitutive gap in possibility but not an absolute measure of appropriation in propriation. We could bullet-point problems of socialization, of property, of masculinism, of gross normativity, of agential deficit, of unthinking, of crass working-class anomie. Yet the moments arrayed try to grasp a dynamic incommensurability. They identify more than spectacular senselessness, even if this is easily captioned or portrayed as such. The dialectical obtuseness of the act is a real abstraction, an antinomy that cannot be solved by senselessness for and in itself. But is proletarian pulsion simply a litany of *méconnaissance* and misapprehension, a frenzy that would in fact confirm a contrasting rationalism of a capital-striated ego (noted in Balram's switching sides)? What looks back at the viewer in these moments? There is violent joy bordering on ecstasy, a laugh or a scream in the face of the inexorable (justice?), but also resignation followed by a more than theoretical line of flight. The disorder of desire can be thought but not adequately composed: the Subject seen is not composed in their composition. The proletarian look is both the viewer's objection as viewer and, in the manner of materialization, the viewer's abjection. Desire lies in relation, literally and metaphorically, that image movement measures in its shortfall. Here it is a cinematic symptom declared but not necessarily represented, even when, or precisely because, its decision is, as Christine puts it, a matter of their skin over hers.

Notes

1 "I'd rather have had our bosses' skin than for them to have had ours," Christine explains at the time of the Papins' arrest. Quoted in Rachel Edwards and Keith Reader, *The Papin Sisters* (New York: Oxford University Press, 2001), 5. More on this case below.
2 There are several translations of this landmark essay. See, for instance, Sabina Spielrein, "Destruction as the Cause of Becoming," in *The Essential Writings of Sabina Spielrein*, ed. and trans. Ruth I. Cape and Jonathan Burt (New York: Routledge, 2019), 97–134.
3 See Paula Rabinowitz, *Labor and Desire* (Chapel Hill: University of North Carolina Press, 1991).
4 Gilles Deleuze and Félix Guattari, *Anti-Oedipus: Capitalism and Schizophrenia*, trans. Robert Hurley, Mark Seem, and Helen R. Lane (Minneapolis: University of Minnesota Press, 1983), 378.
5 See, in particular, Robert B. Reich, *Saving Capitalism for the Many, Not the Few* (New York: Knopf, 2015).
6 See Gilles Deleuze, *Difference and Repetition*, trans. Paul Patton (New York: Columbia University Press, 1994). See above also Deleuze and Guattari on the death instinct in *Anti-Oedipus*, 335–7.
7 Since for Lacan, all drives are death drives, they reappear everywhere Lacan details desire. But see, Jacques Lacan, *Écrits: A Selection*, trans. Alan Sheridan (London: Tavistock Publications, 1977).
8 See, for instance, Chris Harman, *Zombie Capitalism* (Chicago: Haymarket Books, 2009).
9 See Bernie Sanders and John Nichols, *It's OK to be Angry about Capitalism* (New York: Crown, 2023).
10 Sanders and Nichols, *It's OK to be Angry about Capitalism*, 281.
11 Sanders and Nichols, *It's OK to be Angry about Capitalism*, 283.
12 Karl Marx, *Capital: A Critique of Political Economy*, trans. Ben Fowkes (London: Penguin, 1976), 275.
13 Marx, *Capital*, 345.
14 Marx, *Capital*, 355.
15 Marx, *Capital*, 364–5.
16 Lacan, *Écrits*, 68.

17 Lacan, *Écrits*, 51.
18 Peter Hitchcock, "On the Politics of Paranoid Style," *symplokē* 29, no. 1–2 (2021): 75–95.
19 For a fascinating analysis of the case and its coverage, see Rachel Edwards and Keith Reader, *The Papin Sisters* (New York: Oxford University Press, 2001).
20 Edwards and Reader, *The Papin Sisters*, 5.
21 Edwards and Reder, *The Papin Sisters*, 64.
22 Edwards and Reader, *The Papin Sisters*, 15.
23 Lacan, *Écrits*, 85.
24 Lacan, *Écrits*, 223.
25 Lacan, *Écrits*, 224.
26 See Gilles Deleuze, *Cinema 1: The Movement Image*, trans. Hugh Tomlinson and Barbara Habberjam (Minneapolis: University of Minnesota Press, 1986), particularly Chapter Two, but also the commentaries on Bergson.

Works Cited

A Touch of Sin. Directed by Jia Zhangke. Xstream Pictures, 2013.
Blade Runner. Directed by Ridley Scott. Warner, 1982.
Deleuze, Gilles. *Cinema 1: The Movement Image*. Translated by Hugh Tomlinson and Barbara Habberjam. Minneapolis: University of Minnesota Press, 1986.
Deleuze, Gilles. *Difference and Repetition*. Translated by Paul Patton. New York: Columbia University Press, 1994.
Deleuze, Gilles, and Félix Guattari, *Anti-Oedipus: Capitalism and Schizophrenia*. Translated Robert Hurley, Mark Seem, and Helen R. Lane. Minneapolis: University of Minnesota Press, 1983.
Edwards, Rachel, and Keith Reader. *The Papin Sisters*. New York: Oxford University Press, 2001.
Harman, Chris. *Zombie Capitalism*. Chicago: Haymarket Books, 2009.
Hitchcock, Peter. "On the Politics of Paranoid Style." *symplokē* 29. no. 1–2 (2021): 75–95.
Lacan, Jacques. *Écrits: A Selection*. Translated Alan Sheridan. London: Tavistock Publications, 1977.
Marx, Karl. *Capital: A Critique of Political Economy*. Translated by Ben Fowkes. London: Penguin, 1976.
Parasite. Directed by Bong Joon-ho. Universal, 2019.
Rabinowitz, Paula. *Labor and Desire*. Chapel Hill: University of North Carolina Press, 1991.
Reich, Robert B. *Saving Capitalism for the Many, Not the Few*. New York: Knopf, 2015.
Saltburn. Directed by Emerald Fennell. Amazon MGM, 2023.
Sanders, Bernie, and John Nichols. *It's OK to be Angry about Capitalism*. New York: Crown, 2023.
Spielrein, Sabina. "Destruction as the Cause of Becoming." In *The Essential Writings of Sabina Spielrein*, edited and translated by Ruth I. Cape and Jonathan Burt, 7–134. New York: Routledge, 2019.
The White Tiger. Directed by Rahmin Bahrani. Netflix, 2021.
Triangle of Sadness. Directed by Ruben Östlund. SF Studios, 2022.

13

Derrida's Cruelty Drive

Brian O'Keeffe

My objective is to comment on Jacques Derrida's lecture to the States General of Psychoanalysis in the course of which he reflects on Freud's death drive and on what Derrida calls the cruelty drive. This lecture, in Peggy Kamuf's translation, is "Psychoanalysis Searches the State of its Soul: The Impossible Beyond of a Sovereign Cruelty." We may guardedly suppose that Derrida tries to define cruelty's baleful power and characterize the callous deliberateness of inflicted torment and pain. "Guardedly," however, since Derrida hesitates before essential definitions. What is cruelty? Derrida gives multiple responses, that multiplicity being a way to avoid opting for one putatively essential definition. It remains Derrida's question, however, but it's doubled by at least one other, namely whether cruelty can be lessened or eradicated altogether.

To envisage cruelty's eradication, according to Walter Benjamin's "Critique of Violence," one must destroy the state's monopoly on violence and the institutions that perpetrate those violent cruelties. But one must also offer perspectives on what happens after that destruction. Few do so. What remains on the agenda of discussion in the meantime (the prolonged meantime of "politics") is one signal manifestation of the state's monopoly over violence—the death penalty. In Derrida's *Death Penalty* seminar, it's a matter of the "horror that the *cruelty* of execution inspires."[1] But questions concerning cruelty don't just involve institutional and penal frameworks and the apparatuses they cruelly employ—lethal injections or guillotines. They also concern basic human nature. We now verge upon the questions Derrida puts to Freud. Is the cruelty drive as primordial as the other drives Freud describes? Is it as primitive as the death drive, or is the cruelty drive subsumed by the rubric "death," where it's *death* that impels humanity to destruction and the infliction of pain?

What Is Cruelty?

Let me now begin my essay by citing Derrida's preliminary responses to the question: What is cruelty? It is "suffering *just to* suffer; the making-suffer, the making- or letting-oneself suffer *just for* . . . the pleasure of suffering."[2] Derrida contemplates gratuitous cruelty—something one does *just to* do it. Can we think of anything we do *just* for the sake of it? Derrida confides to his audience: "Yes, I am suffering cruelly."[3] What of that adverb "cruelly"? Derrida asks his audience to accept that adverb as if they know what it means. Do they? Do we? The Latin etymology for "cruelty" induces thoughts of bloodshed, but the German words Freud uses (*Grausam, Grausamkeit*) lack that etymology, and hence something is lost in translation. In any case, once spilt blood is deemed a characteristic or consequence of cruelty, then we perforce still tarry with Derrida's assessment of the death penalty's cruelties and non-cruelties. One would like to define cruelty by asserting its negation. If one said what cruelty is not, then perhaps a binary opposition might stabilize. Whether one can rely on the opposition between blood and bloodlessness to assist in that stabilization is one question, therefore. Whether non-cruelty is decisively epitomized by love, or *Eros*, is another.

Derrida invokes Nietzsche: "Cruelty would be without limit and without opposable term. . . . But for Freud, who is nevertheless so close to Nietzsche, as always, cruelty might perhaps be without limit but not without opposable term, that is, endless but not without contrary."[4] For Freud, cruelty might be without limit, but perhaps it can be opposed by the pleasure principle. Derrida continues:

> One can staunch bloody cruelty . . . , one can put an end to murder by blade, by the guillotine, in the classical or modern theaters of bloody war, but, according to Nietzsche or Freud, a psychic cruelty will always take its place by inventing new resources. A psychic cruelty would still, of course, be a cruelty of the *psyche*, a state of the soul, thus still of the living, but a nonbloody cruelty.[5]

Benjamin imagined a divinely annihilating violence that sheds no blood. Such unalloyed violence, if it could be wielded by someone other than God, would blanch its cruelties in the name of a legitimate punishment calibrated to the staunching of blood or else a lethal punishment costing criminals not one red drop. But note "a psychic cruelty will always take its place." The body spills blood, but psychic cruelty presumably concerns the non-body and so blood is hardly a benchmark for that cruelty since cruelty now involves the mind, the unconscious, the soul. Such things apparently live in the body and yet the wounds of psychic cruelty leave no scar but instead wrack the soul into a pain without corporeal trace.

"Would such cruelty, if there is any and if it is properly psychical," Derrida asks, "be one of the horizons most proper to psychoanalysis? Would this horizon even be reserved to psychoanalysis, like the bottomless depth of what it alone would be given to *treat*, the ultimate ground on which one day its figure took shape?"[6] *If there is any*: if the psyche bears no scars, wears no wounds, sheds no blood, then how can we supply probative evidence of such cruelty? Since it's psychoanalysis that speaks of things psychic, can't we ask it about this? Isn't psychic pain its proper subject, a pain for which it proposes therapeutic *treatment*? Derrida says:

> Psychoanalysis would perhaps not be the only possible language or even the only possible treatment regarding this cruelty that has no contrary term and no end. But "psychoanalysis" would be the name of that which, without theological or other alibi, would be turned toward what is most *proper* to psychical cruelty.

> Psychoanalysis, for me, if I may be permitted yet another confidential remark, would be another name for the "without alibi."[7]

Perhaps. Psychoanalysis gives us a language if one wishes to speak of matters psychic, although (to stress translation) questions remain concerning the Freudian *Übertragung*. What, though, is a response "without alibi"? Perhaps a response whereby psychoanalysis doesn't seek strategic alibis in its "science," mythologies, or Mosaic "theology." Derrida turns psychoanalysis toward the "without alibi" in order to hold some feet to the fire. That particularly involves turning psychoanalysis away from the domain it regards as its own and toward the area where psychoanalysis deems itself to have no proper cause to intervene. Politics, that is, where the cruelties of capital punishment seem fundamental to considerations concerning *sovereignty*. Is this the domain—that of sovereign cruelty—where psychoanalysis fears to tread in case it goes beyond the bounds of an area it claims as its exclusive property, namely what is *proper* to the psyche? Will psychoanalysis present itself before the States General of *politics* and plead itself innocent of the fault of never having properly engaged in political matters? Is psychoanalysis's alibi that it was never at the scene of the crime, namely the scene of history and politics—those *theaters* of cruelty where bloody war so frequently plays the starring role? These are some questions Derrida raises in order to prompt psychoanalytic soul-searching. But the main questions remain these:

> My questions will be, rather and later: Is there, for thought, for psychoanalytic thought to come, another beyond, if I can say that, a beyond that would stand beyond these *possibles* that are still *both* the pleasure and reality principles *and* the death or sovereign mastery drives, which seem to be at work whenever cruelty is on the horizon? In other words, altogether other words, can one think this apparently impossible, but otherwise impossible thing, namely a beyond the death drive or the drive for sovereign mastery, thus the beyond of a cruelty, a beyond that would have nothing to do with either drives or principles?[8]

Later we'll see whether Derrida considers that otherwise impossible thing, a beyond the death drive, to be possible. And hence what "translation" of psychoanalytic thought might occur when Derrida speaks in "altogether other words."

Derrida, like Freud, only guardedly proposes hypotheses. What about the "hypothesis of an irreducible death drive that seems inseparable from what is so obscurely called cruelty, in either its archaic or its modern forms? Would there also be, a few steps further beyond the principles, a beyond of the beyond, a beyond of the death drive and thus of the cruelty drive."[9] Already we're programming a step "beyond the beyond," since presumably we're wondering whether remedies are in sight for what seems otherwise *irreducible*—be it the death drive or the cruelty drive. What of cruelty's archaic or modern forms? Can psychoanalysis envisage "new historical figures of an ageless cruelty, as old and no doubt older than man"?[10]

Older than man. What histories or anthropologies could register what is older than man? Could zoology, or even a chemistry of primordial ooze, register a cruelty *no doubt* older than man? Derrida envisages an anarchic, anachronic cruelty that *will have* persisted without that persistence being conditional on man's activities or on the age of man either. Derrida writes: "Cruelty there will have been, before any personal figure, before 'cruel' will have become an attribute, still less anyone's fault."[11] For cruelty to be irreducible, it mustn't be contingent on a *person* being cruel: that would make cruel acts that person's *fault*. Cruelty updates its forms while ever remaining the same. It isn't conditional on human agents being cruel—to another, or to oneself. Rather, the logic involves stripping away human agency. Accordingly, the only terms available to *think* that anarchic irreducibility, that prior-to-all-other-conditions circumstance, are provided by Derrida, rather than by Freud's language of instincts, principles, and *Triebe*. Terms like *différance*, trace, cinder, writing, and mark. Derrida says "Cruelty there is."[12] Compare the formulation "cinder there is," or, in French, "*il y a là cendre.*"[13]

Consider Derrida's *Limited Inc*: "If one admits that writing (and the mark in general) must be able to function in the absence of the sender, the receiver, the context of production etc., that implies that this power, this being able, this possibility is always inscribed, hence necessarily inscribed as possibility in the functioning or the functional structure of the mark."[14]

Would we risk saying of cruelty what Derrida says of the mark? If *one admits* that "cruelty there is," cruelty must be able to function in the absence of human agents. This power must remain a possibility beyond all possibilities premised on someone actually *being* cruel. Cruelty's power to reproduce or iterate itself is *always* and *necessarily* a power it has: it's the power of its own irreducible possibility and potentiality, a power cruelty doesn't need to demonstrate by dint of a factual occurrence of cruelty, nor by relying on human agents to *be* cruel. It's a tough thought to think. But if Derrida brackets out human agents, it's in order to leave room for an examination of cruelty's irreducibility in terms of the inhuman *constat* that "cruelty there is."

Because Derrida considers what is "older than man," he ignores the Freudian essays his audience probably expected reference to—"The Ego and the Id" and "The Economic Principle in Masochism." Yet, in that latter essay, Freud says that masochism is mysterious "from the economic point of view"[15] because if the pleasure principle seeks to avoid unpleasure, then masochistic desire for that unpleasure is incomprehensible. Given Derrida's penchant for an-economic scenarios, one wonders why Derrida didn't exploit that remark. Derrida is also silent about the moment in *Beyond the Pleasure Principle* when Freud traces "the origin of an instinct to *a need to restore an earlier state of things*."[16] Derrida, one suspects, won't allow anyone else to speak of what is "earlier," nor to have the final word on what would be *earliest*. There's no remit for biology, zoology, or even chemistry to have that final word, particularly if such sciences would hamper the characterization of an "ageless" state Derrida wants trace and *différance* to describe and register. "Ageless" doesn't mean "old," moreover. Cruelty, Derrida claims, cannot be fixed to an age called "old," nor induced to return to the moment when it *began*. When Freud speaks of "an *old* state of things, an initial state from which the living entity has at one time or other departed and to which it is striving to return by the circuitous paths along which its development leads,"[17] Derrida avoids that circuitous path because *différance* doesn't lead back anywhere, certainly not back to life's origins. Despite Derrida's own crooked paths, he doesn't take Freud's detours: "These circuitous paths to death, faithfully kept to by the conservative instincts, would thus present us today with the picture of the phenomena of life."[18] Derrida, one suspects, wouldn't let any of those terms pass muster: "faithfully," "kept," "conservative," "phenomena," "life."

If Derrida's commitments are to an irreducibility that warrants the expression "cruelty there is," then, to repeat, such cruelty cannot be conditional on human agents, nor conditional on Freud's instincts and drives. But is there nothing to be done? We must now reply in the name of so-called civilization. Civilization, alas, destroys what it builds (hence civilization's Ozymandias complex, so to speak). But it's surely too bleak to regard the death, aggression, and ruinous drives as paramount, as if unmatched and unmatchable by any counterforce. That's the question one might put to Derrida: Why does he say nothing about *Eros*? Is there no strength left in humanity—as if love is depleted and ethics lacks sinew and a compelling imperative, despite the valiant efforts of Emmanuel Levinas, for instance? One could object that Derrida offers too pessimistic an assessment of the cruel state of things, hardly offering any remedial optimism. But Derrida's point is this: it's not he who presents himself as a therapist entitled not just to diagnose the illness but to *treat* it; it's psychoanalysis that does so. Hence, there is a certain *j'accuse* in Derrida's tone and argumentative thrust—a frankness when Derrida asks what measurable successes psychoanalysis can credit itself for in view of the real world where politics frequently turns cruel, bloody, war-bent, and sometimes genocidal.

Cruelty: What Is to be Done?

So to politics and Derrida's "J'accuse."[19] Consider: "Resistance to psychoanalysis, autoimmune resistance *of* psychoanalysis to its outside and to itself."[20] People assuredly resist psychoanalysis's sex-talk, but what of psychoanalysis's own resistance? Is this resistance to what psychoanalysis considers "outside" its proper domain, namely politics or ethics? Does psychoanalysis *do* ethics? *Pace* Lacan's *Ethics of Psychoanalysis*, I suspect Derrida doesn't think that psychoanalysis has an ethics. If it did, it would have to go beyond (that word again) its objection to war (as in Freud's "Why War?" essay) and encompass the gamut of human malignancies, the gamut of cruelty itself. It would have to *moralize* about the drives and instincts psychoanalysis prefers to consider in a neutral manner whereby the death drive, for instance (or above all), is neither good nor bad, just a fact of life death.[21]

The "autoimmune resistance *of* psychoanalysis" would be this: psychoanalysis resists the invitation to do ethics and politics, but nonetheless, politics and ethics have always-already been topics for psychoanalysis, "inside" psychoanalysis, once it spoke of Oedipus and Moses. Once it did, because it did, psychoanalysis *nolens volens* did politics as much as it did theology. The immune responses within the psychoanalytic body hence involve the expulsion of politics in the name of a ring-fenced specialty—psychic matters—no other discipline is entitled to treat. The autoimmune response, however, concerns that repeated expulsion. Because it is repeated, this confirms that psychoanalysis has always been hovering on the margins of its own desire to intervene in politics.

J'accuse. Derrida castigates psychoanalysis for neglecting the French Revolutionary Terror. Derrida noticed that a body of professional psychoanalysts called itself the States General, and that too easily prompted Derrida to revisit the Terror and the blood-spatter of its oft-used guillotine. Derrida's audience, so to speak, put their necks on Derrida's chopping block. Derrida contemplates the revolutionary States General thus:

> By definition, we will never know whether the States General . . . were destined to condemn or save the king's head, and it matters little, no doubt, because in any case the two gestures, condemning and saving, remain indissociable. They inscribe in the concepts of sovereignty and cruelty an ambiguity that is as unrelievable as autoimmunity itself. It is too late, even for the question. That is perhaps the ultimate signification of any paregicide, of any Oedipus, any totem-and-taboo, any republican or democratic installation of the equality of brothers after some paregicide.[22]

To condemn, to save. Either way, it concerns the king's head. Head-saving or head-severing remains a matter of sovereign executive privilege. The States General, despite having swept away the monarchy, couldn't avoid that aspect of sovereignty since it fell to them to decide whether to save the king's life. Sovereign is he who executes. Sovereign is he who pardons. Perhaps psychoanalysis cannot rid itself of a politics where it's never that kingly heads *aren't* severed. Regicide is the fulcrum of psychoanalysis's intervention into a politics which, let's note, is always royally cast.

Let's retain "unrelievable" from that earlier quote. Why can't we relieve ourselves of cruelty and sovereignty? Consider this in light of Derrida's "What is a 'Relevant' Translation?" and hence contemplate the Hegelian parlance that, as it concerns the term *Aufhebung*, might be translated as "relevant" in French or English. Imagine we asked: What is a "relevant" translation of *Grausamkeit*? A translation into the absolutes of death or the death drive? Does death sublate cruelty or else preserve cruelty at a "higher" level? What matters, besides the cruel confrontation with etymology (Latin and German) that translation and translators suffer, is who or what operates that *relève* or *Aufhebung*. Is it sovereignty? Is cruelty sublated, sublimated, or *relieved* by the death penalty if it can be deemed non-cruel, as if its cruel pain is canceled at this "higher" level, or does cruelty remain at this "higher" level inasmuch as *bodies* remain to feel the pain of death? Bodies can't be sublated away. Bodies remain as obdurate reminders to sovereign politics of its cruelty because death-pain cannot be *relieved* by any implement that deals death in the name of the law.

Cruelty resists and persists because the politics of sovereignty persists and resists the efforts of "democracy" to make sovereignty tremble, falter, or recede into history like the phantom of a bygone *ancien régime*. Derrida links three terms, "*cruelty, sovereignty, resistance*,"[23] speaking of their "spectral silhouette."[24] Democracy hasn't exorcised the ghosts of absolute sovereignty, and (considering American democracy) it cannot as long as the death penalty is retained as a manifestation of state power. It cannot, for that matter, as long as the president has the unconditional prerogative to pardon.

At issue is the sovereign right of pardon and the prerogative to refuse that pardon. To refuse or to grant: either way, the sovereign maintains the puissance of a condign power dealing in *sovereign* cruelty. Sovereignty persists because cruelty persists; cruelty persists because sovereignty persists. Contemplate Geoffrey Bennington's claim, in *Scatter 2*, that "Democracy is—sovereignty failing."[25] Derrida inspects the circumstances where sovereignty *doesn't* fail. It doesn't if sovereign prerogatives resist democracy's impulse to remove them—the president's unconditional pardon, and the state's right to execute people and call that neither cruel, nor unusual, nor murder. Sovereignty doesn't fail, I add, if there's nothing to be done about sovereignty's "spectral silhouette"—it's hard to put specters to death. It's hard to resist the *revenance* of the sovereign *revenant*—it keeps returning to haunt democracy's steps. Specters of sovereignty, you might say.

Obviously, it isn't as easy as abolishing the death penalty and then expecting sovereignty to meet its immediate demise. Here, one must complicate matters vis-à-vis the abolitionist argument and retrieve the *Death Penalty* seminar. In Judith Butler's review of Derrida's first volume, Butler asks, "are abolitionists perhaps seeking to eradicate the death drive—the 'hostility to life,' as Derrida puts it, that is 'inherent to life itself'?"[26] Butler cites Derrida: "'surpassing cruelty by an apparent cruelty,' he continues, 'would be merely a surpassing *in* cruelty, a surfeit of cruelty.'"[27] If Dr. Guillotin was right that the blade's nick is painlessly quick, and hence the guillotine isn't a cruel form of punishment but is rather the most humane way of administering the death penalty, would abolishing the death penalty deprive the state of the only non-cruel means it has for dealing in death and punishment? Without the guillotine, how else to punish capital offenses? If that punishment is replaced by a life sentence, doesn't that prolong the agony and become crueler than what abolitionists nonetheless argue is the supreme cruelty of the death penalty? "Those who oppose the death penalty," Butler observes,

> such as Beccaria and sometimes Bentham, seem to prefer a long, drawn-out form of cruel imprisonment, which raises the question: which camp in this debate stands for the more humane form of punishment? Wary of forms of aggression disguised as benevolence, Derrida asks whether some abolitionists are committed to other forms of cruelty that are masked by elegant moral formulations, ones that rationalize prolonging the time of cruelty and the tenure of sadistic delight.[28]

I simply add that when matters concern cruelty, reflections on *time* are necessary—the time of the instant (the guillotine blade's nick-of-time head-chop) and the prolonged time during which one feels cruelly done to, during which the sadist has tenure. In the *Death Penalty* seminar, Derrida writes: "One cannot think cruelty without time, the time given or the time taken."[29] Freud opposed the death penalty, but in general, Derrida accuses psychoanalysis of having ducked the matter. Because it did, it cannot properly broach the topic of resistance—cruelty and sovereignty's resistance—either. Such is the resistance of psychoanalysis. It resists that topic. Thus:

> Cruelty resists; sovereignty resists. The one and the other, the one *like* the other, pose a resistance *to* psychoanalysis, no doubt, but *just as* psychoanalysis also resists them, in the most equivocal sense of this word. Sovereignty and cruelty, very obscure things, resist differently, but they resist, one *like* the other, both without and within psychoanalysis proper.[30]

At issue is *politics*, which stands outside the psychoanalysis's own domain. But if psychoanalysis repeatedly seeks to expel cruelty to the exterior margins of its own ring-fenced domain, it's trying to expel what already resides within psychoanalysis. Yet if cruelty resists because sovereignty also resists, how can we counter cruelty's resistance if cruelty is irreducible? Derrida nags psychoanalysis for answers: "What does 'cruel' mean? Do we have, did Freud have a rigorous concept of the cruelty that, like Nietzsche, he spoke of so much (as regards the death drive, the aggression drive, or sadism, etc.)? Where does cruelty begin and end? Can an ethics, a legal code, a politics put an end to it?"[31] Perhaps ethics, law, or politics might end it, but the question is whether psychoanalysis, given its resistances, has dealt itself out of the game and has no services to render in the task of ending cruelty. "As I see it," says Derrida,

> psychoanalysis has not yet undertaken and thus still less succeeded in thinking, penetrating, and changing the axioms of the ethical, the juridical, and the political, notably in those seismic places where the theological phantasm of sovereignty quakes and where the most traumatic, let us say in a still confused manner, the most cruel events of our day are being produced.[32]

Can psychoanalysis assist in making that theological phantasm quake and tremble still further—help exorcise the resistant remnants of sovereignty from our democracies? For Derrida, psychoanalysis must update itself in view of the events of *our* day. "What," Derrida asks, "new forms of cruelty could a psychoanalyst of the year 2000 have to interpret at renewed expense, outside or within the institution?"[33] Note "renewed expense": what would it *cost* the psychoanalytic institution to do that? Derrida doesn't consider it trivial, therefore, to ask whether psychoanalysis should relinquish its Comp. Lit. syllabus privileging the Oedipus plays and *Hamlet* and update its course listings to reflect the present age: "Will it be the theater of the same family, an always more or less royal family, rather patriarchal and heterosexual, installed in sexual difference as binary opposition? . . . . Will the theatrical reference of psychoanalysis still tomorrow be Greek, Shakespearean, Elizabethan theater?"[34]

Either psychoanalysis proposes that drives are drives and there's nothing to be done about that, or psychoanalysis thinks there *is* something to do, even if whatever that is cannot involve a rewiring of the human being, soul, or psyche at a level so fundamental as to concern organic life and death (so fundamental that those mythic epitomes, *Eros* and *Thanatos*, would be redundant). Speaking of the ambiguous conditions under which psychoanalysis might address itself to cruelty, Derrida writes:

> On the one hand, these conditions imply an ethics and a politics that correspond to a condemnation and thus tend toward the elimination of this cruelty, to be sure,

> but at the same time and on the other hand, given the originary and ineradicable origin of the death or aggressivity drive, as well as the drive for power and thus sovereignty, one can have no illusions about the eradication of evil.[35]

On the one hand, on the other. Does Freud want it all ways at once? Certainly, Derrida observes, Freud denounces the illusion "of an eradication of the cruelty drives and the drives for power and sovereignty."[36] Let's reluctantly agree: it's deluded to imagine one can eradicate such primary and primitive drives. Nonetheless, Freud does think that it's necessary to fight against such drives. Derrida remarks:

> What *it is necessary* to cultivate (for it is necessary that an "it is necessary," and thus the tie of an ethical, juridical, political obligation, take shape) is a differential transaction, an economy of detour and difference, the strategy, one can even say the method (for it is a question here of path, path breaking, and road), of *indirect* progress: an indirect, always indirect way of combating the cruelty drive. The word "indirect" is articulated like the pivot of this progressivism without illusion. Freud thinks, like the Nietzsche of *Genealogy of Morals*, that cruelty has no contrary, that it is tied to the essence of life and the will to power.[37]

There can be no frontal assault on cruelty, since the theaters of cruelty and of battle keep scene-shifting, inventing new savageries as they do so. The path must be indirect—one of detours, rather than an arrow-straight Roman road. This is also Derrida's path, but much still depends on that differential transaction: Is that a transaction with *différance*? And what is an *economy* of detour and difference? It doesn't mean deferring matters until tomorrow since morally felt *necessities* require that something be done about cruelty *today.*

Resistances of Cruelty

It's all very well for Derrida to critique psychoanalysis's diffidence as regards finding (political) solutions to cruelty. But does Derrida have any solutions to offer? Can't we ask Derrida whether cruelty is as ineradicable as any primordial drive or instinct Freud names? Must we remain with bleak registrations that "cruelty there is" and "cruelty resists," and cherish wan hopes of cruelty's meager alleviation rather than expect something more root and branch? If cruelty resists, does cruelty resist deconstruction, whatever indirect operations, whatever detours deconstruction takes around that apparently abiding fact of human and political life? To answer, one must gather thoughts around aspects of *time*: the never, the forever, and the discreetly potent investment Derrida makes in the *perhaps.* We also need the *à-venir.* We must moreover gather thoughts around impossibility and possibility. Derrida, after all, says that "In other words, altogether other words, can one think this apparently impossible, but otherwise impossible thing, namely, a beyond the death drive, or the drive for sovereign mastery, thus the beyond of a cruelty, a beyond that would have nothing to do with either drives or principles?"[38]

How consequential is that "thus"! Consider "altogether other words": Derrida *translates* matters into his own parlance. *A* cruelty: Derrida avoids a substantive definition of *la cruauté*. *A* beyond, not *the* beyond. This "beyond" would be triggered by an event of the "impossible." Let's anticipate the objection: when he gestures to the impossible event, Derrida extricates himself too easily from the horns of the dilemma on which he has pinioned psychoanalysis. Assuredly, Derrida would hardly let Freud offer the last prospect on the *Jenseits*. Hence the jujitsu move whereby Derrida proposes a beyond of the beyond:

> This originary affirmation of beyond the beyond offers itself on the basis of numerous figures of the impossible. I have studied a few of these elsewhere: hospitality, gift, forgiveness—and above all the unpredictability, the "perhaps," the "what if" of the event, the coming, and the coming of the other in general, his or her or its arriving. Their possibility is always announced as the experience of a non-negative im-possible. The hospitable exposure to the event, to the coming, to the visitation of the unpredictable *arrivant* cannot be made into the horizon of a task, not even for psychoanalysis.[39]

The beyond of which Derrida can speak, but psychoanalysis cannot, concerns the unpredictable event—the event of the other arriving from the *à-venir*. Once that arrival has completed its coming, an event verily takes place. If that event enacts the im-possible (the formulation I prefer), it's because forecasts of the future predict what can and cannot come to pass. The field of the future is therefore saturated by determinations of possibility and hence impossibility as well. But if there's another future—horizon-less, unamenable to the presaged determinations of im-possibility—then it would be the beyond-the-horizon *à-venir* whence might *perhaps* come an event that makes possible cruelty's elimination.

But since Derrida speaks of hospitality as one such event, is Derrida the putative guest, a glad-tidings prophet disguised as the Devil's advocate, announcing cruelty's end to an audience of psychoanalysts? I cannot answer. Derrida: "It is perhaps a piece of good luck, this threat, the moment at which one begins to think, the Stranger would say, I mean the one who, in addressing you, basically does not belong to a presumed inside of the analytic community."[40] Derrida knows he is trying his hosts' hospitality, and perhaps the problem with strange guests is they bring "threat" rather than presents for their kindly hosts. *Luckily*, Derrida bears the beneficent harm of critique psychoanalysis needs to suffer cruelly. You have to be cruel to be kind, isn't that so? Derrida continues:

> If at least others arrive, from close by or far away, from the family or from the most distant strangeness, they do it, like everything that happens, like every event worthy of the name, like everything that is coming, in the form of the impossible, beyond all convention and all scenic control, all pleasure or reality principle, beyond all drive for power and perhaps all death drive. It is a hospitality of visitation not of invitation, when what arrives from the other exceeds the rules of hospitality and remains unpredictable for the hosts.[41]

Scenic control: psychoanalysis struts and frets upon the stage, scene, or theater controlled by drives and principles only it gets to name. Now Derrida comes onstage, like Banquo, interrupting things mightily. Still, the question is whether ending cruelty (and sovereignty) must take the "form of the impossible," namely the form of an event worthy of the name.

But does Derrida really want us to pin everything on the im-possible event that might eradicate cruelty? Is it cruel of Derrida to ask us to hope-without-hoping that a path beyond sovereign cruelty can be laid, broken, or treaded upon at all? Perhaps there is something unsatisfactory about how Derrida fishes out of his back pocket, as it were, his notion of the im-possible event. Still, deconstruction always ventures toward finalities, categorical impossibilities, ineradicable and irreducible situations, but tarries—*performatively*—on the brink of confirming the truth of such situations. Derrida expects-without-expecting the im-possible event to rout what he otherwise regards as cruelty's irreducibility.

Time's Cruelty

Perhaps Derrida's lecture was an exercise in performative bad faith. Does Derrida ever exemplify cruelty? Not quite. Consider, though: "What is this, cruelty? Where does it begin? Where does it end? And what if there were, sometimes, cruelty in *not* putting to death? And what if there were love in *wanting* to give death by twos, one to the other, one for the other, simultaneously or not?"[42] The hint is that we read "Aphorism Countertime," his text on *Romeo and Juliet*, where Derrida writes: "The impossible—this theatre of double survival—also tells, like every aphorism, the truth. Right from the pledge that binds together two desires, each is already in mourning for the other, entrusts death to the other as well: if you die before me, I will keep you, if I die before you, you will keep me in yourself."[43]

Time is cruel. Time asks two lovers to suffer countertime since neither can occupy the same time in which to share their love. Time's cruelties, I think, were Derrida's subject all along. Derrida wanted to make his audience *feel* time's cruelty. He therefore took up his audience's time and never gave it back. Time, once taken, cannot be returned, even as a "gift." We know this problematic from *Given Time*. Remember also the *Death Penalty* seminar: "One cannot think cruelty without time, the time given or the time taken."[44] If cruel is the taking, but not the returning of time, Derrida enacted that cruelty by giving a lecture and performing that cruelty. Derrida does this from the start, saying "If I say right now . . .: 'Yes, I am suffering cruelly,' or again, 'you are being *made* or *allowed* to suffer cruelly.'"[45] Derrida suffers because he is beginning a lecture that took hours to deliver. Derrida makes his audience suffer along with him. But, by inviting Derrida to give that lecture, the audience—masochistically—*allowed* him to take that cruel length of time needed for his lecture.

Ironic, therefore, is Derrida's: "I advance onto the stage of this new theater of cruelty,"[46] and his parenthesis:

> If ever I had a preference about the analytic session, well, you will find out what it is today at your expense, for you are going to suffer from it: it's that I would be resolutely, incorrigibly in favor of long sessions, very long. And despite the patience required, this is not the preference of the patient [man], quite the contrary.[47]

Cruel is the analyst who so lengthily tries the patience of patients!

I don't know whether his audience got the point. In any case, the point was performative: the cruel performance involved Derrida's taking up too much of people's time—time they didn't get back. Derrida, a keen reader of Shakespeare, might have been thinking of Sonnet 60: "And Time that gave doth now his gift confound."[48] Time confounds its apparent gift by steadily taking away the life-time we're given. Such is time's cruelty—it gives time with one hand, takes it away with the other hand. Shakespeare writes, however, "And yet to times in hope my verse shall stand, / Praising thy worth, despite his cruel hand."[49] How to resist time's cruel hand? Writing affords us hope that we might live on, assuming we invest our hopes in librarians prepared to deposit our publications into archives, and hope for readers who will still read our writing. This would be writing that *stands* despite the ravages of time's "sequent toil,"[50] as Shakespeare puts it—the toilsome sequences of time that proceed us all toward a steadily sooner death. Derrida toiled through the sequences of his lecture, visiting masochistic cruelty upon himself and sadistic cruelty on his audience. He proceeded himself and his audience toward the sooner imminence of mortality.

Derrida also hoped to survive thanks to writing that *stands*. Yet, if writing assures a certain postmortem survival, does writing thereby resist the death drive? Derrida doesn't unproblematically grant writing immunity from the death drive, however. That's why he ventures the possibility of writing having its own death drive. In "The Night Watch (Over the 'Book of Himself')," a preface Derrida wrote for Jacques Trilling's *James Joyce ou l écriture matricide*. Derrida informs us that he finished writing that preface just after the States General of Psychoanalysis lecture, adding "writing dreams of sovereignty, writing is cruel, murderous, suicidal, patricidal, matricidal, infanticidal, fratricidal, homicidal and so on."[51] Do sovereignty and cruelty persist because *writing* persists? If psychoanalysis cannot rid itself of death, particularly as it contemplates the deaths of kings and patriarchs, neither, apparently, can Derridean grammatology, even as grammatology grants a wider expanse to the killing at issue. When, in dialogue with Socrates, Phaedrus says "no dead discourse, but the living speech,"[52] where "dead discourse" is *writing*, perhaps that's the point. Writing is lifeless—it cannot *be*. If all life comes to be thanks to a mother, then writing contemplates its lifelessness by mourning its separation from the vital processes by which life is begotten. Or writing furtively fantasizes about matricide in order to kill off the invidious prestige of organic life—life deemed "higher" than any life writing might enjoy or indeed suffer. Can there be redemption for writing's cruelties—its "-cidal" fantasies—and redemption for the sovereignty drive that perhaps lurks at the heart of all grammatologies whereby writing, or the *gramme*, tries to assert its privilege over *living* speech? Is this akin to asking grammatology the question "Is writing without matricide still possible?"[53] It's as if Derrida asks himself whether grammatology neglected its own drive for the sovereign mastery of writing over speech. When Derrida says "Beyond the death drive, beyond every drive for power and mastery. Writing without writing,"[54] what writing-without-writing can grammatology contemplate? What writing lies beyond the death, cruelty, and sovereignty drives of *writing*? "No, mother! Let me be and let me live,"[55] exclaims Stephen Dedalus, but perhaps writing—given its matricidal drive—never lets *mothers* live.

Can writing be redeemed of its cruelties? It could, if one celebrates writing's survival drive—the drive to *stand*. Or else, I suggest, if one appreciates the *translation drive*—the drive texts have, when facing a certain mortality, to live on in translation. This living-on perforce relinquishes the securities of original languages; however, abandons the securities of *mother* tongues, in a perilous exposure to what one might dare call translation's matricidal drive. Recall Benjamin's "The Task of the Translator": "A translation issues from the original—not so much from its life but its afterlife."[56] So while Derrida's writing stands and survives in French, it's appropriate to conclude upon the sequent toils of translators. What cruelties do they suffer? In the lecture's postscript, Derrida refers to "all the virtual translations"[57] he had been negotiating with in light of certain French terms. He adds:

> I already imagine the sufferings of the translator who would like to respect each of these three words. . . . An apparently impossible translation. The French language seems to me the only one that deals out such a fate or such a welcome to the unheard-of and absolutely singular configuration of these words, these very large words, *avoir*, *faire*, *vouloir*, and *mal*.—Am I somehow to blame for this impossibility of translation? For the impossibility of translating word for word?[58]

The French language is a cruel mistress for Anglophone translators. Is Derrida to blame for this impossibility of translation? He replies, dialoguing enigmatically with an unnamed interlocutor: "No, of course not, it's in the language. You inherit it."[59] Is that Derrida's alibi? It's the fault of the French language, not his. "Yes, I am, on the contrary; look what I am doing with this inheritance. I'm betraying its truth."[60] Then: "Is the alibi still avoidable? Is it not already too late?"[61] It's as if Derrida accuses himself of betraying the truth of the French idiom. Too late for exoneration. No alibi. Guilty as charged. Unless Peggy Kamuf found it possible to pardon Derrida for the cruelly long trial of translation he put her through.

Notes

1 Jacques Derrida, *The Death Penalty, Volume 1*, trans. Peggy Kamuf (Chicago: University of Chicago Press, 2014), 48.
2 Jacques Derrida, "Psychoanalysis Searches the State of its Soul: The Impossible Beyond of a Sovereign Cruelty," trans. Peggy Kamuf, in *Without Alibi* (Stanford: Stanford University Press, 2002), 239.
3 Derrida, "Psychoanalysis Searches the State of its Soul," 238.
4 Derrida, "Psychoanalysis Searches the State of its Soul," 239.
5 Derrida, "Psychoanalysis Searches the State of its Soul," 239.

6 Derrida, "Psychoanalysis Searches the State of its Soul," 239.
7 Derrida, "Psychoanalysis Searches the State of its Soul," 240.
8 Derrida, "Psychoanalysis Searches the State of its Soul," 241.
9 Derrida, "Psychoanalysis Searches the State of its Soul," 258.
10 Derrida, "Psychoanalysis Searches the State of its Soul," 270.
11 Derrida, "Psychoanalysis Searches the State of its Soul," 280.
12 Derrida, "Psychoanalysis Searches the State of its Soul," 280.
13 Jacques Derrida, *Cinders*, trans. Ned Lukacher (Minneapolis: University of Minnesota Press, 2014), 3.
14 Jacques Derrida, *Limited Inc*, trans. Samuel Weber (Evanston: Northwestern University Press, 1998), 48.
15 Sigmund Freud, *On Metapsychology*, trans. James Strachey (London: Penguin, 1991), 413.
16 Freud, *On Metapsychology*, 331.
17 Freud, *On Metapsychology*, 310.
18 Freud, *On Metapsychology*, 311.
19 Given the tone and thrust of Derrida's "J'accuse," particularly as regards politics and his somewhat forcible request to the audience that psychoanalysis does some soul-searching, Elizabeth Rottenberg, when she briefly refers to Derrida's lecture in "Cruelty and its Vicissitudes," a chapter of her book *For the Love of Psychoanalysis: The Play of Chance in Freud and Derrida* (New York: Fordham University Press, 2019), perhaps understates the severity of Derrida's critique. Derrida's cruel "love" for psychoanalysis is more complex, as I am trying to show.
20 Derrida, "Psychoanalysis Searches the State of its Soul," 269.
21 I take this formulation from Derrida's seminar *Life Death*, trans. Pascale-Anne Brault and Michael Naas (Chicago: University of Chicago Press, 2020). The absence of any punctuation, for instance a comma, between the two terms is highly important, of course.
22 Derrida, "Psychoanalysis Searches the State of its Soul," 260.
23 Derrida, "Psychoanalysis Searches the State of its Soul," 242.
24 Derrida, "Psychoanalysis Searches the State of its Soul," 242.
25 Geoffrey Bennington, *Scatter 2. Politics in Deconstruction* (New York: Fordham University Press, 2021), 203.
26 Judith Butler, "On Cruelty," *London Review of Books* 36, no. 14 (July 17, 2014), https://www.lrb.co.uk/the-paper/v36/n14/judith-butler/on-cruelty.
27 Butler, "On Cruelty."
28 Butler, "On Cruelty."
29 Derrida, *Death Penalty*, 220.
30 Derrida, "Psychoanalysis Searches the State of its Soul," 242.
31 Derrida, "Psychoanalysis Searches the State of its Soul," 263.
32 Derrida, "Psychoanalysis Searches the State of its Soul," 244.
33 Derrida, "Psychoanalysis Searches the State of its Soul," 257.
34 Derrida, "Psychoanalysis Searches the State of its Soul," 255.
35 Derrida, "Psychoanalysis Searches the State of its Soul," 267.
36 Derrida, "Psychoanalysis Searches the State of its Soul," 271.
37 Derrida, "Psychoanalysis Searches the State of its Soul," 271.
38 Derrida, "Psychoanalysis Searches the State of its Soul," 241.
39 Derrida, "Psychoanalysis Searches the State of its Soul," 276.
40 Derrida, "Psychoanalysis Searches the State of its Soul," 249.

41 Derrida, "Psychoanalysis Searches the State of its Soul," 254.
42 Derrida, "Psychoanalysis Searches the State of its Soul," 280.
43 Jacques Derrida, "Aphorism Countertime," trans. Nicholas Royle, in *Psyche: Inventions of the Other, Volume 2* (Stanford: Stanford University Press, 2008), 132.
44 Derrida, *Death Penalty*, 220.
45 Derrida, "Psychoanalysis Searches the State of its Soul," 238.
46 Derrida, "Psychoanalysis Searches the State of its Soul," 256.
47 Derrida, "Psychoanalysis Searches the State of its Soul," 256.
48 William Shakespeare, *The Sonnets*, ed. G. Blakemore Evans (Cambridge: Cambridge University Press, 2006), 56.
49 Shakespeare, *The Sonnets*, 56.
50 Shakespeare, *The Sonnets*, 56.
51 Jacques Derrida, "The Night Watch (Over the 'Book of Himself')," trans. Pascale-Anne Brault and Michael Naas, in *Derrida and Joyce. Texts and Contexts*, ed. Andrew J. Mitchell and Sam Sloate (Albany: SUNY Press, 2013), 102.
52 Plato, "Phaedrus," trans. R. Hackforth, in *Plato: The Collected Dialogues Including the Letters*, ed. Edith Hamilton and Huntington Cairns (Princeton: Princeton University Press, 1961), 521.
53 Derrida, "The Night Watch," 103.
54 Derrida, "The Night Watch," 102–3.
55 James Joyce, *Ulysses*, ed. Hans Walter Gabler (New York: Random House, 1986), 9.
56 Walter Benjamin, "The Task of the Translator," trans. Harry Zohn, in *Selected Writings, Volume 1, 1913–1926*, ed. Marcus Bullock and Michael W. Jennings (Cambridge, MA: Harvard University Press, 1996), 254.
57 Derrida, "Psychoanalysis Searches the State of its Soul," 279.
58 Derrida, "Psychoanalysis Searches the State of its Soul," 280.
59 Derrida, "Psychoanalysis Searches the State of its Soul," 280.
60 Derrida, "Psychoanalysis Searches the State of its Soul," 280.
61 Derrida, "Psychoanalysis Searches the State of its Soul," 280.

Works Cited

Benjamin, Walter. "Critique of Violence," translated by Edmund Jephcott. In *Selected Writings, Volume 1, 1913—1926*, edited by Marcus Bullock and Michael W. Jennings, 236–52. Cambridge, MA: Harvard University Press, 1996.

Benjamin, Walter. "The Task of the Translator," translated by Harry Zohn. In *Selected Writings, Volume 1, 1913—1926*, edited by Marcus Bullock and Michael W. Jennings, 253–63. Cambridge, MA: Harvard University Press, 1996.

Bennington, Geoffrey. *Scatter 2. Politics in Deconstruction*. New York: Fordham University Press, 2021.

Butler, Judith. "On Cruelty." *London Review of Books* 36, no. 14 (July 17, 2014): https://www.lrb.co.uk/the-paper/v36/n14/judith-butler/on-cruelty.

Derrida, Jacques. *Limited Inc.* Translated by Samuel Weber. Evanston: Northwestern University Press, 1998.

Derrida, Jacques. "Psychoanalysis Searches the State of its Soul: The Impossible Beyond of a Sovereign Cruelty," translated by Peggy Kamuf. In *Without Alibi*, 238–80. Stanford: Stanford University Press, 2002.

Derrida, Jacques. "Aphorism Countertime," translated by Nicholas Royle. In *Psyche: Inventions of the Other, Volume 2*, 127–42. Stanford: Stanford University Press, 2008.

Derrida, Jacques. "The Night Watch (Over the 'Book of Himself')," translated by Pascale-Anne Brault and Michael Naas. In *Derrida and Joyce. Texts and Contexts*, edited by Andrew J. Mitchell and Sam Sloate, 87–103. Albany: SUNY Press, 2013.

Derrida, Jacques. *Cinders*. Translated by Ned Lukacher. Minneapolis: Minnesota University Press, 2014.

Derrida, Jacques. *The Death Penalty, Volume 1*. Translated by Peggy Kamuf. Chicago: University of Chicago Press, 2014.

Derrida, Jacques. *Life Death*. Translated by Pascale-Anne Brault and Michael Naas. Chicago: University of Chicago Press, 2020.

Freud, Sigmund. *On Metapsychology*. Translated by James Strachey. London: Penguin, 1991.

Joyce, James. *Ulysses*. Edited by Hans Walter Gabler. New York: Random House, 1986.

Plato. "Phaedrus," translated by R. Hackforth. In *Plato: The Collected Dialogues Including the Letters*, edited by Edith Hamilton and Huntington Cairns., 475–525. Princeton: Princeton University Press, 1961.

Rottenberg, Elizabeth. *For the Love of Psychoanalysis: The Play of Chance in Freud and Derrida*. New York: Fordham University Press, 2019.

Shakespeare, William. *The Sonnets*. Edited by G. Blakemore Evans. Cambridge: Cambridge University Press, 2006.

14

Black *Ressentiment* and the Politics of the Death Drive

A Fanonian Meditation

Zahi Zalloua

The death drive is a scandal; it is a scandal to anyone invested in the subject, in the grammar of autonomy, in the Kantian ideal of a self-legislating being. To paraphrase Freud, to affirm the death drive is to willingly bring the "plague" to your field or discipline.[1] It is to radicalize further Freud's claim that "*the ego is not the master in its own house*."[2] The death drive—this unruly "inhuman" at the core of the human, *what is in us more than us*—discloses the ideal of self-mastery as nothing but a humanist fantasy. If the death drive points to the workings of an "illogical logic"[3] in human actions, what prospects does it bear for politics? Is any humanist endeavor invalidated from the start by this invariably corrosive idea? If not, how do you then translate the death drive's destructive force, its undermining of the subject's powers (over its own self-interests), into a life-affirming political vision? To put it slightly differently, what are the political stakes in avowing the death drive?

The act of entertaining the possibility of the death drive almost immediately opens up a pessimistic line of thought. It shifts the very foundations of one's political agenda. Witness David Marriott's objection to what he takes to be Achille Mbembe's classical humanist commitment that "there is, in every human person, something unconquerable, fundamentally untameable, that domination—regardless of the forms it takes—cannot eliminate, nor contain, nor repress, at least not totally."[4] Against the West's racist gaze, there is always something beneath that resists, that is irreducible to what white society tells you you *are*. Like Cedric Robinson, Mbembe is invested in recovering and amplifying a critical Black tradition—with Frantz Fanon playing a pivotal role in this anti-racist lineage. Marriott, however, moves to decouple Fanon from Mbembe's humanist enlistment precisely by turning to the notion of the death drive. Marriott questions Mbembe's identification of excess with "creative capacity," his somewhat idealizing alignment of excess with "freedom-as-possibility"; Marriott recasts excess instead as "the lived meaning of a death drive," which, he adds, "is also inalienable, untameable, prior to domination."[5] The death drive paints the Human in a less flattering light. What "we" share is not so much a will for freedom and/as creativity (the would-be basis for a planetary ethics, a commitment to a world in common); rather, what we have in common is a self-sabotaging or short-circuiting foreignness from within. But Marriott is quick to tie the death drive to anti-Blackness in Fanon, who understood the death drive to be "the lived meaning of black social death, a mortification which humanism can only disavow or repress."[6] Thinking the death drive in relation to anti-Blackness frames the Freudian idea in a peculiar light, compelling us to return to the subject and question its universal status and ontological makeup before fearing or celebrating its alleged derailment.

In what follows, I want to pursue what we might call the Black subject of the death drive. In doing so, I will first situate the death drive as social death in Fanon's elaboration of the "zone of nonbeing,"[7] a concept that continues to elicit interpretations from new and seasoned readers of *Black Skin, White Masks*. Second, I will turn my attention to the affective register, to civil society's libidinal economy, attending to the circulation of Black *ressentiment* as a response not only to negrophobia but also to liberal democracy's brand of negrophilia, encapsulated in its promotion of identity politics and neoliberal grammar of victimhood. Lastly, I will return to the politics of the death drive and consider its valences, focusing on the ways supplementing the death drive with a Fanon-inflected, dialecticized vision of Black *ressentiment* ruthlessly troubles narcissistic investments in identity, none more appealing than that of the victim.

On Entering and Exiting the Zone of Nonbeing

In the first couple of pages of his introduction to *Black Skin, White Masks*, Fanon juxtaposes two seemingly incommensurable ideas and moods. The first comes as an implicit response to the question "Why am I writing this book?" Fanon offers his readers a list of possible reasons:

> Striving for a New Humanism.
> Understanding Mankind.
> Our Black Brothers.
> I believe in you, Man.
> Racial Prejudice.
> Understanding and Loving[8]

Opening with "Striving for a New Humanism" both inscribes Fanon's text within a humanist tradition and creates a mood of hope—hope that this new humanism might be able to address the shortcomings of the humanist tradition, in particular its racial politics. This is the legacy of Fanon to which Mbembe adds his name. The second passage follows a provocation to the reader. "Running the risk of angering my black brothers," Fanon writes, "I shall say that a Black is not a man." He then adds:

> There is a zone of nonbeing, an extraordinarily sterile and arid region, an incline stripped bare of every essential, from which a genuine new departure can emerge. In most cases, the black man cannot take advantage of this descent into a veritable hell.[9]

The zone of nonbeing attests to the quasi-permanent effects of anti-Blackness; the inferiority of Blackness gains an ontological reality. There is seemingly ("in most cases") no way out of this ontological inferno. Black people are systematically de-worlded, zombified, denied relationality and community, stripped of individuality without the prospects of becoming something/someone else. Their "human" capacity for transcendence—what renders the existentialist claim for absolute freedom, "existence precedes essence," legible—is indefinitely suspended. The grammar of recognition does not belong to them nor apply to them; they don't qualify for any dialectical upgrades (the movement from Other to Self, modeled after Hegel's paradigmatic Master/Slave dialectic). As socially ostracized creatures, the blackened, the wretched, dwell in a heartless world, sealed in their (non)being.

The rhetorical effect of setting both ideas/moods in tension from the very beginning creates a degree of interpretive uncertainty. Oscillating between optimism and pessimism, the reader ponders, What kind of "human" will this new humanism assume? And will it speak to the deadlock of the zone of nonbeing, the exclusion of *most* Black folks from the benefits of "this descent into a veritable hell"? We can formulate Fanon's predicament in Lacanian terms: the subject's "descent into a veritable hell" is akin to and yet different from the experience of the Real, which is tantamount to the shattering of the subject's symbolic identity. The subject is caught "between two deaths," as Lacan puts it. She is between symbolic death and actual death: socially dead, but biologically alive. What is at stake here is the status of the subject's symbolic identity. It is precisely the givenness of identity that is absent for those racialized bodies relegated to the zone of nonbeing, cruelly subjected to the zombification of life. The zone of nonbeing is not experienced as an ontological interruption (an experience of *de trop*, as Sartre might put it; an experience of the void at the core of my being) but as a quasi-permanent condition. Anti-Blackness is an everyday event. We might say that the zone of nonbeing attests to the banality of racial trauma. To assume that self-destitution (symbolic suicide—"an act of 'losing all,' of withdrawing from symbolic reality, that enables us to begin anew from the 'zero point'"[10]) is available to all is equally to assume that identity is available to all. This assumption—shared by humanists and anti-humanists alike—can reinforce an anti-Black world insofar as the human as such is left under-theorized, divorced from Western modernity's racial and colonial project: its disciplining and categorizing of bodies as human, not-quite-human, and nonhuman.

The death drive is directly implicated in this discussion to the extent that it is also preoccupied with self-destitution and human agency. Commenting on the death drive's relation to the zone of nonbeing, Derek Hook writes enthusiastically that it is "perhaps only with reference to this conceptual supplement [the death drive] that we are able to properly grasp the revolutionary potential [of the] idea of the zone of nonbeing."[11] Hook is relying here on the Lacanian inflection of the death drive as *ethical cause* rather than the Freudian death instinct. The Lacanian death drive as a fidelity to a cause—as embodied in Antigone's heroic resistance to King Creon's cruel authority—recasts the zone of nonbeing as a project straddling the ethical and the political. In this light, the death drive as an engine of change is poised to enable the Black subject to finally take advantage of this descent into a veritable hell and fashion or recreate itself anew. But the same lingering question remains: as with the alleged givenness of symbolic identity, what is the universal force of the death drive in an anti-Black world?

The fact that Fanon says "in most cases" rather than "in all cases" the Black man cannot take advantage of his situation opens up the possibility that this zone of nonbeing is not a fully totalized space. This zone of nonbeing—the condition of Black social death—is not destiny. The death drive is another way to imagine the ontological incompleteness of the Black subject. It registers a gap between the empty subject of psychoanalysis and the social ego. Is harnessing the negativity of the death drive then a viable means to transcend the zone of nonbeing? The question hinges of course on how we understand transcendence. If society relegates Black bodies to the zone of nonbeing, exiting this zone remains an ideological fantasy unless civil society's anti-Blackness is effectively dealt with (the same holds for the idea of a "new humanism"). Transcendence here must be stripped of its existentialist and individualist residue. Exiting the zone of nonbeing—and/as inaugurating a new humanism—will be a collective effort or it will not be.

Black *Ressentiment* and/at the Human

Politicizing the death drive sends us back to civil society's collective unconscious, to its anti-Black libidinal economy: the implicit rules and principles regulating desires and fears, the production, circulation, and consumption of anti-Blackness. A given society's libidinal economy governs our deep sense of who affectively matters, belongs, counts—and who effectively does not. Politicizing the death drive then calls for reckoning with the symbolic order's grammar of the human. I want to return to Fanon's provocative remark that "a Black is not a man." In Richard Philcox's translation, this observation *runs the risk of angering his Black brothers*. The original French version says something a bit different: "Dussé-je encourir le ressentiment de mes frères de couleur, je dirai que le Noir n'est pas un homme." Charles Lam Markmann's translation follows the original more literally: "At the risk of arousing the resentment of my colored brothers, I will say that the black is not a man." My only objection to this rendering is the choice of "resentment" over "*ressentiment*," which risks covering over the Nietzschean register. Though the main point that Fanon seems to be stressing here is the negative emotion that he is expecting from his Black interlocutors, the fact that he chose *ressentiment* (and not *colère* or *rage*, for instance) might not be irrelevant, especially if we examine further the object of ire: the statement that *the Black man is not a man*. Fanon anticipates that his interlocutors will read this claim as a slight, a denigration of their being and a denial that they are worthy of claiming the universal or Republican ideal of the human subject. Their *ressentiment* is a "reaction" to Fanon's critique. To be reactional characterizes the Nietzschean "man of *ressentiment*." Later in *Black Skin, White Masks*, Fanon makes explicit the Nietzschean insight that "there is always *ressentiment* in *reaction*,"[12] before approvingly quoting Nietzsche's posthumous *The Will to Power*: "To induce man to be actional, by maintaining in his circularity the respect of the fundamental values that make the world human, that is the task of utmost urgency for he who, after careful reflection, prepares to act."[13] Fanon imagines his interlocutors not as acting, but precisely as reacting to his observation. Their protestation would take the form of a negation/correction: *the Black is a man*. In other words, their *ressentiment* fuels their defense and preservation of their being—the claim that they are human too. *Ressentiment*, in this instance, is about the defense of identity and laying claim to the man of Western civilization.

What Fanon's hasty readers miss is the full force of his critique. Fanon's aim is clearly not to denigrate his Black brethren, but to expose the social phantasm that passes for the human. Fanon makes this point obliquely when he says that "the black man wants to be white" (and thus is in part responsible for his own alienation), but also adds, "the white man is desperately trying to achieve the rank of man [*une condition d'homme*]." In this sense, the white man is *not* a man either—in the absolute sense of the term, no one *is*. The pure human is a social fantasy. Whoever can claim to embody it relies on a social order, a racial matrix that includes and excludes, that divides and categorizes the human, the not-quite-human, and the nonhuman. The grammar of the human has thus everything to do with power and the regulation of desires and attachments. Forging a new grammar, which necessarily entails a new ontology (since language both reflects and shapes being), is the daunting challenge facing the wretched, the blackened subject of modernity. Without it, a genuine new departure from the zone of nonbeing can never emerge.

Black *ressentiment* seems to be an impediment to the creation of this new grammar. It is a reactionary response to anti-Black racism. It is a defensive posture that seeks to preserve identity and proclaim one's humanity. Black *ressentiment*, as with any form of *ressentiment*, is devoid of invention and life-affirmation. At the same time, scenes of *ressentiment*, scenes that are *ressentiment*-inducing, also pervade Fanon's work, complicating, in turn, the term's narrow Nietzschean meaning. Let's consider a couple of examples from chapter 5 of *Black Skin, White Masks*. In "The Lived Experience of the Black Man," Fanon describes his interaction with a white child, where the boy's ingrained anti-Blackness grossly distorts the meaning of his behavior:

> The Negro is an animal, the Negro is bad, the Negro is wicked, the Negro is ugly; look, a Negro; the Negro is trembling, the Negro is trembling because he's cold, the small boy is trembling because he's afraid of the Negro, the Negro is trembling with cold, the cold that chills the bones, the lovely little boy is trembling because he thinks the Negro is trembling with rage, the little white boy runs to his mother's arms: "Maman, the Negro's going to eat me."[14]

The terrified white boy mistakes Fanon's trembling, due to coldness, for rage. In an anti-Black world, Black being is overdetermined from without. The child doesn't see Fanon; he only perceives a phobic Black man. This is a powerful example of the pervasiveness of anti-Blackness in French society. And yet "the Negro is trembling with rage" can gain an additional meaning. Imagine Fanon—or his wretched readers—rereading this passage. I would argue that this passage is *ressentiment*-inducing. It fuels the rage of the racially excluded. *I was cold, minding my own business, internalizing white society's wickedness, then I encountered this child; I wasn't initially trembling with rage, but now I am.* Fanon/the reader's would-be reaction here, however, is not tied to an identity that the wretched wants to protect or claim. This *ressentiment* is more about saying *No!* to the current order of things, *No!* to appeasing the lovely little white boys of the world!

Shortly after this episode, Fanon tells us of his encounter with a white woman, who quickly praises his appearance:

> Look how handsome that Negro is.
>
> The handsome Negro says, "Fuck you" [*le beau nègre vous emmerde*], madame.[15]

If *ressentiment*, in the earlier example, was a delayed reaction, here it is immediate. He is unwilling to go along, to accept the white woman's backhanded compliment, since she assumes the ugliness of Blackness as the default. Fanon is the exception that proves the rule. His *ressentiment* explodes any sham of politeness or respectability. The effects are telling: "Her face colored with shame. At last I was freed from my rumination [about the crushing white gaze]. I realized two things at once: I had identified the enemies and created a scandal. Overjoyed. We could now have some fun."[16] In an anti-Black world, there is no real difference between white supremacists and white liberals. They both traffic in collective fantasies whose purpose is to separate the Black from the human, to insulate the latter to the detriment of the former. There is something joyful and actional in identifying the white enemy (in all her colors). Black *ressentiment* takes on a combative attitude. It produces a counter-enjoyment, an enjoyment derived from frustrating the sensibilities of white folks. This example also pivots the subject of *ressentiment* away from its Nietzschean status as a slavish, bitter victim. Whereas the champions of identity politics, who feature as the new priests in the Nietzschean sense of the term, engage in *ressentiment* management, guiding the conduct of their alienated constituents (as would-be victims), their actions and modes of thought, Fanonian *ressentiment* proves less prone to cooptation by the liberal proponents of identity politics and its neoliberal grammar of victimhood.

The Death Drive as the Will to De-exceptionalize

It is here that the death drive holds some promise for an alternative anti-racist politics, one that is not grounded in the identity of the victim. This mode of the death drive manifests itself in Fanon's refusal to exceptionalize Black suffering, to identify only with his putative kin. As a Black man, he declines to elevate the status of his subjugated identity, to fetishize, for example, the Haitian Revolution as a Black event:

> I am a man, and I have to rework the world's past from the very beginning. I am not just responsible for the slave revolt in Saint Domingue. Every time a man has brought victory to the dignity of the spirit, every time a man has said no to an attempt to enslave his fellow man, I have felt a sense of solidarity with his act.[17]

For Fanon, Black *ressentiment* does not end with Black folks. Rather, it opens to the plight of others, enjoining them to universalize their grievances, to see their antagonism as cutting across societies, turning personal trauma into a common cause. What Fanon desires is solidarity with the wretched of the earth in their struggles for racial and economic justice, in their struggle for life itself, insofar as to be wretched is to be at war with an inhospitable world, to be in "a permanent struggle against an omnipresent death."[18] In Lacan's terms, Fanon's commitment to liberation is the unconditional demand on which he is not prepared to give way.[19] This is precisely Fanon's "ethical cause." Fanonian solidarity does not follow today's hegemonic dictates of identity politics; it intimates a politics of the death drive, pointing "beyond the pleasure principle," to what is at odds with the conservative and narcissistic logic of identity politics. Žižek has drawn attention to the conceptual overlap between *ressentiment* and the death drive. He writes:

> The true opposite of egotist self-love is not altruism, a concern for common good, but envy, *ressentiment*, which makes me act against my own interests. Freud knew it well: the death drive is opposed to the pleasure principle as well as to the reality principle. The true evil, which is the death drive, involves self-sabotage. It makes us act against our own interests.[20]

Žižek aligns *ressentiment* with the death drive precisely because of its impulse to undermine the sovereignty of the subject. *Ressentiment* and the death drive do make us act against our own interests. But the agency here need not be so unidirectional, positing the self as the hapless victim of his own nature. The subject can embrace these notions and adopt, as I've been arguing, a different attitude toward his own self.

From the standpoint of the advocates of identity politics, who actively nurture the egotist self-love of their constituents, Fanon and Fanonians are committing symbolic suicide, divesting from society's sanctioned model of the victim. They are not only declining what is in their self-interest; they are also refusing legibility and recognition, refusing to follow the identitarian (neo)liberal script for social grievances. A Fanonian rejoinder: Has identity politics really delivered on its goals? Isn't it time to reconsider the values of national, racial, or ethnic particularism? Wouldn't a universal politics—an emancipatory project worthy of its name—require us to move "beyond the pleasure principle," to take actions no longer invested in the preservation of a person or group's given identity and narrow interests?

A politics of the death drive would transform the coordinates of the situation, de-ossifying the field of power. Though Edward Said does not name it as such, he does value what we might describe as Fanon's nonconformity to the pleasure principle. Said underscores Fanon's drive to de-exceptionalize his *parti pris*, the ways he nuances and punctures—as opposed to buttress and reify—his identification with any one political movement or cause. As Said puts it:

> It is inadequate only to affirm that a people was dispossessed, oppressed or slaughtered, denied its rights and its political existence, without at the same time doing what Fanon did during the Algerian war, affiliating those horrors with the

> similar afflictions of other people. This does not at all mean a loss in historical specificity, but rather it guards against the possibility that a lesson learnt about oppression in one place will be forgotten or violated in another place or time.[21]

To recall, Marriott situates the death drive in our anti-Black world, where this Freudian idea is intimately tied to "the lived meaning of black social death," which Fanon understood as "a mortification which humanism can only disavow or repress."[22] Marriott's Fanon puts on display a Black imago that represents the horrors of the human, of a human whose humanity has been obliterated. Blackness is the embodiment of the death drive's destructive effects; it is a sign of the inhuman in the human, precisely what the white humanist gaze willfully ignores in itself but happily recognizes in Black bodies. Aligning Blackness with the death drive reinforces the ontological difference between the Human and the Black. Whereas a human being holds to the potential of transcendence, the Black being is always already banished to the zone of nonbeing. Though Marriott is rightly vigilant against humanist readings of Fanon that tame Fanon's insights, he nevertheless forecloses what a politics of the death might look like for Fanon. His account of the relation of Blackness to the death drive is suggestive but too one-sided. It addresses the persistence of the zone of nonbeing in Black lives; consequently, the zone of nonbeing becomes exclusively a zone where escape and invention are unrealized and unrealizable possibilities.

But Fanon's whole work aims at questioning the political ontology that oppresses the wretched. The language of political ontology is prevalent in the reception of Fanon by Afropessimist thinker Frank Wilderson. For Wilderson, the operative antagonism of civil society is not between white and its racialized others, but between Black and non-Black. To fully appreciate why this world, why civil society is irredeemable, is to take seriously, or even axiomatically, the transformative impact of the transatlantic slave trade on the ontology of Blackness. The Middle Passage generated nothing short of a "new ontology": racial Blackness, an ontological paradox, a kind of (non)being devoid of any relationality.[23] A refrain in the works of Wilderson and other Afropessimists is that Black slavery is "without analog."[24] In the realm of "human" comparison, Blacks are incomparable. Other racialized bodies—such as Jews, Palestinians, Native Americans, undocumented immigrants, refugees, queers, and so on—are all extended the privileges of humanity. There is in place within the juridical framework available to those who are excluded but non-Black—disparagingly named "junior partners of civil society"[25]—a mechanism, however flawed, to voice the wrongs done to them and secure the protection of the law. In contradistinction, to be Black signifies "abject inhumanity," not "degraded humanity";[26] Black folks are without any willing interlocutors capable of hearing their plight: "The collective unconscious is not ready to accept that blacks are human."[27] The zone of nonbeing is another word for the afterlife of slavery.

In relation to modernity's political ontology, Wilderson sees no viable operation in this world other than the call for its destruction. Wilderson frequently turns to a passage from *Black Skin, White Masks* in which Fanon quotes Aimé Césaire's *Notebook of a Return to the Native Land*. Wilderson praises Fanon's praise of Césaire's revolutionary call to begin with "the end of the world," which, he adds, is the "only thing . . . worth the effort of starting."[28] To contextualize a bit, Fanon turns to Césaire's epic poem in order to refute Octave Mannoni's psychological reading of Shakespeare's *The Tempest* in *Prospero and Caliban: The Psychology of Colonization*, where Mannoni theorizes that the colonized identifies with the oppressor, the father figure of the colonizer, as a result of an essentialized "dependency complex." He argues that Caliban, even when plotting against Prospero, can only think of serving new masters (Stephano and Trinculo), never desiring freedom itself, never seeking a life without a master. On Mannoni's reductive reading, all colonized subjects are basically pathologized Calibans, suffering from an intrinsic desire for subjugation.[29] Fanon and Césaire completely reject such a reading of Caliban. Their Caliban is a creature of history who also, and more importantly, embodies the colonized's inextinguishable hunger for freedom.

Recalling this reading of Caliban reminds us to frame the zone of nonbeing as a historical condition; it is a dynamic situation that must not be rigidly ontologized. Black *ressentiment*, as we have seen, is a double-edged sword; it is an endless source of investment and divestment. The well of *ressentiment* can work to lock you in your identity (to produce a desire to preserve or [re]claim your identity) and it can generate an emancipatory form of negativity. In the second instance, the Nietzschean phenomenon of *ressentiment* is negated and preserved, taking on a new, higher, politicized form; it undergoes a semantic mutation. It is no longer about an individualized suffering that can be weaponized by today's managers of pain (the champions of identity politics). The neoliberal personalization of one's, or a group's, narrative is abolished, but the affect's negativity is retained and rechanneled for a truly collective vision. If identity politics largely conforms to the pleasure principle—manage your *ressentiment* and act in such a way to preserve your identity and realize your interests—Fanon's politics guards against the lures of exceptionalism and separatism (the temptation of Afropessimism); such politics stage *ressentiment* as a response and demand for more. Fanon solicits and elicits the *No!* of his readers—an uncompromised and uncompromising *No!* to this world and its deadening possibilities. The saturation of the zone of nonbeing is a problem that touches all of us, but obviously not in the same way. There is no end to this colonized and colonizing world unless the unjust distribution of identities and libidinal attachment to them undergoes mass upheaval, until a reckoning with the symbolic self takes place on an individual and collective level.

Now if the pleasure principle and identitarian politics do work in tandem, which I've been arguing they do, the death drive holds an immeasurable political potential. The death drive can be used to demystify the traditional conception of the subject as fully transparent to itself, predictable in terms of the pleasure principle. As Lacan avers, the death drive's ruthless indocility "challenges everything that exists,"[30] obeys no external authority, and shuns futurology (forecasts about the future from current trends in society); it cannot be placated nor seduced and bribed by the rewards of the social order. It moves the subject of the drive to sacrifice, to defect, and, more generally, to jeopardize its comfort and well-being.[31] The death drive disabuses all humanists of their faith in the subject's powers. A politics of the death drive does not stop here; it builds on the displacement of the subject by harnessing the drive's inventive power, indexing what Lacan describes as its "will to create from zero, a will to begin again."[32] Indeed, Lacan further characterizes the death drive as "will to destruction. Will to make a fresh start."[33] The death drive is a libidinal reset; it clears your unconscious attachments, the psychic investments that tie your identity to the symbolic order. But the injunction "to wipe the slate clean"[34] is not intended to glorify negativity, along the lines of *negativity for negativity's sake*. Rather, the virtue of negativity lies in its capacity to generate new meanings, occasioning the introduction of the new into social existence.[35] An idea that resonates well with Fanon's observation, "I must constantly remind myself that the real *leap* consists of introducing invention into life."[36] The death drive makes leaps happen. It is destructive as it is generative. The death drive disables the workings of egoistical reason, faithful adherence to the pleasure principle, but it also enables the subject to create anew.

To return to a concern raised above: Does this vision of the death drive presuppose a human subject premised on the perpetuation of Black social death? Or to put it slightly differently, is the *will to begin again* nothing more than a white privilege—the luxury of self-destitution? Afropessimists might be inclined to answer in the affirmative. There is no human subject without the abject Black/Slave. Consistent with their purist rhetoric of exceptionalism, Afropessimists like Wilderson adopt a separatist mode of being, marked by Black worldlessness, an exclusive and paradoxical kind of identity politics—which homogenizes and ontologizes anti-Blackness, the evisceration of Black being—that risks reifying the schism between Black and non-Black. Fanon's answer is far more ambivalent. His own apocalyptic call for "the end to the world" points in a different direction. It begins with a will to de-exceptionalize, for which the death drive's self-sabotaging ways—its interest-frustrating propensities—are aptly suited. There is none of the Afropessimists' unqualified investment in the singularity or incomparability of anti-Blackness, and there is nothing more foreign to Fanon than even the whiff of Oppression Olympics—the surplus enjoyment in one's own radical otherness or claim to ultimate victimhood. Rather, Fanon constantly turns to multiracial class-based interventions and labors for a collective or transnational exit from the zone of nonbeing, an exit that understands that there is no genuine exit unless the whole system that has manufactured this heartless zone of disposable beings is itself dismantled (only then can a "new humanism" ever be contemplated). Toward that end, Fanon exerts pressure on the system from all directions, vigorously multiplying rather than restricting *ressentiment*'s negativity, turning a personal expression of frustration (at the Human, at civil society, at the pleasure principle of liberal culture, etc.) into a collective *No!*, a contagious *No!* And, as with Caliban's insatiable and *ressentiment*-infused hunger for freedom,[37] Fanonian solidarity is unimpeachably expansive. To adapt his earlier quote, *every time an individual embraces the will to begin again, every time she wills symbolic suicide by saying no to an attempt to enslave her neighbor, I have felt a sense of solidarity with her acts.*[38]

Notes

1 As Jacques Lacan recounts, Carl Jung recalls Freud claiming upon his arrival in America in 1909 that he and Jung were "bringing them the plague." See Jacques Lacan, "The Freudian Thing, or the Meaning of the Return to Freud in Psychoanalysis," in

Écrits: The First Complete Edition in English, trans. Bruce Fink (New York: Norton, 2006), 336.

2 Sigmund Freud, "A Difficulty in the Path of Psycho-Analysis," in *The Standard Edition of the Complete Psychological Works of Sigmund Freud*, ed. James Strachey, volume 17 (London: Hogarth, 1955), 141.

3 Jacques Derrida, *Rogues: Two Essays on Reason*, trans. Pascale-Anne Brault and Michael Naas (Stanford: Stanford University Press, 2005), 123, 157.

4 Quoted in David Marriott, "The Becoming-Black of the World? On Achille Mbembe's *Critique of Black Reason*," *Radical Philosophy* 2, no. 2 (2018): 66.

5 Marriott, "The Becoming-Black of the World?" 67.

6 Marriott, "The Becoming-Black of the World?" 67.

7 Frantz Fanon, *Black Skin, White Masks*, trans. Richard Philcox (New York: Grove Press, 2008), xii.

8 Fanon, *Black Skin*, ix.

9 Fanon, *Black Skin*, xii; translation modified. Philcox's translation leaves out a crucial comma after "an incline stripped bare of every essential." See Geo Maher, *Anticolonial Eruptions: Racial Hubris and the Cunning of Resistance* (Berkeley: University of California Press, 2022), 20.

10 Slavoj Žižek, *Enjoy Your Symptom!: Jacques Lacan in Hollywood and Out* (New York: Routledge, 1992), 43.

11 Derek Hook, "Death-Bound Subjectivity: Fanon's Zone of Nonbeing and the Lacanian Death Drive," *Subjectivity* 13 (2020): 358.

12 Fanon, *Black Skin*, 197; translation modified.

13 Quoted in Fanon, *Black Skin*, 197.

14 Fanon, *Black Skin*, 93.

15 Fanon, *Black Skin*, 94.

16 Fanon, *Black Skin*, 94.

17 Fanon, *Black Skin*, 201.

18 Frantz Fanon, *A Dying Colonialism*, trans. Haakon Chevalier (New York: Grove Press, 1965), 128.

19 Jacques Lacan, *The Seminar of Jacques Lacan, Book VII: The Ethics of Psychoanalysis, 1959–1960*, ed. Jacques-Alain Miller, trans. Dennis Porter (New York: W.W. Norton, 1992), 319.

20 Slavoj Žižek, *Violence: Six Sideways Reflections* (New York: Picador, 2008), 87.

21 Edward Said, *Representations of the Intellectual: The 1993 Reith Lectures* (New York: Vintage Books, 1996), 44.

22 Marriott, "The Becoming-Black of the World?" 67.

23 Frank B. Wilderson III, *Red, White & Black: Cinema and the Structure of U.S. Antagonisms* (Durham: Duke University Press, 2010), 18, 56.

24 Wilderson, *Red, White & Black*, 38.

25 Wilderson, *Red, White & Black*, 28.

26 Frank B. Wilderson III, "Afro-Pessimism and the End of Redemption," *Humanities Futures. Franklin Humanities Institute: Duke University*, October 20, 2015, https://humanitiesfutures.org/papers/afro-pessimism-end-redemption/.

27 Frank B. Wilderson III, "'We're Trying to Destroy the World': Anti-Blackness and Police Violence After Ferguson," in *Shifting Corporealities in Contemporary Performance Danger, Im/mobility and Politics*, ed. Marina Gržinić and Aneta Stojnić (New York: Palgrave, 2018), 58.

28 Wilderson, *Red, White, & Black*, 28.
29 "Wherever Europeans have founded colonies of the type we are considering, it can safely be said that their coming was unconsciously expected—even desired—by the future subject peoples. Everywhere there existed legends foretelling the arrival of strangers from the sea, bearing wondrous gifts with them." See Octave Mannoni, *Prospero and Caliban: The Psychology of Colonization*, trans. Pamela Powesland (Ann Arbor: The University of Michigan Press, 1990), 86.
30 Lacan, *The Ethics of Psychoanalysis*, 212.
31 "To revolutionize a system," Žižek writes, "is never equal to just eliminating one of its parts." The identities of the white racist as well as that of their Black victim will have to endure "symbolic erasure." See Slavoj Žižek, "Three Fragments on Suicide as a Political Factor," *Crisis and Critique* 9, no. 2 (2022): 424, 423.
32 Lacan, *The Ethics of Psychoanalysis*, 212.
33 Lacan, *The Ethics of Psychoanalysis*, 212.
34 Lacan, *The Ethics of Psychoanalysis*, 210.
35 Slavoj Žižek, *The Ticklish Subject: The Absent Center of Political Ontology* (New York: Verso, 1999), 153.
36 Fanon, *Black Skin*, 204.
37 Recall how Césaire's Caliban captures and translates the rebellious nature of Shakespeare's Caliban, who, far from being servile, turns Prospero's teachings against him by using the language he has learned to curse back. In *A Tempest*, decolonizing the mind begins with a life-affirming *ressentiment*—the purging of Caliban's body, forcibly removing all the venom of colonialism and all the traces of Prospero's discourse: "I'd vomit you up, all your pomp and designs! Your white poison!" See Aimé Césaire, *A Tempest*, trans. Richard Miller (New York: TCG Translations, 2002), 57.
38 This chapter draws on material originally published in Zahi Zalloua, *The Politics of the Wretched: Race, Reason, and Ressentiment* (London: Bloomsbury Academic, 2024).

Works Cited

Césaire, Aimé. *A Tempest*. Translated by Richard Miller. New York: TCG Translations, 2002.

Derrida, Jacques. *Rogues: Two Essays on Reason*. Translated by Pascale-Anne Brault and Michael Naas. Stanford: Stanford University Press, 2005.

Fanon, Frantz. *A Dying Colonialism*. Translated by Haakon Chevalier. New York: Grove Press, 1965.

Fanon, Frantz. *Black Skin, White Masks*. Translated by Richard Philcox. New York: Grove Press, 2008.

Freud, Sigmund. "A Difficulty in the Path of Psycho-Analysis." In *The Standard Edition of the Complete Psychological Works of Sigmund Freud*, edited by James Strachey, volume 17, 135–44. London: Hogarth, 1955.

Hook, Derek. "Death-Bound Subjectivity: Fanon's Zone of Nonbeing and the Lacanian Death Drive." *Subjectivity* 13 (2020): 355–75.

Lacan, Jacques. "The Freudian Thing, or the Meaning of the Return to Freud in Psychoanalysis." In *Écrits: The First Complete Edition in English*, translated by Bruce Fink, 334–66. New York: W.W. Norton, 2006.

Lacan, Jacques. *The Seminar of Jacques Lacan, Book VII: The Ethics of Psychoanalysis, 1959–1960*. Edited by Jacques-Alain Miller. Translated by Dennis Porter. New York: W.W. Norton, 1992.
Maher, Geo. *Anticolonial Eruptions: Racial Hubris and the Cunning of* Resistance. Berkeley: University of California Press, 2022.
Mannoni, Octave. *Prospero and Caliban: The Psychology of Colonization*. Translated by Pamela Powesland. Ann Arbor: The University of Michigan Press, 1990.
Marriott, David. "The Becoming-Black of the World? On Achille Mbembe's *Critique of Black Reason*." *Radical Philosophy* 2, no. 2 (2018): 61–71.
Mbembe, Achille. *Critique of Black Reason*. Translated by Laurent Dubois. Durham: Duke University Press, 2017.
Said, Edward. *Representations of the Intellectual: The 1993 Reith Lectures*. New York: Vintage Books, 1996.
Wilderson III, Frank B. *Red, White & Black: Cinema and the Structure of U.S. Antagonisms*. Durham: Duke University Press, 2010.
Wilderson III, Frank B. "Afro-Pessimism and the End of Redemption." *Humanities Futures. Franklin Humanities Institute: Duke University*. October 20, 2015. https://humanitiesfutures.org/papers/afro-pessimism-end-redemption/.
Wilderson III, Frank B. "'We're Trying to Destroy the World': Anti-Blackness and Police Violence After Ferguson." In *Shifting Corporealities in Contemporary Performance Danger, Im/mobility and Politics*, edited by Marina Gržinić and Aneta Stojnić, 45–59. New York: Palgrave, 2018.
Žižek, Slavoj. *Enjoy Your Symptom!: Jacques Lacan in Hollywood and Out*. New York: Routledge, 1992.
Žižek, Slavoj. *The Ticklish Subject: The Absent Center of Political Ontology*. New York: Verso, 1999.
Žižek, Slavoj. *Violence: Six Sideways Reflections*. New York: Picador, 2008.
Žižek, Slavoj. "Three Fragments on Suicide as a Political Factor." *Crisis and Critique* 9, no. 2 (2022): 414–25.

15

Paraontology and the Death Drive

Nicole Simek

In May 1802, Louis Delgrès, a freeborn man of color who had risen to the rank of colonel in the French revolutionary army in Guadeloupe, led a revolt in Guadeloupe against troops sent by Napoleon to reassert control of France's Caribbean colonies and reimpose slavery where the practice had been abolished. Rallying Black and *mulâtre* troops, as well as sympathizers among the general population, Delgrès, along with Commander Joseph Ignace, a former maroon, and La mulâtresse Solitude (another famous resister celebrated with them today), chose to exhaust every military tactic and fight to the death rather than surrender themselves to slavery, as detailed in a proclamation Delgrès issued on May 10. After splitting their troops to spread the battle across a larger terrain and divert the opposing forces, each eventually became cornered. Ignace was defeated outside Pointe-à-Pitre, and his head was displayed on a pike in the capital city's main square. After sustaining artillery fire at the fort that is today named after him, Delgrès and his 400-some followers, including women and children, fled to the mountain plantation of D'Anglemont, where they mined the terrain with gunpowder and, on May 28, blew themselves up, taking with them as many enemy troops as they could. Solitude survived, was captured, and was executed as soon as she gave birth.

The memory of this 1802 revolt was at first severely repressed, then later depicted through a colonialist lens as an irrational pursuit of personal vengeance. In more recent years, however, this suicidal act has been read variously as a nonevent, as a failed revolt contrasting with Haiti's contemporaneous revolutionary success, or, conversely, as a heroic defense of liberty that inspired Haitian revolutionaries, as a sacrifice of personal interest in the service of universal values, and as a symbol of Black and Guadeloupean agency.[1] These differing interpretations resonate with differing understandings of the death drive and its effects as well: Delgrès's knowledge that his refusal to lay down arms would not only bring about his death but would also fail to win the war reads alternately as a self-destructive sacrifice without any strategic gain for his cause, or, following the example of Antigone's radical commitment, as an ethico-political refusal to take up his designated place in the social order, a refusal whose breach of that order continues to ripple through the social fabric of Guadeloupe today and open up possibilities of living otherwise. In this essay, I would like to investigate further what it means to read the suicidal revolt of 1802 through the lens of the death drive. More specifically, I want to examine how we might bring the death drive to bear on understandings of slavery, its afterlife, and what Derek Hook has described as the particular modes of "death-bound subjectivity" that emerge from a "condition of ontological erasure."[2] How might we situate the death drive in relation to the Critical Black Studies notion of the paraontological—that fugitive againstness or disruptive negativity associated in Fred Moten's work with Blackness—with "a constant demand for an ontology of disorder, an ontology of dehiscence,"[3] "a desire for and a spirit of escape and transgression of the proper and the proposed?"[4] What does it mean to claim, as Moten does, that because it hinges on self-possession, on a sovereignty that stands outside of time and change, "freedom is the inorganic state to which the sovereign subject is supposed to return,"[5] and thus that "the freedom drive is a death drive,"[6] a "(give me liberty or give me) death drive"?[7] What to make of Delgrès's declaration of his intent to live free or die, *vivre libre ou mourir*, through such an optic, which gives the "or" an appositive rather than oppositional valence? And finally, in a contemporary Guadeloupean landscape burgeoning with memorializations of Delgrès, with invocations of his example, what does it mean to repeat Delgrès? Is it to repeat a deathly drive for self-possession? To reenact an instance of subjective destitution? Or, to foster an ethico-politico-libidinal transformation, a reinvestment in an ethical cause?

Liberty, or Death

Delgrès's act resembles the death drive's, as I suggested above, in its unpredictable negativity, in the way it yokes the possibility of social transformation to self-destruction. What we understand this resemblance to mean more precisely depends of course on the notions of self, death, and drive that underpin this reading. Fred Moten's brief invocation of the death drive in his meditation on the drive for freedom echoes Freud's description of the death drive as a drive to return to an inorganic state, or what Žižek calls the "Nirvana Principle" or "craving for self-annihilation,"[8] the yearning for quiescence, a condition free of pain. Moten contrasts this drive for freedom, this death drive, with fugitivity, a drive for escape, a drive that "runs *from*, rather than *to*," as Jack Halberstam puts it.[9] I would like to suggest the possibility of another relation between the drive for freedom and the death drive, one that aligns the parontological force of fugitivity with the emancipatory potential of the death drive. In this light, Delgrès's drive for freedom is a death drive, but one that can break with the dictates of the Nirvana Principle.

Paraontology is a term Moten adopts and adapts from Nahum Chandler to speak of a resistant movement of disruption that differs from nonbeing, or the negation of being, as an ontological predicate. Paraontology points to the inadequacy of "given ontologies," which fail to account for existence, and more specifically for Blackness, understood not as a property of Black people, but as an impulse to resist arising from an anti-Black political ontology. Paraontology, or Blackness, queers the "proper" (being and its humanist grammar, a grammar centering the ideal of the autonomous, self-legislating individual). Paraontology disturbs and unsettles, working against—alongside or apposite to—ontology's form-giving, meaning-making schemas. Marquis

Bey describes paraontology well as "the project of a desedimentation" and "a fissuring besidedness to ontic and ontological meaning making *and* a protection from the regime of ontology, which is to say, defended from the tyrannies of hegemonic, stabilizing subjectivation."[10] In this, it resembles *marronage*, a marooning alchemy, or what Patrick Chamoiseau calls "an alchemy of roundabout resistance [*résistance détournée*],"[11] an oblique mode of transformation that works on and through the given that it desediments.

Subjectivation, for Moten, roots us oppressively in a single, fixed being, fostering violence between self and other as well; "the very idea of the self in its separateness is where the xenophobic comes inexorably on line," he writes in *The Universal Machine*.[12] Blackness stands in opposition to this autonomous individual and to "the very idea of self-determination."[13] Importantly, Blackness, for Moten, is distinct from people identified as Black; it is the paraontological, constitutive otherness or outside created alongside the imposition of subjectivation, which generates a multiplicity and movement of being that cannot be contained by ontology even as it is constrained. Imposition, in other words, generates fugitivity, an impulse to flee that cannot be satisfied by the object of freedom, so long as freedom takes the form of an impossible sovereignty. As Moten puts it in a passage I will quote at greater length here:

> The freedom drive is a death drive, sovereignty's continual (dis)establishment, the repetition of subjection, the repetition rather than remembering of subjectivity's failure to launch, which almost always takes the form of a disavowal of individuation, a submission, let's say, to being held, but which, because it is valued as failure, is repeated as distress. The memory of impossible individuation's disavowal becomes the repetition of a failure to individuate.[14]

Disavowal produces repetition; we seek after an individuation that promises liberation but would arrest us, returning us to the inorganic, the non-generative. Moten's reflection on freedom here follows from a meditation on a case brought by abolitionists to the Massachusetts Supreme Court in 1857 concerning an enslaved woman, Betty, whose "decision" to return to Tennessee with her owners after the court declared her a free person confounds the conventional opposition between freedom and slavery. Freedom, understood as autonomy, relies on the notion of the individual as a temporally self-same agent with the capacity to contract, to make promises about the future as if that future, and future self, were fixed and (self-)determined. Betty's case reminds us that this abstract, transcendental right to self-determination is fraught with paradox, in that it must include the right to relinquish that capacity, the right to alienate the supposedly inalienable. In Betty's "choice" (a term, along with "decision," that Moten puts under erasure), Moten sees an unsettling, Bartleby-like disruption of such static concepts of freedom and slavery, self and other, as separate and opposed. "The threat of a freedom against freedom" that Betty embodies "haunts any and every promise of freedom the law both makes and guards."[15] Betty's nonperformance of autonomy is fugitive. For Moten, because she refuses to take up the role laid out for her, the role of the "mere petitioner" who accedes to a deathly reification in accepting the legal status of free individual that the law proposes, her decision represents "neither her submission to slavery, nor her permission to the state to enforce her legal freedom" but an "obscene" ethical and aesthetic act, in the sense of that which does not appear directly on scene, that which thwarts narration, which runs from, rather than to, a settled representation of itself, to take up Halberstam's language again.[16] "Fugitivity is the realm of the (always anticipatory) afterlife," Moten states, "The social life that now we know as Betty is neither slave nor free but fugitive."[17] In other words, fugitivity can be described as a giving over of ourselves to improvised, unforeseeable multiplicities, to the "organic fecundity" of "the unmade promise, the terrible, beautiful, irreducible futurity that sent us and sends us every day."[18] In short, Moten notes, quoting Édouard Glissant, fugitivity enacts our "consent not to be a single being."[19]

Considered from this perspective, Delgrès's suicidal stand can be read alternately as an embrace of the deathly Enlightenment ideal of the autonomous, sovereign self, or as a fugitive act of disruption, a flight from the living death that is slavery in the name of a freedom from servitude to come, a freedom the resisters refused to give way on, despite the knowledge that they would never live it personally and the possibility that it might never arrive at all. In Massimiliano Tomba's terms, this reading of fugitivity sees in Delgrès's act a refusal of "juridical universalism," an abstract universalism from which Black and Brown folks have been barred, in favor of an "insurgent universality," a particular realization of freedom made concrete through the agency of those—"women, the poor, and slaves"[20]—who assert it. Delgrès conceives of the just outside the limits of Napoleon's law. In doing so, he affirms a subjectivity *à-venir*, a free subjectivity out of joint with Napoleonic hegemony and its call for a return to slavery. This subjectivity remained unintelligible to the French generals who had distinguished themselves fighting for the Republic and against racial equality at the same time, as well as to the first colonial historians to discuss the events, who described the resisters, as Nick Nesbitt has detailed, as cowards or animals unlawfully rebelling against the just and rational social order required for peace, economic prosperity, and French national power.[21]

Delgrès's fugitivity is a response to Napoleon's effort to relegate Black people to what Frantz Fanon calls the "zone of nonbeing." Fanon defines this as "an extraordinarily sterile and arid region, an incline stripped bare of every essential from which a genuine new departure can emerge."[22] But Fanon also stresses, "In most cases, the black man cannot take advantage of this descent into a veritable hell."[23] Writing *Black Skin, White Masks* in 1952, Fanon positions most Black subjects in France in the "zone of nonbeing," recognizing that *formal* equality does not shield one from the crushing reality of social death. While Fanon is talking about Black subjectivity in the postcolonial afterlife of slavery, Delgrès, though born a free man of color, witnessed firsthand the precariousness and limitations of this nominal freedom along with the horrors of slavery and is now confronting its cruel return. Though he had yet to formally reinstate slavery, Napoleon had already banished all Black people to this zone of nonbeing, to the realm of abject nonhumanity, when he launched his military repression. On Mount Matouba, Delgrès and his companions were in a sense already dwelling in the zone of nonbeing. A Black man who claims freedom and access to universality has no place in a Napoleonic social ontology, no home in his racist order of being. Delgrès's suicidal act can be understood, then, as a choice of biological death over social death.

Reading Delgrès's May 10 proclamation, addressed to "l'univers entier" or "the entire universe,"[24] suggests that this choice is not only a preference for a quick death over the slow torture of enslavement but also an expression of the Lacanian death drive, understood, as Derek Hook describes it, as "a mode of surplus life which both underlies an unceasing fidelity to a cause and that delivers a subject to a zone between life and death," a zone out of which revolutionary action can emerge.[25] Giving up one's life for such a cause carries with it the appeal of "symbolic immortality," the possibility that your sacrifice will be remembered and that it will reshape the symbolic order itself.[26] Delgrès's proclamation testifies to this investment in a new future beyond his own. Decrying the perversion of justice and natural right unfolding ironically at "the height of a century forever famous for the triumph of enlightenment and philosophy," Delgrès describes how "a class of hapless people targeted with annihilation must lift its voice to posterity, so that their innocence and misfortunes will be known after they are gone." Addressing Napoleon directly as a "philosopher warrior," he denounces Napoleon's local representatives as rogue abusers of their authority, deplores the fact that the First Consul will learn of their transgressions too late, after the harm is done, and calls upon the "citizens of Guadeloupe" to recognize the justice of their cause, for "resistance to oppression is a natural right" and "even the divinity would see no offense" in their fight to defend it. After swearing to do no violence to Guadeloupe's citizens or their families, Delgrès ends his statement with the line, "And you, posterity, shed a tear for our misfortunes and we will die satisfied."

Importantly, as Hook argues, if the ontological erasure undergone in the Fanonian zone of nonbeing would seem to eradicate political agency, making physical death a passive escape from pain, the death drive's "mode of 'undead' libidinal animation," its impulse to carry on, no matter the costs and without regard for self-preservation, opens up avenues for ethico-political commitments: "What we witness in the death drive—that is, in any drive pursued to the end, despite the costs incurred to the subject's livelihood or well-being—is a willingness to make any sacrifice necessary. When such a drive impulse becomes attached to a political objective, then we are in the ethical domain of death drive as cause."[27] As Hook elaborates, drawing on the examples of Antigone as well as South African anti-apartheid activist Steve Biko to elucidate how agency can emerge out of the zone of nonbeing, it is the very movement into this zombie-like limbo, where one feels one's impending death to be already accomplished, that eradicates one's alienating investments in the existing symbolic order, clearing the terrain to recreate this order differently. "To be the subject of the death drive," as Hook puts it, "not only enables one to disinvest one's self of such lingering unconscious effects of power, it also means that one is able to throw the very underpinnings of the symbolic into question for a broader political community."[28]

This version of the death drive—one that resonates as well with Žižek's vision of the death drive as a radically destabilizing excess that unchains us from mechanical existence and clears the way for creation—is paraontological. Just as Blackness disturbs settled categories of meaning, transgresses the proper, and blurs intelligibility, the death drive names a fundamental excess at the heart of being. As Žižek puts it, the death drive is a "certain excess of destructability that is, as it were, undermining, destabilizing the social order, an excess that is ambiguous in the sense that it can be a source of constructive energy or it can be purely destructive."[29] It is a force that is both sabotaging and self-sabotaging, revealing the self's non-sovereignty. Žižek adds, "this space of excess . . . opens up the space for possible change," exposing "how there is a gap, a failure, a nonfunctioning excess in society."[30] And as I have been suggesting, paraontology explores a similar gap in its pursuit "to be in the name of being otherwise."[31] In its paraontological operations, the death drive involves the "desedimentation of both the given . . . and the possible."[32] Delgrès's act destroys his self-preservation yet preserves, in its enactment, paraontology's and the death drive's constructive force. To accept slavery is to accept Napoleon's law, the new given, and submit to the possible; it is to collapse the distinction between Black and Blackness, and to become permanently sealed in the zone of nonbeing. In Delgrès's case, the death drive arguably enables him "to take advantage of this descent into a veritable hell." He becomes otherwise—not Napoleon's slave, not a copy of Enlightenment sovereignty.

Repeating Delgrès

If such an act has the capacity to disturb the symbolic order, the symbolic order also has the capacity to reabsorb it, to resettle what has been de-sedimented, and in many ways, what is at stake for us today is not so much what we can know of Delgrès's psychic life and impulses, to which we have little access, but rather how the death drive functions in the reception and repetition of the memory of 1802. Can the unsettling, paraontological force of this drive be sustained in contemporary invocations of Delgrès?

The most prominent contemporary public uses of Delgrès's story embody a tension between the creativity of fugitive memory and the pull of ontology. The first and, for me, most striking of these is the *Mémorial du sacrifice de Louis Delgrès* (Memorial to Louis Delgrès's Sacrifice), a publicly commissioned monument by Guadeloupean artist Roger Arékian installed at Fort Delgrès, in Guadeloupe.[33] The memorial occupies a 21-square-meter space. Fort Delgrès is located about 5 miles away from the site where the resisters killed themselves; the monument does not mark the site of death or burial but is instead integrated into the fort that the resisters occupied just before escaping to Matouba, where they made their stand. Using volcanic rocks, concrete, metal, and cobblestones from the fort, this piece emphasizes the explosive fragmentation of Delgrès's body and implicitly links this force to the Guadeloupean landscape and Matouba's location on the slopes of La Soufrière volcano. The mimetically rendered head that sits at the center contrasts with the figural evocations of the unknown fighters spiraling out from that center, which bear engravings of words and phrases found in Delgrès's May 10 proclamation, like "live free or die," "resistance," and "oppression." Delgrès's selfhood is represented here as constituting the body politic in the very act of its dissolution; the dismembered fragments of his corpse that seem to explode outward also remain in orbit around him and become re-membered, reconstituted, as faithful revolutionaries in the two senses of the term, as the movement of the spiral evokes the countervailing pull of the head's gravity and the Republican ideal of liberty around which this violence revolves. This is the movement that the visitor follows as well, since all approaches to the memorial begin at a distance, taking us first to the outer bands and then to the eye of the revolutionary storm. The relatively orderly disposition of the stones and the weightiness of their mass lend the piece a stasis and solemnity that dulls the edge of its movement; yet the fixed, piercing gaze that emanates from the decapitated but still seeing head generates unease, working as a kind of affective stumbling block that thwarts efforts to wash away the violence of this death or channel the viewing smoothly into reverential hero worship.

The motif of partial self-dissolution as the force that forges collective agency is echoed in two other contemporary pieces: a 2001 monument by Jacky Poulier installed at Les Abymes, Guadeloupe (also titled *Mémorial du sacrifice de Louis Delgrès*) that puts Delgrès's dismembered parts in the pose of the thinker atop a pedestal surrounded by fellow fighters, and a 2017 sculpture by Suzel Galya in the Parisian suburb of Blanc-Mesnil (*Louis Delgrès et ses compagnons*, or Louis Delgrès and his Comrades) that figures Delgrès's torso as the prow of a ship built of ribs and the heads of compatriots.[34] In these two pieces, we see more phallocentric representations of heroism. The verticality of both, compared to the horizontality of the Fort Delgrès memorial, falls in line with traditional statuary representations of "great men." Jacky Poulier's sculpture emphasizes sacrifice as a thoughtful strategy that inspires the men and women grouped protectively around the meditative Delgrès; while his dismemberment unsettles, the circle of intact bodies below him testifies to the wholeness of the people's resolve, pointing, like one figure in this circle who raises a fist, to the certainty of triumph. In Galya's piece, we see a muscular, eroticized Delgrès leading a kind of mutiny; his companions retain some measure of individuality yet are reduced to heads all looking up to their leader and rowing in the same direction. The monument seems to play on the figure of the slave ship, one that has been overtaken by rebels and is now steering a new course. The body itself is the ship, enslaved or free, and appears to be sailing, ghostlike, in a state of semi-decomposition, its bones either losing or gaining flesh through the countervailing forces of amnesia and remembrance.

The force and effects of artworks can never, of course, be traced solely to their form. The public sites discussed above, along with a number of other monuments to Delgrès, frequently serve as the backdrop for public commemoration ceremonies, school trips and study projects, tourism, and private contemplation framed by political, pedagogical, historiographical, and labor union discourses, as well as for-profit guidebooks, among other interpretive frameworks. Actors who have taken up the task of commemorating Delgrès include regional government bodies, transnational organizations like UNESCO, and the French state. In Petit-Canal, Guadeloupe, we find a bust of Delgrès integrated into the site known as "Les marches des esclaves," or the Slaves' Steps, which commemorates the various African tribes whose members were brought to this port and auction site by force, as well as maroon resistance (the figure of the maroon being a very popular symbol among labor unions and independence activists). The late 1990s and early 2000s saw an increase in French state interest in Delgrès at a time when France celebrated the 150th anniversary of the abolition of slavery, passed the Taubira Law declaring slavery a crime against humanity, commemorated the bicentennial of Delgrès's 1802 revolt, and admitted both Louis Delgrès and Toussaint Louverture to the Pantheon. State representations seek to foreground a color-blind Republican ideology of equality by conscripting traditionally marginalized figures into a narrative of French national identity. A sign marking a Paris street in the 20th *arrondissement* named after Delgrès specifies, for example, that Louis Delgrès was "a French officer from the Antilles who died for the abolition of slavery" ("officier français originaire des Antilles mort pour l'abolition de l'esclavage").[35] Fort Delgrès itself serves as host to regional political ceremonies and publicly sponsored cultural events, while the memorial has become an inspiration and also a prop, a commodity, for groups and individuals ranging from Delgrès the band, a Caribbean blues trio who describes their music as a "vehicle" for "private experience and family history, as well as . . . the destiny of a part of the world marked by its rootlessness and identity struggles"[36] to social media videos promoting social organizations, individual influencers, tourist companies, and style magazines.[37] As Nick Nesbitt has convincingly argued, if, in the immediate aftermath of 1802, discussions of Delgrès were outlawed, erased from the historical archive, and driven underground, his story remained alive in oral culture, animating Guadeloupeans' critical relationship with the past. And yet the explosion of interest in Delgrès in Guadeloupe after the Second World War represents not an intensification of this relationship, but rather its "entombment."[38] As Guadeloupe is politically integrated into France in the postwar period, it is simultaneously transformed "into a consumer society utterly dependent upon the central French state"; under this horizon, "historical experience is quite literally *consumed*; memory becomes mere representation and comes to serve the paradoxical function of reaffirming a static, ahistorical status quo."[39] The paraontological disorder and dynamism of Delgrès's "complex, conflicted revolutionary act" is repressed or disavowed, covered over with inanimate—inorganic, ungenerative, Moten might say—image-commodities. The complexity of Delgrès's act is negated, ontologized, as its interpretation is sanctioned and reified by official discourse. The lesson, for Nesbitt, is that new forms of critique and aesthetic representations are needed; I read this need as synonymous with reorienting our attention to the paraontological force of Delgrès's act.

One particular intervention I would like to turn to now for the way it endeavors to achieve this reorientation is Fabienne Kanor's poetic novel *Humus*. Kanor works such a desedimentation by engaging what we might describe as the horizon of Delgrès, the figuration of heroic sacrificial death that haunts contemporary attempts to think sovereignty and historical change in Guadeloupean discourse.[40] Composed of chapters named after their narrators' social identities—such as "the mute woman," "the slave," "the amazon," or "the heiress"—*Humus* offers a multivoiced telling of fourteen Black women who leaped overboard together from the deck of the slave ship *Le Soleil* on March 23, 1774. A brief description of the event from the captain's logbook is the only written trace of this jump that remains in the archive. In response to this scant record, *Humus* mobilizes what Saidiya Hartman calls "critical fabulations," speculative narration that functions simultaneously as invention and intervention, a creative attempt to bear witness while keeping in view the erasures and inaccessible details that are impossible to fill. Chapters visually mark leaps in time, train of thought, vantage, and speaker with spatial gaps, asterisks, and typographical modulations. Narrative joints connecting sundered stories and bodies protrude in *Humus*, as does the absence of sutures. In addition to drawing our attention to the aporias of history, however, Kanor's imaginative construction of possible histories responds to the ripples that these women's lives made, traces that can be picked up and followed again by willing listeners. In this sense, as Kanor argues in an interview,

> We should understand this jump . . . as a pretext, the text that precedes the novel to come. It is because these women jumped that Captain Mosnier took up his pen, and that the novel can begin. They jump not because they no longer have anything left to say, but precisely because they need to tell everything that happened. And I use this jump to dive into the narrative, to bring closure to it as well as to rekindle it. . . . It is never a period, but works instead as a comma, an opportunity for speaking [*une possibilité de parole*].[41]

It is this orientation toward the jump as a comma, a paraontological pause that impels further speech, that underpins Kanor's efforts to multiply and densify these women's stories of refusal. To take the jump as a comma is to reopen the telling and linger on how this leap unsettles both the anti-Black social world that enslaved these women in the first place and the model of heroic resistance into which narratives about refusal often congeal—the framework through which acts of resistance, and agency itself, become legible to us as such.

Kanor tells suicide's contribution to the Black radical tradition otherwise by queering the eventalization of the suicide, foregrounding, in turn, the collective and unfinished character of the jump. All the jumpers act out of what Žižek describes as "an irrepressible commandment one feels to do something suicidally heroic—one does it simply because one cannot not do it";[42] the "decision" to leap is neither a fully controlled calculus nor a completely mechanical act. Kanor presents us with multiple Antigones responding differently to the limbo, the living death, of the slave hold. The amazon, a Dahomey warrior, urges the fearful with the Delgrès-like words, "It is better to flee than to submit. Death before slavery!"[43] Yet death itself is not for her the aim, but rather a risk worth taking; she jumps willing to die yet determined to swim to shore and fight, as does the queen, who aims to escape and retake her throne. The slave, recognizing the queen she had served in captivity, follows her into the water only to kill her out of vengeance. The mute woman jumps to end the unrelenting torture of slavery, and La Blanche does so out of despair at being rejected by her sailor lover, while the employee, a guard hired by the captain to spy on the captives, jumps on a spontaneous impulse, in envy and admiration, because "something broke inside [her]" at the sight of their resolve to be free.[44] Their jump, for the employee, is a sublime act that dissolves, at least momentarily, her self-interest and resignation to her symbolic place in this world as a servant of the trade, placing her in the zone of nonbeing.

This dissolution, which enables her to act, to jump, is short-lived for the employee; identity and self-preservation reassert themselves as she drifts back to shore and returns to her usual work on yet another vessel. Some of the other women die in the jump and speak to us from the grave; the rest, fished out of the water, go on to endure servitude, to run away with the maroons, to go mad, to turn to religion for solace, and to witness the Haitian Revolution. In recognizing and dwelling on the density and contradictions of these women's lives, on their undead life after death, Kanor writes not a story of antiheroes, but a non-heroic telling of the death drive's refusals. Humus, the rich soil that decomposition leaves in its wake, captures the conjoined decay and fertility from which this telling springs, and which its critical vision of the past produces, a promise of radical memory and action with no guarantees. In this respect, we might say Kanor repeats Delgrès's call for racial insubordination for an ethical cause: Black freedom. This repetition returns us to the paraontological distinction, disclosing a Blackness that refuses to conform either to the captain's white gaze that fixes Black bodies in their place or to a contemporary color-blind France that celebrates Delgrès's suicidal act only to better contain its destructive force.

Notes

1 Philip Kaisary underscores Delgrès's positive effect on the Haitian Revolution: "Delgrès triumphed in his very defeat, but not where he thought he was fighting." See Philip Kaisary, *The Haitian Revolution in the Literary Imagination: Radical Horizons, Conservative Constraints* (Charlottesville: University of Virginia Press, 2014), 115–16.
2 Derek Hook, "Death-Bound Subjectivity: Fanon's Zone of Nonbeing and the Lacanian Death Drive," *Subjectivity* 13 (2020): 361.
3 Fred Moten, *The Universal Machine* (Durham: Duke University Press, 2018), 150.
4 Moten, *Stolen Life* (Durham: Duke University Press, 2018), 131.
5 Moten, *Stolen Life*, 264.
6 Moten, *Stolen Life*, 263.
7 Moten, *Stolen Life*, 263.
8 Slavoj Žižek, *The Parallax View* (Cambridge: MIT Press, 2006), 262.
9 Jack Halberstam, "Go Gaga: Anarchy, Chaos, and the Wild," *Social Text* 31, no. 3 (116) (2013): 130; emphasis added.
10 Marquis Bey, *The Problem of the Negro as a Problem for Gender* (Minneapolis: University of Minnesota Press, 2020), 12, 18.
11 Patrick Chamoiseau, "Les Secrets de Chamoiseau," *Antilla Special* 11 (December 1988–January 1989): 25; see also Lucien Taylor, "Créolité Bites: A Conversation with Patrick Chamoiseau, Raphaël Confiant, and Jean Bernabé," *Transition* 74 (1997): 138–9.
12 Moten, *The Universal Machine*, 122.
13 Fred Moten, "Blackness and Nothingness (Mysticism in the Flesh)," *South Atlantic Quarterly* 112, no. 4 (2013): 752.
14 Moten, *Stolen Life*, 263.
15 Moten, *Stolen Life*, 247.
16 Moten, *Stolen Life*, 247.
17 Moten, *Stolen Life*, 263.
18 Moten, *Stolen Life*, 264.
19 Fred Moten, "Black Optimism/Black Operation," unpublished paper, 2007, https://lucian.uchicago.edu/blogs/politicalfeeling/files/2007/12/moten-black-optimism.doc. Glissant's phrase is "consentir à ne pas être un seul"; Moten credits Christopher Winks for the English translation here and also adopts this phrase as a title for the trilogy of works including *Black and Blur*, *Stolen Life*, and *The Universal Machine*.

20 Massimiliano Tomba, *Insurgent Universality: An Alternative Legacy of Modernity* (New York: Oxford University Press, 2019), 32.

21 Nick Nesbitt, *Voicing Memory: History and Subjectivity in French Caribbean Literature* (Charlottesville: University of Virginia Press, 2003), 54–62.

22 Frantz Fanon, *Black Skin, White Masks*, trans. Richard Philcox (New York: Grove Press, 2008), xii.

23 Fanon, *Black Skin, White Masks*, xii.

24 Louis Delgrès, "Proclamation de Louis Delgrès le 10 mai 1802," *Comité National pour la Mémoire et l'Histoire de l'Esclavage*, accessed November 29, 2024, http://www.cnmhe.fr/spip.php?article191. Translations from this text are my own.

25 Hook, "Death-Bound Subjectivity," 358.

26 Hook, "Death-Bound Subjectivity," 370.

27 Hook, "Death-Bound Subjectivity," 367.

28 Hook, "Death-Bound Subjectivity," 371.

29 Slavoj Žižek, "Unbehagen and the Subject: An Interview with Slavoj Žižek," *Psychoanalysis, Culture & Society* 15 (2010): 422.

30 Žižek, "Unbehagen and the Subject," 422.

31 "There is cause for optimism as long as there is a need for optimism. Cause and need converge in the bent school or marginal church in which we gather together to be in the name of being otherwise." See Fred Moten, "Black Op," *PMLA* 123, no. 5 (2008): 1747.

32 Nahum Chandler, *"Beyond This Narrow Now": Or, Delimitations of W. E. B. Du Bois* (Durham: Duke University Press, 2022), 7.

33 For photographs and background information on this monument, see "Mémorial du sacrifice de Louis Delgrès," *Réseau Canopé*, accessed November 29, 2024, https://www.reseau-canope.fr/art-des-caraibes-ameriques/oeuvres/memorial-du-sacrifice-de-louis-delgres.html.

34 For photographs, see "Mémorial du Sacrifice de Delgrès," *Guadeloupe Tourisme*, accessed November 29, 2024, https://fr.guadeloupe-tourisme.com/145/memorial-du-sacrifice-de-delgres-les-abymes/; and "Monument à Louis Delgrès," *Foundation pour la Mémoire du L'Esclavage*, accessed November 29, 2024, https://memoire-esclavage.org/monument-louis-delgres.

35 Wikipedia provides a clean archival image of this plaque "Rue Louis-Delgrès," *Wikipédia*, accessed November 29, 2024, https://fr.wikipedia.org/wiki/Rue_Louis-Delgr%C3%A8s, while Google Maps and tourist photos shared online show it as it appears on the street, frequently covered in graffiti and stickers (see, e.g., an image posted on Tripadvisor at https://media-cdn.tripadvisor.com/media/photo-s/14/36/29/56/panneau-de-rue-de-localisation.jpg). A commemorative bench installed by the Toni Morrison Society in 2010 to honor Delgrès (as part of the organization's Bench by the Road Project) can also be found on this street. See "Bench by the Road Project," *The Toni Morrison Society*, accessed November 29, 2024, https://www.tonimorrisonsociety.org/bench.html.

36 Delgres, "Biography," *DelgresMusic.com*, accessed November 29, 2024, https://www.delgresmusic.com/about.

37 One striking example among these is a cardiac health video cosponsored by the *département* of Guadeloupe, its regional public health agency, and a private shipping company, which brings biopolitical management together with neoliberal self-help advice in a walking tour of Fort Delgrès with cardiologist André Atallah. Atallah advises "all Guadeloupeans to visit the site with their families to combine culture and

health" ("Je conseille à tous les Guadeloupéens en famille de venir visiter ce site pour allier à la fois l'aspect culturel et l'aspect santé"; my translation). L'Agence de Santé de Gaudeloupe Saint-Martin et Saint-Barthélémy, Le Département de la Guadeloupe, La communauté d'agglomeration La Riviéra du Levant et la Compagnie Express des Iles, "Sur les pas du Dr André Atallah au Fort Delgrès, Basse-Terre," *Les Iles de Guadeloupe à la trace*, April 16, 2018, video, 6:14, https://www.youtube.com/watch?v=eCzWsTNd468.

38 Nesbitt, *Voicing Memory*, 72.

39 Nesbitt, *Voicing Memory*, 71.

40 I carry out a more extensive study of this text in *Alchemies of Blood and Afro-Diasporic Fiction: Race, Kinship, and the Passion for Ontology* (New York: Bloomsbury, 2023).

41 Jason Herbeck, "Entretien avec Fabienne Kanor," *The French Review* 86, no. 5 (2013): 971; my translation.

42 Slavoj Žižek, *Surplus Enjoyment* (New York: Bloomsbury, 2022), 205–6.

43 Fabienne Kanor, *Humus*, trans. Lynn E. Palermo (Charlottesville: University of Virginia Press, 2020), 65.

44 Kanor, *Humus*, 111.

Works Cited

"Bench by the Road Project." *The Toni Morrison Society*. Accessed November 29, 2024. https://www.tonimorrisonsociety.org/bench.html.

Bey, Marquis. *The Problem of the Negro as a Problem for Gender*. Minneapolis: University of Minnesota Press, 2020.

Chamoiseau, Patrick. "Les Secrets de Chamoiseau." *Antilla Special* 11 (December 1988–January 1989): 23–6.

Chandler, Nahum. *"Beyond This Narrow Now": Or, Delimitations of W. E. B. Du Bois*. Durham: Duke University Press, 2022.

Delgres. "Biography." *DelgresMusic.com*. Accessed November 29, 2024. https://www.delgresmusic.com/about.

Delgrès, Louis. "Proclamation de Louis Delgrès le 10 mai 1802." *Comité National pour la Mémoire et l'Histoire de l'Esclavage*. Accessed November 29, 2024. http://www.cnmhe.fr/spip.php?article191.

Fanon, Frantz. *Black Skin, White Masks*. Translated by Richard Philcox. New York: Grove Press, 2008.

Halberstam, Jack. "Go Gaga: Anarchy, Chaos, and the Wild." *Social Text* 31, no. 3 (116) (2013): 123–34.

Herbeck, Jason. "Entretien avec Fabienne Kanor." *The French Review* 86, no. 5 (2013): 964–76.

Hook, Derek. "Death-Bound Subjectivity: Fanon's Zone of Nonbeing and the Lacanian Death Drive." *Subjectivity* 13 (2020): 355–75.

Kaisary, Philip. *The Haitian Revolution in the Literary Imagination: Radical Horizons, Conservative Constraints*. Charlottesville: University of Virginia Press, 2014.

Kanor, Fabienne. *Humus*. Translated by Lynn E. Palermo. Charlottesville: University of Virginia Press, 2020.

L'Agence de Santé de Gaudeloupe Saint-Martin et Saint-Barthélémy, Le Département de la Guadeloupe, La communauté d'agglomeration La Riviéra du Levant et la Compagnie

Express des Iles. "Sur les pas du Dr André Atallah au Fort Delgrès, Basse-Terre." *Les Iles de Guadeloupe à la trace*. April 16, 2018. Video, 6:14. https://www.youtube.com/watch?v=eCzWsTNd468.

"Mémorial du Sacrifice de Delgrès." *Guadeloupe Tourisme*. Accessed November 29, 2024. https://fr.guadeloupe-tourisme.com/145/memorial-du-sacrifice-de-delgres-les-abymes/

"Mémorial du sacrifice de Louis Delgrès." *Réseau Canopé*. Accessed November 29, 2024. https://www.reseau-canope.fr/art-des-caraibes-ameriques/oeuvres/memorial-du-sacrifice-de-louis-delgres.html.

"Monument à Louis Delgrès." *Foundation pour la Mémoire du L'Esclavage*. Accessed November 29, 2024. https://memoire-esclavage.org/monument-louis-delgres.

Moten, Fred. "Black Optimism/Black Operation." Unpublished paper. 2007. https://lucian.uchicago.edu/blogs/politicalfeeling/files/2007/12/moten-black-optimism.doc.

Moten, Fred. "Black Op." *PMLA* 123, no. 5 (2008): 1743–7.

Moten, Fred. "Blackness and Nothingness (Mysticism in the Flesh)." *South Atlantic Quarterly* 112, no. 4 (2013): 737–80.

Moten, Fred. *Stolen Life*. Durham: Duke University Press, 2018.

Moten, Fred. *The Universal Machine*. Durham: Duke University Press, 2018.

Nesbitt, Nick. *Voicing Memory: History and Subjectivity in French Caribbean Literature*. Charlottesville: University of Virginia Press, 2003.

"Rue Louis-Delgrès." *Wikipédia*. Accessed November 29, 2024. https://fr.wikipedia.org/wiki/Rue_Louis-Delgr%C3%A8s,

Simek, Nicole. *Alchemies of Blood and Afro-Diasporic Fiction: Race, Kinship, and the Passion for Ontology*. New York: Bloomsbury, 2023.

Tomba, Massimiliano. *Insurgent Universality: An Alternative Legacy of Modernity*. New York: Oxford University Press, 2019.

Žižek, Slavoj. *The Parallax View*. Cambridge: MIT Press, 2006.

Žižek, Slavoj. "Unbehagen and the Subject: An Interview with Slavoj Žižek." *Psychoanalysis, Culture & Society* 15 (2010): 418–28.

Žižek, Slavoj. *Surplus Enjoyment*. New York: Bloomsbury, 2022.

Notes on Contributors

María del Rosario Acosta López is Professor of Latin American Studies in the Department of Hispanic Studies at the University of California, Riverside. She obtained her PhD in Philosophy from the Colombian National University (2007). She teaches and conducts research on Aesthetics, Critical Theory, Political Philosophy, and more recently on Decolonial studies, with an emphasis on questions of memory and trauma in the Americas. Her most recent publications are devoted to the Aesthetics of Resistance in Latin American Art, Decolonial Perspectives on Memory and History, Epistemic Injustice and Epistemic Violence, and Transitional Justice and Politics of Memory in Colombia. She has also recently coedited volumes on F. Schiller (2018), Critique in German Philosophy from Kant to the Present (2020), Transitional Justice in Colombia (2023), and Historical Memory in Colombia and Its Legacies (2023). She is currently working on the manuscript of her next book, *Grammars of Listening: Rendering the Unheard-of Audible* (forthcoming in Spanish in 2025), and on the final editions of two forthcoming books, one in Spanish on community in Hegel, Nancy, Esposito, and Agamben (*Narrativas de la comunidad: de Hegel a los pensadores impolíticos*), and one in English, *The Unstoppable Murmur of Being-Together*, coauthored with Jean-Luc Nancy.

Emanuela Bianchi is Associate Professor of Comparative Literature at New York University with affiliations in Classics and Gender and Sexuality Studies. She is the author of *The Feminine Symptom: Aleatory Matter in the Aristotelian Cosmos* (2014), *La naturaleza en disputa. Physis y eros en el pensamiento antiguo* (2022) (in Spanish), editor of *Is Feminist Philosophy Philosophy?* (1999), and coeditor, with Sara Brill and Brooke Holmes, of *Antiquities Beyond Humanism* (2019). She is also the author of numerous book chapters and articles investigating questions of gender, sexuality, nature, matter, and the body in relation to ancient Greek metaphysics and contemporary philosophy and theory. She is the book review editor for *philoSOPHIA: A Journal of transContinental Feminism.*

Adriana Michele Campos Johnson is Associate Professor of Comparative Literature at the University of California, Irvine. Thinking with and from a Latin American archive, she writes most often on media formations and power in situations of coloniality and heterogeneity. Recent publications include "In São Paulo Visible" (*Revista Hispánica Moderna*), "Visuality as Infrastructure" (*Social Text*), "Excess of Visibility/Scarcity of Water" (*Discourse*), "The Impropriety of Piracy" (*Matraga*), and "OffScreen, Unsighted, Unthought" (*Forma*). It also includes a coedited volume with Dan Nemser for *Social Text* entitled *Reading for Infrastructure: Worlds Made and Broken* and a dossier co-edited with Keiji Kunigami on *Black Brazilian Cinema* (*AfterImage*).

Penelope Deutscher is Joan and Sarepta Harrison Professor of Ethics and Justice in the Department of Philosophy at Northwestern, where she is also Associate Director of the Critical Theory Program. She is the author of a number of publications at the intersections of twentieth-century French philosophy, race, gender, and sexuality studies, including, most recently, *Foucault's Futures: A Critique of Reproductive Reason*.

Jeffrey R. Di Leo is Professor of English and Philosophy at the Texas A&M University-Victoria. He is the founder and editor of *symplokē* and Executive Director of the Society for Critical Exchange and its Winter Theory Institute. His books include *Dead Theory: Death, Derrida, and the Afterlife of Theory* (2016), *Higher Education under Late Capitalism: Identity, Conduct, and the Neoliberal Condition* (2017), *American Literature as World Literature* (2017), *Bloomsbury Handbook of Literary and Cultural Theory* (2019), *The End of American Literature: Essays from the Late Age of Print* (2019), *Biotheory: Life and Death under Capitalism* (2020, with Peter Hitchcock), *Philosophy as World Literature* (2020), *What's Wrong with Antitheory?* (2020), *Vinyl Theory* (2020), *Catastrophe and Education: Neoliberalism, Theory, and the Future of the Humanities* (2020), *Happiness* (2022), *Selling the Humanities* (2023), *Contemporary Literary and Cultural Theory: An Overview* (2023), and *Out of Print* (2024).

David Greven is Professor of English at the University of South Carolina. He publishes in the areas of nineteenth-century American literature and Film Studies. His books include *Intimate Violence: Hitchcock, Sex, and Queer Theory* (2017), *Ghost Faces: Hollywood and Post-Millennial Masculinity* (2016), *Gender Protest and Same-Sex Desire in Antebellum American Literature: Margaret Fuller, Edgar Allan Poe, Nathaniel Hawthorne, and Herman Melville* (2016), and *The Fragility of Manhood: Hawthorne, Freud, and the Politics of Gender* (2012). His latest book is *All the Devils Are Here: American Romanticism and Literary Influence* (2024).

Peter Hitchcock is Distinguished Professor of English at Baruch College and the Graduate Center of CUNY. He is also Associate Director of the Center for Place, Culture and Politics. His books include *Dialogics of the Oppressed* (1992), *Oscillate Wildly: Space, Body, and Spirit of Millennial Materialism* (1999), *Imaginary States: Studies in Cultural Transnationalism* (2003), *The Long Space: Transnationalism and Postcolonial Form* (2009), *The New Public Intellectual: Politics, Theory, and the Public Sphere* (2016; coedited with Jeffrey R. Di Leo), *Labor in Culture, or, Worker of the World(s)* (2017), and, most recently, *The Debt Age* (coedited with Jeffrey R. Di Leo and Sophia A. McClennen, 2018).

Sara Lindheim is Professor of Classics at the University of California, Santa Barbara. She is the author of *Mail and Female: Epistolary Narrative and Desire in Ovid's Heroides* (2003) and *Latin Elegy and the Space of Empire* (2021). She is the coeditor with Helen Morales of *New Essays on Homer: Language, Violence, and Agency* (2015), and with Ella Haselswerdt and Kirk Ormand of *The Routledge Handbook of Classics and Queer Theory* (2023). She works primarily on gender and subjectivity in Latin poetry of the late Republic and the Augustan Age, and has published articles and chapters on Catullus, Tibullus, Propertius, Virgil, and Ovid.

Paul Allen Miller is Carolina Distinguished Professor at the University of South Carolina and Distinguished Guest Professor at Ewha Womans University, Seoul, South Korea. He is the author of *Lyric Texts and Lyric Consciousness* (1994), *Latin Erotic Elegy* (2002), *Subjecting Verses* (2004), *Latin Verse Satire* (2005), *Postmodern Spiritual Practices* (2007), *Plato's Apology of Socrates* (2010) with Charles Platter, *A Tibullus Reader* (2013), *Diotima at the Barricades: French Feminists Read Plato* (2015), *Horace* (2019), *Foucault's Seminars on Antiquity* (2021), and *Theory Does Not Exist* (2024). He has also edited volumes of essays on literary theory, gender studies, and topics in classics, as well as published many articles on Latin, Greek, French, and English literature, theory, and philosophy. His new book, *Truth and Enjoyment: Cicero Beyond the Pleasure Principle,* is forthcoming from Oxford.

Shannon M. Mussett is Chair and Professor of Philosophy at Utah Valley University. She specializes in feminist theory, existentialism, German Idealism, and aesthetics. She has published widely on the philosophy of Simone de Beauvoir and G. W. F. Hegel, among others. She is the author of *Entropic Philosophy: Chaos, Breakdown, and Creation* (2022) and is coeditor of both *Beauvoir and the History of Philosophy from Plato to Butler* (2012) and *The Contradictions of Freedom: Philosophical Essays on Simone de Beauvoir's "Les Mandarins"* (2006). She is currently the executive codirector of the Society for Phenomenology and Existential Philosophy.

Daniel T. O'Hara is an Emeritus Professor of English at Temple University, Philadelphia, PA, USA. Author, editor, and coeditor of many books in modernist literature and critical theory, he was a coeditor and review editor of the postmodern journal *boundary 2*. Currently, he is coeditor of the *Journal of Modern Literature* and the *Shining Rock Poetry Anthology and Review.* He is also a contributing editor for *American Book Review* and an advisory editor for *symplokē*. Finally, he is a series editor (with Donald Pease) of *Pivotal Studies in the Global American Literary Imagination*, and a series editor (with Ranjan Ghosh) of *Transforming Literary Studies: Crossing.* His latest monograph is *Yeats and Revisionism: A Half-Century of the Dancer and the Dance* (2022).

Brian O'Keeffe is a senior lecturer in the French Department at Barnard College, New York, USA.

Nicole Simek is Cushing Eells Professor of Philosophy and Literature at Whitman College, Walla Walla, WA, USA. She is the author of *Alchemies of Blood and Afro-Diasporic Fiction: Race, Kinship, and the Passion for Ontology* (2023), *Hunger and Irony in the French Caribbean: Literature, Theory, and Public Life* (2016), and *Eating Well, Reading Well: Maryse Condé and the Ethics of Interpretation* (2008), and the translator of Maryse Condé's *The Belle Créole* (2020).

Mario Telò is Professor of Rhetoric, Comparative Literature, and Ancient Greek and Roman Studies at the University of California, Berkeley. He is the author of *Aristophanes and the Cloak of Comedy* (2016), *Archive Feelings: A Theory of Greek Tragedy* (2020), *Greek Tragedy in a Global Crisis: Reading Through Pandemic Times* (2023), *Resistant Form: Aristophanes and the Comedy of Crisis* (2023), *Reading Greek Tragedy with Judith Butler* (2024), *Roman Comedy against the Subject* (2025), and *The Late Animal: Edward Said, Classicism, and the Limits of Humanism* (2026).

Zahi Zalloua is the Cushing Eells Professor of Philosophy and Literature at Whitman College and Editor of *The Comparatist*. He is the coauthor, with Ilan Kapoor, of *Universal Politics* (2021), and the author of *Fanon, Žižek, and the Violence of Resistance* (2025), *The Politics of the Wretched: Race, Reason, and Ressentiment* (2024), *Solidarity and the Palestinian Cause: Indigeneity, Blackness, and the Promise of Universality* (2023), *Being Posthuman: Ontologies of the Future* (2021), *Žižek on Race: Toward an Anti-Racist Future* (2020), *Theory's Autoimmunity: Skepticism, Literature, and Philosophy* (2018), *Continental Philosophy and the Palestinian Question: Beyond the Jew and the Greek* (2017), *Reading Unruly: Interpretation and Its Ethical Demands* (2014), and *Montaigne and the Ethics of Skepticism* (2005).

Index

Note: Page number with "n" refer to note numbers

abjection, the abject 6-7, 10, 90, 96–8, 100, 104 n.41, 133, 168, 210, 215, 240, 242, 250
abolition (of slavery) 249, 253–4
Adler, Alfred 121 n.9
Aeschylus 96, 97
Afropessimism 7, 12, 166, 176 n.4, 240–2
Alcman 90
allegory 1, 144, 212
Althusser, Louis 159, 212
ambivalence 90–1, 93, 211, 242
anagram 39–40
analysis 12–13, 46, 52, 59, 61, 65–7, 72 n.49, 90, 98, 100, 111, 114, 122 n.21, 145, 154, 178 n.54, 185, 187, 195–6, 209, 211, 216 n.19, *see also* psychoanalysis
Anaxagoras 91
anthropology 39, 40, 48, 55 n.88, 78, 219
anti-blackness 234–42, 248, 255
Antigone 5–7, 11–12, 16, 32–3, 165–82, 235, 247, 251, 255
aporia 90, 99–100, 255
archive fever 166
Aristophanes 4, 31, 81, 90–1, 94
Aristotle 10, 33, 89–106
Atē 5–6, 33
auto-immunity 8, 12, 166–7
auto-repugnancy 12, 185, 190, 193, 197, 199 n.30

Baader-Meinhoff Group 33
Bahrani, Ramin 212–13
Banshees of Inisherin 11, 139–40, 143, 148
Bataille, Georges 39, 49–51, 84 n.5
Baudrillard, Jean 9–10, 39–58
Beller, Jonathan 11, 152, 154–60
Bellow, Saul, *Ravelstein* 10, 147–9
Benjamin, Walter 65, 175, 179 n.76, 217–18, 229
Bennington, Geoffrey 189, 192, 200 n.34, 223
Berlant, Laurent 7
Bersani, Leo 111–12, 120 n.6, 121 n.10
binding (*Bindung*) 29, 64, 99, 142, 144, 192
biology 3, 48–9, 56 n.93, 81, 83, 86, 93, 97–8, 129, 159–60, 186–91, 193, 196–7, 204, 220, 250
Bion, Wilfred 142
biopolitics 13, 40–1, 48, 51–3, 57 n.114, 169, 172, 258 n.37
Blackness 13, 172, 194, 201, 234–42, 248–52, 256
Bloom, Allan 147–8
Bong Joon-ho 210–11
Braidotti, Rosi 8
Braunstein, Nestor 2
breakdown 9, 11, 51, 60, 62, 67, 72 n.54, 78, 99, 152–3, 157, 209
Breuer, Joseph 112, 121
Brown, Norman O. 111
Browning, Robert 142
Buddhism 45
Burke, Edmund 6
Butler, Judith 7, 165–6, 171–2, 175, 176 n.20, 179 n.80, 223

Camus, Albert 1
capitalism 9, 11–12, 40, 44, 51–2, 56 n.106, 57 n.114, 119, 152, 154–9, 166, 204–9, 211–13, 215
Carson, Anne 90
Caruth, Cathy 60, 61, 63, 65–7, 69, 72, 73 n.60
Chamoiseau, Patrick 249

Chile 66
China 45, 207–8, 213
Christianity 43–5, 76, 97
class 12–13, 44, 93, 111, 186, 201, 203–14, 242, 251
Colombia 59, 70
colonialism 152–3, 155–6, 160, 166, 168, 170, 172, 200 n.43, 235, 244 n.37, 250
Copjec, Joan 7
Creon 5–6, 12, 33, 166–72, 178 n.51, 235
cruelty 2, 13, 167, 217–29
cruelty drive 13, 217, 219, 225

Dante 141–2, 145
Dasein 44, *see also* Heidegger, Martin
death 1–3, 5–12, 16 n.46, 24, 26–7, 40–52, 64, 68, 75–85, 86 n.31, 90, 92–3, 98, 100, 112–14, 118, 127, 140–3, 148, 151–5, 157–9, 165–6, 169–72, 174–5, 178 n.55, 179 n.72, 185–6, 194, 196, 207, 212, 220, 224, 227, 229, 239, 254–6
  drive 2–4, 6–13, 14 n.12, 15 n.22, 28, 32–3, 39–48, 51–3, 56–7 n.113, 69, 77, 79, 81–3, 85–6, 92, 96, 101 n.1, 104 n.50, 109–11, 114, 117, 125–6, 131–4, 135 n.4, 139–42, 144, 151–3, 157, 159–60, 161 n.15, 165–6, 168–75, 176 n.7, 178 n.53, 187–9, 191–3, 197, 199–200, 203–6, 208–10, 213–14, 217, 219, 221–3, 226, 228, 233–6, 238, 240–2, 247–9, 251–3 (*see also Todestrieb*)
  social 13, 234, 236, 240, 242, 250
decolonialism 13, 244 n.37
deconstruction 9, 13, 40, 46–7, 52, 225, 227
Deleuze, Gilles 7, 49, 205–6, 208, 210, 214
Delgrès, Louis 13, 247–8, 250–7
Derrida, Jacques 7, 13, 27–30, 33–4, 98, 166, 176, 199 n.28, 200 n.34, 217–32
desire 2–3, 5–8, 12–13, 33, 78, 85 n.23, 89–92, 100, 101 n.1, 102 n.24, 111, 115–17, 119, 126–7, 134, 143, 147, 168, 188–9, 195, 203–4, 206–15, 220–1, 241, 248
Devil, the 45, 226
dialectic 26, 44–6, 77, 95, 97, 100, 102 n.29, 143, 155, 204, 206, 208–9, 211–14, 234–5
différance 23, 25, 27, 199 n.28, 220, 225
disaggregation 10, 90, 92, 98, 151
drives 2, 10, 39, 45–6, 50, 63, 75, 80–3, 85 n.24, 92–3, 96, 141, 143–4, 147, 185, 188, 206, 214, 215 n.7, 217, 219, 221, 224–5, 227, 229, *see also* pulsion and *Trieb*
dust 12, 166, 169–70, 173, 175

ecocide 169–70, 172, 174–5
economic standpoint (in Freud) 3–5, 7–9, 24–8, 32–4, 40, 52, 57, 61, 79, 117, 122 n.31, 220
economics 2, 40, 51, 211
Edelman, Lee 7, 10, 12, 109–12, 119, 125–6, 128, 131, 133–4, 171, 178 n.53, 185–7, 189, 192–6, 198 n.17, 200–1
Ego Psychology 14 n.13
elegy 10–11, 125–37
Empedocles 91–3
enjoyment 2, 4–7, 9–10, 24, 32–3, 130, 186, 195, 238, 242, *see also jouissance*
Enlightenment 25, 250–2
Eros 10, 42–7, 79, 81–3, 85 n.24, 86 n.37, 89–94, 96–102, 147, 151, 165, 189, 192, 200 n.34, 204, 206, 218, 221, 224
Euripides 90
excess 15 n.22, 39, 50–1, 63, 66, 68, 94, 98, 175, 196, 233, 251–2
Exchange 4–6, 8, 24–6, 39–41, 48–53, 57 n.114, 207
existentialism 43–4, 235–6
expenditure 39, 51, 171

Fanon, Frantz 13, 172, 233–42, 250–1
fantasy of the Roman good life 126, 130, 133
fascism 14 n.13, 121 n.10
father, the 5, 95, 97, 118, 142, 241
Felman, Shoshona 60, 69

feminism 110–11, 204
film (and cinema) 3, 11–12, 110–11, 139, 154, 210–14
form 4–5, 7–8, 11–12, 23, 26, 29, 39–40, 47–8, 50–1, 53, 61, 63, 66–7, 69, 76, 82, 84 nn.5, 15, 86, 89–90, 92, 95–7, 103 n.40, 109, 116, 119, 141–4, 148, 151–2, 155–8, 160, 163 n.68, 165, 172, 174–5, 186–7, 193–4, 199 n.31, 203, 205–8, 214, 226–7, 237, 241, 248–9, 253
fort/da game 2, 25–6, 70, 140, 143, 144
Foucault, Michel 3, 33, 49, 51–3, 57 n.114, 110, 119, 120 n.3, 192, 198 n.17
freedom drive 13, 248–9
Freud, Anna 8, 14 n.13
Freud, Sigmund 7–13, 24, 29, 33, 39–40, 43–7, 51–2, 56 n.13, 59–67, 69, 75, 79, 81–3, 84 n.7, 85 n.24, 86, 93, 109–13, 116–19, 120 n.7, 121 nn.8–9, 148, 151, 153, 157–8, 160, 165–6, 169, 174, 188–92, 199–200, 204–6, 210, 217–18, 220–1, 223–5, 233, 239, 242 n.1, 248
  "Analysis Terminable and Interminable" 93, 165
  "Anxiety and Instinctual Life" 42–3, 47
  Beyond the Pleasure Principle 2–5, 8, 10, 12–13, 23–31, 39, 45–6, 59–63, 68–9, 70 n.4, 71 n.21, 75, 77, 80–2, 86, 102 n.13, 104 n.50, 140, 142–4, 151, 167, 187–93, 198 n.25, 199, 200 n.33, 226
  "A Child is Being Beaten" 2, 118
  Civilization and its Discontents 4, 45, 77, 79, 84 n.10, 85 n.23, 86 nn.34, 38, 165, 198 n.15
  "The Economic Problem of Masochism" 117–18, 121 n.21, 220
  The Interpretation of Dreams 104 n.50, 112, 140
  Introductory Lectures on Psychoanalysis 42
  New Introductory Lectures on Psychoanalysis 42–3
  "On Narcissism" 117
  An Outline of Psychoanalysis 42
  Totem and Taboo 5
  The Uncanny 2

Gaia 89, 92, 170
gay 111, 121 nn.10–11, 148, 196
Gaza 11–12, 165–75
gender 90, 101 n.9, 110–11, 120 n.1, 172, 201 n.59, 203–4, 209
Genet, Jean 110, 121 n.10
genocide 165, 169–70, 172, 201 n.46
genus 10, 30, 75, 78–9, 81–3, 85 n.19
germ cells 10, 75, 81–3
gift, the 34, 39–40
Giono, Jean 1
Goethe, Johann Wolfgang von 145
grammar 9, 13, 60, 66–8, 205, 233–8, 248
Green, André 11, 141–8
Grosz, Elizabeth 189, 192, 200 n.34
Guadeloupe 13, 247, 251–4, 257 n.37
Guattari, Félix 7, 40, 205

Halperin, David 101 n.9
Hawthorne, Nathaniel 114–16
Hegel, G. W. F. 10, 75–87, 93, 143, 222, 235
Heidegger, Martin 29, 44, 90
Hesiod 89–90, 92
heteronormativity 127–8, 132–4, 166
homosexuality 93, 101 n.9, 107, 110, 120 n.3, 121 n.10
humanism, new 234–6, 242

idealism 56 n.93, 75–6
identity 13, 76, 109–10, 120 n.3, 125, 151, 157, 176 n.5, 186–7, 194–7, 201, 204, 234–42, 244 n.31, 254–5
imaginary, the 44, 50, 52, 56 n.33, 94–5, 130, 134, 141–2, 144, 154, 156, 159, 186, 212, 214
imago 211, 213, 240
incest 5–6, 93, 115, 195, 209
infrastructure 11, 44, 152–6, 160–1, 173, 175
instinct 4, 12, 27, 42–3, 46–7, 78, 82, 85 n.14, 86 n.26, 96, 117–18,

122 n.21, 151, 165–6, 170, 174, 188, 210, 214, 215 n.6, 220–1, 225, 235
International Psychoanalytic Association (IPA) 8, 14 n.12
Islam 45
Israel 12, 166–72, 174–5, 177 n.23, 178 n.55

James, Henry 10, 109–21
Jameson, Fredric 41
Jews 147, 240
Jones, Ernest 121 n.9
jouissance 2, 4–7, 32, 56 n.93, 98, 100, 104 n.50, 121 n.10, 131, 133–4, 167, 186, 204, 206, *see also* enjoyment
Jung, Carl 121 n.9, 242 n.1

Kanor, Fabienne 254–6
Kant, Immanuel 6, 233
Keats, John 142
kinship 127, 170, 238
Klein, Melanie 7, 14 n.12, 142
Korea 210–11
Kristeva, Julia 4, 6, 32, 90–3, 95–8, 101

labor 12, 39, 129, 131–2, 154–5, 203–5, 207–14, 253
Lacan, Jacques 2, 5–7, 10, 14 n.12, 32, 52, 56 n.93, 94–5, 104 n.50, 114, 125, 128, 131, 134, 135 n.4, 140, 142, 161 n.50, 165, 171, 175, 203–6, 208–12, 214, 235, 239, 241, 251
  Seminar I 7
  Seminar II 7, 34 n.11, 125, 135 n.4
  Seminar VII 5–6, 12, 16 n.34, 32–3, 134, 135 n.4, 165–6, 173–4, 221, 241
language 7, 11, 56 n.3, 66–8, 94, 96–7, 104 n.42, 143, 147, 152–5, 159–61, 165, 169, 171, 192, 206, 209, 218–20, 229, 237, 240, 244 n.37
Laplanche, Jean 172
lesbian 111, 209
liberalism 13, 55 n.88, 110, 242
libido, libidinal 3–4, 13, 40, 92–4, 101 n.9, 117–19, 122 n.21, 188, 199 n.31, 234, 236, 238, 241, 251
life 2, 6, 9–12, 24–5, 27, 29–30, 40, 44–7, 50–2, 59–63, 65, 68–9, 75–84, 85 n.24, 86 n.31, 91, 93–4, 111–13, 117, 126–34, 141–7, 151–2, 154–8, 160, 165–7, 169, 171–72, 174–5, 186–94, 196–7, 198 nn.19, 25, 199–200, 206–10, 213, 221–5, 228–9, 233, 235, 237, 239, 241–2, 244 n.37, 250–2, 256
  instinct 42–3, 170
limit 3–7, 9, 24–6, 30–4, 40, 51–2, 59–60, 98, 205, 218
listening 9, 59–60, 62, 64–70, 72 n.52
looping 1, 133
lusimelēs 10, 89–90, 92–3, 96, 98, 100, 104 n.50
lusis 10, 90, 98–100
Lysis, see lusis

Malabou, Catherine 80–1, 86 nn.30–31, 151–3, 157–60, 163 n.73, 201 n.34
Manichaeism 44–5
Marcuse, Herbert 7
Marriott, David 233–4, 240
Martinez-Ruiz, Rosaura 60, 64–5, 67, 69, 102 n.14
Marx, Karl 12, 50, 154, 162 n.63, 207–9
Marxism 13, 40, 43
masochism 116–19, 142–3, 145, 220
  moral masochism 10, 117–19
maternal body 10, 96–7, *see also* mother, the
matter 43, 64, 75–82, 86 n.31, 89, 91–2, 95, 97, 100, 103 n.40, 104 n.41, 151, 170–1, 190–1, 198 n.25, 199 n.30
Mauss, Marcel 39
McNulty, Tracy 7
memorials (public) 13, 70 n.1, 248, 252–4
metaphysics 8
Mieville, China 153–60, 162 n.63
Miller, D. A. 110
mirror stage (Lacan) 94–6, 219
Modernism 110, 119, 142
Moten, Fred 13, 248–50, 254

mother, the 10, 38 n.93, 69, 94–8, 100, 101 n.9, 133, 140, 142–3, 145–7, 173–4, 228–9

Nachträglichkeit (belatedness) 62–3
narcissism 11, 96–7, 110, 117, 141
nationalism 111
nation-state 12, 166–7, 170, 174–5
nature 10, 43–4, 49, 61, 75–83, 85 nn.14, 22, 86 n.36, 90–1, 93, 98–9, 158, 165, 186–7, 207, 217
Nazis 33
necropolitics 8, 169, 171, 178 n.55
negrophilia 13, 234
negrophobia 13, 234
Nemesis 128–34, 136 n.36
neoliberalism 13, 53, 57 n.114, 147, 166, 212–13, 234, 238–9, 241, 257 n.37
neurosis 59–63, 65–7, 94, 98, 209
Nietzsche, Friedrich 47, 122 n.21, 218, 224–5
Niobe 173–5, 179
Nirvana 42, 46, 248

Oedipal 4–5, 26, 172
Oedipus 26, 118, 221–2, 224
ontology 6, 9, 24–5, 27, 29, 85 n.24, 97, 151, 157, 168–9, 174–5, 194–6, 201 n.49, 206, 234–7, 240, 248–52
opera 3
organism 10, 23, 29, 61, 77–82, 84 nn.12–13, 85 n.14, 90, 93, 95, 97, 104 n.50, 117, 151, 187, 191–2
Orpheus 11
Ovid 11, 95, 125, 133, 179 n.77

pain 2–5, 7–8, 23–6, 29, 32–3, 35 n.25, 69, 79, 93, 117–19, 129, 131, 140, 146, 217–18, 222, 241, 248, 251
Palestine, Palestinian 166–74, 177 n.23, 179 n.80, 200 n.43, 240
Papin sisters 209–13, 215 n.1
paranoia 167, 172, 209–11
paraontology 13, 248–9, 252
Parasite 210–12
pedophilia 3
Petrarch 145
phantasm 11, 48, 50–1, 95, 140–2, 144–7, 172, 185–7, 195–7, 224, 237
philosophy 10, 29, 43, 52, 75–6, 83, 86 n.31, 98–100, 121 n.9, 154, 197 n.10, 251
Plato 9–10, 24, 29–30, 33, 89, 91, 94–6, 101 n.9, 147
  Philebus 9, 24, 29–34
  Symposium 4–5, 81, 89–91
  Timaeus 4, 26, 92
pleasure 1–11, 15 n.22, 23–33, 34 n.11, 35 n.25, 39, 61, 71 n.21, 79–80, 83, 84 n.5, 91, 94, 100, 104 n.50, 114, 117–19, 122 n.21, 131, 140, 148, 157, 191, 217
pleasure principle (*Lustprinzip*) 2, 4–10, 24–9, 33, 34 n.11, 42, 46, 61–2, 64, 79, 86 nn.28, 30, 104 n.50, 140, 157, 159, 170, 188–93, 199 n.31, 200 nn.33–34, 218, 220, 239, 241–2
Poe, Edgar Allen 114
Polynices 5–6, 169–70
positivism 46–7, 209
postcolonialism 250
posthumanism 7
postmodernism 41, 53 n.17
Pound, Ezra 141–3
proletarian 12, 203–15
psychoanalysis 3, 5, 7–9, 12–13, 25, 32, 34 n.11, 39–40, 45, 47–8, 50–2, 56 n.113, 61–2, 89, 93–5, 98, 100, 101 n.1, 110, 140, 142, 152, 158, 171, 203, 211, 217–19, 221–8, 230 n.19, 236
psychology 8, 12, 25, 29, 35 n.25, 83, 86 n.38, 112, 121 n.9, 166, 204, 208
psychosis 94, 98, 141–2, 147, 159, 167, 209
pulsion 47–8, 51, 56 n.106, 96, 204, 206–8, 211–12, 214, *see also* drive and *Trieb*

queer 118, 120 nn.3, 8, 121 n.10, 125–6, 131–4, 178 n.53, 185, 187, 189, 193–7, 200 n.38, 201 nn.49, 52
  theory 7–8, 10, 14, 109–12, 117, 119, 121 n.10, 128, 186

race 49, 104 n.41, 145, 156, 201 n.59, 207, 237, 239–40, 256
racism 155, 208, 233–5, 237, 244 n.31, 250
Rancière, Jacques 7
real, the 3, 6, 12, 26, 31, 33, 41, 50, 52, 56 n.93, 125–6, 128, 131, 134, 166, 179 n.72, 186, 208, 210, 212, 235
reality principle (*Realitätprinzip*) 3–4, 7–8, 24–5, 27–8, 33, 40, 50, 167, 172, 219, 226, 239
repetition 2–3, 8, 15 n.22, 24, 27–8, 46, 48, 50–1, 62, 65, 68–70, 128, 130–1, 133, 166, 197, 199 n.30, 206–7, 249, 252, 256
  compulsion (compulsion to repeat) 7, 9, 26, 42–3, 47, 59, 61, 63, 67, 71 n.21, 79, 83, 140, 144, 151
reproductive futurism 12, 109, 127–8, 133–4, 185, 189
ressentiment 13, 233–42, 244 n.37
reversibility, principle of 39–40, 45
Richard, Nelly 66
Rose, Jacqueline 7

sacrifice 35 n.25, 39, 51, 75–6, 79, 81, 83, 170, 208, 213, 241, 247, 251–3
sadism 117–18, 151, 168, 188, 223–4, 228
Sappho 90
Sartre, Jean-Paul 235
Saussure, Fernand de 39
Schopenhauer, Arthur 43
science 9, 35, 43–4, 47–8, 52, 97, 120 n.8, 189, 191–4, 199 n.32, 219–20
sex 10, 78, 82, 91, 94, 110, 114, 120, 121 n.10, 185, 193, 195, 198 n.15, 209, 221
sexual history 109–10
sexuality 10–11, 29, 33, 47, 109–14, 117–21, 151, 186, 201 n.59
simulacra 41
slave revolts 13, 238, 247, 253
slavery 13, 155, 194, 200 n.43, 238, 240, 242, 247–55
socialism 39–40
Socrates 29–32, 101 n.9, 228
solidarity 44, 207, 214, 238–9, 242
Sophocles 10–12, 166, 172–4
spirit 33, 76–7, 79, 82–3, 84 n.6, 238
sublimation 3, 10, 43–4, 47, 90–1, 100, 141–4, 146, 214, 222
sublime 6, 9–10, 25, 90–1, 100, 148, 213, 255
suicide 4, 13, 52, 93, 132, 145, 165, 185, 228, 235, 239, 242, 247, 250, 255–6
Sussman, Henry 6
symbolic, the 5, 7, 11, 39–40, 48–52, 56 n.93, 98–9, 125, 128–31, 133–4, 144, 161 n.15, 165, 170, 176 n.4, 178 n.51, 179 n.72, 203, 235–6, 239, 242, 244 n.31, 251–2, 255

terrorism 33, 44, 48, 166–8, 170
thanatopolitics 40–1, 52, *see also* necropolitics
Thanatos 12, 42–3, 45–7, 165, 169, 204, 206, 224
Tibullus 10–11, 123–34, 135 n.13
Todestrieb 2, 4, 8, 11
tragedy 3, 6, 90, 95, 99, 169, 212
trauma 3, 5–9, 14, 24, 26, 59–70, 72 nn.52, 54, 73 n.59, 140, 152–3, 157–9, 170, 197 n.10, 224, 235, 239
Trieb 15, 78, 85 n.14, 190–1, 193, 198, 199 n.30, 206, 220, *see also* drive and pulsion
truth 7, 30, 33, 42, 44, 46–7, 65–7, 83 nn.1, 4, 95, 99, 116, 121 n.9, 160, 167, 227, 229

unbinding 10, 40, 98–9, 101 n.1, 104 n.50, 142, 144
unconscious, the 3, 11, 15 n.22, 33, 47, 50, 63, 75, 77–8, 84 nn.6, 9, 118, 140–1, 144–5, 155, 158, 200 n.37, 206, 213, 218, 236, 240–1, 251
unlimited, the 9, 24, 26, 30–2, 34
unpleasure (*Unlust*) 3, 10, 25–6, 28, 34 n.7, 61, 220

violence 3, 6, 9, 12, 39, 47, 59–60, 63, 65–6, 68–9, 70 n.1, 72 n.52, 77–8, 83, 97, 104 n.41, 165–6,

171, 175, 176 n.20, 179 n.77, 186, 194, 196–7, 201 n.56, 204, 211–14, 217–18, 249, 251, 253
voice 9, 59, 65, 67–70, 72 n.52, 73 n.59, 156, 179 n.77, 187, 251

Warren, Calvin 7, 201 n.49
Weatherill, Rob 15 n.22
White Tiger 212–14
Winnicott, Donald 142
women 102 n.9, 116, 133, 145, 185, 196, 209, 247, 250, 253–6
wretched, the 235, 237–40

xenophobia 249

Zionism 165–6, 171, 176 n.8
Žižek, Slavoj 5, 7, 26, 33, 239, 244 n.31, 248, 251–2, 255
zone of nonbeing 13, 234–42, 250–2, 255
Zoroastrianism 45

www.ingramcontent.com/pod-product-compliance
Lightning Source LLC
LaVergne TN
LVHW022320270326
835028LV00003B/52